Globalizing the Postcolony

Globalizing the Postcolony

Contesting Discourses of Gender and Development in Francophone Africa

Claire H. Griffiths

LEXINGTON BOOKS

A division of
ROWMAN & LITTLEFIELD PUBLISHERS, INC.
Lanham • Boulder • New York • Toronto • Plymouth, UK

Published by Lexington Books
A division of Rowman & Littlefield Publishers, Inc.
A wholly owned subsidary of The Rowman & Littlefield Publishing Group, Inc.
4501 Forbes Boulevard, Suite 200, Lanham, Maryland 20706
http://www.lexingtonbooks.com

Estover Road, Plymouth PL6 7PY, United Kingdom

British Library Cataloguing in Publication Information Available

Library of Congress Cataloging-in-Publication Data

Griffiths, Claire.
  Globalizing the postcolony : contesting discourses of gender and development in
francophone Africa / Claire H. Griffiths.
    p. cm. — (After the empire: the Francophone world and postcolonial France)
  Includes bibliographical references and index.
  ISBN 978-0-7391-4382-7 (cloth : alk. paper) — ISBN 978-0-7391-4384-1 (electronic)
    1. Women—Africa, West—Social conditions. 2. Women—Africa, West—Economic
conditions. 3. Social planning—Africa, West. 4. Economic development—Africa,
West. 5. Africa, West—Social policy. 6. Africa, West—Economic policy.
7. Postcolonialism—African, West. I. Title.
  HQ1810.G75 2011
  305.40966'0917541—dc22

                                                                    2010043801

∞™ The paper used in this publication meets the minimum requirements of American
National Standard for Information Sciences—Permanence of Paper for Printed Library
Materials, ANSI/NISO Z39.48-1992.

Printed in the United States of America

Contents

PART III: From the Global to the Postcolony: Data Profiling in Gabon and Senegal

PART IV: In Search of Context and Culture 1: Historicizing Gender

PART V: In Search of Context and Culture 2: Locating Gender

PART VI: Writing Gender and Development: Culture, Context, and Change in Francophone Africa

Preface

Knowledge flows through people yet the discursive journey gender and development has traveled in the first fifty years of its existence has embedded the discourse of change in a theoretical geography beyond culture and context.

In practice, gender and development discourse, though global in reach, began as a largely monolingual affair in the mid twentieth century led by the international institutions created by the victors of World War II. This international community has driven gender and development discourse through a system of conventions and platforms for action dominated conceptually as well as linguistically by the English-speaking world.

Since the Luxembourg Declaration of February 2000, the francophone world has been mounting a linguistic challenge to the old order, advancing a new discourse of gender and development through a French-speaking international development lobby. The new francophone discourse engages with culture, context and change in ways not seen before in the international arena. Francophone discourses have operated at the margins of the development process in francophone Africa throughout the postcolonial era. The extent to which the internationalized francophone discourse will succeed in modifying dominant development paradigms and become a prime influence over francophone African gender and development policy will become clearer as we progress through the twenty-first century.

This book explores these competing discourses of gender and development in the context of francophone West Africa, classified as the least developed region of the world in international gender and development rankings. It maps the international model of gender and development onto countries in the region, highlighting the cultural and contextual gaps in our understanding of what gender and development means in francophone African societies.

The discussion then goes in search of the context and culture of gender and development discourse in the region of West Africa that came under French colonial administration. It examines the history of gender politics in pre-colonial Africa and the legacy of colonization in the region.

The study traces the discursive journey through the postcolonial era with an extensive exploration of alternative discourses of development in the region with particular reference to Senegal. It draws from a range of scientific, social scientific and literary sources to uncover dominant and competing paradigms of gender and development. Competing discourses serve to reveal some of the obstacles that lie in the way of rationalist social policy and highlight the dangers of stimulating social change in the absence of an understanding of culture and context.

The study concludes by evaluating the contemporary agenda for change and the potential for francophone West Africa to generate a more equitable landscape in which to promote social development for all in the twenty-first century.

Acknowledgments

In the course of conducting this study of francophone African gender politics, I received help and assistance from so many members of the francophone African development community that it is now not possible to list them all here. They have all been so generous and without their help I would not have been able to collate the breadth and variety of material on the subject that has been synthesized in this book. I am particularly grateful to colleagues who provided me with their own unpublished or locally published research. I have listed these contributions of unpublished work in the bibliography at the end of this book.

One of the main aims in conducting this research was to push back the boundaries surrounding the discussion of what development means in francophone Africa. To this end, I have included voices and sources from the region not found in other studies of the subject. Included in the bibliography are details of interviews and discussions conducted in Senegal and in Gabon, the latter being a country particularly rich in oral information but still lacking in written gender research.

Francophone African NGOs and agencies were helpful in providing alternative insights, contacts and fresh sources of information, both written and oral. UN agencies in francophone Africa were especially generous in sharing internal documents for this study and in offering critical perspectives on the future of gender and development policy in the region. I am particularly indebted in this regard to the International Labour Organization (ILO) in Libreville and Dakar, to the United Nations Development Programme (UNDP) and the United Nations Fund for Women (UNIFEM) for their help in data collection for the whole of the francophone West Africa sub-region.

    Lastly I would like to reserve special thanks for the African academic
community. Despite the challenging conditions in which many scholars work
in Africa, over the years I have been preparing this study not one academic
colleague declined to give their time, to be interviewed or to advise in one
way or another. In particular I would like to acknowledge Professor Dr. Fatou
Sow for her generosity and leadership in the field of gender and development research in francophone Africa, to Mr. Ibrahima Ba of the Ministry of
Education whose help with the many practical issues of fieldwork has been
invaluable over the years, to Mr. Lamine Sy for all the help he has given setting up meetings with the academic community, to Lilian Baer and colleagues
at Africa Consultants and the Baobab Center in Dakar who at the beginning
of this project helped make the first contacts with the literary community,
to academic friends and colleagues at the West Africa Research Center in
Dakar-Fann for their technical assistance and for the convivial and supportive
environment they generate, and lastly to colleagues working in *IFAN, ENS,
INEADE, MEN*, at the Universities of Cheikh Anta Diop and Libreville, and
in the many other academic institutions and research units around the region
engaged in the study of gender and development in francophone Africa, thank
you for sharing your knowledge and wisdom.

Abbreviations

AAWORD/*AFARD*	Association of African Women in Research and Development/*Association des femmes africaines pour la recherche et le développement*
AU	The African Union
BIT/ILO	*Bureau international du travail*/International Labor Office
CEDAW/*CEDEF*	Convention on the Elimination of All Forms of Discrimination Against Women/*La Convention sur l'élimination de toutes formes de discrimination à l'égard des Femmes*
CIDA/*ACDI*	Canadian International Development Agency/*Agence canadienne pour le développement International*
CODESRIA	Council for the Development of Social Research in Africa
CONGAD	*Conseil des organisations non-gouvernementales d'appui au développement*
CONGO	Confederation of Non-governmental Organizations
CONSEF	*Conseil Sénégalais des femmes* (Senegal)
CSW	Commission on the Status of Women (UN)
DAW	Division for the Advancement of Women (UN)
ECA	Economic Commission for Africa (UN)
fCFA	*franc de la Communauté financière africaine*
FDEA	*Femmes développement et entreprise en Afrique* (Senegal)
GAD/*GED*	Gender and Development/*Genre et développement*

GDI/*IDG*	Gender and development index/*indice de développement et genre*
GDP/*PIB*	Gross domestic product/*Produit intérieur brut*
GEM	Gender empowerment measure
GERDDES	*Groupe d'études et de recherches sur la démocratie et le développement social*
GNP/*PNB*	Gross national product/*Produit national brut*
GPF	*Groupement de promotion féminine* (Senegal)
HDI/*IDH*	Human development index/*indice du développement humain*
HDR	Human Development Report/*Rapport sur le développement humain*
HIC/*PPTE*	Heavily-indebted country/*Pays pauvre très endetté*
IAD	*Institut Africain pour la Démocratie*
IDG/*OID*	International Development Goal (OECD)/*objectif international pour le développement (OCDE)*
IFAN	*Institut fondamental de l'Afrique noire* (Senegal)
IFD/WID	*Intégration de la femme au développement*/Women in Development
IMF/*FMI*	International Monetary Fund/*Fonds monétaire international*
INEADE	*Institut national d'études et d'action pour le développement de l'éducation* (Senegal)
LDC/*PMA*	Least-developed countries/*Pays les moins avancés*
MDG/*OMD*	Millennium Development Goal/*Objectif du Millénaire pour le développement*
MFEF	*Ministère de la femme, de l'enfant et de la famille* (Senegal)
MFPE	*Ministère de la famille et de la petite enfance* (Senegal)
MICS/*EGIM*	Multiple Indicator Cluster Survey/*Enquête par grade à indicateurs multiples*
NEAS	*Nouvelles Editions Africaines du Sénégal*
NGO/*ONG*	Non-governmental organization/*organisation non-gouvernementale*
OECD/*OCDE*	Organization for Economic Co-operation and Development/*Organisation pour la Coopération et le Développement Economique*
OPEC/*OPEP*	Organization of Petroleum Exporting Countries/*Organisation des pays exportateurs du pétrole*
PAFS	*Plan d'action de la femme sénégalaise* (Senegal)

PANAF	*Plan d'action national de la femme sénégalaise* (Senegal)
PANEG	*Plan d'action national d'équité de genre* (Senegal)
PNUD/UNDP	*Programme des Nations Unies pour le développement*/United Nations Development Programme
ppp	purchasing power parity
PRSP/*DSRP*	Poverty Reduction Strategy Paper/*Document de stratégie de réduction de la pauvreté*
ROFAF	*Réseau des organisations féminines de l'Afrique francophone*
SNEEG	*Stratégie nationale pour l'équité et l'égalité de genre* (Senegal)
UN/*ONU*	The United Nations/*Organisation des Nations Unies*
UNDP/*PNUD*	United Nations Development Programme/*Programme des nations unies pour le développement*
UNFPA/*FNUAP*	United Nations Fund for Population Activities/*Fonds des Nations Unies pour la Population*
UNGA	United Nations General Assembly
UNRISD	The United Nations Institute for Social Development
WHO/*OMS*	World Health Organization/*Organisation mondiale de la santé*

I

IS THERE A GENDER AND DEVELOPMENT CRISIS IN FRANCOPHONE AFRICA?

1

Gender and Development in Francophone Africa

The Making of a Crisis

The impact of development policy is a matter of immense importance for people who live in the world's most economically vulnerable regions and within the massive industry that has grown up around international development, the potential for development policy to address poverty and disadvantage is of particular significance for women. Despite half a century of campaigning and legislation, women in Africa still constitute, according to data currently used to measure quality of life indicators in developing countries, the most disadvantaged population group in the world.[1] Reports suggest the situation is once again worsening for these women living in the world's poorest countries, "reversing the encouraging trend over the previous decade."[2]

This is a study of how gender affects development in French-speaking countries in West Africa. It analyses how policies designed to address the gender dimension of social disadvantage have developed in the postcolonial era, and explores the impact of gender and development policies on the lives of the women in the region.

By examining the discourse of development the study reveals the extent to which the theory and practice of gender and development has moved on from the decades of dysfunctional and disappointing initiatives that characterised the early years of the postcolonial era. By the last decade of the twentieth century, the international development community[3] was forced to concede that women living in the poorest regions of Africa were even more vulnerable to poverty and declining living standards than in the past:

> The international economic environment is highly volatile and unfavourable.
> [. . .] The result is increasing poverty and malnutrition, and declining health and

education conditions. These factors must and do eat away the quality of life of every citizen excepting a few elites, and they affect women most seriously.[4]

In the early years of the twenty-first century the situation facing women, particularly in Africa, was growing more threatening[5] under the impact of economic liberalization and globalization. International trade agreements and specifically the multilateral agreement on investments (MAI) strengthened the position of multinational corporations vis-à-vis developing economies and weakened the already fragile hold these countries had over their own productive markets. By facilitating the entry of foreign competitors into local African markets, the MAI had a potentially threatening impact on the livelihoods of vulnerable local producers. The first local producers to go to the wall in these conditions are those who carry the lowest profit margins and the smallest share of the market. In Africa over two thirds of the small-scale local producers are women.[6] While conditions in the mid-decade stabilized, the global recession of the post-2008 period highlighted the risks facing the vulnerable populations of the world's poorest regions. This situation is of particular concern to the countries of francophone West Africa.[7]

In the decades since the fourteen former French colonies of the region gained Independence from France in 1960, all but one of these countries[8] have constituted what international development indicators define as the world's poorest nations. The people living in this region of sub-Saharan Africa have remained particularly vulnerable to the vagaries of the economic environment. A World Bank study of the francophone Sahel conducted in the early 1990s concluded that "despite years of French munificence, particularly in the social sector, the social infrastructure in these countries is woefully inadequate."[9] Subsequent research in the region confirmed that women and girls had become "the main victims of poverty"[10] because they are the most exposed to fluctuations in the economic environment.[11]

While there has been some local research on gender as a factor determining an individual's capacity to participate in development and to experience the improved quality of life that development is expected to offer, gender and development as a research category is in its infancy in francophone Africa. This is in stark contrast to elsewhere in the continent.

RESEARCHING GENDER AND
DEVELOPMENT IN FRANCOPHONE AFRICA

The link between gender and development evolved into an industry in Anglophone Africa in the decades following Boserup's groundbreaking study on the impact of female labor on African development.[12] While the impact of gender on development permeated all levels of policy research and formulation in the Anglophone development research communities both in Africa and globally during the 1980s and 1990s, it has remained comparatively marginalized in French and francophone research communities throughout the postcolonial era.[13] By the year 2000 the discrepancy between Anglophone and francophone research on gender was being seen as a threat to the future of social science research and teaching in the region:

> The many obstacles to women's progress in African societies include the difficulty of engendering social science teaching and research in Africa because of the strong resistance to gender conceptualization particularly in the French-speaking countries.[14]

The resistance to gender theorizing has inevitably left large gaps in the knowledge base. Furthermore, up to very recent times, efforts to fill these gaps have not been universally welcomed. When Senegalese sociologist Awa Thiam exposed the female experience of polygynous marriage, excision and other contentious socio-cultural issues in her book *La Parole aux Négresses*,[15] the publication received a hostile reception in some influential quarters and resulted in the author leaving the country.[16] Hostility to gender theorizing has not been confined to francophone Africa, active and passive resistance to this field of enquiry have resulted in it being a poorly integrated category in social science and humanities research and teaching generally in the twenty-first century.

From the middle of the first decade of the twenty-first century, the situation has been evolving more rapidly and African institutions, including those located in francophone Africa, are addressing gender as a cross-cutting research issue. For its part the *Institut fondamental de l'Afrique noire (IFAN)*, the research institute in which Thiam conducted her research, opened its first gender research center[17] in 2006. Francophone Africa's oldest university, the University Cheik Anta Diop of Dakar (UCAD) likewise responded with a research unit bearing the more traditional title of *Laboratoire femmes, sociétés et cultures* the following year. While the official title of this center may not reflect the current focus on relocating women's studies within gender studies, research being conducted within such institutions responds to wider concerns about the colonial and postcolonial legacies of resistance to gender theorizing. The structures through which knowledge is being disseminated and the gendered nature of the entire knowledge base are under interrogation:

> The Academy is not an abstract carrier of a totality of neutral knowledge, but houses men and women marked by cultures and specific memories [. . .] the institutional and intellectual culture of UCAD has reinforced the masculinisation of the institution. [. . .] The intellectual and political dimensions of gender

[. . .] call into question the ideological character of knowledge as this knowledge renders certain actors and social dynamics invisible.[18]

Meanwhile the need to address the gaps in the knowledge base and the need to re-evaluate the inherited knowledge base in francophone Africa have been addressed in academic-related institutions for some considerable time in both Anglophone and francophone Africa. African women researchers have been identifying the connections between gender and economic and social disadvantage in African societies and disseminating this work in local research networks. The *Association des femmes dans la recherche et le développement*/Association of African Women in Research and Development (*AFARD*/AAWORD), founded a center in Dakar in the late 1970s and went on to build up a membership across the continent. African academics have also been active in forging international networks at the global conferences hosted by the United Nations since 1975.[19] "Feminism," insofar as it signifies an identification of the subordination of women coupled with an active political engagement to promote the position of women, is a widespread reality in Africa, even though the term itself is sometimes rejected as a "Western" construct. As Obioma Nnaemeka has put it:

"Feminism" is an English (Western) word but the feminist spirit and ideals are indigenous to the African environment; we do not need to look far into the annals of African history to see the inscription of feminist engagements.[20]

African women have found themselves in a position of disadvantage, and indeed widespread destitution, not because of a failure to recognise their rights in society or a failure to act upon them. The forces dictating the shape of the African economies are immensely complex, as are the roles of individuals, male and female, within these economies. It has been in response to these issues of pauperization and social vulnerability that the theory and practice of gender and development policy has evolved over the past 30 years.

HOW DID THE DEVELOPMENT COMMUNITY RESPOND TO THE GENDER AND DEVELOPMENT CRISIS IN AFRICA?

The origins of contemporary gender and development policy in the economically less developed countries can be traced to the aftermath of decolonization, when the developing countries and the industrial and former colonial powers created a policy arena within which to regulate their primarily economic interactions. At that stage social development policy in the so-called Third World was conceived as an adjunct of economic development policy, involving little more than emergency aid and relief. Over the decades, it transpired that "economic development" was not translating into improved quality of life among the world's poor. The economic theory of "trickle-down" that prevailed in the 1970s and claimed that increased wealth at the top of society trickles down eventually to the lowest levels of society, was becoming increasingly unsustainable. By 1990 it was acknowledged in the international community that the gap between rich and poor had in fact widened over the previous 30 years. Evidence that the world's poor were not becoming wealthier had become overwhelming, with the number of poor people rising consistently throughout the last years of the twentieth century. Ignacio Ramonet summarized the trend in 2000 noting that whereas in 1960 the richest 20 percent of the world's population was 30 times richer than the poorest 20 percent, by the end of the century the richest 20 percent had become 80 times richer than the poorest 20 percent, and the numbers of poor had grown exponentially to reach some 5.5 billion.[21] Immanuel Wallerstein underlined the point in 2005 in his introduction to *Africa: The Politics of Independence and Unity*: "All statistics point to Africa as not only the poorest continent but, relative to the rest of the world, much poorer than it was fifty years ago (and in many cases in real terms as well)."[22]

While commentators proceeded to chip away at the erroneous belief that economic development automatically brought benefits to the world's poor, social development policy became increasingly integrated into national and international development economics as the means of rectifying this weakness in the prevailing economic system of the market economy. Systematic development data collection was introduced to measure social well-being spread across the whole population, in terms of access to a range of social goods (education, health, life expectancy, etc.). The term *social development policy* was invented as the instrument through which the national and international community could intervene in economic development to promote the quality of life of the population as a whole. As social development established itself as a separate and distinct area, albeit within the field of development economics, the term itself evolved in several different ways within development studies and within development practice.

DEFINING SOCIAL DEVELOPMENT POLICY

Firstly, social development was and still is used to signify a collection of social policy instruments. Usually these include health services, basic education services, and other policy fields such as the provision of transport services, social housing, amenities such as water and electricity, and benefits such as

pensions.[23] Secondly, the term social development is also used more broadly
in social science research: "Social development can be used in a disciplinary
sense, if it is distinguished in particular from economic development."[24] Here
the process of social development has been analysed particularly within the
discipline of sociology where the emphasis has been on evaluating the power
of competing development theories to explain the process of development,
and in offering alternatives paradigms.

Since 1990 a version of social development, known as "human development" has emerged in development economics, largely from the work of
economist and Nobel laureate, Amartya Sen, whose "capabilities" approach
to development economics revolutionised economic development thinking
in the 1980s.[25] The change was one of approach more than substance in that
the analysis of social development shifted focus from the instruments of
social development (policies) and the ideological paradigms within which to
analyse them (structures), to the recipients of social development policy (humans), and to social development policy in terms of developing "human capital" (outputs). The impetus behind the subsequent widespread acceptance of
the human development definition of social development is its compatibility
with market-led economic policies favoured by the international community
in its dealings with the developing world.

> Even the IMF and the World Bank, which used to be against the introduction
> into developing countries of what they regarded as "premature" social welfare
> institutions (especially given their preoccupation with budget deficits), are now
> talking about the need to provide a "safety net."[26]

However, the apparent absence of an ethical argument for social development
underpinning this approach led to criticisms that human development was being used by its proponents to back up neo-liberal economic policy. Amartya
Sen responded by repositioning his human development approach to social
development within a human rights framework wherein he and others argued
that the poor have a human right to experience the fruits of economic development and that wealth redistribution is not only good for the economy but
is also an ethical necessity.[27] This discourse of rights was rapidly integrated
into the discourse of social development in the first half of the 1990s, as the
contribution of Gabon to the first international social development summit
organised by the United Nations in Copenhagen in 1995 illustrates[28]:

> *La nouveauté de l'approche tient ici à la remise en cause par la Communauté
> internationale du «postulat de base: c'est l'économique et le financier qui
> se trouvent au poste de commandement. Le social sera donné de surcroît».
> L'on abandonne ainsi la vision exclusivement quantitative du développement*

pour une vision plus qualitative. L'homme cesse d'être une simple machine à produire des richesses c'est-à-dire un simple capital humain.[29]

WOMEN IN THE DISCOURSE OF HUMAN DEVELOPMENT

The new human development approach, based on the human rights discourse that had evolved since the international community started codifying rights in 1948, claims as one of its outputs "the liberation of women" through access to education and to the other services provided under the human development umbrella.[30] Sen, Nussbaum, and Glover proposed that the education of women was a right but also a way of developing human capital insofar as education constitutes a means of releasing enormous potential for growth into the economy. The belief in the impact on economic growth of knowledge transfer and of technological expertise in the population is supported by the example of East Asian growth during the 1980s and 1990s.

The human development approach currently has widespread influence in the international development community[31] and particularly as it defines gender in social development. The approach is based on a universalistic discourse of rights and markets and in this respect it does not address the cultural context in which development theory is practised and policy implemented. It assumes both the inevitability of globalization and by implication the monocultural character of this process.

This raises the question of whether culture matters in development. This question will be at the heart of the discussion here of how social development policy has been implemented in francophone Africa and how far this policy responds to the social development demands of women in those communities. The discussion begins with an exploration of the history of social development policy as it has been formulated and targeted towards women in the developing world in general. The focus on revealing how social development policy is specifically targeted towards women in the developing world serves to uncover how gender is seen to determine women's position in society from the perspective of the policy-making bodies of the international community, where the main planks of global social development policy are formulated. This understanding of gender as a determinant of social position is reflected in the institutional discourse, the policies and the legal conventions of the international community that are examined in part II. The analysis of these structures reveals a "dominant model" of social development for women in the developing world which has served to guide development policy-making in francophone Africa over the past fifty years. For the purposes of this discussion, a new term has been coined to signify this discourse. The "New York

Consensus"[32] on social and human development echoes the long established "Washington Consensus" coined by development economists to signify the broad consensus in international financial institutions around market-driven economic development models.

The dominant model that emerges from the examination of the discourse of gender and development is then applied to two contrasting case studies from francophone West Africa. Gabon and Senegal provide fundamentally different political and economic environments in which to explore how gender mediates an individual's access to the society-wide outputs of development.

RESEARCHING GENDER AND DEVELOPMENT

Throughout the postcolonial era, Dakar has served as a regional centre for research and development in francophone Africa. Studies on gender in the other countries of the francophone sub-region have been few and far between, even though some of the countries in the region have educational budgets capable of sustaining a high level of nationally funded research and development activity. With annual average per capita income several times higher than the regional average, Gabon is a rich nation that has built its fortune on the export of oil and minerals. It has a relatively tiny population between one and two million people. Despite all its economic advantages, Gabon has not engaged in any sustained study of gender and social development accessible to the international academic community. This belies what appears at first glance to be an official interest in the subject and several government departments and centers devoted to the subject of women and gender.[33] In fact, Gabon, despite its considerable resources to fund higher education teaching and research has produced very few studies of any sort on the subject of women's experience of development, poverty, disadvantage or indeed anything at all to do with the gendered experience of development. The universities in Gabon have contributed a small number of academic theses on topics related to gender but most remain unpublished and are largely inaccessible to the international academic community working outside the West African region. Bilateral missions have over the years undertaken field studies in Gabon[34] but the bulk of the output has been international agency-led and this tends to mean quantitative reports which on the whole are strong on statistics and weak on cultural context and interpretation.[35] As it stands this would suggest that Gabon might not be a good case study. However, Gabon, being a country with strong oral traditions in the knowledge base, was able to provide a rich source of oral information accessible through fieldwork in the country.[36] Notwithstanding these contributions, the lack of sustained local gender and development research over time, and the lack of both quantitative and qualitative information[37] made it impossible to produce the type of in-depth case study of Gabon that has been produced for Senegal.

NEW VOICES, NEW PERSPECTIVES: RELOCATING THE RESEARCH PERSPECTIVE

One of the main aims of this study has been to expand the gender and development research base both intellectually and culturally using a wide range of sources. A significant proportion of the research presented in the discussion that follows is based on fieldwork in francophone West Africa conducted over a ten year period. Throughout this time, the research questions and themes were constantly informed and revised by the rich seam of local academic resources, human and documentary. Though relatively little research has been published on Gabon[38] and substantial body of literature has been generated in Senegal over the fifty years since Independence, and particularly in the past quarter of a century.[39] This literature along with hundreds of interviews and discussions conducted in Senegal between 1998 and 2008, followed by a short period of documentary fieldwork in 2010, provided the basis for the analysis of gender and development discourse and practice in Senegal in chapters 12 to 15. These chapters draw particularly heavily on local research, much of which has not yet been integrated into the international body of knowledge in the field. As well as providing the opportunity to synthesize previously unpublished or unavailable research, the case study on Senegal brings new, culturally specific perspectives to the debate on how gender continues to mediate the quality of life in francophone Africa.

The theoretical and methodological challenges confronting gender researchers working in the francophone African region are considerable given the inconsistency and diversity of the knowledge base across the region. The next chapter considers these challenges and suggests a new methodology for navigating the particularities of this research terrain.

NOTES

1. At a country level, GDP per capita is used to measure relative economic advantage. At the population level, life expectancy, literacy, health, access to drinking water, transport, housing, are added to the GDP variable to give a more sophisticated assessment. According to the UN quality of life indicators, the countries occupying the bottom 20 to 25 places in the world's ranking are consistently African countries, and the most numerous among these are the former French colonies of Africa.

2. United Nations (2009), *The Millennium Development Report* (United Nations Statistical Division), chapter 1 "Eradicating Poverty," 9. The 2009 Report cites ILO predictions on the greater danger women still face in times of global recession.

3. This term here encompasses the multilateral agencies working in the development field (such as the World Bank, the EU and the various UN agencies); the international, national and local non-governmental organizations; and the offices and missions of the individual donor countries. A larger configuration of the "international development community" is developed in chapters 2 and 3 and includes, in response to particular issues, other players in international development, such as the U.S. government and the Vatican.

4. Margaret C. Snyder and Mary Tadesse, *African Women and Development* (London: Zed Books, 1995), 5. Since the 1980s, it has been widely accepted in development studies that women make up two-thirds of Africa's poorest people.

5. Since 2000, UNIFEM (the United Nations Women's Fund) has been publishing a biennial report, *Progress of the World's Women*, in which it traces the socio-economic situation of women in the developing world according to a number of criteria. It argues at the international level for greater awareness of women's pauperization and sponsors local studies. The most recent study of pauperization among francophone West African women was commissioned by the *Bureau Régional pour l'Afrique de l'Ouest Francophone* in Dakar in 2003 and focuses on Senegal, Burkina Faso and Benin: UNIFEM, *Regards de femmes africaines sur la pauvreté* (Dakar: UNIFEM, 2003).

International agencies have been sponsoring studies on the region since the mid-1990s which support the findings of the UNIFEM studies: Bureau International du Travail-ACOPAM *Genre et Développement—analyse de la place des femmes une expérience au Sahel* (Dakar: BIT/ILO, 1996).

6. AAWORD/*AFARD*, *Visions of Gender Theories and Social Development in Africa: Harnessing Knowledge for Social Justice and Equality* (Dakar: AAWORD/AFARD, 2001), 17. This small volume presents papers from a symposium held in Dakar on the impact of gender on social and economic disadvantage in Africa.

7. ILO estimates suggest 85 percent of sub-Saharan African women are vulnerable to the effects of the post-2008 recession.

8. Benin, Burkina-Faso, Côte d'Ivoire, Guinea, Mali, Mauritania, Niger, Senegal, and Togo (formerly *l'Afrique occidentale française)*; Gabon, Cameroon, Congo, Chad and the Central African Republic (formerly *l'Afrique équatoriale française)*. Nowadays these countries have a common identity within the franc zone. Only Gabon has been consistently identified as a middle-income country, the other former French colonies ranking among the poorest countries in the world with mid decade average GDP per capita ranging from pppU.S.$780 a year in Niger to pppU.S.$2,300 in Cameroon.

9. S. C. Mehta, "Social Infrastructure in Francophone Sahel," *Africa Quarterly* 34, no. 1, 1994, 115.

10. AAWORD/*AFARD*, *Visions of Gender Theories*, 13.

11. Fatou Sow, Ngagne Diakhaté, Adama Fall-Touré, and Mamadou Matar Gueye, *Les Sénégalaises en Chiffres* (Dakar: PNUD, 2000), Section 2—*Données*

Economiques. This section provides a detailed presentation of the risks of pauperization facing women in Senegal.

12. Ester Boserup's *Women's Role in Economic Development* of 1970 was revolutionary in shifting the focus on African women from documenting their "domestic" lives (a lens inherited from the colonial academic tradition) to analysing their role as economic agents in African development. From the early 1970s through to the early 1990s this approach dominated gender and development research and theory.

13. With the notable exception of the French Canadian research community since the mid 1990s.

14. AAWORD/*AFARD*, *Visions of Gender Theories*, 17.

15. Awa Thiam, *La Parole aux Négresses* (Paris: Denoël-Gonthier, 1978). Thiam's book contains the raw and disturbing accounts of polygyny and female genital mutilation as experienced by her interviewees. It was seen as a direct and dangerous attack on the institution which up to the end of the twentieth century still affected almost half of all married women in Senegal.

16. These events were recounted to me over twenty years later during interviews in Senegal with academics who had been working at IFAN in the late 1970s and early 1980s.

17. The center was given the title of *Laboratoire genre.*

18. Aminata Diaw, "Sewing machines or computers? Seeing gender in the institutional cultures at UCAD," *Feminist Africa* no. 9, 2007, 5–21 [17].

19. The francophone African countries have been well represented at these "World conferences for women" first in Mexico in 1975, Copenhagen in 1980, and Nairobi in 1985. At the latest in Beijing in 1995 all 14 countries sent a team of representatives. See: United Nations, *UN Report of the Fourth World Conference on Women*, A/Conf.177/20, 17 October 1995, 138.

20. Obioma Nnaemeka, "Urban spaces, women's spaces—Polygamy as Sign in Mariama Bâ's Novels," in *The Politics of (M)Othering*, Obioma Nnaemeka, ed. (London: Routledge 1997), 165.

21. Ignacio Ramonet, "Pour Changer le Monde," *Le Monde diplomatique— Manières de Voir* no. 52, July/August 2000, 1.

22. Immanuel Wallerstein, *Africa: the Politics of Independence and Unity* (Lincoln: University of Nebraska Press, 2005), vii.

23. See, for example, Jean-Pierre Dumont, *Les Systèmes étrangers de Sécurité Sociale* (Paris: Economica, 1988); Arega Yiman, *Social Development in Africa 1950–1985: Methodological Issues and Future Perspectives* (Brookfield, USA: Avebury: 1990); Howard Jones, *Social Welfare in Third World Development* (London: Macmillan, 1990); J. Midgley, *Social Development: The Developmental Perspective in Social Welfare* (London: Sage, 1995).

24. Jan Nederveen Pieterse, *Development Theory—Deconstructions/Reconstructions* (London: Sage, 2001), 116.

25. Amartya Sen, *Commodities and Capabilities* (Oxford: Oxford University Press, 1985).

See also K. Griffin and T. McKinley, *Implementing a Human Development Strategy* (London: Macmillan, 1994).

26. Ha-Joon Chang, *Kicking Away the Ladder—Development Strategy in Histori-cal Perspective* (London: Anthem Press, 2002), 101.

27. See, for example, the discussion of this issue in Martha Nussbaum and Am-artya Sen, *The Quality of Life* (Oxford: Clarendon Press, 1993); and in Amartya Sen, *Development as Freedom* (Oxford: Oxford University Press, 2001).

28. I am grateful to Professor Fidèle Nze Nguéma of the Prime Minister's Office of the Republic of Gabon for providing me with a copy of Gabon's written contribu-tion to the Social Development Summit.

29. Primature de la République du Gabon *Contribution du Gabon au Sommet Mondial pour le Développement Social* (unpublished 1995), paragraphe 1.1.3, 6. "The novelty in this approach lies in the international community's questioning of a basic premise, namely the primacy of the economic and the financial over the social. By no longer positing the social as an added value, we are moving from a purely quantitative to a more qualitative vision of development. Man ceases to be conceived simply as a machine for producing wealth, as human capital." Author's translation.

30. See Martha Nussbaum and Jonathan Glover, *Women, Culture and Develop-ment: A Study of Human Capabilities* (Oxford: Clarendon, 1995); Martha Nussbaum, *Women and Human Development: The Capabilities Approach* (Cambridge: Cam-bridge University Press, 2000).

31. When the United Nations adopted the human development approach at the beginning of the 1990s this had enormous impact on social development politics throughout the world. The history of these developments is discussed in chapter 2.

32. New York houses the main agencies involved in setting the social develop-ment agenda in the international community, foremost among which is the Human Development Report Office at UN headquarters in New York, whose input is evalu-ated in chapter 3.

33. I came across an example of this during a visit to the *Centre de documentation sur la condition féminine* in Libreville. The Ministry official keeping guard over the facility was there to ensure no-one gained access to the collection. When word came down from a senior administrator to open the center it transpired that it housed just a few dusty back numbers of a government-produced glossy magazine called *Femmes gabonaises* and a number of documents of rather tangential interest to *la condition féminine*.

34. Fieldwork in Gabon revealed that the Embassy of Canada has been the most active bilateral agency in commissioning gender research in Gabon. I am particu-larly indebted to Rita Couture and Colette Charpentier of the Canadian Embassy, Maryvonne Ntsame Ndong of *GERDDES*, and the ILO office in Libreville for unpub-lished reports and studies on Gabon.

35. The most comprehensive agency reports from Senegal and Gabon date from the early 1990s coinciding with the big push at that time to fill statistical gaps. UNICEF-*PNUD*, *La Femme et l'Enfant au Sénégal* (Dakar : UNICEF, 1995); Fatou Sow et al. *Les Sénégalaises à l'horizon 2015* (Dakar: PNUD/Ministère de la Femme, 1993); Fanta Diallo Maïga, *L'Accès des filles à l'éducation de base au Gabon* (Dakar: UNESCO, 1993); UNICEF *Analyse de la Situation des Enfants et des femmes au Gabon* (Libreville: UNICEF, 1995—document interne).

36. The President of the Constitutional Council and the Minister of Education made a significant contribution to this study through long personal interviews in which we discussed the situation of women in general and more specifically gender as a factor of social development and/or disadvantage in Gabon. Indeed with consummate tact the President of the Constitutional Council, as a fellow academic, helped steer some of the lines of enquiry towards more useful goals.

37. Entries for Gabon in international information sources are littered with "n.d." (no data) where social statistics appear for other countries in the region. Fieldwork in the country revealed that extensive and sophisticated statistical accounting does take place. Furthermore local statisticians and academics were almost invariably prepared to help in locating or even producing information in situ. I would particularly like to thank Louis Wora of the government's Statistical Service in this regard.

38. The development agencies of the United Nations have recently shown more interest in Gabon, providing significant funding for studies on gender, reproductive health, and other UN priority areas. The UN population fund alone provided almost $2 million to Gabon in the 2002–2006 funding round for gender and population development initiatives.

39. See, for example, Rokhaya Fall, *Femmes et pouvoir dans les sociétés Nord-Sénégambiennes* (Dakar: CODESRIA, 1994); Aissatou Sow Dia, *L'évolution des femmes dans la vie politique sénégalaise de 1945 à nos jours,* Mémoire de maîtrise, Département d'Histoire, Université Cheik Anta Diop, Dakar, 1994–95.

2

Science, Statistics, and Stories

In Search of Methodology

Scrutinizing and criticizing global norms and problematizing dominant discourses are not new activities in this field of social science. As Nederveen Pieterse has put it, the move against universalistic discourses at the beginning of the twenty-first century and the renewed concern with "culture" are evidence of how the academic community tends to:

> rework established discourses. [. . .] Culture comes into development studies at a time of retreat from structural and macro approaches in development theory in favour of micro and actor-oriented approaches.[1]

In francophone Africa, culture has served as a vehicle for articulating development discourses since the early twentieth century.

The focus on cultural integrity versus exogenous universality featured prominently in francophone African thought both within Africa and in the francophone African diasporas in the Interwar period and throughout the anticolonial struggle. As proponents of the *Négritude* movement Léopold Sédar Senghor and Aimé Césaire positioned "culture" as a key instrument with which the new African elite would fashion its resistance to colonial rule. It became a driving force behind the aspirations of the political class of the era: "During the period (1956–60) of the *loi-cadre* and autonomous states within the Community, various versions of *négritude* and African socialism suffused the ideology of all the nationalist movements in French-speaking West Africa."[2] Likewise, the centrality of culture in Fanon's experience of alienation and resistance to colonial paradigms of development influenced generations of theorists of political emancipation in African and Caribbean regions under French colonial rule.[3] In the postcolonial era, the absence of political and economic autonomy from the former colonial power[4] has served to reinforce the primacy of culture. Indeed, the concept of an indigenous unifying culture became an instrument in the hands of the first generation of the African political elite to forge a new identity for the postcolonial State. Here, as in other parts of the developing world, "culture" has been a conveyance through which the State has created a postcolonial national identity in its own image. In francophone West Africa, prestige buildings and monuments erected in capitals across the region testify to a certain idea of modernity as national identity.[5] Supporting a monolithic configuration of State and society, "the nation has been engineered top-down by ideologues and state-sponsored official literature."[6] In this way though culture has been central to the discourse of development in postcolonial francophone Africa, it has served as an instrument of exclusion and marginalization reinforcing the political hegemony of an elite.

That this elite has failed to incorporate into its ranks a cross section of the societies over which it rules is commonplace. Many of those who have numbered among its most long-serving luminaries were the products of the French colonial system which offered to a few local boys and men the opportunity of a French education and "assimilation" into French civilization. It was and still is a system that replicates French, and more generally European, gender norms, and as a result, and as Nederveen Pieterse points out, the way culture has been monopolized and used in the creation of a new national identity in the post-colonial African context has been: "A profoundly gendered process [. . .] nationalism has been a profoundly masculinist discourse."[7]

THE GLOBAL CONTEXT OF CULTURE IN DEVELOPMENT

One of contradictions inherent in this use of a cultural discourse of national politics in francophone Africa becomes apparent specifically in the field of development. The national objectives of development are not defined nor in any sense controlled by the national elites of the developing nations of sub-Saharan Africa. The economic mantra of "modernization" that permeates development politics in this and other developing regions was defined by the Western powers in the aftermath of World War II and institutionalized through the Bretton Woods institutions. This mantra has remained largely unaltered though "there have been heated debates on whether or not these recommended policies and institutions are in fact appropriate for today's developing countries."[8] This model of economic development introduced by the West has been maintained by the international financial institutions[9] which have become even more influential during the recent period of economic globalization. Any development practitioner or academic who has worked in a highly indebted country knows that the World Bank representative is now one of the most, if not the most, influential development policy-maker in the country.

Within this global context, international financial institutions have been imposing uniform economic "solutions" to the ills besetting the impoverished countries of the developing world. The ideological and cultural infrastructure upon which economic liberalism rests, along with the configuration of modernity and the process of modernization that accompanies this model, are imported into the developing world contexts through development packages designed by the international financial institutions. These exogenous structures are layered onto local economic structures redefining not only economic objectives but the whole range of policy fields in which the international community plays an active role (namely all those fields where bilateral or multilateral agencies are the main financial sponsor).

Faced with the expanding role of international structures and the multiplication of policy fields, development research has been showing greater interest in investigating competing or indigenous cultures of development. In the case of francophone West Africa, indigenous cultures have been a privileged site of academic enquiry, particularly in North American and West European institutions, since the 1920s.[10] While these developments have tended to remain confined to ethnographic and literary studies, more recently social anthropology has succeeded in making the disciplinary leap between African cultural studies and social science research in its relocation of culture as the object of study rather than as the agent of change. Likewise, cultural anthropology[11] has advanced a more complex and dynamic view of culture as a network of structures and relations harboring a plurality of cultural realities within a single research site, though admittedly it has not been fully engaged with the gender dimensions of this site. In respect of new research methodologies, recent sociological research in France has made progress towards theorizing interdisciplinary links between literary analysis, cultural studies and social science, notably in the journals *Mouvements* and *Sociétés*, though not specifically in relation to policy-making as I will discuss in more detail in part VI.[12] Notwithstanding these general advances, the incorporation of a cultural dimension into the core research methods of development studies research is still relatively rare.

NEW PERSPECTIVES INTO SOCIAL SCIENCE

Among the many challenges these disciplinary developments set for gender and development research is the elusive goal of finding methods that allow cultural/literary analysis to inform the social science of policy-making.

Achieving this goal would constitute a significant methodological advance and also and most importantly it would integrate hitherto marginalized voices of women who have used non-formal or non-traditional means of political engagement as a result of being excluded from the formal channels of debate on development and change.

Creative writing and other cultural forms have traditionally featured in social science research only as exemplification for findings generated by established social science methods. These cultural products, and the voices that speak through them, have been used as sources of supplementary evidence but not as primary tools for providing social data.

The premise underlying the present study is that there is a possibility of achieving a closer understanding of gender and social development in francophone Africa if we redesign the parameters of social science research in this field to combine literary and social science methodologies. By doing this the empirical and epistemological environment that sustained social development policy-making and implementation in the past can be challenged through the deconstruction of the understanding of social categories and social change. This goes some way towards confronting the conceptual constraints of development economics that have limited what we explore and uncover in research even in the most empirically defined areas, such as numerical data collection:

> [T]he way decision makers interpret current "reality" and trends and conceive their future information needs itself depends upon the existing framework of data collection and presentation [. . .] whether or not statistics are broken down by gender depends on the recognition of women. [. . .] Neither can the choice and definition of what to measure and to report it be treated as a technical issue [. . .] political influences upon the collection and interpretation of statistics must not be ignored.[13]

The hypothesis I am proposing here is that it is possible to access a greater range of understandings of social realities by redefining the limits of social science methodologies to accommodate "non-scientific" texts. I propose an interdisciplinary approach that admits flexibility in the construction of categories and admits cultural variation in our understanding of quality of life issues and social disadvantage. The objective is to present a picture of gender and social development at the intersection of more than one analytical dimension.

The approach does not reject or overturn traditional social science methodology. Though the positivist "empirical" approach has been severely criticized for its heavy reliance on quantitative research methods, it is both unnecessary and undesirable in this study to exclude quantitative research methods. Indeed, it would be counter-productive to eliminate entirely the empirical approach that has generated the vast majority of gender and development findings in the francophone African region, where arithmetic projections of complex social realities continue to dominate debate and research on gender and social change. For the time being, the continued dominance of this approach to researching and understanding social development seems inevitable. As Neylan has argued, policy-makers and bureaucracies use calculative technologies to contain uncertainty: "numbers [. . .] can easily be accepted on face value and be turned uncritically into decision-making rationales."[14] The reliability of these data that claim to record trends in the quality of life of male and female populations in the francophone African sub-region will be subject to closer examination in chapters 6 to 9, which explore the theory and the practice of data profiling in Senegal and Gabon.

A MULTI-METHODOLOGY FOR CAPTURING GENDERED DEVELOPMENT

Far from abandoning the objective/empirical approach, the rationalist method constitutes the first of three distinct methodological approaches providing a multidimensional analysis of the discourse of gender and development and its impact in the francophone region. The second dimension of analysis is drawn from social science research methodology and involves the interpretation of social realities from a social values perspective, in this case the social values perspective is located in feminist research. Lastly, an aesthetic/subjective analysis is drawn from creative/narrative accounts of social realities as they present in the cultural location. Each of the three analytical dimensions contributes different and uniquely useful elements to the present study. Table 2.1 summarizes the three dimensions, their information sources, and their principal methodologies. Each dimension provides a set of findings within its discrete analytical category and contributes to a new set of outcomes generated in the interstices between these dimensions.

It is not the aim of this study to pit disciplines or sources of information one against the other, nor to test the power of social science to describe social realities against the power of creative writing. Rather this study has set out to be genuinely interdisciplinary and to use sources of information in such a way that presupposes their potential for complementary synthesis. In this respect, the traditional boundaries that contain research disciplines have been rejected in favor of an approach that assesses the value of multiple information sources

Table 2.1. Dimensions of Analysis

	Dimension 1 objective/empirical	Dimension 2 social values	Dimension 3 aesthetic/subjective
Example of information type	Quantitative data	Philosophical/ ideological interpretations	Creative writing
Example of information sources	UN "human development" data bank, World Bank catalogue of social indicators	Academic gender studies/feminist research	Social realist fiction/politically engaged novels by francophone West African writers
Primary research method	Quantitative analysis of data	Interview researchers in the field (qualitative data gathering)	Thematic analysis of novels

in relation to the study's objectives and not in relation to its discipline of origin. While the empirical approach focuses on providing quantifiable answers, the social values approach interrogates the ideological foundations of a discursive policy tradition raising questions on the way in which the discourse of gender and development has evolved during the postcolonial era:

> Do socially constructed international human rights advance the economic and social well-being of women? Or do these norms reflect a gender bias that hinders the betterment of women?[15]

Social values research locates such questions in the cultural context and by allowing culturally specific responses to inform our understanding of these issues, enables further layers of knowledge and meaning to be set alongside a globally-established empirical or "universal" language of rights.

Within the cultural location a range of voices has been responding to these globally relevant questions through a multiplicity of national and continental structures. First and foremost, these include influential voices from the Academy,[16] political representatives, and representatives of civil society (lobby groups, pressure groups, NGOs, church representatives) in francophone Africa. But increasingly these voices have included participants not widely recognized as having a role to play in the formal political arena. In the case of francophone Africa, this third tier of participation that has emerged separately from the international community and the national formal political arena, includes politically-engaged writers.

VOICES ON THE MARGINS OF GENDER AND DEVELOPMENT

Francophone African women's writing has demonstrated a political commitment to opening up the debate on the position of women in African society since it first made its mark in the international francophone literary system in the 1970s. Though it can be argued that creative writing has provided a platform upon which African women intellectuals have maintained a constant presence in the debate on gender and development over the past thirty years, the importance of this writing has not been recognized in the policy-making structures.

The role the literary text plays in this study is innovative as is the assumption that social science is not necessarily the most privileged research site within which to evaluate quality of life issues and draw information of relevance to gender and development policy. The unique quality the literary text can bring to a study of discourse and culture in development politics lies in the power it has to contribute the subjective point of view within the relative freedom of literary expression and within a culturally-specific context authenticated by the author. These qualities free the literary dimension from the epistemological constraints of the empirical/objective approach. This approach responds to the concept of the "third space" theorized by Homi Bhabha, and which has since informed much postcolonial literary criticism.[17] It is a space within which marginalized voices can move from their colonial peripheries to a postcolonial centre. In this way, the literary dimension enables marginalized voices from the postcolonial world to participate in an arena up to the present defined and limited by structures and cultures created outside postcolonial francophone Africa. While the limits imposed by the subjectivity of creative writing must be acknowledged,[18] the explicit absence of objectivity in the literary text stops being an automatic bar to the generation of social research findings once the discursive framework of empirical research has been recognized as not of itself "objective."

METHODS: OBJECTIVE, INTERPRETATIVE AND SUBJECTIVE

The research methodology of the present study has been designed around the primary objective of integrating a multiplicity of information sources into the analysis of discourses of gender and social development in francophone Africa. The study sets out to inform the dominant model of social development policy-making with inputs from the recipients of policy, namely women and men who are the targets of policy. In other words, it introduces a "bottom-up" model of policy analysis which provides a different set of findings from the traditional "top-down" model.[19] The bottom-up approach, drawing on local politically-engaged literature (short stories and novels) by women writers, provides the cultural/aesthetic dimension of analysis mapped in the third column of table 2.1. The social values approach operates in a middle ground, engaging with the views of policy-makers and activists (men and women) in the locality from their location in the formal arena of politics and policy-making. These inputs are combined with the more traditional "empirical" social science inputs of statistical data and surveys.

The methodology is interdisciplinary insofar as the results of the quantitative, qualitative and thematic analyses are used to inform each other as well as to add, each in its own manner, to the knowledge base in this field. Ultimately, the aims of this study are both substantive and theoretical. In terms of theory, it uses a multi-methodological and interdisciplinary framework of analysis that combines existing but discipline-distinct dimensions of analysis. In this respect, the study adds to our knowledge and understanding of the limits and possibilities of discipline-specific methodologies.

Though the study is innovative in the combination of three dimensions of analysis, disciplinary constraints are respected within the separate dimensions, and as such established research methodologies and procedures are used. Where the study contributes to our understanding of methodology is in synthesizing findings rather than methodologies. By combining outcomes from literary and social science research the study will result in a more culturally-embedded understanding of how gender impacts upon social development in the francophone West African context.

RATIONALIST DEVELOPMENT METHODOLOGY

The methodology used in the first empirical analytical dimension aims primarily at identifying the key social variables that make up the dominant discourse of gender and development. The tools it uses to measure these variables are drawn from traditional social statistical quantitative analysis. In this dimension, the factors of analysis are economic and social indicators, and social development is measured in terms of variance from a numerical representation (1.0) of "social/human development." The degree to which a woman experiences social indicators (for example, access to primary education) reveals the degree to which she is experiencing "social development" as defined within this paradigm. The data used in the empirical analysis are population-wide social statistics produced mainly though not exclusively within the UN system. During fieldwork in the region, locally produced statistical material was gathered to fill gaps in the UN data. The data are assembled to produce new quantitative findings presented in the form of country-specific data profile tables for Senegal and Gabon.[20]

Within the empirical/objective dimension of analysis, the motor for change is the market economy which in turn drives the process of modernization. Here modernization is posited as the necessary condition for social development and in this perspective "modernity" is a fixed concept. In the second dimension of analysis, the social values approach, the concept of modernity is not fixed. The presentation of modernity as based on a market economy generating capital surplus in the economy and an increasingly urbanized economic environment—in other words a Western model of economic growth and development—can be accepted or rejected. The social values perspective recognizes that all the categories under examination are constructed, and therefore can be subject to change over time and space. From within the social values dimension of analysis, research methods are designed to "deconstruct" the dominant model of modernity and social development. This deconstruction of the dominant model is carried through in the case study of Senegal in part V.

Within the aesthetic/cultural dimension of analysis, the concepts of gender and social development are not articulated in the "scientific" discourse of quantitative and qualitative social research. There are no explicit references to gender and development or "exogenous concepts of modernity" in even the most politically-engaged women's literature from francophone West Africa. The literary expression of social issues is composed in a quite different language in the social realist novels examined in part VI.

In the literary context, the key themes are typically the position of women in the family and the impact of Westernization on women's lives. These themes provide the literary equivalent to the key variables and policy fields analysed in social science research. The literary text focuses on the individual and the subjectivity of that person's gendered experience of development.

EXPANDING THE RESEARCH BASE

As each dimension operates within a different conceptual framework, the target of analysis differs in each case. The empirical objective dimension uses quantitative data to report on large numbers of women who share certain characteristics, as defined by the researcher. Women are identified in this model as a single social entity. In this sense hundreds, thousands and even millions of individuals can be reported as a single group. This single group then becomes the "target population" of social policy.

Social values research in the field of gender and development also uses population-wide studies but with a different objective. Here the structures and categories that make up the population-wide data are problematized and alternative categories identified. These are evidenced by dividing the population-wide group into sub-groups which are then invited to express fundamental divergence from the dominant discourse. Through the research design, these groups are empowered to voice alternative identities and development goals.

For its part, the literary text does not labor under the constraints defined by population size or competing identities. The literary text does not need to concern itself with numerical issues, or with issues of identity at the level of the individual as opposed to the population, or whether the data produced at either level can be triangulated. Being free from the constraints and limitations of social science methodology, the text is also freed from the problems of causality in social science methods, such as the problem of survey or interview questions that tend to produce certain answers and conclusions.

Literary representations of social realities are used in this study as a means of accessing the subjective perspective on social experience in a specific cultural locality. The question here becomes whether the creative text can firstly represent a present reality, and secondly indicate where society is heading. In other words, can literature provide a lens through which we can view a generalized present and a conditional future? Given that the author of the creative text may choose to deliver a vision of what is *desired* as opposed to what *is* in society, using the literary form as a platform to articulate alternative views in that society, I would propose that the literary text cannot be used to reflect a "universal truth," whereas it can be used as a tool for illuminating the subjective perspective on social experience and, importantly, it can also be used to help ground knowledge gained from social science methods within a specific cultural location. The hypothesis being tested here proposes that while social science can provide a statistical extrapolation of current trends as an approximation of the future based on current events, and qualitative "social values" research can deliver information on the aspirations of a society or an individual within the context of the research project as defined by the researcher, the literary lens is uniquely endowed to contribute a perspective on the present and a vision of the future that draws from lived experience and intellectualizes that experience in a subjectively drawn account of the way gender and development is lived in the local environment, and that such subjective accounts can contribute to the construction of social policy theory.

THE RESEARCHER AS RESEARCH OBJECT?

Exploring the gender dimension of social policy in francophone West Africa provides a position from which a non-African researcher/observer is marginalized in multiple ways. Identifiable as an outsider, culturally alien to the community, the researcher without ostensible African origins will be racially "othered" as well as experiencing further "otherings," such as being a non-Muslim. All of these characteristics in the researcher can extend the cultural distance between the incomer and the environment.

However, the fact of being externally perceived as an outsider in the culture can offer the researcher a privileged vantage point on the margins of society. Occupying an unfamiliar location in the environment, being non-African, non-Muslim, non-male, and not ostensibly representing any established power center, can be as productive as it is challenging, protecting the researcher from prejudice, while providing a shield behind which she can take shelter from her own and the community's preconceptions of the process and outcomes of developmental research.[21]

To this extent externality has as much potential to be creative as to be a minefield of ignorance. As Brown and Rhodes (2003) have argued, the ethics of the research process and its outcome (in their case, writing research) is a process that is determined as much by the agency of the observed as by the intentions of the observer:

> Following Levinas, Derrida suggests that the responsible subject (in our case the researcher) be regarded as a host or a guest who, rather than being self-sufficient, is defined by the welcome offered by the Other. [. . .] An ethics of research writing emerges through the characterization of the relations between self and Other in the text. As such, the Other is not considered as an object under the scientific gaze of the writer or as an entity than can be represented unproblematically.[22]

Notwithstanding these efforts to relocate the subject and object of research within a postmodern paradigm, there are those who warn us that an individual who is external to a given culture/society has no right to trespass into its territory and even less to try to interpret its social realities. Postcolonial theorists have also quite rightly interrogated the methodologies of Western research that involve viewing one culture with the tools and viewing instruments produced by another culture, particularly when that other culture is a "dominant" and universalizing one.[23] Those of us with francophone and Anglophone origins are products of two of the most dominating and universalizing cultures in history, and as such must pay particular heed to the historic tendency within our cultures (and Greco-Roman cultures in general) to ignore cultural difference or where we do see it to target it for obliteration in the misguided belief that our culture and civilization is global. We are compelled to listen to those, like Huma Ibrahim, who warn against Western researchers positioning themselves in a role she has characterized as:

> I, white academic feminist, claim you, Third World woman, not being able or desiring to carry the class label of feminist, as victim. I, white feminist, name you victim in defining/calling you victim.[24]

Ibrahim's warning, that we must not fall into the trap of assuming that any woman from a developing country is necessarily more of a victim than a "Western" woman, is a salient one in West Africa as the discussion in part VI on the origins of gender politics reveals. While the dangers of making such assumptions are clear, it is equally inadvisable to take this warning to extremes by designating even the worst excesses of gender discrimination in Africa as "cultural practices" on which no judgment can be passed. This academic fashion is a form of intellectual censorship, one which it is equally important to avoid in a field exploring the gendered nature of disadvantage. Teresa Brennan warned against such tendencies to over-interpret the postmodernist position. Feminist scholarship can be a discourse as well as a space in which to reflect on social problems:

> Is it simply the case that as Women's Studies becomes more institutionalised, feminist scholars are defining their concerns in relation to those of their colleagues in existing disciplines? This could account both for an often uncritical adherence to a postmodernism that negates the right to act, if not speak, and to the distance between feminism in the institution and outside it.[25]

Approaching gender identity and experience as a cross-cultural issue, does not require gender identity and experience to be monolithic or identical across the globe. The experience of women in the developing world can serve to uncover what in the industrialized world may lie beneath the materialism that often disguises gender inequalities within our own nuclear families and beyond entry-level access to professional careers.

Further, the creativity that is required by women from economically poor countries to formulate and implement modes of resistance could, at the very least, be a source of inspiration for those who experience marginalization, fixity and containment in their more economically comfortable societies. Ibrahim's warning could be recast for the white Western researcher entering the West African research community into a call for collaboration and collective action:

> I, European feminist, claim you, African feminist, as a person able to and desiring to carry the label of feminist and able to teach me not only about your feminism but about mine too.

NOTES

1. Jan Nederveen Pieterse, *Development Theory—Deconstructions/Reconstructions* (London: Sage, 2001), 60.

2. Immanuel Wallerstein, "Elites in French-speaking Africa: The Social Basis of Ideas," *Journal of Modern African Studies* 3, no. 1 (1965), 25.

3. Frantz Fanon, *Les Damnés de la Terre* (Paris: Maspero, 1961); Frantz Fanon, *Peau Noire Masques Blancs* (Paris: Seuil, 1998) [1952]. Fanon opposed *Négritude*'s essentialist and ethnographic conceptualization of culture using political experience as a starting point from which to theorize African culture. Sam Oluoch Imbo discusses "ethnophilosophy" versus hermeneutics in twentieth-century African philosophy in *An Introduction to African Philosophy* (1998).

4. There is not the space here to discuss the degree to which the politics of francophone African countries have been influenced by France in the postcolonial era. Suffice it to say that stakeholders and commentators have defined the relationship very differently. Where Francois-Xavier Vershave wrote of neocolonialism in his exposés of *"la FrançAfrique,"* the term *"coopération"* has been favored by the French political class. This notion of *coopération* has survived largely unchallenged by politicians during the postcolonial era bar a few exceptions such as Jean-Pierre Cot in the early 1980s and Lionel Jospin in the late 1990s.

5. Dakar has not escaped this trend, a recent example being the Millennium Park on the *Corniche-ouest*, but Abidjan and Libreville are better examples with their skylines punctuated with high-rise, energy-guzzling, air-conditioned glass and concrete constructions.

6. Dominic Thomas, *Nation-Building, Propaganda, and Literature in Francophone Africa* (Bloomington: Indiana University Press, 2002), 2.

7. Nederven Pieterse (2001), 62–63. The masculinist discourse extends out of the construction of the francophone African *polis* into its critique: See Achille Mbembe's "Provisional Notes on the Postcolony" (1992), *On the Postcolony* (2001) and "On the Postcolony: A Brief Response to Critics" (2005). Mbembe's analysis of the structural and ideological dimensions of contemporary francophone African politics helps inform the present discussion of the conceptual limits of the discursive landscape (the "imaginary") in which social priorities are laid down and acted upon.

8. Chang, Ha-Joon. *Kicking Away the Ladder: Development Strategy in Historical Perspective* (London: Anthem Press, 2002), 1.

9. In development politics the IFIs are led by the World Bank and the International Monetary Fund (IMF) and are supported by the developed nations through the Development Assistance Committee (DAC) of the OECD, and through other economic groupings such as the "Paris Club" which brings together the leading lending nations of the world.

10. The interwar period in France saw the rise in ethnographical studies of French West African cultures. In the more recent past, there has been a huge growth in francophone African studies, for a large part literary studies, in the United States, Canada and the UK, as well as in French-speaking countries. The interest in this field has rolled out throughout the Academy, as testified by the number of new courses in

francophone North African, West African and Caribbean studies launched over the past 15 years.

11. J. Clifford and G. E. Marcus, eds., *Writing Culture: The Poetics and Politics of Ethnography* (Berkeley: University of California Press, 1986).

12. See, for example, P. Christias, "Du littéraire et du social—le double: recherche pour une métaodon," in *Sociétés* 64, no. 2, 1999, 67–75; and B. Ricard, "Pour un rapprochement de la littérature et de la sociologie," *Sociétés* 62, no. 4, 1998, 5–7.

13. Roy Carr-Hill, *Social Conditions in Sub-Saharan Africa* (London: Macmillan, 1990), 179–80.

14. Julian Neylan, "Quantifying Social Entitites: an historical-sociological critique," *Journal of Sociology and Social Welfare*, December 2005, 23.

15. William F. Felice, *The Global New Deal: Economic and Social Human Rights in World Politics* (Lanham, MD: Rowman & Littlefield, 2003), 157.

16. See Arturo Escobar, *Encountering Development—The Making and Unmaking of the Third World* (Princeton, N.J.: Princeton University Press, 1995); Lourdes Benaría, *Gender, Development and Globalization—Economics as If People Mattered* (New York & London: Routledge, 2003).

17. See, for example, Valérie Orlando, *Nomadic Voices in Exile* (Athens: Ohio University Press, 1999), 3.

18. The implications of these limitations are discussed in chapters 16 to 18.

19. The human development approach is an example of a top-down model, which starts from the level of the policy-maker determining goals and outputs which are then delivered or passed down to the recipient in the developing world.

20. The new tables are incorporated into the discussion of numeric approaches to mapping the quality of life in chapters 7 and 8.

21. This was a reality that I found consistently advantageous in conducting this research. Whenever possible I conducted my fieldwork ostensibly unassisted. Given the topic of the enquiry being a female academic generated generally positive responses, and being perceived as racially different from the majority and working apparently independently without a team of colleagues or assistants in tow, most often incited a willingness among my interlocutors to engage in the project and help. It was very rare to encounter suspicion, resentment or rejection among the people from whom I sought information and advice.

22. A. D. Brown and C. Rhodes, "Writing Responsibly: Narrative Fiction and Organization Studies," *Organization* 12, no. 4, 505–529.

23. For the origin of this discussion see Gayatri Spivak, "Can the Subaltern Speak?" in *Colonial Discourse and Post-colonial Theory*, Patrick Williams and Laura Chrisman, eds. (New York: Harvester Wheatsheaf, 1993), 102; and Lata Mani, "Cultural Theory, Colonial Texts: Reading Eye-witness Accounts of Widow Burning," in *Cultural Studies*, L. Grossberg, C. Nelson, and P. Treichler, eds. (New York: Routledge, 1992), 403.

24. Huma Ibrahim, "Ontological Victimhood," in *The Politics of (M)Othering,* Obioma Nnaemeka, ed. (London: Routledge 1997), 157.

25. Teresa Brennan, series editor, "Preface," in *The Politics of (M)Othering,* Obioma Nnaemeka, ed. (London: Routledge 1997), xii.

II

WHEN GENDER AND DEVELOPMENT
WENT GLOBAL

3

The Origins of a Global Discourse, 1945 to 1990

The discursive journey development that has traveled in francophone Africa began in the last months of the Second World War when the industrialized world laid the groundwork for its relationship with the developing world at the Bretton Woods and Dumbarton Oaks. With the United States at the helm, the victors of World War II fashioned a raft of new institutions in the image of the Western powers. In this new global political community, France struggled to find a position from which it could continue to exert a global influence. It was a dilemma facing both the superpowers of the imperial age. France and Britain were accommodated onto the supreme body of the United Nations, as permanent members of the UN Security Council, while having effectively already lost their global role in the interwar period to the superpowers of the twentieth century. As Soviet Russia became increasingly isolated in the years following World War II, the United States assumed the mantle of world leadership and defined the political culture in which the "supranational" project for the developing world would henceforth be conducted.

As the age of empire reached its end in many parts of the world, development became a supranational theatre of policy-making. The years immediately after World War II saw Britain withdraw from Burma, Siam and the Indian sub-continent and in the following decade from its African dominions. The geographical space in which this new project could be played out expanded exponentially. It was with reference to the Anglophone regions of the developing world that the discourse of development first evolved, and it was during this period just before the liberation of the French developing areas that the language of development became resolutely English. The impact of language culture on the framing of this discourse is revealed in the direction that gender and development has followed in the sixty years of development politics in francophone Africa.

THE UNITED NATIONS AND THE FRAMING OF A DISCOURSE

The UN has served as the international community's main platform for debating gender issues since the entry into force of the founding Charter of the United Nations in the autumn of 1945. The Preamble to the Charter set out the commitment of the UN to uphold "the equal rights of men and women" in all the member states of the new international community. Despite this commitment, the case for equal rights has traveled a slow and uneven path in the six decades since the founding charter was signed and the Universal Declaration of Human Rights confirmed the international community's commitment to gender equality.[1]

At the outset, responsibility for defining and monitoring equal rights between men and women had been allocated to one of the founding organs of the United Nations, the Economic and Social Council. It was through the Economic and Social Council that the many commissions and committees were set up to report on matters related to the well-being of women (and men) across the globe. These structures included from 1946, the Commission on the Status of Women (CSW). It was the responsibility of CSW to oversee not just the definition but more importantly the implementation of the international community's commitment to equal rights. In its early days, the CSW focused much of its effort on generating the legal framework for defining, promoting and protecting the human rights of women. The primary instrument used by the United Nations system for translating the discourse of rights into practice was the international legal convention.

The conventions have generally preceded rather than reflected political developments at the national level of the member states, as such they assumed a pro-active role to promote gender and social development throughout the international system. One of the earliest conventions of this type was the "Convention on the Political Rights of Women" adopted by the UN in 1952 and coming into force from 1954. The 1952 Convention states:

Article 1   Women shall be entitled to vote in all elections on equal terms with men, without any discrimination.

Article 2   Women shall be eligible for election to all publicly elected bodies, established by national law, on equal terms with men, without any discrimination.

It is both ironic and revealing of the lag that exists between discourse and practice that Switzerland, the seat of several UN institutions, failed to comply with Articles 1 and 2 of the Convention on the Political Rights of Women for almost two decades after the convention was adopted. In 1971, Switzerland lifted the ban on women voting in national elections. It is notable that at the time of the 1971 reform, over 30 percent of the Swiss electorate, including some women's groups, opposed enfranchising women.

The Convention on the Political Rights of Women addressed primarily the problem of institutionalized sexism in the formal political arena. The next major legal instrument created by the international system was the "Convention on the Consent to Marriage" of 1962, a particularly contentious and ground-breaking document in that it confronted cultural and religious practices that were deemed discriminatory. This convention is still not complied with in many Member States of the UN in the twenty-first century. There has been an on-going dispute in the Muslim areas of the world, including francophone West Africa, around whether the Convention on the Consent to Marriage contravenes religious law. The contention centers on whether the teachings of the Koran state that agreement to a marriage must be *sought* and not *imposed*. Islamic scholars insist that denying a Muslim (female or male) the right to consent in marriage is a contravention of the Koran while Islamic politicians and many clerics continue to cite Sharia Law as a reason for not ratifying the 1962 Convention on the Consent to Marriage.[2]

In Africa, the decolonization of British and French possessions in the 1950s repositioned the continent on the UN development agenda, encouraging a more pro-active role for the international community spearheaded by the Economic Commission for Africa (ECA) from 1958. The ECA began to highlight the issue of the status of African women by commissioning reports and studies that focused primarily on the former British colonies.[3] For its part, the Commission on the Status of Women produced the long-awaited "Programme of Concerted International Action for the Advancement of Women"[4] that marked a change in thinking on the connection between gender and disadvantage in Africa and signaling a more holistic approach to policy-making from 1970.

Meanwhile the Commission on the Status of Women's preoccupation with the codification of women's rights resulted in the UN agencies coming together to draft a new convention addressing what they saw as all aspects of women's rights. The result was the "Convention on the Elimination of All Forms of Discrimination Against Women" (CEDAW),[5] adopted in 1979 and in force worldwide from September 1981.

The process by which CEDAW is implemented in the countries[6] that are party to the Convention is overseen by the Committee for the Elimination of

Discrimination against Women. The Member States are required to report at regular intervals to the CEDAW committee on the progress they are making in implementing CEDAW in their countries. The CEDAW committee, made up of 23 women elected by the signatory countries, reviews, during its twice-yearly meetings, a number of country reports every year. From these reports, the Committee draws up its own report and submits this to the Economic and Social Council. It falls to the Economic and Social Council to make a yearly statement on the implementation of CEDAW to the UN General Assembly.

On the face of it, the UN system cannot be faulted in its efforts to set up a framework to promote women's rights throughout the world. The critical flaw in the framework is that it contains no element of coercion. At no point in this procedure can the UN enforce observance of the Convention on any member state, regardless of whether this country has signed, ratified and publicly committed itself to implementing the Convention. The CEDAW Committee can make recommendations and suggest ways for improving progress, but it has no powers to go further than this. Notwithstanding this significant impediment, the CEDAW Committee has described the Convention as "legally binding" and cites it as "the basic legal framework to protect . . . the human rights of women."[7]

The problem of implementing CEDAW is an ongoing issue throughout the world and not least in francophone Africa. The *Réseau des organisations féminines de l'Afrique francophone* (*ROFAF*) regional conference of 2009 addressed the theme in terms of *La Situation des droits des femmes et de l'égalité des sexes en Afrique francophone.*[8] Participants presenting at this conference evaluated the degree to which countries in the region have been implementing CEDAW and observing Article 18 paragraph 3 of the African Charter that requires all African States parties[9] to implement CEDAW in a timely fashion, a commitment reiterated by an African Union (AU) Heads of State communiqué in 2006. The case of Mali is representative of the situation in much of the region. While Mali had signed and ratified CEDAW by 1985 two major obstacles continue to undermine its implementation:

> *La jouissance effective des droits humains des femmes se heurte à plusieurs facteurs dont les plus importants sont les pesanteurs socioculturelles et la pauvreté. [. . .] Comme dans la plupart des pays de la sous-région du Sahel, les lois religieuses et les coutumes s'appliquent au Mali. Ces traditions heurtent parfois la Constitution et les lois maliennes elles-mêmes tout comme elles entrent en conflit avec les engagements internationaux pris par le Mali.*[10]

Notwithstanding these obstacles, all fourteen former French colonies of West Africa ratified the Convention on the Elimination of All Forms of Discrimination Against Women between 1982, Guinea and Congo being the first to sign, and 2001 when Mauritania finally ratified the text. The Anglophone African states have followed an almost identical pattern of compliance between 1984, when Kenya led the field, and 2004 when Swaziland adopted CEDAW. The obstacles to implementation have likewise crossed the linguistic divide, with poverty, conflict, and institutional biases constituting some of the more intractable barriers to compliance in sub-Saharan Africa.

INTERNATIONALIZING GENDER DISCOURSE AT THE WORLD WOMEN'S CONFERENCES

As the problems of implementing international conventions at the national level became increasingly clear, the Commission on the Status of Women turned its attention to exploring other mechanisms through which to facilitate the protection and advancement of women's rights. By the early 1970s, CSW was particularly focusing on how to address the problems women were facing in the developing world. This led to a series of international events designed to bring the situation of women in the developing world to the top of the political agenda. The launch of these events took place in 1975, designated by the UN as "International Women's Year," at the first UN World Conference on the Advancement of Women held in Mexico City. The first UN "Decade for Women" 1975 to 1985 was punctuated by a second World Conference on the Advancement of Women held in Copenhagen, Denmark, in 1980, and its end was marked by a third world conference in Nairobi, Kenya, in 1985.

The first world conference focused on alerting the world to the persistence of poverty in the developing world, and particularly on highlighting the gendered nature of poverty. It provided evidence from around the world revealing that women make up over two-thirds of the world's poorest people. Out of this conference came the first global women's fund, UNIFEM. In the 30 years following its establishment, UNIFEM went on to earn a reputation in francophone Africa and Africa generally as the key advocate in the UN system. The discourse generated by UNIFEM in collaboration with feminist and women's organizations around the developing world has been pro-active and recognized as leading the debate in the UN system in advance of more traditionally conservative elements such as UNESCO, and the more cautious stance of agencies such as UNFPA (the UN's Population Fund). The UNFPA is a fund that, like UNIFEM, depends on voluntary contributions from Member States. UNFPA rarely adopts a political stance on women's rights and so attracts little adverse publicity.[11] It usually receives about ten times the contributions Member States are prepared to offer UNIFEM.

UNIFEM has taken a lead in advancing many aspects of the gender in development debate including women's economic empowerment. This theme rose to the top of the agenda at the third world conference in 1985. The outcome of the Nairobi conference was a 15-year plan called Forward-Looking Strategies for the Advancement of Women. These Forward-Looking Strategies contained 372 paragraphs that attempted to address discrimination in every aspect of women's lives in society.

The prominence given to economic empowerment from the late 1970s and through the 1980s led to an upsurge in scholarly publishing in the field, first in Scandinavia, then more generally in Western Europe, Canada and the United States. Much of the research focused on evaluating the implementation of the Forward-Looking Strategies. Research revealed that progress was, in some areas, imperceptible. In short, it was slow and in almost all cases falling far short of the objectives and the schedule set at Nairobi. Indeed, the global commodities crises in the late 1970s and early 1980s led to a worsening in the economic position of women in developing countries, and particularly in Africa.

It was in this context that CSW encouraged the UN General Assembly to call a fourth world conference to evaluate the crisis. The proposal was accepted and it was decided that the world's most populous country should host the conference.

THE 4TH WORLD WOMEN'S CONFERENCE, BEIJING, 1995

The fourth World Conference on Women held in Beijing in September 1995 generated unprecedented worldwide interest and attendance. There were 189 delegations,[12] and some 50,000 participants discussed the situation facing women around the world as the twentieth century was drawing to a close.

The primary aim of the Beijing summit was to look at where countries had got to in implementing Forward-Looking Strategies adopted in Nairobi. The opening document of the conference testified to the lack of progress:

> 10 years after the Nairobi Conference, equality between women and men has still not been achieved. On average, women represent a mere 10 per cent of all elected legislators worldwide and in most national and international administrative structures, both public and private, they remain underrepresented. The United Nations is no exception. Fifty years after its creation, the United Nations is continuing to deny itself the benefits of women's leadership by their under representation at decision-making levels within the Secretariat and the specialized agencies.[13]

The point was underlined more succinctly in paragraph 42: "Most of the goals set out in the Nairobi Forward-looking Strategies for the Advancement of Women have not been achieved."[14]

In the light of this, the mission statement of the Beijing Conference set out the main objective as:

accelerating the implementation of the Nairobi Forward-looking Strategies for the Advancement of Women and removing all the obstacles to women's active participation in all spheres of public and private life through a full and equal share in economic, social, cultural and political decision-making.[15]

The statement then proceeded to identify twelve "critical areas of concern" in which governments, the international community, civil society and the private sector had to take action as a matter of urgency. These critical areas of concern were:

1. Poverty and the increasing burden it inflicts on women.
2. Women's access to education and training.
3. Women's access to health care and related services.
4. Violence against women.
5. The impact of armed conflicts on women.
6. Women's access to economic resources.
7. Women's access to power and decision-making.
8. Mechanisms for women's advancement.
9. Women's human rights.
10. How women are represented in the media, and their limited control over the media.
11. Lack of access to environmental management
12. Violations of the rights of the girl-child.[16]

These twelve priority areas were duly debated and incorporated into the "Beijing Declaration," the outcome document of the conference signed by over 95 percent of the UN member states.

The Beijing Declaration contained few concrete and measurable targets. Article 182 engaged governments in ensuring that at least 30 percent of decision-making positions were occupied by women, and Articles 80 and 81 stated that all girls must be given access to primary education and governments must act to close the gender gap in primary and secondary education. Outside these there was little for the CSW to monitor and measure.

The action plan that came out of Beijing exemplifies how the UN as a body operates less as an agency for change and more as a mouthpiece for emerging debates. These capture the aspirations of a global community that the agencies then map onto discursive instruments, including the legal Conventions, Declarations and Resolutions. The action plan can act as the vehicle for the international community to interpret what it perceives as the general will of the member states of the United Nations. But the UN agencies cannot act for Member States who have their own agenda on female empowerment. While climate change, environmental politics, and global terrorism have revealed deep divisions among the Member States of the UN there is no area of debate and activity in the global community that sparks as much controversy and fundamental disagreement than gender equality and the role of women in society.

BEIJING+5: REVIEWING PROGRESS ON GENDER EQUALITY IN 2000

The gap between the discourse of gender and development and the engagement of some Member States of the UN system to promote women's rights had been apparent from 1975. This gap had widened particularly in parts of the world experiencing a rise of politico-religious fundamentalism. The 23rd Special Session of the United Nations General Assembly held in New York in the summer of 2000 marks the point at which the gap between the discourse of gender and development and the engagement of Member States reached crisis point.

While the discourse of development articulated by the many organs and agencies of the international development community had moved on from theorizing socio-economic disadvantage in relation to "women" as a distinct category of humans, and disadvantage was increasingly being theorized in relation to wider social forces and structures, the 23rd Session stopped well short of taking that step forward.

The Review of 2000, known officially as *Women 2000: Gender Equality, Development and Peace for the 21st Century*, attracted fewer than half the participants who had traveled to Beijing five years earlier.[17] In all, 178 Member States participated along with over one thousand NGOs.

Beijing+5 was preceded by months of controversy. After weeks of difficult negotiations over wording, inclusions and exclusions, the document, entitled "Further Actions and Initiatives to implement the Beijing Declaration and Platform of Action," was released. It was met with a barrage of criticism from international women's organizations. The pressure group, Center for Reproductive Rights, reacted to the review document by accusing the international community of backsliding on its commitments:

The Review Document falls short in meeting the most fundamental priorities of women's rights organizations for Beijing+5: commitment of financial resources and adoption of time-bound targets, indicators, and concrete benchmarks to foster accountability and increase political will.

The Review Document adds just three time-bound targets to the Beijing Platform's anemic twelve paragraphs. These are: ensuring a non-discriminatory legal environment by 2005; the incorporation of ICPD+5's time-bound goals[18]; and the improvement of adult literacy by 50 percent by 2015. This stands in contrast to the ICPD+5 negotiations in1999, at which governments agreed to an additional thirteen targets and benchmarks, including one on financial resources. This anomalous situation shows that governments continue to resist setting concrete goals and committing adequate financial resources to further women's equality and human rights.[19]

Although the Review Document fell far short of the demands of some participants, the 23rd Special Session did bring to the fore the relation between poverty and gender. It was recognized that since the Nairobi and Beijing conferences, the social, economic and political situation of women had worsened in many countries and particularly in the less-developed countries of Africa:

Among the new challenges . . . [the participants] cited globalisation and increased disparities in the economic situation among and within countries, coupled with a growing interdependence of States. Structural adjustment programmes and high costs of external debt servicing had worsened the situation in many developing countries.[20]

To highlight the worsening living conditions of women, UNIFEM launched a report entitled *Progress of the World's Women*[21] at the 23rd Special Session. This UNIFEM report revealed that only Sweden, Denmark, Finland and Norway had met all the Beijing targets set in 1995. In addition, Iceland, Netherlands, Germany and South Africa had at least achieved equality of access to secondary education and 30 percent representation of women in parliament.[22] Meanwhile, in much of the developing world, the situation had deteriorated. The representative from Women in Law and Development in Africa stated that the situation of women in Africa had deteriorated in all sectors of development since 1995. She also alerted participants to the threat hanging over the 23rd Special Session of a backlash against commitments made at Beijing, a threat that had materialized in arguments over wording prior to the Session opening. The Executive Director of the UNFPA, Nafis Sadik, brought the problem into sharp relief by questioning some delegations' objections to the paragraphs on gender-based violence and particularly the abduction of girls, rape as a war crime, and sexual abuse:

> The lack of agreement on segments of the final document is puzzling. Is there
> anyone who is in favour of rape, sexual slavery, enforced prostitution, forced
> pregnancy or sterilisation? Does anyone support their use as weapons of war?
> Why is the language of this document still being negotiated?[23]

Objections raised by delegations from the Holy See, Iran, Sudan, Nicaragua, Algeria, Pakistan, Syria, Libya, Morocco, and, on occasions, Iraq, were interpreted at the conference as a ploy to bring acquired rights back to the negotiating table. The threat became so real that then UN Secretary-General Kofi Annan intervened to warn Member States that commitments agreed at Beijing were not up for re-negotiation.

As it transpired, the balance of power at the UNGA shifted in favor of the progressive contingent thanks to the intervention of a group of Latin American countries. The move was precipitated by the decomposition during the Session of the developing world's main negotiating bloc, the G-77. A group of Latin American countries refused to accept the conservative position of the G-77 on women's rights and started to express their position through a regional negotiating bloc, called the "SLAC."[24] On this platform they began to campaign more vocally for debt-relief and women's human rights. The SLAC bloc grew during the negotiations as CARICOM[25] countries joined their position. The enlarged bloc, SLACC,[26] then liaised with the long-standing southern African regional group, the SADCC,[27] and with other independent countries in Africa, and out of this the developing world formed a new and powerful negotiating group. The shift in the balance of power temporarily disabled the conservative Christian and Islamic forces who had been at the forefront of efforts to undermine the Beijing Declaration at the 23rd Session but it also diverted attention away from making progress on existing rights. The outcome document came as a great disappointment to some participants, including the Senegalese delegation whose representative endorsed the outcome document but expressed her delegation's regret that the outcome was so lacking in ambition.

In the end, the 23rd Special Session closed with the international community's reaffirmation of its commitment to the Beijing Declaration and its Platform for Action. The delegations signed the closing document and a number then submitted their "interpretative statements." The United Arab Emirates, Kuwait and Saudi Arabia all submitted written statements reaffirming the position of Sharia Law in their countries and indicating that their governments would "endeavor to implement the outcome"[28] but in a manner that did not contradict their interpretations of Islamic law. The United States submitted its usual disclaimer to the effect that the outcome of the 23rd Special Session consisted of recommendations on how governments could and should promote the rights of women but they interpreted these as "not legally binding."

BEIJING+10, MARCH 2005

One of the few proposals that met with unanimous approval at the 23rd Special Session of the UNGA was the decision to have another meeting in 2005 to review progress.

As neither a world conference nor even a special session of the UNGA was organized for this purpose, the CSW used its own 49th Session in March 2005 to carry out the review.

No sooner had the session begun than it hit a crisis. It had been preceded by objections raised within the Republican administration in the United States to a number of issues, most notably surrounding reproductive rights. U.S. Ambassador Ellen Sauerbrey, the head of the U.S. delegation, tabled an objection to the conference discussion document, which, she claimed, sought to extend women's reproductive rights to include the right to abortion. After several days of well-publicized debate, the U.S. representative withdrew the objection. It had been made clear that the document did not provide women with abortion rights in countries that denied them such rights; in other words the paragraphs in question were not enforceable in any of the States parties to the Declaration.[29]

Just as UNIFEM had launched its widely publicized report *Progress of the World's Women 2000* at Beijing+5, another high profile publication was launched five years later at Beijing+10. The formal review and appraisal of the implementation of the Beijing Declaration was the business of the permanent UN department responsible for such matters, the Division for the Advancement of Women (DAW), but it is not without significance that the most high-profile publication to be launched to coincide with Beijing+10 was prepared at the UN Institute for Social Development (UNRISD). The UNRISD Bejing+10 Report was a critical evaluation of the key policy issues and an attempt to highlight the gender implications of the move from the original Keynsian approach to development to the more neo-liberal economic reforms that characterized development programs in many regions by the early 2000s. In essence, it aimed at providing an analysis of the gender aspects of the changing political economy of development and the social development implications of this from a gender perspective.

GENDER AND DEVELOPMENT IN
THE TWENTY-FIRST CENTURY

What emerges from this overview of the UN world conferences and the subsequent reviews is that the theorizing around gender and development in the thirty years since gender and development became a global debate in 1975, had advanced significantly over the period but failed to follow through in the implementation stage. From 1975 to 1995, "women in development" (WID) had enjoyed an uninterrupted rise to prominence on the international community agenda. During this period the academic community and the research arm of the international development community had been moving theory on from a women-centered approach to a more fundamental critique of the economic, cultural and political structures that operate to the disadvantage of women and the way in which these structures resisted change. This new debate on gender and development called into question the way in which powerful political and economic players were actively or passively excluding women from decision-making roles. The new approach not only called the powerful to account, but also addressed the ordinary man and woman in the street with questions about labor, responsibilities and power in the home, thereby problematizing their domestic space.

In the final years of the twentieth century and the early years of the present century, the new discourse of gender and development passed from the theoretical to the applied side of development. By this point, as theory threatened to become practice, the discourse had become too radical for some of the world's decision-makers and resistance to change became vocal at the UN.

In the early years of the twenty-first century, and particularly in the aftermath of the terrorist attacks in the United States on 11 September 2001, the international community's political agenda changed. While environmental and social issues had risen up the list of international preoccupations in the late 1990s, the tragic events of 9/11 brought issues of global security and terrorism to the centre of the world stage. Notwithstanding 9/11, women's advancement and gender and development (though gender was never the theme of any of the world conferences) had been rapidly losing their salience in the international decision-making forums from 1995. During the second half of the 1990s, the idea of social or human development became increasingly the focus of international community policy-making and programs.

To an extent, the social development debate that took place in the last years of the twentieth century evolved from issues raised at the international women's conferences not least among which was the rediscovery of poverty. The social development initiative would serve as a non-gendered platform on which to explore the implications of the failure of trickle down to deliver development to all sections of the developing world population. In this sense, social development took the gender and development discourse forward, but to a place where gender could either be excised from the international development discourse or mainstreamed. The following chapter traces the fate of gender in the international social development discourse into the current century.

NOTES

1. The United Nations adopted the International Declaration of Human Rights in November 1948.

2. Before proceeding further in this exploration of how the discourse on gender entered the international political system, a distinction needs to be made between international legislation and international legal conventions. The legal status of a convention adopted by the members of the UN system is subject to individual Member States ratifying the convention in their own national parliaments. Once ratified the Conventions face yet another hurdle, notably implementation at the national level. Consequently, a very long period of time can elapse between the adoption of a Convention at a UN General Assembly and the application of this convention in the Member State.

3. Economic Commission for Africa, *Status and Rôle of Women in East Africa* (Addid Ababa: United Nations Economic Commission for Africa, 1967).

4. Margaret Snyder and Mary Tadesse, *African Women and Development* (London: ZedBooks, 1995), 33.

5. *La Convention sur l'Elimination de toutes formes de discrimination à l'égard des Femmes (CEDEF)*.

6. By 2010, 186 of the 193 Members States of the United Nations Organization had signed and ratified the Convention. http://treaties.un.org. Accessed 08/08/2010. Seven countries have still not ratified the Convention: the United States; Iran; Somalia, Tonga, Palau, Nauru and Sudan. http://www.cedaw2010.org/index. Accessed 08/15/2010.

7. United Nations. *Progress Achieved in the Implementation of the Convention on the Elimination of all forms of Discrimination against Women* (Report by the Committee on Elimination of Discrimination against Women) A/CONF.177/7, 2.

8. *ROFAF* Regional Forum, Lomé, Togo, 23–26 March 2009.

9. The term is used by the international community to signify a country that has signed up to an international convention.

10. Djingarey Ibrahim Maiga, "La Situation des droits humains des femmes au Mali," in *La Situation des droits des femmes et de l'égalité des sexes en Afrique francophone* (Compilation des Communications du Forum régional du *ROFAF*), Lomé, Togo, 23–26 March 2009, 12–13. "There are numerous factors that undermine women's ability to exercise their human rights fully, the most important being poverty and socio-cultural constraints. In common with other countries in the Sahelian sub-region, there are religious laws and customs in force in Mali that are sometimes not compatible with the laws and Constitution of the country as well as international agreements Mali has signed up to." Author's translation.

11. In 2002, the Bush administration accused UNFPA of funding abortion services and suspended its annual contribution to the fund estimated at around $34 million.

12. UNIFEM documents cite 188 participating member states, UN press releases from the period recorded 189.

13. United Nations. *Womanwatch—Summary Report on the Fourth World Conference on Women* (New York: United Nations, 1995), 7.

14. United Nations, *Womanwatch*, 10.

15. United Nations, *Fourth World Conference on Women,* A/CONF.177/20, 17 October 1995, 4.

16. United Nations, *Womanwatch*, 10–11.

17. Around 2,300 delegates registered for the Beijing+5 Review.

18. This refers to the UN's International Conference on Population and Development 5-year review held in 1999.

19. Center for Reproductive Rights. *Beijing+5—Assessing Reproductive Rights,* November 2000, http://www.crlp.org/pub_art_beijing5.html.

20. United Nations. *UN General Assembly Press Release* (2000), paragraph 7.

21. UNIFEM. *Progress of the World's Women 2000* (New York: UNIFEM/ UNDP, 2000).

22. UNIFEM, *Progress of the World's Women*, 11.

23. United Nations. "Contributions from Participants," in *UN General Assembly Press Release* (2000), no page number.

24. Some Latin American countries.

25. CARICOM is an economic community of Caribbean countries.

26. Some Latin American countries and CARICOM.

27. The SADCC, Southern African Development Co-ordination Committee, operates as a regional economic development community.

28. United Nations. "Contributions from Participants," in *UN General Assembly Press Release* (10 June 2000), no page number.

29. Canada and a number of West European members argued against this interpretation and in opposition to the U.S. delegation at this conference.

4

"Good Governance" for Development, 1990–2000

The fall of the Berlin Wall in 1989 signaled a turning point in African politics as well as the end of an era in Eastern Europe. The Cold War had dragged vast tracts of the developing world into the superpower theatre of war. From Congo-Brazzaville to Guinea, Africa bore the scars of the global power struggle that had pitted the forces of the Warsaw pact against the NATO allies, with France positioned on the fringes of the latter[1] and operating as an independent source of military muscle for the first generation of francophone African heads of state after independence in 1960.

The arrival of the media age had brought with it the global political event. Television pictures of Berlin during those heady days of November 1989 flashed around the world and the impact of the scenes of popular resistance resonated in the developing world and particularly in Africa. With the end of the Cold War, the talk immediately turned to a hoped-for "peace dividend." In theory, the industrialized nations from both sides of the Cold War conflict would stop spending billions of taxpayers' dollars on the arms race and spend it instead on peaceful endeavors such as funding development in Africa.

In 1992, the UN called the industrial nations to turn their attention to the matter and announced it was convening a global summit on development in 1995. It was called the Social Summit and required all the Member States of the UN system to focus on the fight against poverty, both in their own countries and in the developing world. Social development as a concept had been present in the language of the UN since 1946, but this was the first time in the history of the UN that heads of state and government had been called upon to bring poverty and disadvantage to the top of the international agenda.

Not surprisingly, the call met with opposition. For advocates of economic liberalism, the issue implied more social policy and this would mean more

47

social spending. Financial recovery packages of the 1980s and 1990s, primarily in the form of Structural Adjustment Programs (SAPs), had required poor countries to cut back on government spending, including social spending. This had exposed vulnerable people, those without ready access to income such as the elderly, the sick, and children, to poverty.

> In the 1980s and 1990s, most African countries [. . .] felt forced to bend their policies to accommodate the new exigencies [of structural adjustment]. However, very few governments saw a positive result from giving in to these demands. On the contrary, the new policies led quite often to the dismantlement of some of the few economic achievements gained from the previous policies of these same governments.[2]

Even in relatively prosperous developing countries, SAPs had caused social and economic problems. Morocco was required under the terms of its SAP to abolish the state subsidy on bread. Coupled with high unemployment, the result was not a tidy improvement in economic output but an explosion of political unrest.[3] With developing countries increasingly locked into a cycle of debt, a Social Summit following on from a long period of economic recession in the developing world, threatened to expose the damaging social consequences of the application of unfettered market economics in developing countries.

The voices of opposition failed to hold sway in the face of global concern over the "rediscovery" of poverty.[4] The chair of the Social Summit's Preparatory Committee, Juan Somavia, announced that the United Nations was "exercising leadership in this matter by addressing issues that ran against the everyday current."[5]

By the early 1990s, not only had poverty been rediscovered but also theories of development through globalization were coming under attack. While globalization offered wealth and opportunities to the industrializing developing world in Asia, the appearance of foreign and international operators in the markets of the least developed nations had put local producers and suppliers out of business. The smallest producers of the developing world suffered particularly, not being in a position to compete with the massive investment machinery and scales of production sustainable by multinationals and other big economic players. Indeed, in many cases the small producer has no capital at all for investment. In francophone Africa, the vast majority of women had no access to credit or capitalization at all.

Faced with this realization, it was clear that the well-being of people living in the least-developed countries was not going to improve unassisted. At this point, the UNDP, the UN's development agency, set up an observatory in their headquarters in New York to monitor the social or "human" side of economic development in the world. It called it the Human Development Report (HDR) office.

If the world conferences on women had provided the vocabulary for a global discourse of gender and development to emerge, the UNDP provided the grammar. The rules of engagement were defined by the Human Development Report (HDR) office of the UNDP and published from 1990 in a series of annual reports.[6] It quickly became the most influential document in global gender and development politics.

By the time the third Human Development Report came out in 1992 the UNDP had managed to capture the attention of development policy-makers and governments the world over. The focus of the 1992 Report was poverty.

The extent of extreme poverty in the developing world was not new knowledge to the international community. But now it was being argued that there were sound economic and political reasons for eliminating poverty over and above the more obvious ethical and humanitarian grounds for intervention.[7] The UNDP drew attention to the damage that poverty was inflicting on countries, and how this damage can extend well beyond a country's borders, posing a threat to political stability and economic development in the wider region.

GOING INTO THE 1995 SUMMIT: 10 COMMITMENTS TO SOCIAL DEVELOPMENT

The aim of the Social Summit of 1995 was to engage heads of state and governments in a common vision of global social development. The contents of this vision were articulated in "Ten Commitments" adopted for the conference:

Commitment 1	Provide the environment for social development.[8]
Commitment 2	End world poverty.
Commitment 3	Achieve full employment.
Commitment 4	Protect everyone's human rights
Commitment 5	Support the advancement of women.[9]
Commitment 7	Integrate social development planning into future Structural Adjustment Programs.
Commitment 8	Use development aid more effectively.
Commitment 9	Bring national social policies in line with UN priorities.
Commitment 10	Provide education and basic health services for all.

References to women, gender and development were scattered throughout the Ten Commitments, thus marking a sea change in the language of discussion

documents prepared for the previous UN conferences. At the first environment conference (UNCED) held in Rio de Janiero in 1992:

> [N]ational and international women's groups had a tremendous impact on the
> document that emerged from UNCED. [. . .] Initial drafts had only two references
> to women, but due to intensive advocacy efforts, the final draft had over 172
> references to women and an entire chapter on women's role in the environment.[10]

The plethora of studies published since the 1970s on the relation between
poverty and gender had clearly had an impact on the international development community, and the fact that most of the world's poorest people were
women informed thinking in all areas of social development and had made its
way into the 10 Commitments for discussion at the Conference.

As freedom from poverty was now being presented as a human rights issue,
Commitment 4 attracted interest in Africa. This resonance was all the stronger
in the former French colonies where African men and women living under
French rule had been denied the rights afforded some French citizens under
the Declaration of the Rights of Man and the Citizen of August 1789. As the
1789 Declaration granted full citizenship rights to certain classes of men it was
a deeply flawed and fundamentally discriminatory document from the outset, a
fact illustrated by the fate of Olympe de Gouges, one of the rare human rights
and anti-slavery campaigners of her day, who presented Declaration of the
Rights of Woman and the Citizen to the French National Assembly in 1793
only to perish for her efforts on the guillotine a few months later. More than
one and half centuries passed before the Universal Declaration of the Rights
of Man of 1948 extended rights to cover almost all categories of citizens, but
again implementation encountered intractable obstacles. It was not until 1993
the year of the UN's global summit conference on human rights, that the rights
of women became officially recognized as human rights.[11] While Commitment 4 was clearly important for women's advancement Commitment 5 was
designed to commit parties to eliminating discrimination against women in all
aspects of public life and made reference to the whole range of issues from
political representation to economic empowerment.[12]

The Social Summit produced an outcome document, the "Program of Action," indicating how countries would realize the goals set out in the Declaration.

AN ACTION PLAN FOR THE SOCIAL SUMMIT

The Social Summit Program of Action was set out in five chapters, which
addressed the need to:

Chapter 1: Create a global context for development and change
Chapter 2: Eradicate poverty
Chapter 3: Maximize productive employment for workers
Chapter 4: Promote human rights
Chapter 5: Remove obstacles to implementation

The theme of gender, so visible in the Commitments, disappeared from sight in the Program of Action. This lack could be attributed to the fact that the Beijing women's conference was taking place just a few months later in September 1995 and therefore would act as the UN's policy document on gender. That "gender" is not synonymous with "women" was not generally understood. Gender was used then, as it often is today, to denote issues affecting women.

WHAT DOES GENDER EQUALITY MEAN TO THE INTERNATIONAL COMMUNITY?

The Program of Action was endorsed by the participating delegations of the Social Summit and by the end of the conference many gender-sensitive issues had been debated. But in the final 83-page version of the Program of Action there were few explicit targets for achieving progress. Chapter 2, paragraph 36 of the final Program of Action contains the clearest definition of the Summit's thinking on gender in social development:

36. Governments should implement the commitments that have been made to meet the basic needs of all, with assistance from the international community consistent with Chapter V of the present Programme of Action, including inter alia the following:
a) By the year 2000, universal access to basic education and completion of primary education by at least 80 percent of primary school-age children; closing the gender gap in primary and secondary education by the year 2005; universal primary education in all countries before the year 2015;
[. . .]
d) By the year 2000, a reduction in maternal mortality by one half of the 1990 level, by the year 2015, a further reduction by one half;
h) Making accessible through the primary health-care system reproductive health to all individuals of appropriate ages as soon as possible and no later than the year 2015,
[. . .]
k) Reducing the adult illiteracy rate—the appropriate age group to be determined in each country—to at least half of its 1990 level, with an emphasis on female literacy.[13]

Access to formal primary education and improvements in maternal health came out of this Summit as the priority social development issues for women and girls. What is important to note here is that the economic and political aspects of women's advancement and social development which were so present in the 10 Commitments (Commitment 5) were not incorporated into the Action plan.[14]

REVIEWING SOCIAL DEVELOPMENT IN THE YEAR 2000

The 24th Special Session of the UN General Assembly reviewed progress towards the 1995 World Summit on Social Development five years on.

The review started in May 1998, when the Secretary-General's office was invited to compile a report on how far the member states had gone in meeting the social development targets set in 1995. The Secretary-General called on each of the 118 governments that had attended the Copenhagen Summit to submit a progress report by 30 June 1999. Eighteen reports were received by the deadline. The deadline was extended to 1 December 1999 by which point 74 reports had been received. Fifteen sub-Saharan African countries provided updates,[15] including Benin, Burkina Faso, Cameroon, Côte d'Ivoire, Mali, Niger and Mauritania.[16] Commenting on the sub-Saharan African reports, the Secretary-General suggested that "existing paradigms may not provide adequate strategies and new insights should be sought by examining the situation from diverse viewpoints."[17]

The apparently bland statement strikes a significant and discordant note in a dominant discourse that brooked no cultural or local variation from the established UN policy framework. In this statement, the Secretary General, himself a West African, recognized that the dominant model of social development policy operating in the region was flawed, and the principle flaw lay in the universalism of its discourse. However, rather than interrogating the model itself, the Report went on to criticize the way African member states were implementing policies. Notwithstanding, the Report did acknowledge that SAPs in West Africa were failing to accommodate social development targets agreed at the Social Summit. Indeed, it noted that SAPs were having a negative effect on political stability and social development: "Some Governments have generally been weakened by policies to restrain public expenditure under stabilisation and structural adjustment programmes."[18]

The Secretary-General's report did not focus on the gender issues raised in the original Ten Commitments. References to gender appear in the national reports, but even here there is little emphasis on gender as a key factor of social development. One Southern African report mentioned the high number of girls enrolling in secondary schools, which translated into: "girls have been enrolled in school at higher rates than boys"[19] in the Secretary-General's report. At this time, in Benin, Burkina-Faso, Cameroon, Côte d'Ivoire, Mali, Niger and Mauritania the percentage of secondary enrolments taken up by girls had barely moved into double figures.[20] As regards the feminization of poverty, the last sentence of the summary report on the eradication of poverty simply read: "There are more poor women than men."[21] As for the development of language, it is interesting to note that this document, published in 1999, did not include the term "gender" in any title, heading, or sub-heading in the entire 157-page report.

Six weeks before the member states of the UN came together to review how effectively they were implementing their obligations to promote social development, nearly half the paragraphs of the discussion document were still under debate (or "square bracketed" in the jargon of the UN). Four weeks before the Session opened 40 percent was still in square brackets.

Despite all the difficulties, the 24th Special Session of the UN General Assembly entitled: "World Summit for Social Development (WSSD) and Beyond: Achieving Social Development for all in a Globalizing World" opened in Geneva on 26 June 2000. Only 35 heads of state and government along with some 7,000 delegates attended. As usual, the main business involved reaching agreement on an "outcome document." The document contained the Ten Commitments, these were substantially the same with "Gender Equality" remaining as Commitment 5 but undergoing some significant changes that signal how gender and development discourse in the international community had changed between 1995 and 2000.

In the closing plenary of the UNGA's 24th Special Session, member states endorsed the Outcome Document, following which Costa Rica and Malta, countries where anti-abortion legislation is in force, stated that their countries' approval of the Commitment to universal health care services excluded any commitment to providing abortion services. In similar vein, the Holy See reaffirmed its anti-abortion stance. Meanwhile Bangladesh regretted the Outcome Document's failure to foreground gender issues more effectively and particularly in relation to globalization.

The 24th Special Session highlighted the widening split between developing countries and the developed world over globalization and the global economic order. While the developing world was calling on the developed world to assume some responsibility for the impact of globalization and to buffer the developing world from its negative effects, the representatives of the developed world reaffirmed their belief in the free market economy as the best means to achieve global economic development.

The position of the leaders of the industrialized nations was encapsulated in a glossy 28-page brochure called *A Better World for All*[22] jointly authored

by the OECD, the UN, the World Bank and the IMF and launched with some
fanfare at the 24th Special Session. The disgust felt by some participants at
the content of this report was captured on camera at the official launch which
saw representatives of developing world organizations gathering up piles of
the glossy brochures and unceremoniously dumping them in waste paper
baskets in front of the world's press. Disappointment was expressed, particularly by African delegates, that the Secretary-General, as a West African, had
chosen to associate himself and the UN agencies with this publication.

A Better World for All encapsulated the way the industrial powers were
now prepared to envision "development." The book contained nine chapters,
each one devoted to a "priority area" for development, along with one chapter of quantitative indicators on progress towards international development
goals. The third chapter—"Gender Equality"—was two pages long. Half
of the first page was taken up with a large photograph of a beautiful young
Asian woman in traditional costume. The remaining half page contained col-
orful charts indicating that there were now more girls going to school than in
the past. The second page contained two more charts also indicating global
trends in the registration of girls in school.[23] The chapter contained no mention, nor any illustrative material, on women's political empowerment though
a 30 percent share of seats in parliament had been an agreed international
target since the Beijing conference of 1995. There was also no mention of
women's economic empowerment. Perhaps even more surprising was the
absence of the oldest and least controversial target of all: improving maternal
and child health. The document had reduced "gender equality" to entry-level
access to formal education.

The brochure produced a storm of protest, but not because of its treatment
of gender. The storm blew around the failure of the rich nations to state how
social development was going to be funded.

Meanwhile the Outcome Document of the 24th Special Session did address
gender but confined it to Commitment 5 which called on governments to:

1—close the gender gap in primary and secondary education by 2005;
2—increase women's and girls' access to education at all levels;
3—ensure free compulsory primary education for girls and boys by 2015;
4—achieve a 50% improvement in adult literacy levels by 2015;
5—increase women's participation in the labor market;
6—achieve a balanced representation of men and women in all sectors of the
    labor market and close the gender gap in earnings;
7—reduce maternal mortality and morbidity;
8—eliminate all forms of violence against women in the domestic and public
    spheres;

9—promote programs to enable women and men to reconcile work and family responsibilities and encourage men to share household and childcare responsibilities equally with women;

10—promote international co-operation to support national efforts to develop gender-related analysis and statistics;

11—promote action-orientated programs at national level to implement Beijing and Copenhagen agreements.[24]

The changes in the wording of Commitment 5 in 2000[25] compared with Commitment 5 in 1995[26] reveal a new position on gender, a position expressed in language more cautious and conservative than that used in 1995. In essence, the changes indicate a shift of emphasis away from the issue of personal empowerment towards structural responses, such as reinforcing the social development infrastructure, particularly in health and education for women and girls. This is significant in that it marks a return to the "Women in Development" (WID) approach of the 1970s and 80s which focused on dealing with females as a separate population within apparently gender-neutral structures. The "Gender and Development" (GAD) approach that became widely accepted in the 1990s advocated a shift away from focusing on structures and services towards issues of power, marginalization and social exclusion. In other words GAD suggested that policy initiatives should address the causes of gender inequality rather than simply seek to alleviate the consequences of gender inequality. As such the outcome document of the 24th Special Session is a step backwards in the international community's discourse on gender disadvantage and gender equality.

Though gender had all but disappeared in all sections of the 2000 Outcome Document outside of Commitment 5, this did not provoke any sustained demand to reinstate it. There were several competing explanations for this, among which three came to the fore. Typically, participants from industrialized countries argued that the principle of gender equality had been accepted, that opportunities for girls and women to progress towards gender equality had been provided, and so essentially the battle had been won.

Arguing against this case, feminist scholars and activists in the developed world pointed out that access to formal education and entry-level access to most areas of employment had not delivered equality in pay or conditions.

Development specialists put forward a further explanation: "gender fatigue." There had been too much talk about gender since the 1980s, and as this had not led to any perceptible change in the status and position of women, discussants were either fed up with it or had given up on it.

Women's groups participating at the 24th Special Session offered a third explanation. They talked about a "backlash," led by conservative cultural

forces working to promote and sustain fundamentalist religious and patriarchal structures and neo-liberal economists who understood only too well that
female servitude (unpaid female labor) was critical to sustaining the economies of the least-developed countries.

The new minimalist discourse on gender and development was confirmed
at the first international summit of the new century. The Millennium Summit
of 2000 set the framework for development for the twenty-first century.

NOTES

1. Between 1966 and 2008 French forces were not integrated into the NATO
command structure, while in practice France remained within the NATO alliance
throughout the Cold War and beyond.

2. Immanuel Wallerstein, *Africa: The Politics of Independence and Unity* (Lincoln: University of Nebraska Press, 2005), xiii.

3. For a discussion of the impact of this policy in the1980s, see Claire H. Griffiths,
*Social Development in Francophone Africa: The Case of Women in Gabon and Mo-
rocco* (Boston: Boston University Working Paper No. 211, 1998).

4. One of the biggest surprises to come out of this era of re-evaluation of development had been the discovery that there was more money flowing out of Africa into the
international banking system than was going into Africa in the form of aid.

5. United Nations, *Round-up of Session*, SOC/4336, 30 January 1995, 1.

6. This is normally an annual report, exceptionally the 2007 edition covered the
period 2007–2008.

7. United Nations, *Round-up of Session* SOC/4336, 1.

8. The structures were not in place to do this and it required another conference—
the International Conference on Financing for Development—held in Monterrey,
Mexico, in 2002 before the question of how to create the environment was addressed.
See www.un.org/esa/ffd for further information on the outcomes of this conference.

9. This commitment caused much controversy, the negotiators being unable to
agree on language related to reproductive rights and services for women.

10. UNIFEM, *Progress of the World's Women 2000* (New York: UNIFEM/
UNDP, 2000).

11. As enshrined in the outcome document of the UN international conference on
Human Rights, Vienna, 1993.

12. See Appendix A for the full text of Commitment 5 of WSSD 1995.

13. United Nations, *Report of the World Summit for Social Development,* A/
Conf.166/9, 19 April 1995, 54–55.

14. See Appendix A for the full text of Commitment 5 of the 1995 outcome document.

15. The list of countries submitting reports can be found in Annex 11 of the *Comprehensive Report on the Implementation of the Outcome of the World Summit for*

Social Development—Report of the Secretary-General (New York: United Nations, 1999), 156.

16. Mauritania is officially an Arabic-speaking nation and a member is the Cairo-based Arab League, but within Africa it is also considered part of francophone West Africa having been colonized by France and having gained its independence at the same time as the other territories in the region between 1958 and 1960.

17. United Nations, *Comprehensive Report*, paragraph 95, 23.

18. United Nations, *Comprehensive Report*, paragraph 100, 24.

19. United Nations, *Comprehensive Report*, paragraph 766, 127.

20. The UN website, www.un.org, provides links to the *Human Development Reports* published from 1990. Each annual report contains the statistics on educational enrollments for all the countries of francophone Africa.

21. United Nations, *Comprehensive Report*, paragraph 768, 128.

22. IMF/OECD/UN/World Bank. *A Better World For All* (Washington, D.C.: Communications Development, 2000).

23. Research on the relation between educational access and empowerment give a complex picture not reflected in these simplistic charts. See, for example, Claire Robertson's study of African women and education in the mid-1980s quoted in Christopher L. Miller, *Theories of Africans: Francophone Literature and Anthropology in Africa* (Chicago: Chicago University Press, 1990), 269; and Sheila Bunwaree, "Education and the Marginalisation of Girls in post-GATT Mauritius," *Compare* 27, no. 3, 1997, 297–317.

24. Summary of the 24th Special Session of the General Assembly *Earth Negotiations Bulletin* 10, no. 63, 3 July 2000, 11. The full text of Commitment 5 is reproduced in Appendix B.

25. Contained in UNGA Resolution S-24/2 and cited in full in the Appendixes.

26. Commitment 5 contained in the Outcome Document of the WSSD 1995, the commitment is cited in full in the Appendixes.

5

The Millennium Summit and Beyond

Writing Women Out of Development?

The Millennium Summit of September 2000 set the development agenda for the twenty-first century in eight Millennium Development Goals (MDGs[1]) to be achieved by the year 2015. Gender equality figures as the third of these global goals. The definition of gender equality in this Goal reflects the position the leadership of the United Nations assumed between the conservative and progressive forces that had clashed over gender equality at the Beijing+5 and the Copenhagen+5 reviews three months earlier in June 2000.

While the acrimonious debates that characterized those meetings had almost brought proceedings to a standstill, the Secretary-General made it clear to the opponents of the Beijing program of action that gender equality would not be removed from the international development agenda. However, as the Millennium Development Goal 3 would testify, the definition of equality could be recast in such a way as to render it acceptable to even the most conservative regimes.

As the following summary of the outcome of the Millennium Summit illustrates, the discourse that had been resolutely progressive in inspiration and Anglophone in articulation for more than half a century, entered a period of stagnation. Far from consolidating the discourse of social justice, human rights and gender equality of the 1990s, the year 2000 would mark a rupture in this discursive journey. It was during this year that a flaw in the existing architecture of gender and development was revealed. It collapsed when subjected to the dual pressures of rising fundamentalism and globalization. This collapse opened up the possibility for new discourses of gender and development to be heard. It was an opportunity that the francophone world would be ready to embrace.

WHEN THE ANGLOPHONE WORLD
LOST THE GENDER DEBATE

The work of the Millennium Development Summit was set out in a report compiled by the Secretary-General's office called *We the Peoples—The Role of the United Nations in the 21st Century*.[2] The Report identified four themes that would guide international development policy into the future: Freedom from Want; Freedom from Fear; A Sustainable Future; and Renewing the United Nations. Table 5.1 lists the seven chapters that make up this Report indicating the number of times gender and development terminology appears under these headings.

In only two of the seven chapters is the issue of gender in development broached. While the introductory chapter makes no specific reference to gender it does remind the international community on two occasions of its commitment to equal rights between men and women.

Chapter 1 states that men outnumber women in the world's population. It is striking that the Report does not add any comment to the effect that men outnumber women only because more than 100 million girls and women have died prematurely as a result of gender discrimination.[3] Female infanticide, parental neglect and failure to provide medical care continue to diminish the population of baby girls the world over.[4]

Table 5.1. References to Gender in "We the Peoples" Report 2000

Chapters	References to "Gender"	References to "Women"	References to "Girls"	References to "Men"
Introduction: New century, new challenges	none	2	none	2
Chapter 1: Globalization and governance	1	4	none	1
Chapter 2: Freedom from want	6	10	7	[2*]
Chapter 3: Freedom from fear	none	3	none	none
Chapter 4: Sustaining our future	none	none	none	none
Chapter 5: Renewing the United Nations	none	none	none	none
Chapter 6: For consideration by the Summit	none	[4*]	[2†]	[4*]
Total	7	19 + [4*]	7 + [2†]	5 + [4*]

* References to "fellow men and women.
† References to "boys and girls."

The second chapter of the Report focused on the campaign to eliminate poverty and consequently—given the strong correlation between female gender and poverty—there are more references to gender in this section than anywhere else in the report.

While chapter 3 recognized that women and girls are particularly vulnerable to violence and sexual exploitation in times of war,[5] no gender analysis of this situation is offered. This is an issue which will be taken up by the francophone world as it develops its discourse of gender and development in the rest of the decade.

Chapters 4 and 5 address how the world will manage its future in the twenty-first century. They contain no reference to the gender dimensions of resource management in either of these chapters.

The failure of the Report to integrate gender into the core business of development reflects a failure within the architecture of the UN system itself to mainstream gender. The only agencies to have implemented the Beijing targets for achieving gender equality in the workplace are those specific organs within the UN system mandated to manage the UN's gender in development portfolio of operations. Otherwise, the UN was still patently masculinist in character. By the year 2000 none of the key decision-making bodies of the UN had acted upon the equality-at-work targets agreed at Beijing in 1995.[6]

RESTORING GENDER TO THE MILLENNIUM DECLARATION

While the absence of gender referencing in *We the Peoples* attracted criticism, the outcome document of the Summit, the Millennium Declaration, was peppered with references to human rights and gender equality. Though devoid of targets for action, the discursive value of the Declaration lies in its definition of gender equality and the contrast between this and the definition used in the action plan that will eventually come out of the Millennium Summit:

> Equality: No individual and no nation must be denied the opportunity to benefit from development. The equal rights and opportunities of women and men must be assured.[7]

The promising introduction was not followed through in the substantive sections that followed. Section 2, "Peace, security and disarmament," referenced conflicts but with no gender analysis. The D R Congo war had been under UN observation by MONUC[8] since November 1999, at which point the use of rape as a weapon of war against civilians was already recognized as endemic to the conflict. The Congo crisis reflects the absence of an integrated gender policy framework in the international system. Ten years into the UN's mission in D R Congo, despite African and Western media efforts to push the issue up the international agenda,[9] the rape crisis still raged unabated in the Congo.[10] The gendered nature of this violence was undisputed: "We don't know why these rapes are happening, but one thing is clear they are done to destroy women."[11] This failure to provide a gender analysis of contemporary conflict in Africa would be taken up in the course of the first decade of the twenty-first century by the newly emerging francophone development community.[12]

Meanwhile, the Millennium Declaration continued to veer from discursive sophistication to an over-simplification of policy requirements. Section 3, "Development and poverty eradication" contained two references to gender, both asserting the rights of girl children to access formal education.[13] While there is considerable evidence suggesting female literacy and numeracy has a powerful impact on economic growth, there is little research on the relation between access to formal education and gender equality.[14] On the contrary research has indicated that access to the lowest levels of formal education undermines female autonomy whereas "[f]emale schooling at the secondary level is more consistently and strongly associated with increased decision-making and mobility for women than schooling at the primary level."[15] There are indications that access to higher education can have an impact on women's perceptions of their rights in society but whether this extends into the domestic subordination of women is not established.

Meanwhile the discourse makes a brief return to the argument that women are human capital—give them more skills and they perform better in the economy; in the words of the Declaration, governments should promote gender equality and the empowerment of women to combat poverty, hunger and disease and to stimulate development that is truly sustainable.

Section 4 of the Declaration "Protecting our common environment" contained no gender reference or analysis, while Section 5, "Human rights, democracy and good governance," simply resolved to implement the CEDAW.

This was the last reference to gender or women's empowerment to appear in the Millennium Declaration. The Millennium Declaration was not an outcome document of the type produced at Beijing or Copenhagen. The 189 countries that signed up to the Declaration did so with no clear agenda for action.

Recognizing the danger of leaving the Member States to implement policies at their own pace, the UN General Assembly called on the Secretary-General to produce a "road map" for global development in the twenty-first century. The result was the eight "Millennium Development Goals" (MDGs) for the twenty-first century.

THE MILLENNIUM DEVELOPMENT GOALS:
A ROAD MAP FOR DEVELOPMENT IN
THE TWENTY-FIRST CENTURY?

In one sense, the Millennium Development Goals returned gender equality to the top of the international community's development agenda by including it as one of the eight development goals.

The Millennium Development Goals for the year 2015:

MDG 1   *Eradicate extreme poverty*
MDG 2   *Achieve universal primary education*
MDG 3   *Promote gender equality and empower women*
MDG 4   *Reduce child mortality*
MDG 5   *Improve maternal health*
MDG 6   *Combat HIV/AIDS, malaria and other diseases*
MDG 7   *Ensure environmental sustainability*
MDG 8   *Develop a global partnership for development*

Indeed its reappearance was interpreted as a victory by pressure groups that lobbied for this during the Millennium Summit. However, gender equality as it was presented in Millennium Development Goal 3, was merely a reprise of the bid to deliver universal formal education already set out in *A Better World for All*. The only two targets set for this goal were entry-level access to formal education. The minimal character of this definition of equality was matched only by the weakness of the language used to commend the Goal to the international community. Heads of State and government were called on to "promote" women's advancement while the other MDGs were couched in forceful language, compelling leaders to meet agreed targets.

The absence of a political consensus at the international level had stripped gender equality discourse of its flesh, leaving a skeleton on which to rebuild a platform of action for the twenty-first century.

THE MILLENNIUM SUMMIT AND
THE FRANCOPHONE DEVELOPMENT DISCOURSE

In the decades leading up to the Millennium Summit of 2000, the international community represented by the agencies and structures of the United Nations organization created a discourse of development that was Anglophone in origin and universalist in inspiration. While the dominance of the English-speaking world over development theory and practice threatened to

deepen existing political cleavages separating the Anglophone and francophone regions of West Africa, the emergence of new players in the gender
and development policy-making field offered a third way out of the traditional colonial regional identities.

In the 1990s, the Canadian development agency CIDA/*ACDI* became an
increasingly prominent and influential voice in regional gender and development policy operating across the linguistic divide, supporting local academic
and NGO activity as well as funding its own gender and development policy
for the region. Further south, the Belgian diplomatic mission in Gabon was
conducting primary research into gender and development in the region
within a research framework inspired by the international Anglophone research community.[16]

The rise of a francophone gender and development discourse and practice
in Africa led to pressure for change at the global level. The challenge was
taken up by the administrative organ of the francophone world, the *Organisation internationale de la francophonie*. The OIF convened the first World
Conference of Francophone Women in February 2000. The conference followed in the tradition established a quarter of a century earlier by the first
World Conference of Women held in Mexico City in 1975. Its work focused
on the production of a single outcome document capturing a common platform for action resolved at the Conference. The resulting *Déclaration de
Luxembourg* was for the most part an endorsement of the Beijing Declaration
translated into French:

> *Lors de la 1re Conférence des femmes de la Francophonie, tenue à Luxembourg
> les 4 et 5 février 2000, les Etats et gouvernements membres avaient adopté une
> déclaration finale dans laquelle [. . .] ils précisaient que les engagements pris
> à Pékin lors de la 4ᵉ Conférence mondiale sur les femmes [. . .] demeuraient les
> objectifs majeurs pour la francophonie.*[17]

The Declaration went on to acknowledge the linguistic gap that had opened
over the decades as the international community composed its gender and
development discourse in English, and charged the *Agence intergouvernementale de la francophonie (AIF)* with the task of devising:

> *une terminologie française en matière d'égalité des femmes et des hommes et
> de droits des femmes. [. . .] proposant des équivalents terminologiques français
> aux termes anglo-saxons les plus répandus.*[18]

The task confronting the *AIF* was twofold. Firstly, it was explicitly charged
with "catching up" with the Anglophone world, and secondly, implicitly its

role includes accommodating the specificity of gender theorizing in its own language culture. The seriousness of the task was emphasized at the 10th World Summit of *la Francophonie* in November 2004 when the Heads of State and Government confirmed their commitment to the *Déclaration de Luxembourg*.

Three months later at the Beijing+10 review[19] in New York, the *AIF* organised a francophone platform chaired by the French Minister of Parity and Professional Equality, Nicole Ameline, charged with delivering a concerted francophone position on Beijing+10. Declaring themselves *Partenaires pour Pékin+10*, the francophone representatives submitted a *Contribution de la Francophonie* in which they both reaffirmed the francophone world's commitment to the Beijing platform of action and began redefining the discursive parameters of gender and development at the global level:

> *Nous confirmons notre attachement à la diversité des pratiques sociales et culturelles, notamment en ce qui concerne les femmes et leur place dans la société, et nous affirmons qu'elles ne doivent pas faire obstacle au respect intégral des valeurs, normes et principes consacrés par la Charte des Nations unies, la Déclaration universelle des droits de l'Homme[20] et la Convention internationale pour l'élimination de toute forme de discrimination à l'égard des femmes.[21]*

In this document, the francophone world set out a platform for gender and development in a discourse that seeks both to accommodate the universal discourse of human rights that guided international gender and development theorizing through the 1990s, and to introduce cultural specificity into that discourse:

> *en accordant une attention particulière à l'élimination des toutes entraves à la pleine participation des femmes [. . .] y compris les mutilations génitales féminines, les crimes d'honneur et les mariages forcés.[22]*

The potential of this new discursive framework to accommodate alternative and competing discourses of development will emerge in the course of the twenty-first century only if the international community succeeds in accommodating what have to date been considered competing discourses, namely universalism versus cultural relativism. The latter has been marginalized not simply because it is a minority discourse in the Anglophone world, but primarily because of a fear that a cultural discourse will undermine the *droits acquis* of gender and development. There are also practical objections to moving away from the universal discourse of gender and development. A culturally diverse approach to defining women's advancement is difficult to contain within a single definition and less susceptible to being monitored by the mechanisms the international community has set up to measure and report on advancements towards gender equality in Africa and elsewhere in the developing world. This is a serious consideration and one that will be explored in detail in the next chapter, which applies the established global definition to Gabon and Senegal.

Notwithstanding the importance of setting minimum standards for human rights globally, the argument against accommodating cultural diversity in gender and development discourse and practice needs to be interrogated in two key respects.

Firstly, the new discourse opens up the potential for taking the gender and development discourse forward from the universal human rights discourses popularized in the 1990s. By the end of the first decade of the twenty-first century, Amartya Sen, the most influential voice in the human rights discourse of the early 1990s, was himself moving social justice theorizing away from abstract models towards grounding the theory and practice of social justice in social evidence. In *The Idea of Justice* (2009) the marginalized and the dispossessed populations of the world provide the privileged site in which to theorize social disadvantage, poverty and exclusion.[23]

The model of gender equality that finally emerged from the World Conferences was the model considered most likely to help the most marginalized and dispossessed of the world's women to participate in development. It was a model based on objectives that the global community could and would sign up to (access to formal education, paid work, political participation and health care) contained in a set of targets the development agencies could monitor over time. In this perspective, it is crucial that the objectives contained in the model can be effectively measured and monitored worldwide and particularly in the poorest countries of the world where the needs of the world's most disadvantaged population are perceived to be greatest.

Furthermore, the international community feels that through monitoring mechanisms it can exert pressure on delinquent governments who sign international conventions, declarations and platforms for action and then fail to follow through. By setting measurable targets and publishing the progress Member States are making towards realizing those targets, the CSW can aim to ensure minimum standards. However, what is far from certain is whether these monitoring mechanisms do in fact deliver the measures needed to carry out both these tasks—exert pressure where necessary and track the advancement of women.

The next chapter applies the mechanisms used to evaluate the application of the universal (dominant) model of gender and development to countries in francophone Africa to test how effectively these mechanisms are delivering on these two objectives.

CONCLUSION: WHO IS DRAWING THE ROAD MAP
FOR TWENTY-FIRST CENTURY GENDER EQUALITY?

Progress towards meeting the Millennium Development Goals was reviewed at the World Summit during the 60th session of the UN General Assembly in September 2005. The conclusions confirmed that the international community was not on track to meet its Millennium Development commitments by the year 2015.

Several UN agencies, including UNDP, UNFPA and CONGO (the International Confederation of Non-Governmental Organizations) went further, warning that most of the problems addressed by the MDGs have worsened since 2000, the most severely affected populations were the poorest African countries, and within these countries women continued to suffer disproportionately from poverty and exclusion from development.[24] In short, if there is a UN "road map" for women's empowerment, it is not a road along which participants are moving either swiftly or in a straight line.

The debate on gender equality and women's advancement has undoubtedly progressed, but it has also reached a critical phase in its development. On the one hand, significant progress has been made in the terms of establishing legal instruments designed to defend women's rights. However that legal discourse has not translated directly or uniformly into legal practice.[25] CEDAW has been criticized for its "silence as regards gender-based violence"[26] and for the structural paralysis that has gripped much of the gender architecture of the United Nations system in recent years:

> As of March 2002, there were 257 overdue state reports to the Women's Rights Committee. If all these delinquent states were to report, the current system could not handle it; in fact, the committee can not even keep up with the reports it does receive.[27]

Likewise in the field of social policy-making the international community created a common language and a common model through which to deliver development to the world's women. The lack of progress on the Nairobi *Forward-looking Strategies* and then the Beijing Platform led commentators, particularly from the UN agencies, to suggest that the main obstacles to getting results lay at the national rather than the international level. These problems have not been restricted to the outcome documents of the women's conferences. In 2003, the UNDP, the agency most closely implicated in the measuring of results, stated:

> In the Alma Ata Declaration of 1977 the world committed to health care for all people by the end of the century. Yet in 2000 millions of poor people died of

pandemic and other diseases, many readily preventable and treatable. Similarly, at the 1990 Summit on Children the world committed to universal primary education by 2000. But that target was missed.[28]

In response to these missed targets, the UN agencies have been pushing for more auditing in developing countries. Both the Director of UNIFEM and the Chief Administrator of the UN's development program have advocated not only more auditing but also more targets.[29] The UNIFEM position on monitoring and measuring progress differs from its parent agency, the UNDP, in the emphasis UNIFEM places on the need for qualitative information and on political and economic empowerment.[30]

When at the end of 2008, the international structures through which gender and development discourse had been formulated throughout its history came under attack, it appeared that the patience of the international women's organizations worldwide had expired. As 2009 progressed, increasing numbers of developing world organizations joined the "Gender Equality Architecture Reform" (GEAR) campaign calling for a fundamental review of UN gender policy structures. The inability of these structures, including UNIFEM, OSAGI, DAW and INSTRAW, to stem the worsening conditions faced by the women in the world's poorest regions was attributed to the lack of power invested in these agencies. The campaign called for radical reform and the establishment of a single powerful authority within the UN to coordinate and implement gender policy.

The difficulties the international community has faced in reaching its gender and development objectives have given the issue of monitoring and measuring results ever greater significance. Since the Millennium Declaration of 2000 and the World Summit review of 2005, the international community is still committed, for the foreseeable future, to producing statistical accounts of movement towards development goals. Indeed if the advice of the UN development agencies is followed, there will be more emphasis placed on the monitoring and measuring process in the twenty-first century than in the past.

The nature of these measuring tools and their effectiveness in the measuring and monitoring of women's advancement towards development and equality are examined in the next chapter in francophone Africa.

P.S. WHAT HAPPENED TO THE "PEACE DIVIDEND"?

In the end the predicted "peace dividend" did not materialize in Africa. In fact, from 1990 there was a fall in donor funding to poor countries. The major ODA donors (with the exception of the United States) have signed up to

Table 5.2. Official Development Assistance (ODA) in the 1990s

Donor Country	ODA as a Percentage of GNP	
	1991	*1998*
Japan	0.32	0.28
United States	0.17	0.10
Canada	0.45	0.29
France	0.54	0.40
Germany	0.41	0.26
Belgium	0.42	0.35
Netherlands	0.88	0.80

Source: UNDP, *Human Development Report 2000* (Oxford: Oxford University Press, 2000), Table 17, 218.

donate at least 0.7 percent of their GNP to development aid. Table 5.2, listing the main donors to francophone Africa since 1991, illustrates that not only did six of the seven fail to meet the UN target, but their funding levels actually dropped after the Cold War ended.

The peace dividend theory proved doubly illusory in that military spending did fall as predicted after the collapse of the Soviet Union. The biggest military spender, the United States, reduced its military budget by about U.S.$107 billion a year throughout the decade. By 1999, even a medium-sized player like France was saving in the region of U.S.$4.5 billion a year.

When in the post-9/11 era, the downward trend in military spending reversed,[31] again the relation between military spending and development budgets failed to correlate. The U.S. ODA[32] budget increased during the two Clinton administrations (1993–2001), and continued to rise through the first Bush administration from 2001 to 2004, relatively and in real terms. In 1998 the United States was spending $29 per capita of U.S. population a year on ODA, by 2002 this had risen to $46 per capita. The international assistance budget increased from $21.8 billion in 2001 to $23.3 billion in 2002, reaching $24.3 billion in 2003.[33] However, as the next chapter will testify, statistics can be misleading. Behind the gross figures significant changes in the use of ODA were taking place:

> For 2003, the President's Budget includes [. . .] a $1 billion increase on 2002. Increased funding has been allocated based on three broad goals:
> 1) to support our highest priority foreign policy objectives, especially the war on terrorism;
> 2) to enhance security for American personnel and facilities;
> 3) to advance the effort to connect resources to performance.[34]

NOTES

1. *OMD* (*objectifs millénaires pour le développement*).

2. Kofi Annan, *We the Peoples—The Role of the United Nations in the 21st Century* (New York: United Nations Department of Public Information, 2000).

3. The Indian economist and Nobel laureate, Amartya Sen, brought this fact to the world's attention in 1990 when he published his landmark article, "More Than 100 Million Women Are Missing," in the *New York Review of Books* 37, no. 20, 1990. http:/ucatlas.ucsc.edu/gender/Sen100M.htm. Accessed 08/25/2009.

4. For a recent update on the situation in Asia see Isabelle Attané, "L'Asie manque de femmes," *Le Monde Diplomatique*, July 2006, 16–17. In this article French sinologist Attané notes how little attention has been paid to this phenomenon in the international community since the appearance of Sen's article in 1990.

5. Kofi Annan, *We the Peoples*, chapter 3, 5.

6. The persistent inability of the UN to act upon its own gender discourse led Secretary-General Ban Ki-moon to issue a circular to UN section heads in April 2008 stating that "at current rates of progress, it would take until 2120 to reach gender balance at some levels (P-5)." See *Gender-related UN Secretariat Policies*, Office of the Special Advisor on Gender Issues (OSAGI), April 2008

7. United Nations, *Resolution 55/2*, section 1, paragraph 6.

8. The *Mission de l'Organisation des Nations Unies au Congo* initial mandate ran from November 1999 to 31 December 2009.

9. See coverage in the *New York Times*, for example, "Rape Epidemic Raises Trauma in Congo," published 7 October 2007, in which it interviewed John Holmes, the United Nations Under-Secretary-General for humanitarian affairs: "The sexual violence in Congo is the worst in the world. The sheer numbers, the wholesale brutality, the culture of impunity—it's appalling."

10. François Grignon, "Rape as a Weapon of War in Congo," *Der Spiegel*, 11 June 2009.

11. Dr. Denis Mukwege, gynecologist at Panzi Hospital, South Kivu Province, the epicenter of Congo's rape epidemic, interviewed in the *New York Times*, 7 October 2007.

12. See *infra* for a summary of the evolution of the gender and development discourse under the aegis of the newly reconfigured francophone development community.

13. United Nations, *Resolution 55/2*, Section 3, paragraph 19.

14. The lack of research on the impact of education on the life goals and aspirations of women applies to developing and industrialized counties. See Linda J Sax of the Higher Education Research Institute, University of California at Los Angeles, introduction to research study: *Reinforcing Difference: College and Gender Gap* (book in progress).

15. R. Pande, A. Malhotra, and C. Grown, "Impact of Investments in Female Education on Gender Equality" Paper presented at the XXV IUSSP International Population Conference, Tours, France, 2005, quoted in *Education from a Gender Equality Perspective*, Equate, USAID, May 2008, 4.

16. The author acknowledges the help and unpublished research of Mmes Rita Couture and Colette Charpentier of the Belgian Diplomatic mission in Libreville collated in Gabon in the mid-1990s.

17. Roger Dehaybe, *Egalité des sexes et développement—concepts et terminologie* (Agence intergouvernementale de la francophonie, July 2009) http://genre .francophonie.org. Accessed 08/25/2009. "At the first *Francophonie* women's conference of 4–5 February 2000, member states and governments adopted a final declaration which stated that the major objectives adopted at the 4th World Conference for Women held in Beijing would remain the prime objectives of this conference." Author's translation.

18. Roger Dehaybe, *Egalité,* 1. "French terms for equality between men and women and women's rights [. . .] and offering French equivalents for the most widely used English terms." Author's translation.

19. 49th Session of the Commission on the Status of Women of the United Nations, New York, 28 February–11 March 2005.

20. While documents written in French refer to human rights as *Droits de l'Homme*, the term *Droits humains* is being used to signal a commitment to gender equality in human rights.

21. Agence intergouvernementale de la francophonie, *Contribution de la Francophonie à l'examen décennal de la mise en œuvre du programme d'action de la Conférence mondiale sur les femmes de Pékin* (Paris: Agence intergouvernementale de la francophonie, 2005), 3. "We confirm our commitment to social and cultural diversity as regards women's place in society and we likewise confirm that this diversity should not constitute an obstacle to respecting the norms and values contained in the Charter of the United Nations, the Universal Declaration of Human Rights and the Convention on the Elimination of all forms of Discrimination Against Women." Author's translation.

22. *Agence intergouvernementale de la francophonie, Contribution,* 5. "Paying particular attention to eliminating all obstacles to women's full participation, including female genital mutilation, honor killings and forced marriage." Author's translation.

23. Amartya Sen, *The Idea of Justice* (London: Allen Lane, 2009).

24. *International Gender and Trade Network,* http://www.igtn.com. See, for example, Salma Maoulidi, "African Women on the MDGs and Poverty," 6 June 2005. In this article Maoulidi presents findings from interviews and discussions conducted through May 2005 with 250 women from 18 African countries on progress towards MDGs.

25. Women living in Member States that have signed the Optional Protocol of the Convention on the Elimination of all forms of Discrimination against Women since 1999 are able to bring complaints about women's rights abuses in their countries directly to the Committee of CEDAW.

26. UNIFEM, *Progress of the World's Women,* 40.

27. William F. Felice, *The Global New Deal: Economic and Social Human Rights in World Politics* (Lanham, MD: Rowman & Littlefield, 2003), 164.

28. UNDP, *Human Development Report 2003,* 29.

29. United Nations, "Contributions from Participants," Press Release (2000), no page numbers.

30. For policy and advocacy documents see http://www.un.org/undp/unifem.

31. Stockholm International Peace Research Institute military expenditure database http://www.sipri.org.

32. Official development assistance.

33. Office of the President of the United States, *Budget of the United States Government: Fiscal Year 2003—Department of State and International Development Assistance* (Washington, D.C.: Executive of the President of the United States, 2003), 252.

III

FROM THE GLOBAL TO THE POSTCOLONY: DATA PROFILING IN GABON AND SENEGAL

6

Mapping Gender and Development

The Tools of the Trade

The four chapters in part III translate the theoretical configuration of gender and development derived from the global discourse into a numeric mapping of this discourse. The mapping is presented first as a control table (table 6.1) and then applied to produce a gender and development profile of Gabon (table 7.1) and a gender and development profile of Senegal (table 8.1).

Using data over a long period enables a longitudinal analysis of gender and disadvantage (exclusion from development), which serves as the principal monitoring tool for this dominant model of gender and development. The picture that emerges from the data has an impact not only on how we understand gender and development issues in a developing world context, it also serves to set the limits within which we define and formulate policy in these areas.

QUANTIFYING GENDER AND DEVELOPMENT: THE ROLE OF THE HUMAN DEVELOPMENT REPORT

Since 1990, the development specialists at the United Nations Development Programme (UNDP) in New York who have been publishing social development statistics and commentary annually in the Human Development Report, have seen their publication grow into the most influential source of data in contemporary development policy. By the mid 1990s the Human Development Report was being described by the chief administrator of the UNDP as "the crown jewel" of the agency. Renowned economist and Nobel laureate, Amartya Sen, described the Human Development Report as one of the most important sources of information and understanding of the social and economic world available to the international community today,[1] while a special

commission of the UN convened to investigate charges of inaccurate reporting in the 1999 Human Development Report (HDR) came to the conclusion
that:

> the HDR is an influential document that may be unrivalled among UN publica-
> tions in terms of the media and popular attention it receives. Its messages appear
> to influence national and international policy activities. Its techniques, and its
> statistics, are replicated widely and inspire national development reports.[2]

Anecdotal evidence from development workers, researchers, policy-makers,
NGO workers in African and other developing countries testify to how influential the Human Development Report has become in forming opinions
and influencing development policies and programs in developing countries.

In 1995 the HDR team, recognizing the impact of gender in development,
and particularly the impact of gender on social development, prioritized gender data and research in the 1995 Human Development Report. Since this
edition it has collated and included data on the impact of gender on social
development in all the HDRs.

There have been other influential sources of quantitative information on
gender and social development published within the international community since 1990, notably UNIFEM's *Progress of the World's Women 2000*,
the first of what is intended to be a regular series of reports on women's
advancement and on the implementation of all the international conventions
and resolutions and declarations. However, the role of the HDRs remains
unchallenged by these other reports and publications because of the regularity
with which they have been published, namely every year since 1990,[3] and,
importantly, in what appears to be the same format. The purpose has been to
provide information to national governments, policy-makers and interested
parties in the international community on social development trends over
long periods of time. The trends form a key element in agency and government understanding social development needs.[4]

For the purposes of this study, a non-country specific mapping of gender
and development has been constructed from all the gender and social development data published consistently in the HDRs from 1990 to 2005. This
control table brings together all the gender-sensitive and gender-comparative
indicators that can be used to draw up a gender and development profile for
a developing country. Table 6.1 contains the variables that were identified as
the main vehicles of women's advancement during the international community's discussion of gender and development from 1975 to 1995, and included
in the international community's platforms for action.

From 1995 onwards the Human Development Report Office has emphasized the importance of gender as a key factor in a person's access to develop-

ment. Accordingly table 6.1 includes more variables from the second half of the 1990s than the first half. For purposes of clarity, eight exemplary reports are selected from the period 1990 to 2005.

GENDER AND SOCIAL DEVELOPMENT IN *HUMAN DEVELOPMENT REPORTS*

The first table in the HDR[5] is always the Human Development Index table which ranks the Member States of the UN according to the level of human development they have achieved. Each country receives a grade between 0 and 1 indicating how far along a scale from 0 (no human development) towards 1 (maximum human development) it has traveled. Those countries reaching scores nearest 1 are ranked at the top. The countries of francophone West Africa invariably find themselves at the bottom of the list.

The HDI ranking is calculated according to the Member State's performance against 10 "quality of life" indicators ranging from life expectancy, adjusted GDP per capita, access to sources of knowledge and learning; and the living standards of the population as a whole. As such, the Human Development Report statistical section focuses primarily on population-wide parameters and indicators and the information used by the HDR Office is gathered largely from national census data and annual statistical audits. In the case of the middle- and high-income countries these are almost invariably comprehensive audits. The situation for low-income countries is quite different. Statistical technologies in developing countries are not highly developed outside of the financial sector. Social information has to be gathered, or commissioned, from whatever sources are available and the presentation of the data is often not compatible with international equivalents. So quantitative analysis of low-income country data must always be undertaken with a degree of circumspection. Following the widely-publicized critique of the quality of data published in the 1999 HDR, the UN convened a special commission to investigate the reliability of the reporting. The Commission gave the Human Development Report a clean bill of health, but issued the following warning:

> The powerful impact of statistics creates four caveats in their use:
> 1. Overuse—statistics alone cannot capture the full picture of rights and should not be used as the only focus of assessment. All statistical analysis needs to be embedded in an interpretation drawing on broader political, social and contextual analysis.
> 2. Underuse—data are rarely voluntarily collected on issues that are incriminating, embarrassing or simply ignored.

[. . .]
3. Misuse—Data collection is often biased towards institutions and formalized reporting.[6]

Following this verdict, the HDR Office included a whole chapter on the use and abuse of statistics in its millennium edition of the Human Development Report. In it it argued that statistics, when ill-used, were misleading and that in order to be fit for purpose statistics have to fulfill at least the following four criteria. Statistics must be:

1. Policy relevant—giving messages on issues that can be influenced, directly or indirectly, by policy action;
2. Reliable—enabling different people to use them and get consistent results;
3. Consistently measurable over time—necessary if they are to show whether progress is being made and targets are being achieved
[. . .]
4. Possible to disaggregate—focusing on social groups, minorities and individuals.[7]

The application of the statistical model to Gabon and Senegal in the two chapters that follow will be a test of these requirements.

CREATING THE MODEL OF GENDER AND DEVELOPMENT FOR FRANCOPHONE AFRICA

All the statistics related to gender and development that could be deemed "fit for purpose" by the standards listed above appear in table 6.1. The table includes variables that are "policy relevant" to the gender dimension of development in a developing world context; "possible to disaggregate" so we see the impact of gender within the specific variable; "consistently measurable over time" only variables appearing several times between 1990 and 2005 are included. The issue of "reliability" has not been prioritized here as the control table is not country-specific. The very real problem of data reliability in an African context will be discussed in relation to the findings from Gabon and Senegal.

In table 6.1, the variables in the left-hand column are those that appear most consistently. Those that do not appear are absent because they did not appear sufficiently frequently in the Reports over time and were not prominent in the discourse from which HDRO are drawing the variables. Some variables were reasonably consistent while being absent from some annual Human Development Reports, in which case the data symbol ■ is absent for the year in which that variable did not appear in the Report. There were other variables which fulfilled the first and second criteria but were excluded because they had not

Table 6.1. Gender and Social Development in the HDRs, 1990–2005

Variable	1990	1994	1997	1998	1999	2000	2001	2005
Women's life expectancy	(■)[1]	■	■	■	■	■	■	■
Female adult[2] literacy	■	■	■	■	■	■	■	■
% of parliamentary seats held by women	(■)	■	■	■	■	■	■	■
net primary enrolments (girls)	■	■	■	■	■	■	■	■
% share of primary school places occupied by girls		■	■	■			■	(■)
Girls' secondary school enrolments (gross)	■	■	■	■			■	(■)
Female higher education enrolment (gross)	■	■	(■)	(■)		■	■	(■)
Mean years of schooling		■						
GDI[3] rank			■	■	■	■	■	■
GDI value			■	■	■	■	■	■
GEM[4] rank			■	■	■	■	■	■
GEM value			■	■	■	■	■	■
Women in the labor force as % of total	■	■	■	■				(■)
Estimated average female income						■	■	■
Women's % share of earned income			■	■			■	(■)
% of managerial posts held by women		■	■	■	■	■	■	■
Female unemployment					■	■		
Female GDP per capita in ppp$[5]					■			
Female unpaid family workers			■	■	■	■	■	(■)
% of ministerial level posts held by women			■	■	■	■	■	
use of contraceptives		■	(■)	■	■			(■)[6]
average age at first marriage (female)		■						

Source: UNDP *Human Development Report* (New York and Oxford: Oxford University Press.)

[1] (■) = data provided but in another form, e.g., as a ratio of the male average whereas before given as a percentage of the female population, or gross enrolment given in one year and net in another. In all these cases further information is required before data can be converted to a form comparable with other years.

[2] Adult = aged 15 years and over.

[3] GDI = Gender development index

[4] GEM = Gender empowerment measure

[5] Parity purchasing power expressed in US dollars

[6] Contraceptive prevalence rate is not disaggregated by gender, but use of condom in "high risk" sex is.

been present either sufficiently regularly and/or in a consistent form over time and so were incapable of indicating a trend. Variables were usually excluded if they appeared only once over the period.[8] Several variables were included that fail at some or several points in the period to be measurable over time due to the fact that the form in which they were presented was inconsistent. The years in which they are incompatible with a trend established earlier are indicated by the data symbol in parentheses, (■). If the three criteria of statistical reliability had been strictly adhered to, table 6.1 would have contained only two variables: levels of literacy in the adult female population and net enrolments of girls in primary education.[9]

The data variables are listed in the order in which they appeared regularly from the earliest Reports. In essence, table 6.1 provides a snapshot of what the HDR Office has identified as the salient factors influencing women's experience of development compared with men in the developing world as these emerged from the gender and development debate over recent years.

There are obviously other data sources for this period but consistent coverage of gender as a factor in social development is minimal in these alternative sources compared with the Human Development Reports.[10] Other sources began later and cannot offer the longitudinal view of gender and development in the world context contained in the HDRs. Supplementing these data, the UN Statistical Division (UNSD) "Millennium Indicators" website has been charting progress towards MDGs and targets since 2000.[11] MDG 3, "gender equality," targets the elimination of gender inequality in education by 2015 and includes four indicators. Among these four indicators is the reduction of female unemployment in the non-agricultural sector. In theory this could be a useful addition to HDR data from 2000 where female unemployment, surely a key indicator of female quality of life for millions of women in the developing world, has been recorded inconsistently since 1990. Throughout the period 1990 to 2005, the HDRs have failed to include any data from francophone Africa beyond female economic activity rate (the percentage of the female population in receipt of earned income). In practice, the Millennium Development database also provides no indication of female unemployment trends in Senegal and Gabon. The absence of consistent socio-economic data on francophone African countries has been a problem common to all these international databases.[12]

MAPPING THE QUALITY OF A WOMAN'S LIFE

What is immediately apparent from the distribution of data in table 6.1 is that the selection of salient variables has changed over time. Indeed both the number and the nature of the variables have changed.

As expected there are more returns in the right-hand columns than the left, reflecting the HDRO's ability to pick up on developments in the international debate on gender in development and inject new variables into the model. It also shows an ability to adapt and modify UNDP/HDRO thinking in response to emerging issues. As gender rose up the agenda of the international community in all the international summits after 1992, the HDRO responded to this by translating this emerging understanding of the many dimensions of gender in development into variables. This is both laudable and problematic in that as new variables are introduced and others dropped, the power of the reports to reveal trends over time diminishes. There are just four indicators for mapping women's advancement through social development that have remained largely consistent over the period. These are life expectancy; adult female literacy; girls' access to and progress through lower levels of formal schooling; and the percentage of seats held by women in the national parliament. With the exception of employment data, these variables taken together reflect what emerged over the years as a universal "model" for female social development, the central pillar is access to education and literacy, and the secondary pillars are access to positions of influence in national politics and decision-making and access to good[13] employment.

The position of women in paid employment suffered from inconsistent reporting with data being presented in such a variety of forms as to make trends almost impossible to identify, this despite the emphasis on income and paid employment at all the international women's conferences from Mexico City in 1975 through to Beijing in 1995.

Up to 1997 the employment variable was presented essentially in terms of how many women gained access to the paid labor market. From 1997 the focus shifted from women's presence in the labor force to their share of earned income, though here again the indicator has not been used consistently. It was included in 1998, dropped in 1999 and again 2000, and then reintroduced in 2001. A new variable was introduced in 2000 that, if developed, could fill a large gap in our knowledge of women's experience of employment and prove a powerful indicator of women's socio-economic status. This new indicator offers an estimate of average income disaggregated by gender. The focus here is on what women take away from the job market and not solely what they contribute. For this indicator to be useful the HDRO will need fuller information on how much men and women are paid, and not simply on how many men and women are active in the labor force.

This new focus on women's experience of work is reinforced in a table that appeared for the first time in the 1995 Report under the title "Burden of Work by Gender, Selected Developing Countries."[14] It appeared again in the 1999 Report and in the 2000 report, this time as "Gender Gaps in Work Burden and

Time Allocation,"[15] only to disappear again in 2001. Capturing the amount of time men and women work on "market" (paid) and "non-market" activities is highly relevant to their relative socio-economic position. However the data in these tables are of no practical use in evaluating the employment situation for women in francophone sub-Saharan Africa as not one country from the region was included in the HDR tables listed above. The data cover just 22 countries, Kenya being the only sub-Saharan African state included with a data set dating from 1986. Indeed some of the "Gender Gaps in Work Burden" data dated from the 1970s. In a study of contemporary trends, data of that age is normally considered obsolete.[16] In 2002 the same ageing data were used in table 26 "Gender, Work Burden and Time Allocation."[17]

Later in the decade the table, re-titled "Gender, Work and Time Allocation,"[18] introduced new data and one country from francophone Africa (Benin). The data have not appeared frequently enough to present a trend that could be included in a longitudinal analysis but the findings are interesting. They suggest that women living in the urban areas of Benin are paid for half their daily workload compared with men who receive pay for an average of 78 percent of their working day. There are a number of explanations such as the norm among women to provide unpaid domestic service (typically just short of three hours a day per adult women, in addition to family duties such as child care). Women living in towns and cities in Benin provide child care for on average 35 minutes a day while, for men, their daily commitment to child care lasts on average four minutes.

Although the earlier "Gender Gaps in Work Burden and Time" tables do not offer useful and policy-applicable statistical insights into the situation of women's work in Africa, they are interesting in what they indicate about how HDRO and its parent agency, the UNDP, translate thinking on gender in the workplace into variables in the Reports. In its role as advocate for gender and development policy, the UNDP through the Human Development Report drew attention to the emerging debate around unpaid labor, both in ethical terms and in terms of national employment auditing. A significant proportion of work undertaken daily throughout the world is not paid for and therefore falls outside a country's official labor market and employment statistics. By stressing the gender dimension of work burdens, the HDR is also drawing attention to the fact that unpaid labor is largely carried out by women. This issue was discussed at the Beijing Conference and a statement was included in the 1995 Platform of Action, but as UNIFEM pointed out during the Beijing+5 conference in 2000:

> The Platform of Action commits governments to develop a methodology to
> measure unremunerated work but does not specify how to use such data in

macro economic policy-making or how to redress the inequities uncovered by the data.[19]

The variables that have been incorporated into the Human Development Report over the years and presented here in table 6.1 were included in the Reports with the explicit aim of providing policy-makers with a source of reliable knowledge on access to social development in all the poorest countries of the world. The intended outcome was an improved knowledge base on which to develop social policies that would help those most marginalized people in the poorest countries access the outputs of development and become less vulnerable to poverty and social exclusion.

According to the international community's auditing of social development, women in francophone West Africa have had less access to the outputs of development than any other regional population group globally. With this in mind, the significance of the mission of the Human Development Report to provide policy-relevant information on gender and development is particularly salient.

The question then becomes how policy relevant and useful are the data when applied to this least developed region of the world? The next two chapters test the model of data profiling mapped out in table 6.1 by applying it to two very different countries from the francophone African region: Gabon and Senegal.

NOTES

1. Quoted by Ian Castles in the introduction to his critique of the Human Development Reports presented to the 2000 meeting of the United Nations Statistical Commission. The minutes of this meeting were accessible in 2000 at http://www.undp.org/hdro/FOC.report.pdf, 37.

2. United Nations, *An Assessment of the Statistical Criticisms Made of the Human Development Report 1999*, 26–27, and http://www.undp.org/hdro/FOC.report.pdf.

3. There has been a recent exception: the September 2007 edition covered the period September 2007 to September 2009.

4. The Human Development Reports, originally available only in English and French, are now produced in a number of world languages.

5. Data are presented in the Human Development Reports in tabular form as single records of national averages or aggregates. There are 25 to 35 tables in each Report, preceded by a substantial commentary focused on a theme. The 1995 Report focused on gender in development and the 2000 Report on Human Rights.

6. United Nations, *An Assessment of the Statistical Criticisms*, 26–27, http://www.undp.org.hdro/FOC.report.pdf. Accessed 11/2000. (The file was subsequently withdrawn.)

7. UNDP, *Human Development Report 2000* (Oxford: Oxford University Press, 2000), 90.

8. An exception was made in some cases, such as the last variable, these having emerged during fieldwork in West Africa as important gender and social development variables. The question of what was omitted from this list will be returned to at the end of this part.

9. Even this variable is not immune to inconsistency. In 2005 it was presented as a ratio rather than as a percent of the school population.

10. Social Watch, an international monitoring organization, provides commentary as well as advocacy but does not have the level of access to national audits afforded to the official representative institutions of the international community. For Social Watch data see http://www.socialwatch.org.

11. http://millenniumindicators.un.org/unsd/mi.

12. The 2005 World Summit resolved to improve data provision after 2005 but there are still gaps throughout the sub-Saharan Africa region and the former French colonies remain the least well audited of any region in the world.

13. At the end of the first decade of the twenty-first century the international agencies were talking increasingly of decent and reliable employment as opposed to any employment.

14. *Human Development Report*, 1995, Table 4.1.

15. *Human Development Report*, 2000, Table 30.

16. The statistics for Guatemala date from 1977, those for Nepal from 1978, and those for Colombia 1983. The most recent date from 1992. *Human Development Report*, 2000, Table 30, 263.

17. *Human Development Report*, 2002, Table 26.

18. *Human Development Report*, 2007/08, Table 32.

19. UNIFEM, *The Progress of the World's Women 2000* (New York: UNDP, 2000), 55.

Senegal

A Monitoring Model for Francophone Africa?

Have the Human Development Reports published since 1990 produced data of sufficient quantity and quality to show how women have been experiencing the social and human dimensions of development in Senegal over this period and to assist policy-makers in identifying policy outcomes? The following experiment in data profiling attempts to answer these questions.

Table 7.1 is a repeat of the model presented in chapter 6 with the difference that in this case all the data symbols have been replaced with the real data returns Senegal provided for the years included in the table. The process of replacing the theoretical model with a real case generated several logistical and methodological issues.

Firstly, collating data in the Least Developed Countries poses considerable problems. Auditing technologies are expensive to install and maintain. A country like Senegal with a GDP per capita of less than $1,800 a year and falling,[1] does not have the capacity to respond to this bureaucratic imperative of auditing the social and economic life of the country in a fully comprehensive fashion. The implications of this for the quantitative model of gender and development are evident at first sight in table 7.1. The control table 6.1 contains 114 data cells. In theory, therefore, a country should return a maximum of 114 items of data to provide a picture of gender and development in the period 1990–2005. Table 7.1 contains only 80 records.

This discrepancy is not unusual, a differential of 34 data items is low by African standards. Senegal is relatively well endowed with statistical infrastructure and data production when compared with other countries in the francophone sub-region. This former French colony served as the centre of administrative, legal and academic operations during the life of the French

Table 7.1. Gender and Social Development in Senegal, 1990–2005

Variables	1990	1994	1997	1998	1999	2000	2001	2005
Women's life expectancy	[107.3]^a	49.7	50.9	51.3	54.2	54.6	54.8	56.9
% adult^b literacy in female population	19	26	21.2	23.2	24.8	25.8	26.7	29.2
% parliamentary seats held by women	11.7^c	12	12	—^d	—	14	14	19.2
% of girls enrolled in primary school (net)			42	48	53.6	53.6	55	54
% female share of primary places	69	—		79			85	(0.89^e)
% of girls enrolled in secondary (gross)	10	11			[15.5]^f	[15.5]	—	(—)
% women enrolled in tertiary (gross)	1.2	1.2	117^g	142		140	—	—
mean years of schooling		0.5^h						
GDI rank			160	158	153	128^i	130	120
GDI value			0.309	0.326	0.417	0.405	0.413	0.449
GEM rank			—	—	—	—	—	—
GEM value			—	—	—	—	—	—
Women workers as % of total force	39.7	26	42	42	[38.1]^j	[61.3]^j	[61.3]^j	[61.8]^j
Average female income ($ppp)						917^k	996	1,175
Female share of earned income			35.7^l	35.1			—^m	(0.55)^n
% senior admin. posts held by women	—	—	—		—		—	—

Unemployment			—	—		—	—
Female GDP per capita in ppp$		1,253°					
Unpaid family workers		—	—	—	—	—	
% ministerial posts held by women		4	4	6.7	3.3	15.6	20.6
Use of contraceptives	7		13	13			(11)ᵖ
Age at first marriage	18.3						

ᵃ Not comparable with subsequent years as female life expectancy is expressed here as a % of the male average.

ᵇ Adult = 15 years and older

ᶜ Women's participation is expressed as percentage of male participation in 1990 not as a percentage of seats allocated. So it is necessary to find out the number of parliamentary seats and calculate what the percentage represents.

ᵈ This indicator appears in the Gender Empowerment Measure table but no data was included for Senegal in 1998 (*HDR 1998* p. 136) and 1999 (*HDR 1999*, p. 145).

ᵉ This is a ratio of the male value of 1.

ᶠ 1999 and 2000 show **net** secondary enrolments of girls.

ᵍ Records for 1997, 1998 and 2000 indicate the number of women university students per 100,000 women in the population.

ʰ The 1994 figure is an average for the population aged 25 plus calculated in 1992.

ⁱ This gives the erroneous impression that Senegal is rising through the ranks whereas only 143 countries were included in the rankings in 2000 compared with 175 in 1997.

ʲ 1999, 2000, 2001 and 2005 are expressed as a percentage of the adult female population NOT as a percentage of the total workforce.

ᵏ This is an estimate by HDRO, see *HDR 1999*, table 21, p. 213, footnote e, for further details.

ˡ 1997 and 1998 records are also an *HDRO* estimate (see *HDR 1997*, p. 151 footnote d).

ᵐ For countries where data is given, the data are presented as a ratio of 1 (1 being the male average). Some compensation for the lack of comparability with earlier records is to be found in a new column which appeared in the 2001 GDI table (pp. 210-213) giving estimated earned income in ppp$ for men and women.

ⁿ This is a ratio of male income at a value of 1.

ᵒ Again the HDRO can only provide an estimate (see *HDR 1999*, p.141 footnote e).

ᵖ This percentage value is not disaggregated by gender.

West African Empire and the legacy of this colonial history is still visible in the administrative culture of Senegal.

The second problem that becomes apparent when applying the theoretical model is that in addition to the issue of missing data for certain years, there are data missing for the entire period 1990 to 2005. This means that key variables are missing from the country profile that were identified as crucial to women's advancement by the international community during the decades it spent debating and discussing women's advancement in development. The model rests on women being able to access key structures of development and demands that they acquire better access to existing social, political, educational and economic outputs. The data from Senegal do not report on all these dimensions of development. The "snapshot" presentation of female social development provided by table 7.1 excludes information on how women are faring in the job market. With the exception of female economic activity rate as a percentage of the male economic activity rate, the information in table 7.1 does not provide a clear picture of the trends in female employment during the first fifteen years this reporting mechanism has been in operation.[2] The fact that employment data are less deficient in the latter part of the decade illustrates the increased importance attributed to this variable after 1995 within the international community. As access to paid employment was one of the key variables enshrined in the Beijing Platform of Action in 1995 this increased demand for data from the international auditing agents, in this case the Human Development Report Office.

The third main problem facing the quantitative approach is that the form in which the data comes in from the Senegalese auditors is not always comparable and compatible. For the budgetary reasons mentioned above the government cannot prioritize data collection over other pressing social and economic demands facing a less developed country. This means that at times these data cannot be used in longitudinal studies.

In spite of all the gaps in the data and the caveats on the quality and comparability of data, table 7.1 does manage to provide a picture of women's experience of development in Senegal that could be of some potential use to policy-makers. The table provides a clear indication of trends in life expectancy; enrollments in educational institutions; adult literacy; number of seats in parliament held by women; and since 1997 the Gender Development Index (GDI) trend.[3]

LIFE EXPECTANCY, GENDER, AND HEALTH

The clearest statistical representation of an improvement in the quality of life of a population is provided by the life expectancy records. With the exception of 1990, when a woman's average life expectancy was given as a percentage of a man's, the trend in Senegal can be easily read from the Reports from 1991 to 2005. We can see that in the early 1990s a woman could expect to die before reaching the age of 50, 15 years later her life expectancy had risen to almost 57. However, this recorded average life expectancy of 57 signals another problem in Human Development reporting. The actual life expectancy in 2005 for Senegalese women was 64.4 years and 60.4 years for Senegalese men[4] but there is a significant time lag in getting up-to-date statistics into the annual reports. This is of considerable significance in countries exposed to the HIV/AIDS pandemic where careful monitoring of life expectancy helps trace the impact of the spread of the disease through the female population of sub-Saharan Africa. The level of infection reported in Senegal in 2007 was the lowest in sub-Saharan Africa. The Senegalese government adopted a pro-active stance on HIV/AIDS early in the crisis launching publicity campaigns and targeting information at strategic populations[5]; however, the gender dimension of this infection profile remains unclear.[6] There are many possible explanations for a low infection level that cannot be identified from the aggregate data in these Reports. An *Education à la vie familiale et en matière de population* program introduced into schools a decade earlier might be a factor. The program was rolled out gradually from 1991 through 1998 throughout the ten regions of Senegal and included lessons on family planning, marriage regimes, and other issues of direct relevance to the spread of HIV/AIDS.[7] The education statistics reported here would not be able to pick up on this type of provision.

Up-to-date life expectancy data are also crucial to monitoring the Millennium Development Goal 5 aimed at improving maternal health. Half of all deaths in childbirth globally occur in sub-Saharan Africa where it appears that the level has scarcely dropped at all over the period from 1990 to 2005. Senegal reported significant improvements in maternal mortality rates in the 1990s, estimated at 1,200 deaths per 100,000 births in 1990[8] and falling to 560 deaths per 100,000 live births by 1998.[9] However, as half the population during this period had no access to health services at all, this picture is hard to verify. The data are not included in the variables reported in tables 6.1 and 7.1 because they are not comparable by gender.

LITERACY AS A QUALITY OF LIFE INDICATOR

Literacy in the over 15 population has been reported consistently in the Human Development Reports over the whole period. In 1990 it was calculated that only one in five Senegalese women over the age of 15 could read and write in any written language. This usually meant literacy in French or Arabic before the introduction of the Senegalese national languages programme in the early 1990s to promote the countries' main oral languages (Wolof, Mandinka, Joola, Sereer, Soninka, Pulaar) and their use as the medium of instruction in the new *Ecoles communautaires de base* (rural community schools admitting pupils outside the normal primary school age range) and adult literacy classes. Since the early 1990s literacy training has been delivered through a growing number of projects and structures in Senegal with the result that by 2000 one in four adult women in Senegal was literate, a figure that continued to rise at a similar rate throughout the first decade of the twenty-first century.

The trend reflects efforts on the ground to improve the literacy situation particularly in certain highly Islamized regions, such as Diourbel, and regions heavily dependent on female agricultural labor such as Tambacounda.[10] In these regions, the vast majority of girls and women have not traditionally had access to formal schooling.[11] Literacy has been steadily rising throughout the country despite data from the middle of the decade that infer a fall in literacy between 1994 and 1997. One of the weaknesses of quantitative representations is the lack of explanatory commentary. An anomaly like this could only be resolved through further investigation in the data-providing agencies in Senegal.[12] Separate discussions with the Ministry of Education's Department for Literacy and later at the Ministry's statistics unit in Dakar revealed that two different data sets were being used for reporting during the period, each providing a different starting value for female literacy in 1990. The two sets were reporting identical trends, consistently upwards throughout the decade but it appeared the two data sets had been confused on their way into the Human Development Report. The lower of the two starting points is the more realistic of the two, so the starting point was probably 16 percent rather than the 19 percent reported for 1990 in table 7.1.

Variables which contain a large amount of composite information and socio-economic non-numeric variation are very prone to encounter problems in calculative methodologies. On the other hand, there are variables which are reliable, such as the formal political participation data. Here the Human Development Report Office can draw on data from the Inter-Parliamentary Union/ *Union interparlementaire*, a global institution funded by the parliaments of the world.[13] The IPU reports the number and percentage of women elected to political and legislative bodies around the world and publishes these on its comprehensive and up-to-date website.[14] It is therefore unsurprising that the Beijing targets of improving women's access to and representation in formal positions of political influence and power is well documented in the Human Development Reports for all the countries of francophone sub-Saharan Africa.

Figures in row 3 of table 7.1 show the percentage of seats occupied by women in the Senegalese national parliament. With 13 percent representation in 1994 compared with 14 percent in 2001, it could be inferred that little change had occurred in women's access to positions of power and influence in national politics in this period. In fact nothing could be further from the truth. Profound changes took place in parliamentary democracy in Senegal, the first wave being initiated by the National Conference on political democracy held at the beginning of the 1990s, with its remit to widen access to the parliamentary process and extend democratic participation. In theory these changes should have had an impact on women's representation in politics by increasing their representation. In practice, the changes operated differently. Widening participation and access to parliamentary politics did not increase women's participation but rather culminated in the overthrow in March 2000 of a regime which had been in power since Independence in 1958, firstly, under the leadership of Léopold Sédar Senghor, and then under his deputy and successor in 1983, Abdou Diouf.

During this period of Socialist Party rule, women had formal representation both within the ruling Socialist Party and theoretically in the National Assembly. The *Parti socialiste* had adopted a policy to allocate 25 percent of seats in the national assembly to women but in practice failed to get even half way towards this goal. When Abdou Diouf was overthrown in 2000, female participation in formal politics increased due to the personal intervention of the new President Abdoulaye Wade. Representation continued to rise through the decade reaching 22 percent for the parliamentary term 2007–2012. However, an increase in female representation in the formal arena of national politics does not translate directly into the advancement of the female population in general. Nor does greater representation at the national level play out in predictable ways in the local community. Before 2000 women tended to win parliamentary seats only where they had received the backing of the ruling *Parti socialiste*, which gave them the seat in the expectation they would follow the party's lead and not an independent or feminist platform. Post-2000 local political elites have not responded positively to pressures to increase female participation.

In the euphoria following the overthrow of the Diouf regime, the new President could exercise a degree of freedom in choosing his cabinet. The IPU data on governmental posts show a four-fold increase in the percentage of women reaching the higher echelons of the Senegalese government in the aftermath of the 2000 elections. If the HDRs included a variable indicating the gender of the Prime Minister, the 2001 Report would have revealed a historic change. In late 2000, President Abdoulaye Wade promoted his Justice

Minister, Mame Madior Boye, to the head of the government, making her Senegal's first woman Prime Minister.[15]

ACCESS, EDUCATION AND EMPOWERMENT

Just as the data on the rising trends in political appointments of women give no insight into how power is mediated, the rising trends in education do not reveal how girls and women are translating access to education into human development goals. By far the greatest number of cases recorded in the HDRs relate to access to and progress through formal education. Not only are these data the most prolific they are also the most consistent in terms of the form they take and the number of years they have been reported. The picture that comes through from these statistics is of an increasing number of girls of primary school–age attending school. The percentage of school-age girls attending primary schools in Senegal appears to have risen from 41 percent in 1993 to 54 percent in 2005. The picture also shows that the ratio of girls to boys in primary schooling has been evening out. In 1990 a teacher with a class of 37 pupils would expect to see 15 girls and 22 boys in the classroom. This same teacher would have seen on average 17 girls and 20 boys in a class of 37 pupils during the school year 2000–2001.

However, the rate of increase at primary level does not continue through into the secondary sector. There are clearly significant factors governing the low level of progression from primary to secondary education, but again there is nothing in the statistical tables that can help explain this phenomenon. Age at first marriage, which might be considered influential in this matter, has not been reported in the HDRs since 1994. In that year, it was reported that Senegalese girls generally married around the age of 18. The regular national demographic surveys[16] confirm this figure, suggesting that the average age rose from 16 in 1978 to around 18 in 1997.[17] In some regions of the world, marriage at this age would not be expected to have an incidence on primary school attendance. However, the average age of a primary school pupil in some parts of francophone Africa is far higher than in other parts of the developing world. The former French colonies of Africa inherited an education system whereby progression to the next year of study is dependent upon successful completion of a set of end-of-year exams. A pupil who fails these exams has to retake the school year. African children, and particularly girls, frequently have familial responsibilities and calls on their time which interfere with attendance at school and particularly agricultural duties that occur in the end-of-year-exam period. A young rural girl can spend much of the day working in the home, with extra unpaid agricultural duties to perform she will have even less time to attend school. The resulting impact on exam performance among rural children in general and among girls in particular means that it is not at all uncommon for pupils to have to retake a year several times in their school career.

The low availability and use of contraceptives is another factor that bears upon secondary school attendance. This factor has also not been monitored consistently in the HDRs. Fear of pregnancy is high on the list of criteria militating against sending girls to secondary schools in the nearest town or city. Hours of travel or boarding arrangements far from the family home are required. These and other cultural and social impediments to girls' education are not revealed in these quantitative data.

The emphasis on education data in the global discourse of gender and development has overlooked the issue how education might or might not encourage girls and women to analyze their own situation and promote their own advancement:

> *Les manuels utilisés dans l'enseignement primaire francophone mettent en évidence certains faits: [. . .] A quelques exceptions près les femmes apparaissent comme des personnes douces. [. . .] Leurs responsabilités sont limitées. Pour toute décision importante, tant du point de vue matériel qu'éducatif, les pères entrent en scène, faisant figure d'autorité. Dans leur profession, elles sont décrites comme des auxiliaires, tandis que les hommes apparaissent aux postes de responsabilité.*[18]

The scenario is a familiar one to former pupils of Western education systems and to those who have inherited Western educational cultures from the former colonial power. In seeking to preserve a status quo, conservative education cultures inculcate traditional gender stereotypes. In Senegal *INEADE*, the national education institute, started reviewing gender stereotypes in primary school textbooks in the 1990s, with a view to removing derogatory gender stereotyping from educational material in Senegal.

The argument that assumes that formal education is beneficial regardless of its content has particular weight in Africa where there has been a continent-wide campaign running since 1990 to provide entry level formal education for all. Questions about how education affects the life of the individual are subordinated to those that assess the impact of general education, particularly on the economy and society. In this context, it is not surprising that it is very difficult to find information on women's access to higher education, despite the mass of education statistics that have been generated in the continent.

Higher education data do appear in the Human Development Reports but the form they take are not directly comparable year on year. In one year access to higher education is presented as the number of university students per

100,000 head of population, elsewhere they are presented as a percentage of the adult population. The lack of attention paid to higher education is not excusable on the grounds of the expense of auditing technologies alluded to earlier in this chapter. Education enrollments constitute simple numeric data and are readily available from university authorities in Senegal and throughout the francophone region.[19] The regional office of UNESCO, the agency responsible for collecting and disseminating educational data for the UN system, could not provide for this study and at the time of asking the higher education data for Senegal. The data had been available for the previous 12 years at the Registry of the University of Dakar, disaggregated by gender and by faculty for the period from 1988 to the present, and the Registry was also able to supply registration data for the country's second university, Gaston Berger in Saint Louis.[20] As this illustrates, the quality of auditing can be determined as much by cultural as structural factors.

Two gender-comparative indicators that have been included consistently in HDRs since 1995 are the Gender Development Index (GDI), and the Gender Empowerment Measure (GEM). However, as almost all of the data used to make up these measures are missing for Senegal, no GEM value or ranking is recorded. The gender development index includes information on life expectancy, literacy and access to knowledge, all of which are reasonably well documented in the case of Senegal. However, it also includes a standard of living index calculated, like the HDI index, on male and female per capita incomes and these data have not been supplied consistently in Senegal.[21]

After access to education and alongside political representation, women's access to paid work has been the third pillar in the international definition of female social development since the first World Conference on Women in Mexico City in 1975 when the rediscovery of income poverty was used to launch the UN campaign for female economic advancement around the world. The importance of this variable is reflected in table 7.1. Women in the labor force has been reported each year, but the form of reporting has changed between 1990 and 2005. In early reports, the female labor force was represented as part of the total labor force. In later reports women workers were presented as a percentage of the adult female population.

The qualitative changes occurring in the way women's work is being discussed is also evident in the Senegal table. Table 7.1 provides some information on the quality of female employment. We can see that there was a four-fold increase in the percentage of high-level government jobs held by women, and from this it is possible to deduce that women's independent incomes in this section of the elite are rising. Likewise the growth in the percentage of working women suggests that women's share of earned income has also risen.

While these data provide some interesting insights, there are other cases in the table that look less secure. The mid-decade trend in female employment is counter-intuitive. As Senegal suffered an employment crisis throughout the 1990s the sudden drop and rise in female employment between 1990 and 1997 looks unreliable. What we do know is that in times of economic crisis women are more vulnerable to unemployment than men. In the first months after the financial crash of 2008, male employment dropped more rapidly than female. However, from early 2009 the female unemployment rates began to rise and by the mid-year review the trend in greater female unemployment was confirmed.[22]

Secondly, a growth in the number of women recorded as economically active is difficult to interpret in an economy such as Senegal's where many working women operate in what is termed the informal economy and remain undocumented. Thirdly, even if there has been a rise in the number of women in paid work we cannot automatically deduce from this that women are gaining a larger share of earned income. It is safe to assume that women generally earn less than men in Senegal,[23] in equivalent fields women in the UK still earn up to 20 pence on the pound less than men; women in the United States, though faring considerably better than their British counterparts, still earn 11 cents on the dollar less than men.[24] The lack of reliable and useable employment data is not helped by the administrative culture in Senegal, which resists disaggregating employment data by gender, particularly in the powerful centralized *Administration*, the super-sized civil service that runs the state apparatus and the education system. The team of social scientists preparing the UNDP-sponsored sociological study of the position of women in Senegal in 2000[25] had to resort to personal contacts and anecdotal evidence to produce "best guess estimates" of the number of women and men in different professions.

Notwithstanding all the problems mentioned above, when compared with other countries from the francophone West African region, Senegal actually represents one, if not the best, case scenario for data profiling the gender and development status of women in francophone West Africa. Senegal is one of the poorest countries in the region, indeed one of the most underdeveloped on the continent, but it is data-rich in comparison with many countries in the region. By contrast, Gabon, a small oil-rich nation that has enjoyed the enviable position of being one of Africa's most prosperous countries, presents quite a different set of challenges for data profiling, as the next chapter reveals.

NOTES

1. The effects of the global financial recession began to appear in the sub-Saharan African economies in job losses during the winter of 2008/09 reflected in overall GNP for 2009/10.

2. The Human Development Reports published after 2005 contained no data that could fill these gaps for Senegal beyond new information on rising unemployment rates among women in the second half of the first decade of the twenty-first century. In the absence of real data on female share of earned income this continued to be calculated as a percentage of male income.

3. The GDI ranks are misleading because the number of countries included in the ranking varies from year to year. More countries were included in the later Reports of the first decade of the twenty-first century. In the 2007/08 Gender Development Index Senegal was ranked 135th out of 157 countries, placing it third highest of all the former French West African States. (Mauritania came in top at rank 118, Togo second at 134; Niger as usual occupied the bottom place among the francophone countries at rank 155, just above Guinea-Bissau and Sierra Leone.)

4. The 2005 data are included in the *Human Development Report 2007/2008*, 328.

5. An example of this could be seen around Dakar in 2000 on large billboards bearing explicit pictorial messages on how and why to use condoms.

6. The government's response to the HIV/AIDS crisis is discussed in the case study of Senegal.

7. Interview with M. Mamadou Wone, Director of the *Education à la vie familiale* program at the Ministry of National Education, 16 June 2003.

8. United Nations Population Division, *Charting the Progress of Populations* (New York: United Nations, 2000), 86.

9. UNDP, *Human Development Report 2000* (Oxford: Oxford University Press 2000), table 9, 189.

10. Of the ten administrative regions of Senegal, Dakar records the highest levels of literacy and schooling. Thiès is the second most literate region, followed by Saint Louis, Fatick, Kaolack, Ziguinchor, Louga, and Kolda.

11. Fernande Mime, *Les Filles à l'école sénégalaise—de l'égalité des chances à l'inégalité sociale: l'école en question.* Mémoire DEA, Ecole Normale Supérieure de Dakar, 1996–1997, 37.

12. The author thanks the Directorate of Literacy and the Directorate of Statistics at the Ministry of National Education of Senegal for access to their disaggregated primary data on literacy and educational trends during fieldwork 2000 through 2004.

13. Established as an Anglo-French initiative in 1889, the IPU/*Union interparlementaire* has since gained global coverage and serves as an advocate for gender parity in parliaments worldwide.

14. http://www.ipu.org.

15. This is not the first time in Senegalese history that women have had access to the highest positions of state. Women played a central role in politics in this region before European colonization, and, though records are even more scarce for earlier periods, it is suggested that women also played a greater role in public life prior to Arab colonization 400 years earlier. This history is explored in part IV.

16. *Etude démographique et de santé (EDS)*.

17. Fatou Sow, Ngagne Diakhaté, Mamadou Matar Gueye, and Adama Fall-Touré, *Les Sénégalaises en chiffres* (Dakar: PNUD, 2000), 16.

18. Mime, *Les Filles à l'école sénégalaise,* 38. "Almost all the textbooks being used in French-speaking primary schools present women as gentle creatures . . . with limited responsibilities. When any important decision has to be made, about education or on more material matters, the man appears as the figure of authority. In the workplace, women are shown occupying subordinate roles while the men are in charge." Author's translation.

19. The University Cheik Anta Diop of Dakar and the University of Gaston Berger in Saint Louis keep annual accounts of enrollments.

20. See also C. H. Griffiths, "Education in transition—policy and process in Gabon and Senegal," in *Education in Transition: International Perspectives on Policy versus Process,* R. Griffin, ed. (Oxford: Symposium Press, 2002), 239–258.

21. Fatou Sow et al., *Les Sénégalaises en chiffres,* 119. Sow explains that disaggregated employment data are virtually impossible to find in Senegal.

22. ILO figures reported in the *Millennium Development Progress Report 2009,* 9.

23. There are no reliable data so the Human Development Report Office uses the male income level for Senegal and estimates the female rate at about 75 percent.

24. According to the U.S. Government Accountability Office (GAO) the pay differentials have fallen dramatically in the past 20 years; female pay reached 89 percent of male pay (11 cents on the dollar) by 2007.

25. Sow et al., *Les Sénégalaises en chiffres.*

8

Gabon

At the Limits of the Data Profile

Almost two decades ago, the first Human Development Report sent a clear message that human development is about enlarging people's choices, allowing them to develop their full potential and lead productive, creative lives in dignity and in accordance with their needs and interests. The HDR report has helped shift the debate away from gross domestic product (GDP) per capita as the only measure of development [to] a country's achievement in attaining a long and healthy life, access to knowledge, and a decent standard of living.[1]

In some countries, efforts of the Human Development Report to highlight development trends can encounter obstacles the magnitude of which threatens to capsize its core function. While the lack of financial means to invest in calculative technologies in the world's least developed countries leads to inconsistencies and gaps in the data, by way of contrast, Gabon, a small oil-rich country straddling the equator on the west coast of Africa, is the wealthiest of France's former African colonies. Endowed with a natural abundance of the world's most sought after energy resources, Gabon began off-shore oil production while still a colony of France. Uranium was also discovered in the last decade of the French Equatorial African empire.[2] Coupled with rich reserves in uranium and manganese, the oil industry has provided Gabon with a higher level of export revenue per capita of population than any other country in sub-Saharan Africa throughout the postcolonial era. According to government opponents,[3] this revenue has served to create a wealthy elite rather than a population with access to all the social goods expected of a middle-income country.

Up to 1990 Gabon's record on social development was largely unknown. The reality came to the world's attention in a storm of bad publicity in the mid-1990s. While the Human Development Report had been heralded around the world as a major new tool for social development at its launch in 1990, the profile of this report soared in 1994 as governments worldwide prepared their submissions for the UN's first Social Summit in 1995. In the last Human Development Report before the Summit, it was revealed that Gabon had the worst income to human development ratio of any country in the world. In other words Gabon had been amassing an income fortune without investing a normal proportion of this revenue in the social development of its population. Ranked 42 out of 173 countries for *per capita* income, Gabon's human development ranking put it at 114 out of 173, 72 places lower than its income ranking.[4] The situation lasted only one year. In the 1995 Human Development Report, Gabon's place on the statistical ranking for human development rose dramatically and this remained the case for over a decade. Then, at the end of 2008, the gap suddenly returned. National income calculated by head of population suddenly rose from around ppp$7,000 in the first decade of the twenty-first century to over ppp$14,000 in the second half of the decade. This is even more significant to international observers in that Gabon had already been singled out as a poor performer in the 2007/2008 Human Development Report. Comparing Gabon with Vietnam, another former French colony, the 2007 HDR commented on how countries with the same GDP per capita income could produce a very different social development profile for its population as a whole. Vietnam's Human Development Index ranking was 18 places higher than its GDP per capita ranking that year, signalling that it had been expanding educational opportunities, improving health services, providing affordable housing, and developing a public transport system, beyond what would be expected of a country at this level of economic development. The opposite was noted in the case of Gabon.

Gabon has also benefited during the postcolonial era from additional income in the form of official development assistance, and particularly from France. France reaffirmed its close economic relationship with Gabon in accords signed by Presidents Sarkozy and Bongo on the occasion of the French President's first State visit to Africa in July 2007, a visit that included just two former colonies, Senegal and Gabon. Their inclusion was seen as historical in the case of the former, a French zone of influence since Louis XIV acquired political rights over the western seaboard of Senegal in the late seventeenth century, and strategic in the case of the latter, France having drawn on Gabonese natural resources for its energy requirements since the mid 1950s.[5]

The development environment of Gabon changed dramatically over that period and particularly since the 1970s. In 1975, Gabon had a population a shade over 600,000 with 43 percent still living in rural areas. By 2005, the population had doubled and the share of rural residents had dropped to 17 percent. This is significant for gender and development in that the type of modernization that has occurred in the Gabonese economy brought with it a culture of modernity anchored in the Western economic liberalism. While in much of francophone Africa the agricultural economy combined with the "informal" economy (that part of the urban and semi-urban economy that operates outside the fiscal system) still constitute a significant part of the national economy, in an export-driven economy like Gabon, the majority of the labor force work in the industrial salaried sectors. Theoretically this creates the potential for more comprehensive accounting of the pattern of social development in the male and female populations using the measuring and monitoring tools employed by the international community in its social development auditing.

FROM AUDITING TO PROFILING

The model of gender and development mapped out in table 6.1 has been applied to Gabon using the same methodology and sources used for the data profile of Senegal. The result overturns all expectations. For the fifteen-year period in this review, only 46 records were returned for Gabon, as illustrated in table 8.1, compared with 80 for Senegal.

It is immediately apparent that this experiment in data profiling barely reaches the minimum level of information on female social development as defined by the international community and captured in its conventions and platforms for action. In order to be "policy-relevant" in the UNDP's terms, the data profile needs to reveal longitudinal trends combining a number of factors. Along with the key variable of access to formal schooling, the data profile needs at least to reveal whether women are living longer than they did in the past, whether more of them are literate, whether they enjoy political representation and whether they are being paid for their labor.

Table 8.1. Comparing Development Assistance with per capita GDP Francophone Africa, 2008/2009

Country	ODA per capita	GDP per capita
Gabon	39	14,208
Benin	51	1,058
Burkina Faso	47	1,084
Cameroon	23	2,043
Chad	37	1,470
Côte d'Ivoire	7	1,632
Mali	59	1,058
Niger	39	612

Source: Statistics drawn from OECD-DAC and UNDP-HDR databases. 2009.

Table 8.2. Gender and Social Development in Gabon, 1990–2005

Variables	1990	1994	1997	1998	1999	2000	2001	2005
Women's life expectancy		54.2	55.8	56.2	53.8	53.7	53.8	55.2
Female adult literacy	53[a]	50	51.8	53.3	56.8	—	—	—
% of parliamentary seats held by women	(13[b])	6	6	—	9.6	9.2	10.9	11.9
Net primary enrolments (girls)	—	—	—	—	—	—	—	—
Girls' % share of primary school places								(0.99[c])
Girls' secondary school enrolments (gross)	—	—						(—)
Female higher education enrolment (gross)	2.8	2.2						5
Mean years of schooling		1.3						
GDI[3] rank			102	112				
GDI value			.546	.551				
GEM[4] rank					—	—	—	—
GEM value					—	—	—	—
Women in the labor force as % of total	37.7	38	44	44				(77[d])

Estimated average female income in ppp$					4765
Women's % share of earned income	37.3	37.1		—	—	(0.59^e)
% of managerial posts held by women	—	—		—	—	—
Female unemployment			—	—	
Female GDP per capita in ppp$			5678		
Female unpaid family workers	—	—		—	—	(—)
% of ministerial level posts held by women	3	3	3.3	3.4	12.1	11.8
Use of contraceptives	—	(—)	—	—		(33^f)
Average age at first marriage	17.7					

Note: (—) = data provided but in another form, e.g., as a ratio of the male average whereas before given as a percentage of the female population, or gross enrolment as opposed to net enrolments in school. In all these cases further information is required before data could be converted to a form comparable with other years.

a Two values are given in tables 5 and 6 of this *HDR*, 53 percent in the former and 58 percent in the latter.

b This value is absent from the *HDR 1990* but given in table 30 of *HDR 2005*.

c This is a ratio of female to male; it means there is almost parity in numbers.

d Percentage of the male employment rate in adult (15+) population.

e Ratio of estimated female to male earned income

f This value of 33 percent is not disaggregated for gender. The same value of 33 percent is given for condom use at last high-risk sex among women, as opposed to 48 percent reported for men.

LIFE EXPECTANCY

Gabon, like most of francophone West Africa, has seen a steady rise in life expectancy for women and men throughout the post-Independence period, but the rate of rise slows in the 1990s. The first row of values in table 8.2 shows the impact the HIV/AIDS pandemic has wrought in most of sub-Saharan Africa since the disease was identified there in the 1980s. Senegal registered very low levels of infection in the early years of the pandemic, simultaneously witnessing a high level of proactive preventative activity by government and civil society.[6] Gabon, like its neighbours in central Africa, has been registering levels of infection many times higher than that of Senegal and this is reflected in the temporary stagnation in life expectancy.[7] Recent estimates put the rate of HIV infection at around 10 percent in Gabon[8]; in Senegal it has barely reached 1 percent[9] of the adult population. In general, West Africa has not been as badly affected as the south and the southeast where the infection rates are the highest in the world,[10] furthermore the upward trend in new cases slowed in francophone central Africa after 2002.

The global HIV/AIDS statistics hide a great variation in the vulnerability of individuals to contract the disease. Sex workers are clearly the most exposed to risk. A survey among female sex workers in Mali in 2006 reported a 35 percent HIV prevalence rate. Likewise, a survey among 463 male sex workers in Dakar revealed that 22 percent of them were living with HIV/AIDS.[11] Outside professional sex work, gender has been shown to be the most critical factor in HIV/AIDS transmission. The primary source of infection in Africa is through heterosexual sex, and more women than men have become infected with the disease. More than 60 percent of people living with HIV/AIDS are women (27,000 in Gabon and 38,000 in Senegal).[12] The Human Development Reports are not incorporating a variable on HIV/AIDS vulnerability in the gender and development data,[13] but other UN sources reveal that in Gabon the highest incidence of infection has been identified in the population of young women aged 15 to 29.[14]

MOTHERHOOD: A MAJOR CAUSE
OF DEATH IN CENTRAL AFRICA

While the rate of increase of HIV/AIDS cases in Gabon slowed in the first decade of the twenty-first century, the danger it presents to young women is cause for concern, not least given the high maternal mortality rate facing this section of the population. Maternal mortality rate data are particularly policy-relevant in a middle-income, modernizing economy and easy to trace in a female population fewer than one million.[15] Deaths in childbirth were estimated at 500 per 100,000 live births in 1990.[16] By the end of the decade, the reported rate had risen to 600 deaths.[17] Given the margin of error, even in mortality rates, estimates of 500 or 600 probably indicate a stable rate, as the rate reported through the first decade of the twenty-first century hovered around the mid-500s mark. The rate remains high for a middle-income country. In Morocco, the maternal mortality rate was estimated at 230 deaths per 100,000 live births at the end of the decade,[18] Algeria recording 180 deaths and Tunisia 100 deaths per 100,000 live births in 2008.

One of the prime objectives of the French colonial medical service in Africa was to tackle the high maternal and infant mortality rates in the territories.[19] The modalities of colonial health services were passed on to postcolonial regimes in francophone Africa who have continued to invest in modern infant and maternal health care, and Gabon has invested more heavily than most in this area.[20] Health personnel in Gabon attend more than 8 out of 10 births, and as table 8.2 indicates, the fertility rate in Gabon is comparable with countries recording far lower rates of maternal mortality.

The variation in social phenomena that lie behind national aggregates is not revealed by the data-profiling approach illustrated in tables 6.1, 7.1, and 8.2. Where numeric data are being reported, as in maternal mortality rates, numbers of literate women, numbers of seats in parliament, their usefulness lies primarily in signalling anomalies and areas for further investigation. Over-reliance on the surface picture distorts this approach and its capacity to provide background information on factors that have a deep impact on quality of life in the developing world.

Putting aside the arguments for or against capturing this type of information in national audits, one of the practical outcomes of the series of UN

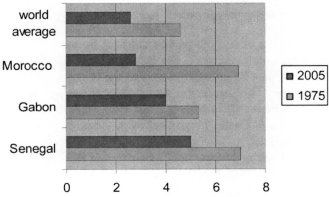

Figure 8.1. Gross Fertility Rates, 1975 and 2005

summits held in the 1990s was their impact on the consistency of auditing. The Social Summit in 1995 required a comprehensive social development report from each Member State. This report had to be updated for the Copenhagen+5 Special Session in 2000 and for the World Summit in 2005. As a result, social development data have become more complete. However, this does not mean that all Member States of the UN system necessarily wish to provide the UN agencies with data. As table 8.2 amply demonstrates, the Gabonese government has not been inclined to release socio-economic data to the international community.

ADULT LITERACY

One numeric factor that can be communicated accurately in the data profile is the number of women who have learned to read and write. Given the lamentable situation inherited from the departing French in 1960, Gabon has achieved a high level of literacy in half a century. At Independence, less than 5 percent of the female adult population were educated to literacy.[21] The small population and Gabon's advanced statistical accounting facilities has made the process of monitoring progress from that very low starting point a relatively easy undertaking.[22]

POLITICAL REPRESENTATION

En Afrique francophone en particulier, la visibilité des femmes en politique reste réduite alors que celle-ci s'est confirmée en Afrique anglophone. Pour prendre l'exemple du Gabon, l'accès au Gouvernement ou au Parlement relève encore d'un exploit pour une femme.[23]

While the proportion of seats in parliament held by women can be tracked with ease through numeric data, the trend in political representation of women in Gabon must be interpreted against the background of an evolving political landscape. This landscape changed significantly during the early stage of the period covered in table 8.2 and even more dramatically in 2009 following the death of Omar Bongo Ondimba, the longest-serving president of postcolonial Africa.

Firstly, the percentage of seats held by women in the national assembly of Gabon during the period 1990 to 2005 fell sharply after 1990. From a high of 13.3 percent[24] in 1990, the percentage fell to less than half that level throughout much of the 1990s.

The statistics hide a number of factors that go some way to explaining the low levels of political participation in Gabon. The sudden drop in female representation in the National Assembly after 1990 coincides with the end of monopartism. The era of *bonne gouvernance* in francophone Africa ushered in by President François Mitterrand at the Francophonie summit of 1990 signalled the end of *de jure* single party rule in Gabon. The ruling party, le *Parti démocratique gabonais*, in power since 1960, had established a women's section in 1975 from which it had selected representatives. Women were appointed to various administrative and political offices by the ruling party. This clientelist system was temporarily disrupted by the entry of new parties into the political arena in 1990. A majority of these political parties then reformed into a group around the *Parti démocratique gabonais* effectively recreating presidential majority.[25]

While this served to exclude and marginalize the majority of Gabonese women, it did not stop some female politicians coming to power at the top end of government during this period. Gabon witnessed a dramatic increase in the number of women in power, in fact a 400 percent increase over the period from 3 percent in 1994 to around 12 percent after 2000. Unlike Senegal, this did not coincide with a change of leadership at the top.[26] The distribution of political power in Gabon was centralized and regulated by the executive under the aegis of President Bongo. Though Bongo was not noted for his efforts to promote gender equality, when the Constitutional Court was established in 1992, a woman lawyer[27] was appointed to head the highest court of the Republic. Four years later a woman was serving both as Minister for Education and as spokesperson for the Gabonese government,[28] and in February 2008 a woman was elected President of the Upper Chamber for the term 2008 to 2014.

When the new government was formed in June 2009 following the death in office of the President, the Constitution required the interim presidency be assumed by the speaker of the Upper House. This ensured an uneventful transition as Madame Rose Francine Rogombe, an old political ally of President Bongo who had served in the women's section of the PDG and then as a junior minister for the promotion of women and human rights, took the helm. Rogombe covered the vacancy until the end of August 2009 when a presidential election confirmed the former Head of States's son, Ali Bongo, as the next president.

Far from signalling a radical change in the political landscape, the political structures run by women in Gabon had limited success in breaking down the barriers to women's participation in politics, nor has the appointment of women to high office in the State administration brought any perceptible change in the political culture generally.[29] Observers have even noted a decline in female participation and activism in Gabon: *"Depuis quelques années, nous remarquons un relâchement de l'action des organisations féminines gabonaises."*[30]

THE ECONOMIC FACTORS OF SOCIAL DEVELOPMENT

The other key factor in gender and development where the statistics and the narrative can tell radically different stories is in the economic data profile of the female population. On the surface, the Gabonese trend looks very similar to that of Senegal. However, the nature of the two economies differs significantly, to the extent that the position of women in the labor force is barely comparable.

On the one hand, Gabon operates a modern economy, exporting petroleum, wood, uranium, manganese and other minerals and ores to developed nations, notably to the United States, and to its former colonial power, France.[31] Since Independence in 1960, the economic landscape has changed dramatically. From 1960 to 1985 was a period of almost uninterrupted boom. The period was brought to an end when the price of crude fell in the mid-1980s, pushing the Gabonese economy into decline. During this period businesses went bankrupt, unemployment rose and the IMF intervened with a structural adjustment program that included cuts in social spending. The period 2001 to 2007 saw a turn around in the economy with a sharp rise in GDP from 2005 to 2007.

According to the Gabonese Government Department for Statistics, the government has failed to invest adequately in regular data collection.[32] Renewed efforts since 2000 to monitor progress towards the Millennium Development Goals brought attention to bear on economic data and their ability to measure efforts to reduce poverty, particularly among women.

Senegal, with its predominantly rural economy coupled with a large "informal" sector in the urban economy, cannot generate employment statistics that are as comprehensive and stable as wage data from the salaried sectors integrated into a national taxation system. The rates of female employment might be far higher in Senegal than in Gabon but this would not be reflected in a statistical picture of the labor force. A woman market trader in Dakar will appear in the labor statistics if she has declared herself as economically active. As this can incur taxation there is an incentive to self report as economically inactive, or as an unpaid dependent family worker. By contrast, in Gabon only 8.8 percent of the labor force is engaged in family work, the majority (over 60 percent) being employed in the small business sector. Gabon has a sizeable State administration employing a quarter of workforce and the multinationals employ a further 15 percent.[33] Within the last two sectors, average earnings are high by African standards, indeed average female earnings in Gabon exceeded ppp$U.S. 8,000 by the mid-2000s and before the 2008 financial crisis. While many of the cells in table 8.2 lie empty, the earnings data are uncharacteristically plentiful. Notwithstanding these, the data for all other variables have been so irregular and scarce that the data profile for Gabon fails to meet the UNDP's own criteria of fitness of purpose, namely to be:

> *Policy relevant*—giving messages on issues that can be influenced, directly or indirectly, by policy action;
> *Reliable*—enabling different people to use them and get consistent results;
> *Consistently measurable over time*—necessary if they are to show whether progress is being made and targets are being achieved;
> [. . .]
> *Possible to disaggregate*—focusing on social groups, minorities and individuals.[34]

From the evidence collected in table 8.2, Gabon has not met any of these criteria. In this respect the Human Development Reports have not succeeded, on their own terms, in producing a picture of the social development status of women in Gabon that is useful for policy purposes. The picture presented of the situation in Senegal is statistically more complete and consistently more measurable over time. Presumably, the data are therefore more policy-relevant.

Unfortunately, this is not necessarily the case as the lack of consistency in the model itself, as illustrated in table 6.1, means that even an optimal result can provide only the crudest indication of social development trends. Whether such crude indications can go on to be useful depends on two factors:

1. the purpose of the indicator: whether it is being used to express a numeric value, such as seats in parliament, or an expressive value, such as political power (its ability to express the latter is very limited);
2. the interpretation of the indicator: the ability of policy-makers to read the data in such a way as to identify issues that need further investigation.

As far as Senegal is concerned, the Human Development Reports 1990 to 2005 claim to identify certain broad trends in how "female social development" is progressing in that they offer an indication of the trend in the GDI[35] values recorded for Senegal in all reports published between 1997 and 2005. The overall picture suggests a positive development, Senegal has moved from a GDI value of 0.309 in 1990 to a GDI value of 0.449 in 2005 in its journey towards the ideal GDI value of 1.0. In this sense, the model provides a progressive interpretation of social development and gender. This general picture is the subject of close examination in part V that brings together information from various sources in Senegal to test this progressive interpretation of social development and gender in Senegal.

In the case of Gabon, the Human Development Reports could not identify the direction social development and gender empowerment had been moving in the 15-year period up to 2005. The *HDRs* recorded no data against the GDI and GEM variables in 1999, 2000, 2001 and 2005,[36] and as such the data cannot be interpreted as having served usefully either for advocacy or policy-making.

CONCLUSION: THE LIMITS OF SCIENCE AND STATISTICS

While the Human Development Report is not aimed solely at highlighting the gender dimension of social development, it does have a brief to focus on gender and claims particular expertise in this field. On the other hand, UNIFEM's *Progress of the World's Women*,[37] launched in 2000, is a gender-specific publication. Like the Human Development Reports, it puts considerable emphasis on quantitative statistics arguing that:

> [N]umerical indicators have proven to be powerful tools when linked to the fulfilment of specific commitments regarding women's progress. This report therefore emphasizes statistical measures, following the precedent of the Human Development Reports and Social Watch in presenting indicators derived from statistics in existing international databases.[38]

It produces a statistical "scoreboard" from the 38 gender-sensitive indicators in the UN's development assistance framework (UNDAF). However, the UNIFEM scoreboard has proved no more powerful than the Human Development Report in revealing the social development status of the female population in Gabon, and simply confirms the HDRs' conclusions on Senegal.

The international discourse of gender and development has encouraged an over-reliance on statistical representations of quality of life indicators. In an effort to secure a minimum standard of living for women worldwide, the international community has been drawn along a route that has led to an over-simplification of the meaning of advancement and equality. It has mapped this meaning on to a simplistic statistical model that in practice only produces a clear and reliable picture in the countries already experiencing high levels of female advancement in the terms defined by the model.

UNIFEM and other advocates for change are aware of the limitations of this approach but have adopted them *faute de mieux* while stressing the in-

Table 8.3. UNIFEM "Progress of the World's Women" Scoreboard 2000, Gabon and Senegal

	GABON	*SENEGAL*
Education	(not known)	GAIN
Employment	(not known)	(not known)
Parliament	LOSS	GAIN
Per capita income	LOSS	No change
Income equality	(not known)	(not known)
Debt reduction	LOSS	GAIN

Source: UNIFEM (2000). 83.

ability of statistics to communicate the "subjective dimensions of women's empowerment."[39]

The application of the statistical model of gender and development to Senegal and Gabon has revealed some of the surface problems inherent in applying Western calculative technologies to development contexts. Before going on to explore the social values and subjective dimensions of gender and development in francophone Africa, the final chapter in this part looks at the implications for francophone Africa of the globalized discourse of goals and targets.

NOTES

1. UNDP, *Human Development Report Statistical Updates 2008*, December 2008, http://hdr.undp.or/HDI_2008.

2. At Independence in 1960 production passed into the hands of a joint French-Gabonese consortium. The French retained a 65 percent interest managed by its energy authority, Cogéma, and the Gabonese State retained 25 percent. Under its control the *COMUF* uranium mines produced 25,000 tonnes of a total national production of 27,000 tonnes between 1956 and 1999 when the mines were declared exhausted.

3. Several of these were operating in exile, especially after the mid-1980s brought a clampdown on the opposition following revelations of financial mismanagement.

4. *PNUD, Le Rapport mondial sur le développement 1994* (Paris: Economica, 1994), 142.

5. Following the decline of the coal industry in the mid-twentieth century and uranium reserves in 1980s, France increased its uranium imports from Gabon and Niger to develop its nuclear energy industry. Under the premiership of Charles De Gaulle (1958–1969), France withdrew from the NATO command structure in the 1960s and developed the French independent nuclear strike force, increasing dependence on nuclear fuel imports. The French military have a permanent presence in the area at their base near Libreville, Gabon.

6. The Catholic Church, not known for a pro-active stance on HIV/AIDS elsewhere in the world, began providing advice and counselling on HIV transmission in Senegal through its *centres SIDA* in 1992. Likewise Senegal led the regional initiative in 2009 to strengthen a coordinated HIV/AIDS strategy for West and Central Africa for the second decade of the twenty-first century.

7. The 2009 *HDR* reported a life expectancy of 61.5 for women and 58.7 for men.

8. Statistics on HIV/AIDS prevalence vary for Gabon, ranging from 5.9 percent to 11.5 percent. The higher end is considered more accurate.

9. UNAIDS estimate for 2009.

10. The worst affected area is Swaziland with a general infection rate above 25 percent of the population.

11. UNAIDS, *Sub-Saharan Africa—Regional Report 2009*, http://www.unaids.org.

12. Data taken from UNAIDS country profiles 2008.

13. The tables included in the section *Achieving Equality for All Women and Men*.

14. The Human Development Reports have not tracked the evolution of the pandemic in data disaggregated for gender, so UNAIDS database has been used to supplement this analysis.

15. The population is approximately 1.45 million, 51 percent of whom are female.

16. United Nations Population Division, *Charting the Progress of Populations* (New York: United Nations, 2000), 86. These data are obviously not gender-comparative (men do not have a mortality rate in childbirth) and so these variables are not included in a gender-comparative table. They are nevertheless very relevant to women's social development insofar as this depends upon state of health.

17. UNDP, *Human Development Report 2000*, table 9, 188.

18. To put this in a global perspective, the U.S. maternal mortality rate was calculated at 8 deaths per 100,000 live births at this time, just a little behind the UK at 7.

19. Denise Savineau, *La Famille en AOF—condition de la femme 1938*, Etude et présentation de Claire H Griffiths (Paris: Editons l'Harmattan, 2007). This summary of a series of mission reports from 1937 to 1938 reveals the centrality of maternal and infant health services in the *cliniques de brousse*. For a discussion of the colonial priorities in health from the point of view of the provider see also ASNOM, *L'Oeuvre huminataire du corps de santé colonial français*, http://www.asnom.org.

20. UNDP, *Human Development Report 2005*, table 6, 238. Data for the period 1995–2003.

21. C. H. Griffiths, "Education in Transition in Francophone West Africa," in *Education in Transition: International Perspectives on the Politics and Processes of Change*, R. Griffin, ed. (Oxford: Symposium, 2002), 239–258.

22. However, even in this field recording is not always reliable. In the 1990 Human Development Report, table 5 recorded a female adult literacy rate of 53 percent while table 6 on the following page recorded a level of 58 percent. The lower figure is more consistent with the literacy records for the rest of the decade in Gabon.

23. Pierrete Oyane Nzue, *Femmes et participation politique: L'exemple du Gabon*. Communication au Forum régional du *ROFAF*, 2009, 1. "Unlike Anglophone Africa, very few women have been appointed to governmental posts in francophone Africa.

For example, getting a seat in government or parliament in Gabon would constitute a major feat for a woman." Author's translation.

24. Inter-parliamentary Union database, http://www.ipu.org.

25. These client parties were known as *les partis gazelles* in Gabon.

26. Omar Bongo Ondimba acceded to the presidency as Albert Bongo in 1967. He ruled unopposed until 1990. Pressure from within and from France led to the introduction of elections. OBO stood for a third elected term in office and in December 2007 began his third term as president. He died in Spain of cardiac arrest in June 2009.

27. Madame Marie-Madeleine Mborountsou.

28. Madame Paulette Missambo.

29. In an interview with the President of the Constitutional Court of Gabon, Marie Madeleine Mborontsou pointed out the considerable lag between legislative change and implementation of the law, particularly in rural Gabon.

30. Reporting in March 2009 on the work *of l'Observatoire des Droits des Femmes et de la Parité* to the regional forum of *ROFAF* (*Reseau des organisations féminines de l'Afrique de l'Ouest*), Pierrette Oyane Nzue noted this lack of progress towards gender equality in Gabon in spite of the number of women in high office and a long tradition of structures attesting to the country's engagement with gender and development issues.

31. Being the largest importer of Gabonese oil, the United States is considered Gabon's most important trading partner. As France owns 57 percent of Elf-Gabon, a large percentage of oil sourced from Gabonese oilfields and entering France will not feature in the external trade figures.

32. Minette Ntsame Engonga and Jean-Pierre Zima Mefe, *Comment appréhender l'emploi au Gabon,* Ministère de la Planification, République du Gabon, 2007.

33. Engonga and Mefe, *Comment appréhender l'emploi.*

34. UNDP, *Human Development Report 2000*, 90.

35. Gender and development index.

36. From 2009 this is being reported as a period of virtual stagnation around the 0.75 mark.

37. UNIFEM, *The Progress of the World's Women 2000* (New York: UNDP, 2000).

38. UNIFEM, *Progress of the World's Women*, 62.

39. UNIFEM, *Progress of the World's Women*, 10.

9

Measuring Gender and Development

Challenges for Francophone Africa

Since the international community began its mission over half a century ago to "reaffirm faith in fundamental human rights, in the dignity and worth of the human person, in the equal rights of men and women and [. . .] to promote social progress and better standards of life,"[1] it has succeeded in committing the governments of the world to the principle of equal rights, at least on paper. Between 1982 and 2001, all the former French colonies of Africa signed the Convention on the Elimination of all forms of Discrimation against Women. Every francophone African country sent a delegation to the Beijing summit and its five-year review in 2000 but progress towards the agreed goals has been almost imperceptible in some of these countries even regarding educational rights for girls. The commitment to educational access was reinforced at the UN Global Education for All Conference in Dakar in the spring of 2000, yet still the francophone African region records the lowest levels of access to education in the world. Now as we progress through the early years of the twenty-first century, large numbers of women living in this region face increasing vulnerability to poverty, discrimination and exclusion from development.

Viewing this process within a postcolonial perspective, policy-making and implementation has uncovered a cultural dislocation separating theory from practice throughout the post-war era. The international community's commitment to gender and development evolved as a response to a tangible situation confronting women in a developing world context. However the policy framework developed as an ill-defined reconfiguration of women's emerging status in industrialized countries where gender equality has come to mean entry-level access to education, paid employment, and political representation. In other words, the concepts that drive the international debate are elaborated in a culture where the goal of delivering equality has not materialized. Indeed in practice the goal of equality has been replaced by the goal of providing the potential for equality.[2] Women are increasingly gaining opportunities to enter the structures that accommodate power in society, primarily the institutions of knowledge, finance, and political influence, and some succeed in occupying positions of power. This has led to claims that equality has been achieved in the West, that we can now live in the "post-feminist" era. Conversely in francophone Africa gender equality remains a burning issue in an environment of persistent material disadvantage where Western notions of equality and feminism have permeated the development discourse but fail to deliver results.

IS GENDER EQUALITY A GLOBAL CONCEPT?

Economic independence through paid employment has long been identified as one of the principal social development indicators for women globally. However, there is little consensus on the value of female paid employment around the world. On the one hand there is active resistance from both radical and conservative forces in society to what is construed as the intrusion of Western feminist ideology into local culture. In practice, conservative social groups in both industrialized and non-industrialized societies continue to dictate the roles many women play in society, restricting these to the domestic space, requiring women to provide support services for husbands and families. The uneven distribution of these responsibilities between men and women undermines equal access to the labor market.

Social development goals for women have been formulated as a response to a growing recognition in the international community since the 1970s that conditions of life are tougher for women in countries undergoing postcolonial economic development. However the policy responses have not developed out of a growing understanding of the nature of those difficulties. It is now, five decades later, a matter of some urgency that efforts to address the socioeconomic difficulties faced by women in developing world contexts are still failing to reach their targets, and by a wide margin in the case of the 2015 development goals.

MILLENNIUM DEVELOPMENT GOAL 3— EQUALITY THROUGH EDUCATION?

Access to formal education has not received the level of overt opposition from conservative groups and governments in the international decision-making arena that the more politically oriented goals of paid employment and political representation have attracted. However even relative consensus among political elites on the value of education has not given predictable results in this policy area.

On the one hand, the expansion of formal education is uneven. While in most of francophone Africa overall levels are rising, population pockets can escape the overall trend. NGO workers in Niger were noting a drop in female education around the middle of the first decade of the twenty-first century,[3] and generally in sub-Saharan Africa, cuts in public expenditure in times of recession tend to prefigure a fall in girls' attendance in schools.[4]

The emphasis on education has come as a result of the position education holds in the discourse of empowerment. There is an assumption made in international social development thinking that a direct, causal, relationship exists between access to education on the one hand and equality and women's empowerment on the other. Not all evidence points in this direction. For several years now there have been more Saudi women holding PhDs than Saudi men, but few would argue that this has led to female emancipation in a kingdom where adult women are not allowed to vote, drive cars or go out alone. Likewise, the impact of education on economic status is far from straightforward. In the United Kingdom girls are now, on average, outperforming boys throughout their educational careers but in the world of work women's earnings remain considerably less than their male counterparts.[5] Furthermore in many countries the role and activities assumed by an "uneducated" woman are virtually identical to those assumed by an "educated" woman.

On the other hand, without formal education it is enormously difficult for women to formulate and engage in a discourse for change. In Saudi Arabia the discourse for change has become more audible in the twenty-first century due to the weight of numbers of highly-educated women. But even where such discourses emerge, change will depend upon an evolution of social, economic, educational, psychological, cultural, and above all political factors. Empowerment is not a one-dimensional variable, it relates to a network of relations operating throughout a society, most significantly in the family, in marital institutions, in relation to community structures and in the workplace. While rights to education and reproductive health can have a considerable impact on the quality of life of the individual, they do not of themselves change structural relations of inequality between people in society. Furthermore, power relations in the public arena change at a different pace from those operating in domestic/private spaces, in all parts of the world.

EMPOWERMENT THROUGH POLITICS?

The international women's conference held in Beijing in 1995 called for 30 percent of decision-making positions to be occupied by women by 2000. This target failed to materialize in most countries around the world, with the exceptions of Denmark, Finland, Germany, Iceland, Netherlands, Norway, South Africa and Sweden.[6] Then Rwanda rose to the top of the international leader board of women parliamentarians through the first decade of the twenty-first century and by 2009 more than half of Rwandan parliamentary seats were occupied by women. But even here statistics can be deceptive. Putting aside the impact of the genocide on the political landscape, reports from Rwanda have suggested that the relation between political representation and female empowerment is complex. Some of the women parliamentarians have been shown to be serving as the mouthpiece of powerful local ethnic organizations and political parties still controlled by men. However, notwithstanding these barriers to change, social entities are not static and the emergence of a critical mass of women in positions of potential influence can effect political change. The process of participating in the democratic institutions of the State has an impact on women's perception of their own position and roles in society, and, as the case of Rwanda demonstrates, this experience can have unexpectedly radicalizing effects.[7]

WHAT DOES "FRANCOPHONE AFRICAN WOMEN" MEAN NUMERICALLY?

International development politics have been dominated by numerical significations of knowledge, encapsulated in the quantitative tables explored in the previous three chapters. The weakness, indeed failure of this approach derives in part from the inconsistency and unreliability of data—as the cases of Senegal and Gabon highlighted—from the instability of definitions of equality, as discussed above, but also from methodological flaws.

The heterogeneous character of the target populations of gender and development policies has been seriously underestimated and simply ignored in the evaluation of quality of life issues in the region, as the case of Senegal exemplifies:

> *Les situations de vie des femmes rurales sont manifestement très différentes des femmes urbaines des classes moyennes .... Les femmes rurales disposent de moins d'argent et ont un niveau de vie plus bas, elles sont moins à même de recevoir une éducation formelle. [. . .] Une femme n'est pas «juste une femme», elle est également, dans le même temps, une femme rurale, wolof, castée, vivant dans le Sénégal néo-colonial, etc.[8]*

A close examination of these differences would require the whole monitoring and measuring procedure used by the international community to be revised, and consequently there is little enthusiasm in official circles to engage with this problem.

Current measuring and monitoring systems calculate quality of life of female populations at best from national aggregated data and at worst from "guesstimates" deduced from studies and surveys in the countries.[9] However, the populations represented in the data are not homogenous. Indeed, populations in developing world countries as a whole have become increasingly heterogeneous over the past half century. The rich have become richer and the poor have become poorer, both relative to the rich and in absolute terms. This becomes increasingly true in the least-developed countries, including most of the African countries that were once territories of the French African empires.[10] Women make up the majority of Africa's poorest inhabitants; with this figure reaching two out every three poor people in the francophone African region, gender has been a key factor in pauperization.

The variation in living standards, as defined by disposable income, in this population group makes the issue of identifying a typical woman even more elusive. Policy-makers are confronted with a significant challenge if their goal is to produce a national policy based on the concept of the "average woman." Socio-economic status is affected by factors that are not recognized in the (Western) data collection systems used by data gatherers in sub-Saharan Africa. Taking the example of income data, people living in this region are mostly poor in income terms though a substantial middle class has emerged. In a Western perspective, these salaried individuals have a better standard of living than their rural cousins. However the salaried employee can have financial responsibilities to the extended family that are so demanding that the salaried individual is as poor as the rural relatives receiving the income transfers.[11] Furthermore the salaried employees often live in an urban or urbanizing environment, where being cash poor presents particular difficulties.[12] This will make the experience of income poverty different in the most westerly parts of the francophone region, where more than half the female population lives in towns and cities, compared with the eastern region where three quarters of women in Niger live in rural communities.[13]

The reduction of a population to a set of statistical data is fraught with problems and undesirable outcomes. It encourages policy-makers to formulate policy in standardized models that are then difficult to implement successfully in local conditions. This has raised the question of whether attempts at quantifying social entities should be abandoned.

SHOULD STATISTICAL APPROACHES BE ABANDONED?

While publicly deploring the increasing over-reliance on data that evolved in the 1990s, UNIFEM[14] published its own statistical report, *Progress of the*

World's Women in 2000. It noted that targets and indicators have been defined and designed in the field of education and reproductive health, "[b]ut
we lack comparable targets and indicators for women's economic empowerment and economic rights."[15] UNIFEM urged the international community to:

> press for participatory monitoring and evaluation at the country level, making
> use of qualitative as well as quantitative indicators, to relay women's experi-
> ences from the village, or township or city neighborhood to national and inter-
> national policy arenas.[16]

It is undeniable that indicators have been useful for raising awareness and
most important they have helped legitimize a discourse for change. However
they do not of themselves generate social development. Indicators, whether
they are qualitative or quantitative, only help generate change where they
are harnessed to effective and applicable policies. As we have seen during
the five decades the international community has been designing social development goals for women, governments sign up to targets at international
summits and then either ignore them or are unable to pursue them once they
return to the daily crisis management involved in governing a low income,
highly indebted country.

   While number-based signifiers of social knowledge have their place in
international development, the limits of this approach have been exposed.
Nevertheless, the global community values quantitative interpretations over
any other form of reporting. The approach has the advantage of offering
concrete "evidence" of whether regimes are complying with international
targets on access to education, political representation, maternal health care,
and other factors undergoing monitoring. The appropriateness or suitability
of the targets to all contexts tends not to be discussed, or at least remains
unaddressed while the search for more effective measuring, monitoring and
reporting procedures continues.

CAN CULTURE BE A VARIABLE IN
GENDER AND DEVELOPMENT POLICY?

As populations are agents as well as subjects of change, they receive policies
in differing and in some cases unpredictable ways. These ways will be all the
more unpredictable where the policy-makers cannot accommodate cultural
and historical factors that influence gender and development in the real world
context.

   The importance of accommodating cultural variables to development practice re-emerged in international development discourse in the 1980s and in

policy during the 1990s in "participatory development" initiatives. However, instead of broadening the development debate, these initiatives resulted in increasing the number of people using the dominant discourse of development.[17] It appeared that the structures that make up the international development industry absorb new agents more easily than new concepts.

UNIFEM's argument that the quantitative approach alone cannot be relied upon to provide a good tool for advocacy or policy-making has been amply demonstrated in sub-Saharan Africa where data reporting is poor and unreliable. However, advocates of a cultural approach to development would argue that poor data reporting is not the principal problem. The weakness of the current approach is that it reduces heterogeneous populations to homogenous statistical aggregates and does not admit socio-economic and socio-cultural variation. The challenge that faces both discursive approaches is conceptual and methodological. If numeric data are insufficiently powerful signifiers of social realities then new methods must be found to capture culturally-specific data.

For their part the authors of the Human Development Report have sought to encourage a more reflective and culturally-sensitive approach to quantitative analysis by placing "interpretative" chapters before the tables of the Human Development Report and adopting a theme of advocacy for each annual publication.[18] By raising specific issues and revealing their gender dimension, the authors have sought both to shape and inform the international debate on gender discrimination. However the approach has defined the limits of the discourse and gender and development policy-making which in practice has been reduced to the few measurable variables agreed upon at the international summits.

It is notable that serious quality of life issues, such as female genital mutilation,[19] forced marriage, child marriage, slavery, and domestic violence, all of which have a clear gender dimension, have been absent from the international discourse and targets for women's social development in francophone Africa for most of this period until the emergence of the francophone *genre et développement* discourse since 2000.[20]

It has been argued, somewhat cynically perhaps, that so long as a social development issue is not officially recognized there is no obligation to monitor it or report on it to the international statistical authorities. On the other hand, there is ample evidence to suggest that by excluding "cultural" and politically-sensitive issues, it has been possible to build a universal albeit minimal model of gender and development that can be applied worldwide. On a practical level, policy-makers argue that if ending female genital mutilation (FGM) and like practices[21] were included as goals, then social development in general would be vetoed because of disagreement over a few contentious issues. According to this reasoning access to formal education is a shared goal but eradication of FGM is not. There are grounds to argue that the fear of bringing the "cultural domain" into international policy-making is misplaced.[22] The 2003 meeting of the African Union adopted a Protocol to the African Charter on Human and Peoples' Rights to outlaw the practice of FGM on the African continent,[23] and by 2008 it had become criminalized throughout francophone West Africa.[24]

The practical objections to including cultural practices reflect what post-colonial critics of international development policy consider a fault inherent in the policy-making process. Policy is formulated at a site remote from the site of implementation. In the case of gender and social development, policy is made by the international development community, frequently through its multilateral operating center in New York. This policy is then implemented in target countries without these populations being involved in the formulation process in any effective way. As such it is imitating the policy-making process that governed relations between center and periphery during the colonial period.

The contemporary era offers alternative approaches to policy-making. Policy formulation could be a shared process operating out of the multiple sites, or it could be a process that is directed from the policy-making center (paymasters do, after all, expect to retain some control over the processes they are funding) and exported to the periphery in a form that admits more cultural diversity.

The rest of this study is devoted to exploring diversity in the culture and context of gender and development. Going beyond the limits of quantitative social enquiry, it investigates the history of gender and development politics in the region and the legacy of this history in francophone Africa today.

NOTES

1. Preamble to the Charter of the United Nations, 1945.

2. The Gender Equality Duty legislation passed by the British parliament in April 2007, and in force nationally from April 2010, has started to address this issue in the UK, which, like the United States, Canada and other highly industrialized countries, remains marred by a poor gender equality record at the top echelons of working life.

3. Interviews conducted by the author in Niger in 2005.

4. Schooling of girls fell in the region during the IMF's Structural Adjustment Programs of the 1980s.

5. Reports published in 2008 suggested that the earnings of women academics in UK universities had reached about 80 percent of their male counterparts.

6. UNIS, *International Status Report: Only 8 Nations Close Gender Gap* UNIS/WOM/480, 7 June 2000, 1.

7. Claire Devlin and Robert Elgie, "The Effect of Increased Women's Representation in Parliament: The Case of Rwanda," *Parliamentary Affairs* 61, 2, 2008, 237–254.

8. Fatou Sow uses examples from North Nigeria and Senegal to explain this diversity. See "Introduction" in *Sexe, Genre, et Société*, Ayesha Imam, Amina Mama and Fatou Sow, eds. (Paris: Karthala, 2004), 30.

9. All members of the UN system feature in these reports. Where data is not forthcoming from member countries they are still included in the indices and tables and the missing data entered as *n.d.*

10. The countries from the region that combine both low income development and low human development are Senegal, Guinea, Côte d'Ivoire, Mali, Burkina-Faso, Benin, Niger, Chad, and CAR.

11. Information collated for the Senegalese national living standards survey of 1997 suggested that salaried women were less subject to these demands for income transfers than salaried men, irrespective of marital situation.

12. There is some statistical evidence from Senegal showing that women are less subject to the demands of extended families than men, and indeed tend to benefit from intra-familial transfers rather have to provide these.

13. Maurice Albarka, *La situation de la femme au Sahel,* Archives des Documents de la FAO, n.d. http://www.fao.org. In the same report Albarka notes that 63 percent of Niger's population live below the poverty line and 73 percent of those are women and girls.

14. UNIFEM serves as the international community's agency for the promotion of women's social, political and economic development worldwide.

15. UNIFEM, *The Progress of the World's Women 2000* (New York: UNDP, 2000), 5.

16. UNIFEM, *Progress of the World's Women*, 58.

17. This issue is returned to in the concluding chapter, which discusses thwarted efforts to extend the debate into localities. See chapter 19, 261–262.

18. Interviews with dozens of government and agency policy-makers across the francophone West African region between 1998 and 2008 revealed that among those who read the publication the overwhelming majority focused on the statistical data and rarely, if ever, read the qualitative section.

19. FGM is also known as female circumcision, or "female genital surgery," to those sympathetic to the practice.

20. Alternative francophone discourses are discussed in the next section, which focuses on gender discourse and practice in the African context.

21. There are various forms of intervention, from excision to infibulation, that undermine a woman's ability to experience sexual pleasure and permanently affect the use of genital, reproductive and excretal organs.

22. World Health Organization, *Eradicating Female Genital Mutilation—An Inter-agency Report* (Geneva: WHO Press, 2008). There are over 130 million women worldwide who are known to have undergone FGM and francophone West Africa is

one of the two sub-regions, along with the horn of Africa, where this practice is most prevalent.

23. World Health Organization, *Eradicating Female Genital Mutilation*, 31.

24. Legal prohibitions have been enacted in most francophone African countries including Central African Republic (1966), Burkina Faso (1996), Côte d'Ivoire and Togo (1998), Senegal (1999), Guinea (2000), Benin, Chad and Niger (2003) and most recently in Mauritania (2005). Center for Reproductive Rights, Item F-027: *Female Genital Prohibitions, Legal Prohibitions Worldwide*, January 2008.

IV

IN SEARCH OF CONTEXT AND CULTURE 1: HISTORICIZING GENDER

10

Sex and Status in Pre-colonial Africa

By its own standards of accounting, the international discourse that framed the gender and development program in the developing world has failed. By not delivering on its minimum ambitions in francophone Africa, alternative discourses of gender and development are emerging with new understandings of how gender mediates the allocation of power and social goods in the francophone African context. Looking beyond the conceptual parameters of the predominantly Western discourse explored in the previous chapters, the rest of this discussion looks at the emergence of new knowledges[1] and endeavors to uncover the limitations of old knowledge of gender and development in Africa.

This discussion starts with a re-evaluation of how gender operated in Africa as a political and social signifier in the pre-colonial period, before moving on to evaluating how the fact of sex difference was used by the European colonizers to re-configure gender in the African context. This historical re-evaluation then concludes with an analysis of how these gender ascriptions were integrated into the discursive architecture of a colonized state and how at Independence they survived the passage into the post-colonial era.[2]

EXPLORING GENDER BEYOND THE WESTERN DISCOURSE

Efforts to investigate gender relations in pre-colonial African societies are undermined by the fact that gender has not featured as a category in historical research until relatively recently and those efforts continue to confront institutionalized prejudices: *"l'absence de réelle légitimation de l'histoire des femmes et du genre dans la discipline académique n'aide pas à combler le fossé existant.*"[3] With the exception of Egypt, the written historical archive of pre-colonial Africa has been sparse, and much oral history did not survive the transition to the modern era.

In some parts of West Africa social histories have been successfully passed on by old and important women, and development of scholarship within and outside Africa over the past half century has begun to provide a base upon which to anchor a history of women, gender and power in Africa.

Given the comparative scarcity of early accounts and studies of African societies, scholars have used what might otherwise be considered prejudiced or unreliable evidence. These sources are interpreted using various postcolonial techniques, notably by reading them "against the grain."[4] It is in this vein that Iris Berger and E. Frances White interpret the observations of the medieval Islamic scholar, Ibn Battuta,[5] who traveled around West and Central Africa in the fourteenth century recording those aspects of political and social life to which he had access. Ibn Battuta had clear views on what he considered acceptable behavior from women, and he described with evident distaste what he saw as the immodest dress and insubordinate behavior of West African women. Exogenous accounts of African women, which focused on their bodies and presumed sexuality, became increasingly prolific in the nineteenth century. Simultaneously white Westerners, missionaries or representatives of their governments were reporting from their travels in Africa that women had an inferior status in African society. This perspective was not subject to any effective interrogation until relatively recently:

> How inferior were West African women really? To what extent did Western observers take time to understand the complexity of social relationships in West African societies? Firstly, their Western middle class ideas about the dependence of women were never really applicable to West African women in particular. The women of this area have been long established in farming, specialist crafts, petty and long distance trading.[6]

THE INFLUENCE OF WESTERN MARRIAGE TRADITIONS IN THE TELLING OF AFRICAN HISTORY

In similar vein, anthropologist Niara Sudarkasa has drawn on oral histories from a variety of pre-colonial African societies to conclude that if one can generalize at all about gender relations in traditional African societies there was only one context in that women generally deferred to men, namely marriage.[7] This is an important finding in itself, but all the more so in the African context because, as she explains, marriage was not the most important social relation for African women:

Western students of African societies have not only focused unduly on the husband-wife relationship in describing African kinship, they have also sought to define that conjugal relationship in terms of parameters found in Western societies. . . . [the example of] "woman-to-woman" marriage . . . signifies most of all that gender is not the sole basis for recruitment to the "husband" role in Africa; hence, the authority that attaches to the role is not gender-specific.[8]

Frances White takes up this theme of pre-colonial marriage institutions. She describes for instance how rich Igbo[9] women married slave "wives," and how the labor of these "wives" and the children they produced would come under the Igbo noblewoman's authority. An Igbo woman could also occupy a role, which, in traditional Western ways of thinking, could be described as the role of a "male daughter," namely a daughter who is granted the same rights of inheritance as those given to the sons.[10]

On the other hand, Coquery-Vidrovitch has characterized gender relations using a more binary model.[11] Working within a discipline and language culture that has a strong tradition of casting women as a distinct social category of historical enquiry, she has argued that rural society made clear distinctions between men and women at all levels. African men, she argues, were valued differently from women, men for their physical prowess, aggression and eloquence, women for fecundity, flexibility and co-operation, and their capacity for work. She suggests that there was very little interaction between men and women in Africa, especially in polygamous societies. Coquery-Vidrovitch has also argued that women were, generally speaking, subjugated in African society, in essence:

L'éducation des filles était une formation à la soumission au pouvoir mâle. On leur enseignait, depuis leur plus jeune age, à ne pas parler en public, à ne jamais adresser la parole en premier à un homme, ni à le regarder dans les yeux (ce qui serait effronté ou insolent).[12]

Marriage is presented in her work as a central institution, indeed as a key economic and political system, run by male elders, where women were goods to be bought, sold or even lent to other men.[13] One of the examples she cites is the case of King Njoya of the Bamoum (Cameroon) who reputedly had 1,200 wives and 163 children when he died in 1930.[14]

The prominence of the marriage institution in the telling of these stories is consonant with the great significance marriage holds for women in Western societies. By comparison, White points to evidence from pre-colonial Africa supporting the view that marriage was not necessarily the defining socio-economic condition for women. For example, before the most recent Islamic and European colonizations of the region, the rulers of the Songhay people of West Africa were always the sons of unmarried women. These women chose their lovers from among the previous generation of rulers, and exercised tremendous power in a vast kingdom located in what later became French West Africa.[15] Taking another example from the Ogooué region of western equatorial Africa, she describes how young girls had to become pregnant before marriage to prove their fertility. The family of the father of the child would take financial responsibility for any male children born, awaiting the arrival of a baby daughter which would seal the marriage contract. By contrast further north in coastal regions of West Africa (present day Senegal), pregnancy before marriage was, and still is, a serious social misdemeanor.

From research in French and Belgian Africa earlier in the century, French anthropologist Denise Paulme developed a nuanced view of gender relations in African societies. According to Paulme, the idea of the African woman being wholly under the authority of men, legally dependent upon male relatives, with no possessions and no sexual freedom outside of marriage to a polygynous male, was

> a fondly entertained masculine ideal that does not tally with the realities of everyday life. On the other hand, it would be equally erroneous to imagine that masculine dominance is entirely mythical.[16]

Paulme maintained that French colonization had in many cases eroded women's economic position in West African societies, an argument endorsed in subsequent work by Vidrovitch. Paulme also went so far as to argue that women lost status in almost all aspects of social and political life and tended towards the view that African women had exercised far more power, influence and equality than was generally ascribed to them in Western scholarship.[17] Introducing the English translation of the collection of essays that make up *Women in Tropical Africa*, Paulme noted that:

> The first thing that strikes one on reading these contributions is how widely varied the modes of life are which they describe. [. . .] All the more remarkable then is the persistence of certain common features in the life of women. Almost everywhere a large measure of pre-marital sexual freedom is permitted to girls—provided they use it with discretion. Almost everywhere too a married woman shows an enduring attachment to her natal family, while the members of her husband's family, among whom she lives, continue to be strangers to her, and often hostile strangers. Marriage is regarded as a lesser evil.[18]

She went on to state that in "traditional" African societies where girls are betrothed in marriage from birth, they have the possibility later on to reject the suitor, whereas boys, also betrothed from birth, would not have the right to reject the girl chosen by his elders. She identifies an exception among the Wolof people of West Africa to the pre-marital sexual freedom allowed to girls[19] and attributes resistance to female sexual freedom here as a corollary of extensive Islamic colonization in the region from the fourteenth century.[20]

Like Sudarkasa, Paulme also held the view that Western scholarship has been too ready to draw hasty conclusions about gender relations in African societies, based largely on Western ideas of marriage:

> African marriage customs have often been condemned on the grounds that they debase women. [. . .] The usual conclusion drawn is that women are oppressed and exploited . . . In this judgement by the outside observer there lurks a hidden assumption: that any divergence from the Western ideal necessarily implies a lower status for women.[21]

Polygyny has been a particularly contentious site in which to explore and articulate gender relations in African societies. Having been described by African and Western observers alike as inhumane and oppressive, and more rarely as a relatively open form of marriage, Paulme for her part interprets it as inherently dysfunctional rather than inhuman:

> Polygyny, because of its uneven sex ratio, tends to encourage adultery, for if a wife were to insist upon remaining faithful to her husband, she might run the risk of going childless. So she may seek a lover in order to have a child by him. The arrangement will then be accepted by the husband, who will be the legitimate father—for are not children the greatest wealth of all? [. . .] In Africa a married woman has an independent life of her own.[22]

Paulme lists ways in which wives can control a polygynous husband, while acknowledging that jealousies and conflicts arise between wives and between their offspring. However, for her the real "defect" of polygyny is the lack of intimacy between husband and wife, along with the distrust and discord that this engenders in the family as a whole.[23]

Paulme's observations reinforce the point Sudarkasa makes about the dangers of interpreting African social structures within a Western prism. The politics of marriage operate differently across African societies and the various forms and institutions of marriage are structured around different cultural norms.

Mona Etienne argued in similar vein after living for a time with the Baule people in Côte d'Ivoire.[24] She refuted the commonly held view in French Africa that African women living in areas that came under French colonial rule were subservient to male relatives, arguing that "[t]he absence of relations of domination-subordination between husband and wife was one aspect of the generalized absence of such relations in Baule society."[25] She learned that Baule marriage involved "mutual rights and obligations" but virilocality conferred on men greater access to political power as the sacred treasures of the group could never be moved, so women who married and left the family home could never aspire to high office and inheritance of the sacred treasures.

It has been argued that reproductive roles had in many cases a far greater influence over the relative position of women in society than did marriage. Women's capacity to bear children gave them such a critical role in society that this led to females of childbearing age being subjected to a range of social controls, while men being less central to the survival of the group, escaped such constraints. The Asante Empire, for example, closed its military ranks to pre-menopausal women, which effectively excluded the women of childbearing age from a key source of political power in the highly militarized state. Women's ability to bear children also affected their position at the other end of the social hierarchy. There were more women kept as slaves in West Africa than men because of the former's capacity to bear children for their masters and mistresses.[26]

GENDER AND POLITICAL POWER IN PRE-COLONIAL AFRICA

These social controls led to political subjugation in some societies but subservience did not characterize relations between men and women in all societies. The Hausa city-states[27] were ruled, before Islamic colonization, by women. The most famous of these Hausa monarchs was Amina, a celebrated soldier Queen of the late fifteenth century. At the head of her 20,000-strong army she extended her empire up to the Niger River by waging war incessantly for 34 years.[28] She did not marry and chose instead a principal lover from among men of each city that she conquered. She was one of a dynasty of seventeen women rulers of the Zaria Empire.[29]

Many of these powerful women have only recently started re-entering African history both in Africa and abroad. Cheikh Anta Diop alerted a generation of African and Africanist scholars to the need to re-configure the geography of African history.[30] Within two decades, scholars were drawing on his redefinition of the geographical boundaries to question the parameters of Western gender theorizing on Africa:

> Dr Diop writes that during the entire period of Egypt and the Pharoahs African women enjoyed complete freedom, as opposed to the condition of segregation experienced by European women of the classical periods.[31]

Not only was the absence of great tracts of African history distorting the historical gaze, this gaze could be doubly skewed when projected through a white male lens. If the idea of an African woman exerting political power did not ring true in the culture of the observer it would not necessarily be recognized or recorded in his history of the region.

As historiography has become increasingly aware of the race and gender of the Western historical archive, the gaps in its records are being addressed. Scholars have been re-acquainting themselves with a traditional body of knowledge on classical African history and interrogating that knowledge from a feminist perspective:

> The later Ethiopian Queens (300 BC–AD 300) which we have come to know as the Candaces, were among the greatest of the African builders, erecting magnificent palaces and tombs. [. . .] The most memorable among them is Amanirenas who struck back at the Roman invaders under Augustus Caesar. [. . .] This warrior queen led the Kushite army [. . .] and routed their garrisons. They were not only masters [sic] of the state but masters of the spiritual capitals as well.[32]

Quoting Wimby, Van Sertima points out that Ethiopian queens ruled in their own right and quite differently from Egyptian queens who tended to be "the power behind the throne" which was occupied by a male figurehead.[33]

The lack of documentary (as opposed to oral) evidence has multiplied the opportunities for excluding or misinterpreting these histories of powerful women and recasting those that have survived as myths. Furthermore the impact of exogenous gender politics on the telling of African history has operated through African scholarship as well as through exogenous channel. Igbo sociologist Ifi Amadiume illustrated this when she characterized Chinua Achebe's presentation of women in pre-colonial Igbo society in his internationally acclaimed novel *Things Fall Apart* (1958) as drawing on a Westernized vision of African women. In this work, which the author himself subsequently recognized as populated with erroneous gender stereotypes, the European colonial tradition of casting women from this part of Africa as politically subjugated and subservient to male power permeates the entire story.[34] Coquery-Vidrovitch's research illustrates the gap between such gender myths and historical realities in this case, describing the allocation of political power in Igbo society in the following terms:

> Among some western Igbo groups, the omu or queen of the village or a group of villages had a position similar to that of the obi or king. Yet she was not his mother or wife or even his female relative; she was the female equivalent of male power in the community. [. . .] She chose her own aides and counselors and gave them titles similar to those of their male counterparts.[35]

Coquery-Vidrovitch's chapter "Powerful Women" contains evidence which tempers the picture she presents elsewhere of African women as an oppressed and subjugated category. At the same time we need to recognize that with the exception of the matrilineal Baule people, whom Vidrovitch describes as "remarkably" egalitarian,[36] the life histories of the powerful women rulers described do not represent the experience of the mass of the women they ruled. As regards non-noble women, scholars have long argued that the political position of women was influenced by the nature of succession or lineage, but here again Sudarkasa notes that there is a danger of over-emphasizing gender in patrilineal and matrilineal societies:

> In both patrilineages and matrilineages, interpersonal relations on a daily basis tend to be regulated by seniority, as determined by order of birth, rather than by gender. Hence senior sisters outrank junior brothers. Where males prostrate before their elders, they do so for females, as well as for males.[37]

More generally Sudarkasa reveals, "Many other areas of traditional culture [. . .] suggest that Africans often de-emphasize gender in relation to seniority and other insignia of status."[38] She argues that the "public domain" was not "a man's world" in traditional West African society:

> The public domain was one in which both sexes were recognized as having important roles to play. Indeed the positing of distinct public and domestic domains does not hold true for pre-colonial West Africa.[39]

Women were excluded from male secret societies, which were politically important in some communities. They were also occasionally excluded from councils of chiefs but this was rare and generally "their participation through their spokespersons paralleled the participation of males through theirs."[40] It is possible that the identification of seats of power in these societies has been mapped too closely on the Western democratic model.[41] Outside the parameters of traditonal Western theorizing, Hadiza Djibo identifies the power that accompanied the realm of sorcery, a supernatural power that both resided in and was passed down through the female line.[42]

FEMALE POWER: FROM MYTH TO MATRIARCHY

Just as African scholars frequently warn against the tendency to look for "female" political power and interpret gender relations in relation to the Western institutions or manifestations of gender differentiation, by the same token they warn against basing interpretations of gender relations in African societies on Western conceptions of motherhood. Whereas Vidrovitch describes as "ironic" that a post-menopausal woman who has "lost the source of her original power, her ability to procreate"[43] could be valued in African society, an African observer might point to the factor of seniority as opposed to gender being the core signifier of status in such a case. The importance attributed to motherhood in Judeo-Christian societies has been as great as the importance attached to maternity in African societies. In the latter case exceptionally high rates of infant and maternal mortality in tropical zones along with labor-intensive systems of production combine to maintain considerable social pressure on girls and women to bear children. In such conditions, a high birth rate is integral to the survival of a society.

"Matriarchy" is another example of a misleading Western reading of African social relations. The existence of matrilineages gave rise to a belief among some nineteenth-century Western explorers and observers that some African societies were run by "matriarchies."[44] Indeed, it is possible that the political interpretation of a matrilineage as a "matriarchy" was part of a general mythologizing of indigenous African cultures as being dangerous to white Western "civilization." A "matriarchy" is conceived as the binary opposite of the dominant Western form of social organization, namely "patriarchy, and as such it could be seen as a threat to the political foundations of European society.

Despite the mythologizing around matriarchy, the dominant image of "the African woman" in European colonial cultures was of a woman living in almost abject subjugation, with the mythical matriarch or obsolete warrior classes of women being the exception that proved the rule.

Annie M. D. Lebeuf, a French political sociologist working in Central and Southern Africa in the middle of the twentieth century, recognized the currency this representation had gained in Western scholarship and provided evidence to the contrary:

> By habit of thought deeply rooted in the Western mind, women are relegated to the sphere of domestic tasks and private life, and men alone are considered equal to the task of shouldering the burden of public affairs. This anti-feminist attitude, which has prevented political equality between the sexes from being established in our country [France] until quite recently (and even so the equality is more de jure than de facto)[45] should not allow us to prejudice the manner in which activities are shared between men and women in other cultures, more particularly, so far as we are concerned, in those of Africa. And we are entitled to ask ourselves if it is not an attitude of this kind that is at the bottom of many erroneous ideas about the very real authority exercised by women in African political systems; and whether it has not contributed, to a certain extent, to the initiation of policies which deprive women of responsibilities that used to be theirs.[46]

It is plausible to assume that women in pre-colonial societies exercised more rather than less political influence compared with their contemporary counterparts.

POWER AND TRADE

Likewise, evidence from studies of traditional economies in Africa indicates a high degree of participation by women in local, national and regional economic systems. Baule women from the Côte d'Ivoire have always, or at least since the 1600s, pursued entrepreneurial ventures and amassed wealth in their own names. Etienne explained the position of Baule women in the Ivorian economy in the 1970s in terms of their historical role in the regional economy:

> Baule women's pursuit of wealth in the framework of contemporary urban migration is not simply a response to new and unprecedented opportunities. It is deeply rooted in history and in the traditional models that govern their sense of identity and their goals.[47]

Indeed there is evidence not just of participation by women in traditional economies but also of widespread economic equality between men and women, Sudarkasa goes as far as to say:

> I have never heard of an indigenous African society in which differential value was attached to the labour of women and men working in the same line or in which women and men were differentially rewarded for the products of their labour.[48]

It is not difficult to find examples of Sudarkasa's conclusion in West Africa. Lebou women have been running fish-processing industries along the Atlantic coastline of Senegal for centuries. To the southwest, Bété women managed the kola nut trade and ran gold prospecting businesses. Trade in pre-colonial Africa operated largely within regional networks, which display different gender cultures operating at the level of transnational economies. In central Africa trade was largely monopolized by men, while in East Africa in the period before the Kikuyu-Masai wars, women were heavily involved in the regional economy. On the other hand, from her experience of the western and central parts of francophone Africa,[49] Vidrovitch argues that men never worked for the benefit of women, only for the benefit of men who ruled over those women. She supports this argument by citing the case of the very hierarchical Tutsi and Hutu peoples of central Africa, stating that while noble Tutsi women did oversee the work of Hutu men, all of them were working for Tutsi male nobles. She also notes that women constituted the majority of the slave labor force of West Africa. Some of these women slaves were bought as extra wives with no access to divorce, extra-marital affairs and the other rights and practices that can make an African marriage so different from its

Western counterpart. By 1900 a quarter of West Africa's population were slaves.[50] Calculating what proportion were women is complicated by the fact that non-African historians at that time did not always recognize enslaved women as being slaves as opposed to wives.[51] The numbers involved are further complicated by the multiplication of forms of slave labor[52] that emerged in the period after the legal abolition of slavery.[53]

Just as there are problems with interpreting marital, reproductive and productive functions from an external perspective, the formulation of gender differentiation has also been misinterpreted. While sources insist that in pre-colonial Sudanese society gender differentiation was very marked at all levels of society, from slaves through to the rulers, they also insist that these gender signifiers worked in more complex ways than merely to oppress the majority:

> Gender differentiation should not be confused with gender subjugation. For example, in all the commercial urban centers which developed around Yorubaland in the 18th century, there was a female ruler who dealt with women's trade and marketing, as well as a male ruler.[54]

The spheres of economic activity in pre-colonial society did not mirror the public/private split we are familiar with in the capitalist industrial model. The economic lives of women within the household, the local market and the external economy were integrated as well as varied. Women ran households, took responsibility for extended families as well as overseeing trading activities and some of them also ran community associations and cults. All this allowed African women more scope for generating wealth from a variety of sources and it afforded them greater opportunities for exercising authority outside of the home.[55]

In conclusion, what can be established about the lives of African women in pre-colonial West Africa from these sources casts doubt on commonly held conceptions of the African woman having always been little more than a beast of burden, or at least always subjugated to male power. It is clear that women held many different roles in pre-colonial societies and colonization would bring unprecedented changes to the lives of these women. Islamic colonization in the fourteenth century and later the jihad, led by Uthman dan Fodio in West Africa in the nineteenth century, led to a series of significant changes in the definition of male and female roles articulated particularly in a gendering of physical space in the social environment. The introduction of seclusion (still prevalent in the Hausa lands of northern Nigeria and southeastern Niger), along with other mechanisms of control, limited women's activities to confined physical locations and subjected their behavior outside the home to the watchful eye of men.

In the century prior to the second wave of Islamic colonization, developments in trade and state formation in West Africa had begun undermining the
economic and political position of women living in many parts of the region
throughout the 1700s. In some respects, this would subsequently be coun-
tered by the influence of Uthman dan Fodio who taught that women had the
right under Islam to education, and furthermore they had the right to disobey
husbands or male relatives who refused them access to education. This led
to the emergence of a class of women intellectuals, some of whom became
"free thinkers."[56]

No such principle of equality of access to education underlay the second
wave of colonization later in the nineteenth century. When France and Britain
subjected almost the whole of West Africa[57] to colonial rule, the colonizers
brought with them the social values of European capitalist society at the
height of its dominance over the global financial and industrial system. The
impact of this material and cultural invasion is explored in the next chapter.
It examines how the importation of French political culture into the French
West African colonies succeeded in transforming every aspect of economic
and political life, changing forever the way women and men structured their
relations in societies across the West Africa region.

NOTES

1. The Foucauldian use of the plural is appropriate when re-evaluating how we
signify the postcolony.

2. It should be stated at the outset that the Western-inspired chronology employed
here does not preclude non-Western ways of perceiving the significance and impact
of gender in social relations over time. Other ways of understanding development
provide the focus for the discussion in the case study of Senegal.

3. Anne Hugon, ed., *Histoire des femmes en situation coloniale* (Paris: Karthala,
2004), 5.

4. An early example of reading historical archives against the grain developed in
Indian subaltern studies. See Lata Mani, "Cultural Theory, Colonial Texts: Reading
Eye-witness Accounts of Widow Burning," in *Cultural Studies,* L. Grossberg, C.
Nelson, and P. Treichler, eds. (New York: Routledge, 1992), 392–408.

5. Iris Berger and E. Frances White, eds., *Women in Sub-Saharan Africa* (Bloomington: Indiana University Press, 1999), 65.

6. Josephine Beoku-Betts, "Western Perceptions of African Women in 19th and
early 20th centuries," in *Readings in Gender in Africa,* Andrea Cornwell, ed. (London: James Currey, 2005), 20–25, [22].

7. Niara Sudarkasa, "The 'Status' of Women in Indigenous African Societies," in
Women in Africa and the African Diaspora, R. Terborg-Penn, and A. Benton Rushing, eds. (Washington, D.C.: Howard University Press, 1996), 73–87.

8. Sudarkasa, "'Status' of Women," 78–79.

9. The Igbo lived in a geographical area subsequently colonized by the British and now part of modern Nigeria.

10. Berger and White, *Women in Sub-Saharan Africa*, 84.

11. Catherine Coquery-Vidrovitch, *Les Africaines: Histoire des femmes d'Afrique noire du XIXe siècle au XXe siècle* (Paris: Editions Desjonquères, 1994), translated by Beth Raps and published as *African Women—A Modern History* (Oxford: Westview Press, 1997).

12. Coquery-Vidrovitch, *Les Africaines*, 99. "Girls were educated to submit to male authority. They were taught from a very young age not to speak in public and never to address a man first before he had spoken to them nor to look him in the eye (this would have been considered insolent)." Author's translation.

13. Coquery-Vidrovitch, *African Women*, 37.

14. Coquery-Vidrovitch, *African Women*, 35.

15. Berger and White, *Women in Sub-Saharan Africa*, 65.

16. Denise Paulme, ed., *Women of Tropical Africa* (London: Routledge & Kegan Paul, 1963), 5.

17. Paulme's work was translated by H. M. Wright and published by the University of California in 1963 but despite this attempt at ensuring wider dissemination, her work is judged to have been undervalued.

18. Paulme, *Women of Tropical Africa*, 3.

19. About two-thirds of the population of Senegal are Wolof.

20. In recent national surveys, over 90 percent of the Wolof population of Senegal describe themselves as practising Muslims.

21. Paulme, *Women of Tropical Africa*, 4.

22. Paulme, *Women of Tropical Africa*, 8.

23. It may or may not be of relevance that Paulme conducted much of her research in Africa from 1937 in the company of her devoted friend and husband, André Schaeffner. She had lost her first fieldwork colleague during World War II. Deborah Lifchitz was deported from France to Auschwitz, where she was killed by the Nazis.

24. Mona Etienne, "Gender Relations and Conjugality among the Baule," in *Female and Male in West Africa,* Chritine Oppong, ed. (London: George, Allen and Unwin, 1983), 303–319.

25. Etienne, "Gender Relations," 305.

26. Berger and White, *Women in Sub-Saharan Africa*, 71.

27. Now part of Nigeria.

28. Berger and White, *Women in Sub-Saharan Africa*, 68.

29. Fatou Sarr also points to the economic impact Amina exerted on the region. It was she who brought the kola nut into production. *La reconstruction du mouvement social féminin africain et la production d'une pensée politique liée à la lutte des femmes.* (unpublished essay, n.d.), 6.

30. In *Antériorité des civilisations africaines: mythes ou vérité historique* (Paris: Présence Africaine, 1967), Cheikh Anta Diop succeeded in reinserting the history of Egypt into the history of the continent.

31. John Henrik Clarke, "Black Warrior Queens," *Journal of African Civilizations* 6, 1, 1987, 124.

32. Ivan Van Sertima, "Black Women in Antiquity," *Journal of African Civilizations* 6, 1, revised edition September 1987, 6.

33. This could explain why Queen Hatshepsut introduced her new science of "rulership" in Egypt by assuming the outward appearance of a male. (She sported a false beard and insisted her courtiers used language denoting male gender when addressing her or speaking about her.)

34. Noted by Florence Stratton in *Contemporary African Literature and the Politics of Gender* (London: Routledge 1994), chapter 1, 22–38. See also Ifi Amadiume, *Male Daughters Female Husbands: Gender and Sex in an African Society* (London: Zed Books, 1987).

35. Coquery-Vidrovitch, *Les Africaines*, 38.

36. Coquery-Vidrovitch, *Les Africaines*, 35.

37. Sudarkasa, "'Status' of Women," 77.

38. Sudarkasa, "'Status' of Women," 83.

39. Sudarkasa, "'Status' of Women," 80.

40. Sudarkasa, "'Status' of Women," 81.

41. In this context, it needs to be remembered that classical Athenian democracy offered participation in political process to a very restricted number of Athenian males. They amounted at any one time to little more than 12 percent of the population. Women and slaves were excluded *de facto* and *de jure* from "democracy." In this system the *demos* was not "the people" but a small male elite.

42. Hadiza Djibo, *La Participation des femmes africaines à la vie politique: Les exemples du Sénégal et du Niger* (Paris : Harmattan, 2001), quoted in Sarr, *La Reconstruction* (n.d.). In Anglophone Africa, Mariane C. Ferme's work on Sierra Leone confirms the differences in gender significance, where the *mabole* character, whose gender lies somewhere between male and female, serves as an example of the absence of a clear binary gender distinction in West Africa, cited in Mbembe, *On the Postcolony*, 166.

43. Coquery-Vidrovitch, *Les Africaines*, 36.

44. Denise Paulme contended that the notion of "matriarchy" in African society is a Western invention. Paulme, *Women of Tropical Africa*, 5.

45. She is referring here to the recent reform in France allowing women to vote in national elections and expressing the view that it takes more than the an extension of the franchise to dismantle the architecture of inequality in which French women live.

46. Annie M. D. Lebeuf, "The Role of Women in the Political Organization of African Societies," in Paulme, *Women of Tropical Africa*, 93.

47. Etienne, "Gender Relations," 307.

48. Sudarkasa, "'Status' of Women," 82.

49. Coquery-Vidrovitch, *Les Africaines*.

50. Coquery-Vidrovitch, *Les Africaines*, 45.

51. The European Union funded *EURESCL* (*Europe-Esclavages*) research and dissemination project 2008–2012 is attempting to address the many gaps in the global history of slavery and its legacies.

52. Babacar Fall, "Forced labor and Labor Laws in French West Africa 1900–1946," *Social History in French West Africa* (Amsterdam/India: SEPHIS/CSSSC, 2002), 5–13.

53. The Abolition Bill was passed in the National Assembly on 27 April 1848.

54. Berger and White, *Women in Sub-Saharan Africa*, 69.

55. Paulme, *Women of Tropical Africa*, 8.

56. Berger and White, *Women in Sub-Saharan Africa*, 81.

57. France and Britain were the undoubted victors of the European "Scramble for Africa" in this part of the continent with Germany, Portugal and, to a lesser extent, Spain managing to secure only a few pockets of coastal West Africa in the Berlin Act of 1885.

11

Engendering the Colony

France in Africa

The region of West Africa colonized by France from the seventeenth to the twentieth centuries formed a crescent-shaped swathe of land stretching from the dunes of northern Mauritania eastwards across the Sahel. It extended another five hundred miles beyond Lake Chad before descending through the forest region of western equatorial Africa into the southern hemisphere following the course of the River Congo into the Atlantic Ocean. By colonizing some three million square miles of the western African continent, France laid claim to a region over twelve times its own size, which it then divided into two colonial empires.

The first two hundred years of French colonization saw French interests in Africa anchored in a trading triangle that linked the commercial wealth of Europe to the exploitation of labor and land in Africa and the Americas.[1]

The triangular trade defined relations between France, Africa and the New World and allowed France to establish the richest single colony on earth (Saint Domingue, later Haiti).[2]

The impact of the Slave Trade on gender relations was immense. The differential value attached to the reproductive and productive roles of male and female slaves at the point of sale, and later in the plantation colonies of the Caribbean, redefined relations between individuals in the enslaved environments. The rapid rise of the Slave Trade from the late 1600s through to legal abolition in 1848 would also have deep economic and social ramifications on the African mainland. As "legal" abolition reduced the slave labor force in West Africa, alternative forms of forced labor emerged which drew particularly heavily on the male population.

The status of the slave thus changed from export product to producer of raw materials. [. . .] In the end and despite strong pressures from abolitionists, the three methods devized to solve the shortage of labor were all derived from or related to slavery. [. . .] These three forms of labor marked the transitional phase between the slave era and the period of forced labor that would emerge later by French decree.[3]

The economic imperative driving the industrial revolution in France provided a motor for colonial expansionism through the second half of the nineteenth century. Before the middle of the century the French had shown little interest in colonizing lands in the equatorial zone. Demand for primary products increased and the capitalist imperative to develop new markets intensified during the Second Empire, bursting into a flurry of activity after 1870. Coupled with this the passion for empire was enflamed by ignominious military defeat at home, this time at the hands of the Prussians who in 1870 brought the Second Empire to an ignominious end.

As a virile breed of colonial explorers set off for the tropics, the picture Greater France began to reflect of itself was a far cry from the figure it cut on the battlefields of Europe. Headed by Pierre Savorgnan de Brazza, a young officer in the French Navy, an expeditionary force embarked from the equatorial trading post of Libreville[4] on the conquest of the interior. In 1880, Brazza, representing the French Republic at the signing of a treaty with King Iloo I of the Tio, acquired land on which Brazzaville, the future capital of French Equatorial Africa, would be built.[5] Back in metropolitan France, the Congo Acquisition Treaty, as it was called, was ratified enthusiastically in the National Assembly in 1882. The colonial lobby's star was in the ascendancy. Léon Gambetta[6] had acceded to the presidency of the Chamber of Deputies in 1879 and two years later, on assuming the premiership of France, he secured the colonial lobby's position at the apex of the French political power structure. With Gambetta's untimely death in 1882, the responsibility passed to Jules Ferry to keep France's imperial mission in Africa and Asia at the top of the political agenda. Following the Berlin Conference of 1884–1885, convened by France and Germany to regulate what had degenerated into a "Scramble for Africa" among the colonial powers, the French government turned its attention to the occupation and settlement of its overseas possessions. By 1895 it had established *l'Afrique occidentale française*, followed fifteen years later by its second sub-Saharan empire, *l'Afrique equatoriale française*. The formalization of imperial France was accompanied by the introduction of a thrusting and ambitious colonial administrative system operating under the aegis of a supreme male commander, the Governor-General, supported by an extensive military-administrative apparatus. The influence of French political and social mores began to permeate the vast interior.

THE POLITICS OF GENDER UNDER COLONIAL RULE

European imperialism in Africa and the rapid economic changes that accompanied this in the late nineteenth and early twentieth centuries had an
immense and immediate impact on gender relations.

> *Quelle qu'ait été l'origine des prérogatives des femmes en Afrique, et quelle que
> puisse être la difficulté de reconstituer d'une manière précise l'état des relations
> entre les sexes dans les temps précoloniaux, il est possible d'affirmer que ce qui
> a conduit à la perte des privilèges de la femme, au renforcement de l'hégémonie
> masculine et à l'aggravation de l'assujettissement féminin, est à chercher pour
> une large part, dans le bouleversement des structures économiques, sous l'effet
> du choc provoqué par les facteurs exogènes.*[7]

Political life in pre-colonial African societies was complex and this was
reflected in the multiple social and political roles held by members of the
community:

> [T]he political element is merged with functions of another kind, social, eco-
> nomic, or ritual—thus providing multiple opportunities to individuals and to
> groups for participation in the general life of the community. Everywhere too
> the functioning of these institutions has been abruptly disturbed by the imposi-
> tion of the colonial system.[8]

Sociological research on this system suggests that these disruptions had a
differential impact on men and women. Changes in the central political and
economic structures of the colonized territories had ramifications that were
felt throughout societies, resulting in fundamental shifts in power and in a
reconfiguration of the economic system:

> Researchers working within an historical dialectical frame of reference have
> argued that whereas women had relatively high status in many pre-industrial
> (and pre-colonial) societies, their positions declined as a result of colonialism
> and capitalist based modernization.[9]

The introduction of the French legal code also had a considerable impact on
African women living in the occupied regions at the beginning of the twentieth century, when they suddenly found themselves reduced "to the status of
minors, the status accorded to wives in the French Civil Code."[10] Indeed, since
the French Revolution of 1789, the French political elite had been allocating
civil and political rights unequally between women and men.[11]

Subsequent legislation introduced in the colonies exacerbated the fall in
women's social and economic status. Between 1904 and 1906 land registration

laws were introduced in French West Africa which required all privately owned land to be registered by the head of household. Land that was not registered could eventually be claimed by the French colonial authorities. Under the Civil Code the head of a household was a man. By refusing to recognize women as heads of households, colonial law undermined what would later be recognized as *le droit coutumier* (traditional law). Thus French law caused women to lose traditional rights of ownership, such as land given to a couple by the woman's family on the occasion of her marriage. In pre-colonial society this practice had acted as a kind of insurance policy against any misbehavior on the part of the husband or the husband's family. Similarly taxation had the effect of marginalizing women and undermining their economic position.

While the impact of the French civil code on the position of women in African societies living under French rule was considerable, the changing nature of the economy under colonial rule exerted a dramatic influence over the economy of the entire region.

THE ECONOMIC IMPOVERISHMENT OF
WOMEN UNDER COLONIAL RULE

When the French arrived in West Africa a high proportion of working women were subsistence farmers. Under colonization and the introduction of import-export trade, subsistence farming became an increasingly marginal activity in the list of national economic priorities. Lands traditionally cultivated by women were taken over for the production of exports crops destined for overseas markets. The alienation of women from land was so "normal" in the exogenous culture as to pass almost unnoticed and "[t]he inherent strains between matrilineal systems of inheritance and cash-cropping created new *de facto* lines of transfer of property."[12] As women were losing their most fertile land, they witnessed their male labor force disappearing into the export economy and the industrial mining sector. The French employed an almost exclusively male labor force in these industries, and women were not usually engaged in the modern economy other than as servants (cleaners, cooks, nannies, etc.). As mining developed in the early twentieth century, the problems facing subsistence farmers worsened. Farmland around mines was commandeered by the mining companies to grow high carbohydrate crops to feed the miners. As more arable land was taken over the subsistence farmers (women) were pushed further and further out into the poorer lands. In essence, the economic transformation which took place in the last quarter of the nineteenth and the first quarter of the twentieth centuries depleted both arable land and the reserve of male labor. Traditionally men had engaged in a number of agricultural tasks that were crucial to subsistence farming. In a country like Gabon, the role of men in subsistence farming was particularly important. In this equatorial zone they took responsibility for some of the heaviest physical tasks such as wood clearing, of prime importance in a region where the vast majority of land is densely forested.

The growth of the import-export trade also undermined traditional trade networks, some of which were run by women. The salt industry along the Atlantic coast was crippled by the import of cheap European salt. The palm-oil industry was decimated by the introduction of kerosene lamps. The use of manufactured tools rather than locally produced items led to the closure of local factories and the disappearance of traditional sources of employment under African control. Nutrition was also affected by the overuse and depletion of arable land, and the extra work burdens taken on by women meant they could no longer devote the time needed to produce the variety of crops they had traditionally cultivated. The result was a diet that became over-reliant on poor staples such as cassava, which, though quick and easy to grow, was less nutritious than the range of products previously grown.[13]

Even relations in the egalitarian Baule society were affected. Husbands and wives traditionally collaborated over the production of cotton cloth. Women were considered the owners of the cloth and they employed the men in its manufacture. When the French wanted to increase cotton production in French West Africa for export to the European market, they introduced French employment practices into the local economy. To take the example of the Gonfreville textile factory, which started operations in the French Ivory Coast in the1920s,[14] Gonfreville employed local men to produce the raw cotton as a cash crop. The men who produced the raw cotton sold it on to the Gonfreville mill, and if they wanted to buy spun thread to weave into cloth they could buy the mechanized product, also from Gonfreville, and bypass the women. In this way, women's control over the cotton trade diminished as the trade was colonized and a male labor force, including child labor,[15] came to dominate the industry.

The development of cocoa plantations in the area further disrupted regional trade and production by re-allocating the workforce to cash crop production. In areas where men relied on women for the provision of fish and meat, they in turn had responsibilities to provide heavy agricultural work. With the drop in the availability of indigenous slave labor,[16] men turned to their wives to work on their cocoa plantations, causing friction within households and an increase in divorce. In 1929 the cocoa market collapsed causing widespread poverty and hardship. The number of divorced and unmarried women living apparently unsupervised by male relatives was a particular concern to the colonial authorities who did not readily conceive of women operating independently from marital or paternal authority.[17]

The French were not the only colonizers to have such a profound impact on traditional gender relations. A similar situation to the one facing women in colonial Côte d'Ivoire emerged in the British Cameroons where Beti women had been the principal producers of cocoa. Between 1918 and 1939 men took over control of cocoa plantations because the British colonial authorities were regulating plantation ownership by taxing land. Like their French counterparts, the British identified men as landowners and taxpayers. The same pattern of gender differentiation occurred when cocoa plantations were set up in Ghana.[18] Throughout the West African region the impact of colonial economic expansion on relations within families and village networks went beyond the industrial sector into the economy in general. It led to increased competition for farming land that caused changes in century-old customs, such as the inheritance of farming equipment in equatorial Africa. At the beginning of the twentieth century in an environment where women were already increasingly impoverished and powerless, the tradition of passing farming equipment down the female line was abandoned.[19] Henceforth on the death of a husband the farming tools could become the property of the husband's family. At a time when increasing numbers of men were already leaving the rural areas to work in colonial mines and in plantations, the outbreak of World War I in Europe accelerated the exodus of rural manpower as African men were called up as porters or enlisted into the colonial African regiments. Over 200,000 colonial men, the majority drafted from the African colonies, swelled the ranks of the French army.[20] After the Great War and throughout the 1920s, the rural exodus gathered pace as men left to seek work in the cash economy.

THE EXCLUSION OF GIRLS FROM
THE COLONIAL EDUCATION SYSTEM

In the face of multiplying disadvantages, women were handicapped in their efforts to fight economic discrimination in the colonies. It was particularly difficult for them to find a place in the changing environment, having been denied access to the colonizer's education system. Apart from entering the military, which operated total gender segregation, the only relatively advantageous career path offered to African colonial subjects was in administration. A formal French education was the essential first step on the ladder towards a civil service career. The way in which education was structured and delivered under colonial rule led to a deepening of gender inequalities.

When French schools for girls started appearing in West Africa in the early nineteenth century, they were run for the most part by missionaries in single-sex establishments where the girls' curriculum mirrored the objectives of religious education in France. The most developed education system was to be found, for historical reasons, in Senegal where a Catholic teaching order began its mission in the 1820s. The Sisters of St. Joseph de Cluny were given permission by Governor Jean Roger to set up schools for girls following a visit to Senegal by the Order's Mother Superior in 1822.[21] As it transpired the motivation for this initiative was as much moral as intellectual. Jean Roger and the Mother Superior were concerned, not to say outraged, by what they considered the extraordinary morals of some Senegalese women and particularly the influential businesswomen who ran a trading center on the small island off the Cap-Vert peninsular. By the eighteenth century the Gorée island economy had come under the control of a local mixed-race population known as Signares.[22] These women had built up fortunes from their many economic activities, not least amongst which was slaving. But the one habit that engaged the attention of the French authorities above all else was their preference for choosing their lovers from among the passing Europeans and refusing to marry them. These women eschewed the traditional Catholic marriage institution, preferring to live in *unions libres*. Seemingly bewildered by this, contemporary French chroniclers described the Signare's preference as "unique in all the Universe."[23]

The rejection of Catholic marriage customs by the powerful Signares, alongside widespread polygyny among African men, were factors believed by the French authorities to be creating a dangerously immoral environment in which to develop a European settlement. Between 1822 and 1852 the Order of the Sisters of St. Joseph were granted the freedom to provide girls' education in Senegal according to its own traditions. The nuns opened two schools on Gorée Island and one in Saint-Louis. The curriculum delivered by this teaching order was a traditional program of study dating back to the middle of the eighteenth century when it had been designed to respond to the social demands of the French nobility. It was intended to instruct and inspire its pupils and though the curriculum was not as academic as that offered to boys at this time, it was by no means devoid of intellectual content. In colonial Senegal it failed to attract many pupils.

After the 1848 Revolution the curriculum taught in girls' schools in West Africa was radically reformed. Sewing replaced history, housekeeping replaced music, henceforth schooling for girls focused on domestic service skills. It quickly became clear that, in the colonies, these skills appealed more to local parents and to French administrators than a training of the mind.

While the nuns had attracted a mere twenty or so pupils to their schools before 1848, during the Second Empire the numbers of girls being educated under the new curriculum swelled to over three hundred.[24]

Legislation introduced in 1866 required all French communes of more than 500 inhabitants in metropolitan France to provide a school for girls, but this law was not exported to the African colonies, and the next major change in French schooling for girls came in the wake of the general administrative re-organization of French West Africa in 1904. At this point the State assumed responsibility for education and began removing subsidies from the religious teaching institutions. Many Catholic girls' schools closed for financial reasons or were closed for failing to teach the secular State-approved curriculum. To get around these new constraints some institutions dropped the title of "school" and started calling themselves *ateliers* (workshops), but in doing this they had to give up all academic aspirations and concentrate solely on teaching the girls how to provide domestic services, such as sewing and ironing. It was hoped that this type of school would be more attractive to Muslim parents who were apparently reluctant to expose Muslim girls to French education. As it transpired those Muslims who had resisted providing girls with access to education did not have much to fear from the French colonial education. As George Hardy, Inspector-General of Education for French West Africa, would testify:

> [O]ur official education [. . .] respects the doctrines of Islam and in no sense aims [. . .] to emancipate the woman or modify the fundamental bases of the Muslim family.[25]

The French authorities needed the compliance of powerful Muslim brotherhoods to secure their colonizing ambitions in Senegal. In fact this support was not universally forthcoming in the region and Georges Hardy would later promote the cause of women's education in West Africa as a means of obviating male resistance to French colonial rule. In *Une conquête morale, l'enseignement en AOF*, his major work on colonial education published in 1920, Hardy argued that neglecting the formal education of African women ran the risk of seeing these women rebel at some stage in the future against the modernizing influence of France. Furthermore he calculated that educating women made sound economic sense as one educated woman goes on to educate her whole family. The same could not be expected from a man.[26]

During the 1930s the view that the lack of education of girls constituted an economic and political constraint on colonization became more widespread. In left-leaning quarters, critics argued that African girls and women were not benefiting from what the colonizers saw as the unique rewards of French civilization.

The coming to power of the first left-wing government in France in the spring of 1936 brought the issue of colonial women onto the French foreign policy agenda for the first time. The representative of the *Front populaire* government in French West Africa, Marcel de Coppet, served as Governor-General from 1936 to 1938, during which period he commissioned an official enquiry into the impact of French colonization on African women.[27]

The report responded to a growing understanding in international circles of the gender dimensions of colonization. Concern over the poor conditions of life for women in the African colonies was voiced in the League of Nations Assembly, where a resolution was passed in 1935 calling for efforts to improve the situation for "native women" in the African colonies, engaging the ILO[28] to undertake an information-gathering exercise and a political campaign to initiate reforms.[29] The Popular Front government under the leadership of Léon Blum provided the impetus for these proposals to be followed through in French West Africa while the response in British West Africa came somewhat later. In 1943 Miss G Plummer, an Education Officer working in the British Cameroons, filed a report entitled "Notes on the Education of Girls in British Cameroons,"[30] where she catalogued the deplorable state of education for girls and the overwork of women in the Cameroons. These issues were taken up by the Cameroons Development Committee, which asked the Nigerian colonial government to send them a "lady education officer" to respond to the problem. The Resident in Cameroon supported the view that the education of women was a precursor to economic growth, a discussion that would re-emerge in international development arena around the world in the 1980s.

For its part the French West African administration acted quickly after commissioning its report on the situation of women and girls in its territories and opened the first teacher training and midwifery college for girls in Rufisque, Senegal, in September 1938.[31] In the first year it enrolled 44 girls: 28 were Catholics, 24 came from civil service families, 11 were Muslim girls, and all came from what has been described progressive family backgrounds.[32]

French schools in the African colonies were typically located first in the capital cities and then in the main county towns. This made it difficult for girls from rural areas to attend school. There was also a general problem of recruiting qualified teachers for the colonies, particularly female teachers. Sub-Saharan Africa was not attracting either colonists or career civil servants in significant numbers. By the eve of World War II, out of a population of approximately 23 million, only 90,000 French nationals were resident in French West Africa.[33]

THE 1945 FRANCHISE: MARGINALIZING A MAJORITY

By the time decolonization began in French West Africa in the late 1950s, African men had acquired the right to vote in French elections. This had initially been offered to African women in 1945, at the same time French women were given the vote, but it was subsequently so severely circumscribed by conditions of eligibility as to be rendered effectively inoperable. Principal among these conditions was literacy. The vast majority of African women were "illiterate" in the sense of formal training in reading and writing and so this extension of the franchise actually served to deepen the divide between male and female colonial subjects. There were inevitably exceptions to the rule, but these only served to camouflage increasing inequalities. Daughters of elite families were held up as examples of a new progressive post-war era. Born into a prosperous Senegalese family, journalist and broadcaster Henriette Bathily[34] was employed by the French colonial broadcasting authority to present her own show on Radio Mali in the 1950s. After Independence she continued a glittering career in the arts and journalism in Senegal during the premiership of her close personal friend Léopold Sédar Senghor. On her death in 1984, President Senghor took the unprecedented step of cancelling the April 4 Independence Day celebrations to mark her passing. Bathily and Senghor both exemplifed the African cultural elite fostered and supported by France both before and after Independence.

GENDER AND INEQUALITY IN THE POSTCOLONIAL ERA

Most women were marginalized from the formal political process throughout the centuries of colonization, with the result that the process of decolonization had a greater initial political impact on the male population. As Hugon notes: "*Les grandes dynamiques de l'histoire des femmes ne sont pas forcément dépendantes des coupures politiques.*"[35] Key areas of gender discrimination, notably exclusion from education, from political representation and the cash economy, were not prioritized by the African political elite who emerged from the French colonial system to inherit the reins of power in 1960. Diane Barthel, writing over a decade after independence, concluded from her research on gender and development politics in francophone and Anglophone West Africa in the 1970s that, overall, "development" since Independence had not opened up opportunities for women. Indeed she noted that in many cases opportunities had closed down.[36] Increased differential access to education was causing social dislocation and economic development was reproducing and even exacerbating social inequality rather than reducing it. Contemporary studies from East Africa, where inequalities in access to education were far less pronounced, showed that even where women had been through university education, they were still not gaining access to professional careers.[37]

Where efforts have been made to address gender inequality in the post-Independence era, these efforts have tended to be confined to improving access to the lowest levels of formal education. Access to higher education has risen very slowly throughout the francophone region, particularly since the international community turned a spotlight on this in the mid-1990s. But as research has shown, access to the institutions of knowledge does not automatically result in an increase in the level of graduate recruitment across the economy.[38] Unemployment among university graduates generally has been high throughout the region, and little effort has been made by any government in francophone West Africa to improve graduate employment opportunities specifically for women.

On the other hand there have been numerous national, regional and continental efforts to prioritize access to primary and secondary schooling for girls. A pan-African conference on education for girls, held in the capital of Burkina Faso in 1993, resulted in the "Ouagadougou Declaration." This collective agreement engaged francophone African governments and politicians in an effort to make the education of girls a priority and set targets to achieve it.[39] These targets were reiterated at the global education summit in Dakar in April 2000 and again at various reviews since 2000, all of which confirm an upward trend in access to formal education across the region, though the rate was unstable even before the global economic downturn.

Any discussion of education as a vehicle of social change needs to take into account that formal education in Africa is not confined to national education systems. Religious education has also been a primary vehicle through which children have been educated into gender roles. Christianity and Islam have both played a role in the construction of gender discrimination in West Africa. Arguing that teaching in both religions downgrades the status of women, Florence Ebam Etta[40] points to the use of the Adam and Eve stereotypes in Christian education to indicate women's subservience, and to Islam's use of the fourth Sura verse 34 of the Quran[41] that is widely interpreted as indicating that men have authority over women because Allah made one superior to the other.[42]

Sudarkasa also notes that progress towards gender equality has been elusive: "In contemporary Africa, the relationship between women and men has moved decidedly in the direction of a hierarchical one."[43] The persistence of gender discrimination has been sustained and even exacerbated by the development policies pursued by postcolonial African elites. Economic development has favored urban expansion over the development of rural areas, to the disadvantage of women. In the first three decades after Independence the rural exodus continued to be a predominantly male phenomenon, creating gender imbalances between urban and rural areas in many parts of franco-phone Africa. It was noted in the 1980s that Baule women were among the few to have prospered in the urban environment. Through various routes, and sometimes in conflict with social and religious norms, they have retained their independence in the urban environment where a significant number run their own households as single women:

> This type of situation is not unusual in [. . .] West Africa, and has been the ob-ject of many studies, the earlier ones, often superficial, with undue emphasis on "prostitution" as a source of revenues.[44]

Throughout this period since Independence, formal literacy has tended to be the norm in the urban salaried employment market. In the absence of policies designed to correct existing structural imbalances, this has meant fewer op-portunities for women.

INTERNATIONAL MODELS MEET REGIONAL REALITIES: SCHOOLING, WORK AND POLITICS IN CONTEMPORARY FRANCOPHONE WEST AFRICA

Far from living up to the expectations of the women who fought alongside men for independence in the 1950s, postcolonial African states did not look to correcting the socio-economic disadvantages their female populations inherited from colonization. On the one hand the elite in power inherited the system of their colonial forebears for distributing political power in the mod-ern state. Political figures like Arame Diène, for thirty seven years a political activist and often referred to as the mother of the Senegalese *Parti socialiste*, had to wait until the end of the Senghor era to win her own seat in parliament. As she confided in a series of interviews in the mid-1990s,[45] her accession to parliament could only have come about after Abdou Diouf succeeded Léo-pold Senghor as President. Diène went to see Diouf shortly before the 1983 legislative elections:

> I said to him: Mr President, I have come to see you because I heard that you were going to name eight women for the deputies' list and I am a regional leader. When Senghor was in, our movement[46] carried enough clout to elect me, but if I had wanted to be deputy, he would have rejected my request because he only believes in people with diplomas.[47]

With the exception of Guinea, where Sekou Touré actively sought to incorporate women into the national development process,[48] and for a short period in Burkina Faso during Sankara's regime, women throughout francophone Africa continued to be excluded from the seats of national political power in the decades following Independence. In the 1970s the issue of sex discrimination was forced onto the agenda of these governments by the international community.[49] This led to the creation of political structures with responsibility for the social development specifically of the female population. Ministries of the *Condition féminine*[50] multiplied around francophone Africa in the aftermath of the Franco-African summit at la Baule in 1990 where the "new relationship" between France and its former colonies was launched.[51] When François Mitterrand sent explicit warning shots across the bows of African regimes that conditions attached to development aid were going to change from 1990, he signaled that these changes included being seen to comply with international norms on "good governance." In practice "good governance" criteria meant building political structures that conformed to the Western model and responding to the international community's development priorities of the day. However, the creation of the *Ministères de la Condition féminine* did not in themselves translate into progress and change for the female populations of the countries in which they were established.

EDUCATION FOR CHANGE OR CONTINUITY?

Just as political structures do not generate policy results, formal education systems do not automatically produce social and political equality. Though independence brought more opportunities for girls to enter the formal education system, the effect of this has not been seen as universally emancipating. It has been argued that throughout francophone and Anglophone West Africa, the objectives that dictated the content of schooling for girls in the colonial period, namely to prepare girls for marriage and motherhood, have been largely retained in African education systems.[52] As Assie-Lumumba explains, "Education is a social institution whose main function is to transmit technical skill, values and norms, is in essence conservative."[53] Not only was the education system founded during the colonial era in francophone Africa conservative, but it was grounded in a discriminatory educational culture:

In France, for example, the Church had a tight control over higher learning, and academic endeavours. [. . .] In accordance with some church dogmas, women were excluded from the intellectual forum, production of knowledge and policymaking. [. . .] African universities, even those that were created after independence, still share these European socio-historical marks, as they were modelled after the old Western traditions.[54]

In other words education can serve as a powerful arm for conservative forces; it can prevent change as well as promote it.

It has been noted that in Africa "formal education of European origin plays a major role in policymaking, as the leadership is formally educated in this inherited system, specifically at the higher education level,"[55] and it also plays a crucial role in determining access to paid employment, particularly in the modernizing sector. The pattern of employment in this sector also mirrors the European norm. In Africa as elsewhere, it is unusual for women to access the highest positions in their professions. The norm remains that they congregate at the lowest levels, be these in teaching, the civil service, the law, medicine, or politics, with the exceptions proving the rule in the highest levels. Though women are increasingly well educated those accessing salaried employment are typically engaged in support roles as secretarial, administrative or nursing staff.

GENDER IN THE POLITICAL SYSTEM
IN FRANCOPHONE AFRICA

In the face of these enduring obstacles, the search for change in the political systems of francophone Africa invariably starts in the parliaments of the region. The most frequently cited political indicator in the battle against discrimination is the number of women a country has elected to its house of representatives. At the end of the first decade of the twenty-first century approximately four out of every five politicians in the world were men. A snapshot of female representation in the fourteen former French colonies in West Africa in 2009 showed that only two of the countries had reached this average of 20 percent female representation in parliament. Table 11.1 illustrates a wide variation across the region with the overall percentage of parliamentary seats occupied by women remaining well below the global norm.

If the earlier discussion on the lack of correlation between structural reforms and transformative processes in society were not enough to alert the reader to the dangers of an overly simplistic reading of change in numeric values, the position of Mauritania at the top of this table should give sufficient pause to consider what is being recorded here, and what exactly these statistical representations of complex sociological realities can or cannot reveal. The position of Senegal alongside Mauritania can be used as further evidence of the standardizing effect number-based signifiers have on what can be quite significant socio-political differences.

Table 11.1.   Women in Parliament in France and Francophone West Africa, 2009

Rank	Country	Year of Election	Number of Seats	Seats Held by Women	% of Women in Parliament
47	Mauritania	11 2006	95	21	22.1%
48	Senegal	6 2007	150	33	22.0%
65*	France	6 2007	577	105	18.2%
72†	Gabon	1 2009	120	20	16.7%
78	Burkina Faso	5 2007	111	17	15.3%
84	Cameroon	7 2007	180	25	13.9%
90	Niger	12 2004	113	14	12.4%
97	Togo	10 2007	81	9	11.1%
98	Benin	3 2003	83	9	10.8%
100	CAR	3 2005	105	11	10.5%
101	Mali	7 2007	147	15	10.2%
107	Côte d'Ivoire	12 2000	203	18	8.9%
114	Congo	6 2007	137	10	7.3%
122	Chad	4 2002	155	8	5.2%

Source: The Inter-Parliamentary Union 'Women in Parliament' database, 2009, at http://www.ipu.org.

* Guinea would have been placed above France if this snapshot had been taken in December 2008 prior to the death in office of President Lansana Conté and the military coup that followed. Before its suspension the Guinean National Assembly numbered 114 deputies, 19.3% of the seats were held by women.

† The figure for Gabon indicates female representation in the last parliament of President Omar Bongo before his death in June 2009.

EXPLODING MYTHS OF AFRICAN WOMANHOOD?

Efforts to reconfigure concepts of gender come into conflict with powerful forces in society as they attempt to protect custom and tradition in the name of social and political stability. "Traditional" interpretations of the roles of men and women and their "natural" place in society became embedded in the region before and throughout the period of the Islamic and European colonizations of Africa. Indeed Islamic and European knowledge systems were integrated into indigenous systems as part of the process of colonization. Having created new understandings about the place of men (and women) in society, discursive norms were introduced to sustain these interpretations. In this way, the discourse on African women that has configured them as an eternally subjugated and impoverished race fails to engage with the economic and political impact of colonization. The poverty suffered by the majority of women in the continent is seen more as a reflection of a centuries-old historical state, rather than as a result of recent political, social and economic upheavals.

This simplified narrative still has much currency in Western and African development culture. It employs a singular configuration of gender as a social signifier. This is particularly inappropriate in the African context where the concept of "gender" has historically not operated in a singular form and has evolved from a base quite dissimilar from that which unites societies of Greco-Roman cultural origins. "Female and male . . . are clusters of statuses for which gender is only one of the defining characteristics."[56] The lack of emphasis on gender as the primary signifier is reflected in the way some African languages employ non-gender-specific pronouns. Explicit gender pronouns are replaced by other signifiers indicating, for example, the age and family relationship of an individual. These distinctions would not necessarily be perceptible or even recordable in European languages. The term for "wife" in Yoruba cannot be translated into French or English using a single synonym, as the term signifies more than a marital relationship between a man and a woman. A woman can refer to the wife of her brother as her "wife." Likewise the term "husband" "refers specifically to a woman's spouse but also generally to the males (and females) in her husband's lineage."[57]

Beyond these fundamental differences in linguistic cultures lie intellectual traditions that determine how social information is identified and incorporated into knowledge systems.[58] The Western intellectual tradition of reasoning in binary form, defining in terms of opposites, white skin as the opposite of black skin, male as the opposite of female, heathen as the opposite of Christian, did not equip the Western observer with an intellectual toolkit apt to identify, reflect upon and illuminate the complexity of relationships operating between men and women living in different cultural universes. The result has been the construction of a knowledge base that is as partial as it is incomplete.

Part V addresses the political dynamics of these issues by exploring knowledge across linguistic and cultural boundaries. The discussion draws from a variety of sources that articulate the relationship between gender and social development from within the multilingual and multicultural societies of the region we call francophone Africa. With the collaboration of academics, politicians, civil society activists, agency workers, journalists and local literary figures in Senegal, the discussion focuses on providing a culturally-located discussion of how gender mediates the development of a nation.

NOTES

1. Great Britain played the primary role in constructing the "Trade," particularly after 1713 when the Treaty of Utrecht passed the *Asiento*—the right to supply slaves to the Spanish colonies in the Americas—to the British.

2. Christopher Miller, *The French Triangular Trade: Literature and Culture of the Slave Trade* (Durham and London: Duke University Press, 2008), ix. Details of the French slave voyages can be found in *The Transatlantic Slave Trade Database*, launched on the Emory University website in December 2008.

3. Babacar Fall, "Forced Labour and Labour Laws in French West Africa 1900–1946," *Social History in French West Africa,* (Amsterdam/India: SEPHIS/CSSSC, 2002), 5.

4. The town of Libreville had been established some 21 years previously in 1849 at the *Comptoir du Gabon*, a trading post set up in the early 1940s to provide support to the French and British efforts to intercept slavers along the Atlantic coast. The town was named after its first settled population, former slaves liberated from the *Elizia* (or *Ilizia*) in 1846 who had spent three years in Dakar awaiting their final destination.

5. Patrick Manning, *Francophone Sub-Saharan Africa 1880–1995* (Cambridge: Cambridge University Press, 1998), xx.

6. Léon Gambetta (1838–1882), founding father of the Third Republic and leader of the French Republican party, was a key figure in the development of the colonial movement in France. He died of a ruptured appendix ten years before the colonial movement transformed itself into a political party in the National Assembly.

7. Hadiza Djibo, *La Participation des femmes africaines à la vie politique: les exemples du Sénégal et du Niger* (Paris: Harmattan, 2001). "Whatever the prerogatives were that women enjoyed in precolonial Africa, and notwithstanding the difficulties in establishing the exact nature of relations between the sexes at that time, what is clear is that the loss of privileges traditionally enjoyed by women and the rise in male hegemony and female domination can be attributed in large part to the collapse of economic structures caused by the impact of foreign intervention."

8. Lebeuf, "The Role of Women," 94.

9. Christine Oppong, ed., *Female and Male in West Africa* (London: George, Allen and Unwin, 1983), 372.

10. Rokhaya Fall, *Femmes et pouvoir dans les sociétés Nord-Sénégambiennes* (Dakar: CODESRIA, 1994), 17. Author's translation.

11. Following the passage of the legislation on the "Rights of Man and the Citizen" through the National Assembly in August 1789, Olympe de Gouges led a moderate campaign for the "Rights of Women" as a result of which she was executed at the guillotine in 1793. A timely reminder of this largely forgotten human rights activist was published as a supplement to *Le Monde diplomatique* November 2008 edition.

12. Immanuel Wallerstein, "Elites in French-speaking Africa: The Social Basis of Ideas," *Journal of Modern African Studies* 3, no. 1, 1965, 14.

13. For a discussion of traditional crops see Manning, *Francophone Sub-Saharan Africa*, 5–8.

14. The Gonfreville spinning and textile mill, founded in 1921 by Frenchman Robert Gonfreville in Bouak, Côte d'Ivoire, started production as *Filatures Gonfreville*. Since 1995, the business has been operating as *Filature Tissage Gonfreville*.

15. Claire H Griffiths, *Denise Savineau—La Famille en AOF Condition de la Femme,* Etude et présentation (Paris: Editions l'Harmattan, 2007), 67.

16. Slavery was made illegal in French West Africa under Governor-General Roume in 1906.

17. Berger and White, *Women in Sub-Saharan Africa*, 102–105.

18. Coquery-Vidrovitch, *Les Africaines*, 109–118.

19. Coquery-Vidrovitch, *Les Africaines*, 108.

20. Tyler Stovall, "Love, Labor, and Race: Colonial Men and White Women in France during the Great War," in *French Civilization and its Discontents—Nationalism, Colonialism, Race.* Tyler Stovall and Georges van den Abeele, eds. (Lanham, Md.: Lexington Books, 2003), 302.

21. Diane Barthel, "Women's Educational Experience under Colonialism: Towards a Diachronic Model," *Signs* 11, no. 1, 1985, 140.

22. In the second half of the fifteenth century and the first half of the sixteenth century Portugal dominated trade in these islands off the Atlantic coast of West Africa. The term *signare*, a corruption of the Portuguese *senhora*, is believed to date from this period.

23. Jean Delcourt, *Gorée—Six siècles d'Histoire* (Dakar: Editions ClairAfrique 1984), 48.

24. Barthel, "Women's Educational Experience," 141.

25. Quoted by Barthel, "Women's Educational Experience," 144.

26. J. P. Little, *Georges Hardy: Une conquête morale, l'enseignement en AOF* (Paris : Editions l'Harmattan, 2005), 65.

27. Griffith, *La Famille en AOF*, xv-xxiv.

28. International Labour Office/*Bureau international du travail.*

29. Resolution 27/9/35 cited in Richard Goodridge, "Women and Plantations in West Cameroon since 1900," in *Engendering History—Caribbean Women in Historical Perspective*, Verene Shepherd, Bridget Brereton and Barbara Bailey, eds. (London: James Currey, 1995), 392.

30. EP19848CSEI/85/9872, National Archives of Nigeria, Enugu, Nigeria, cited in Goodridge, "Women and Plantations," 395.

31. It is now the *Lycée Germaine le Goff* named after the founder and first head of the school. Notable alumni include Mariama Bâ, who trained as a teacher in this school from 1943 to 1947.

32. Barthel, "Women's Educational Experience," 146–147.

33. Betts, *France and Decolonisation*, 116.

34. The national *Musée de la femme* on Gorée Island was named after Henriette Bathily.

35. Hugon, *L'Histoire des Femmes*, 10. "The major dates in the history of women's advancement do not necessarily coincide with major political changes." Author's translation.

36. Barthel, "Women's Educational Experience," 150.

37. Barthel, "Women's Educational Experience," 151.

38. For a discussion of gender inequalities persisting through education see Fernande Mime, *Les filles à l'école sénégalaise—de l'égalité des chances à l'inégalité sociale: l'école en question.* Mémoire DEA, Ecole Normale Supérieure de Dakar,

1996–1997, and Aminata Diaw, "Sewing machines and computers? Seeing gender in institutional and intellectual cultures at Cheikh Anta Diop University, Dakar," in *Feminist Africa* 9, 2007, 5–21.

39. Florence Ebam Etta, "Education and Development in sub-Saharan Africa— Gender Issues in Contemporary African Education," *Afrique et Développement* 19, no. 4, 1994, 59–60.

40. Etta, "Education and Development," 70.

41. Men are the protectors and maintainers of women because Allah has given the one more strength than the other and because they support them from their means.

42. West African Islam is not the only version of Islam to interpret the words of the prophet as implying that men have authority over women. Islamic scholars have argued that the example as well as the words of the Prophet demonstrate that He did not promote this view. The Prophet's wife, Khadija, was the breadwinner of the household and he did, after all, appoint a woman to lead the faithful in his absence. See Patricia Mohammed, *Daughters of Khadija* (2001) at http://www.cgds.uwi.tt for a discussion of the issue.

43. Sudarkasa, "'Status' of Women," 83.

44. Etienne, "Gender Relations," 303–304.

45. These interviews were conducted as part of the oral history workshop at Cheikh Anta Diop University and published in the paper: "Women and Senegalese Political Life—Arame Diène and Thioumbe Samb: A Portrait of Two Women Leaders 1945–1996," in *Social History in French West Africa,* Babacar Fall (Amsterdam /India: SEPHIS/CSSSC, 2002), 66–80.

46. She is referring to the ruling *Parti socialiste* and its affiliates.

47. Fall, "Forced Labor and Labor Laws," 76.

48. See Elizabeth Schmidt, *Mobilizing the Masses: Gender, Ethnicity and Class in the Nationalist Movement in Guinea 1939–1958* (Ohio: Ohio University Press, 2007).

49. For a discussion of this process see William Felice, *The Global New Deal: Economic and Social Human Rights in World Politics* (Lanham, Md.: Rowman & Littlefield, 2003).

50. The language of these institutions reflected the traditional European notion of women having by nature a fixed social condition.

51. Victor T. Le Vine, *Politics in Francophone Africa* (Boulder, Co.: Lynn Rienner Publishers, 2004), 247 passim.

52. Alphonsine Bouya, "Education de filles: Quelles perspectives pour l' Afrique subsaharienne au XXIème siècle," *Afrique et Développement* 19, no. 4, 1994, 11–34, [p. 14].

53. Ndri Thérèse Assie-Lumumba and CEPARRED, "Gender, Access to Learning and Production of Knowledge in Africa," in *Visions of Gender Theories and Social Development in Africa: Harnessing Knowledge for Social Justice and Equality* (Dakar: AAWORD 2001), 98.

54. Assie-Lumumba and CEPARRED, "Gender, Access to Learning," 100–101.

55. Assie-Lumumba and CEPARRED, "Gender, Access to Learning," 97.

56. Sudarkasa, "'Status' of Women," 75.
57. Sudarkasa, "'Status' of Women," 79.
58. See Barry Hallen's article "African Meanings, Western Words," *African Studies Review*, 40, no. 1, 1997, for a more detailed discussion of the philosophical and conceptual distance that separates Yoruba from English.

V

IN SEARCH OF CONTEXT AND CULTURE 2: LOCATING GENDER

12

Speaking the Language of Gender and Development in Senegal

Mum leen rek, yef yi bu may dem yeen la koy bayyee.[1]

The discourse of gender and development has traveled a global route over the past half century. During that time it has grown from a few ambitious conventions and charters into a development industry. This industry has generated a vocabulary that is now used the world over, from New York to Niamey and from Ottowa to Dakar, the central pillars of gender and development constitute a platform from which politicians—regardless of political complexion or credentials—articulate their gender pitch. Offering political power to women is now a commonplace, translating that vocabulary of power into results on the ground is the challenge that still confronts populations and their politicians throughout francophone Africa in the twenty-first century.

The case study of Senegal that follows examines the groundwork that has been laid for this challenge to be met in one country from the francophone sub-region. The data profile constructed in chapter 7 revealed that Senegal, despite immense and apparently intractable economic difficulties, has engaged with the discourse and monitoring of gender and development since Independence and has achieved a relatively high level of statistical reporting. The data-rich profile of Senegal is replicated at national level in a wealth of documentation on "women's issues," and more latterly "gender issues." Indeed, the saliency of gender in postcolonial Senegalese political culture makes it a particularly illuminating example of how gender discourse and praxis has developed in francophone Africa.

The national context for social policy-making in Senegal in the post-Independence era shares some characteristics with other highly-indebted countries of the sub-region. They have operated under enormous financial constraints making social policy-making a site of contention and intense competition for limited resources. At all times this process has been subject to external intervention. Since the early 1980s the country has known the constraints of the structural adjustment programs which imposed cutbacks in social sector spending while maintaining debt repayments. External debt remained a heavy burden on the economy up to the early years of the twenty-first century, by which point debt was consuming over 4 percent of GDP.[2]

While per capita incomes remain among the lowest in the continent, demographic indicators reveal a major shift in the profile of post-Independence Senegal as rural inhabitants have migrated to the towns. In 1995, 60 percent of the population was living in rural areas and 40 percent in urban areas.[3] In 2000, the percentage had dropped to around 51 percent in rural areas, with just over 5 million people living in villages and just under 5 million in towns. Two years into the twenty-first century and the balance had shifted in favor of towns and cities. The feminization of the urban areas has kept pace with the rate of rural exodus. Just over half the population (around 52 percent) are female, and around half of the residents of the urban areas are women and girls.

However, behind these rather neat binary indicators, Senegalese society is highly heterogeneous. On the surface there appears to have been some homogenization since Independence in 1960, as a result of the so-called wolofization of Senegalese society. Two-thirds of Senegalese people classify themselves as Wolofs or Lebu-Wolofs, and this major ethnic group has increased its influence over Senegalese society during the postcolonial era. Wolof society is based on a hierarchical social caste system, the base provided by the artisan trades and the nobility forming the apex. Wolof society is also strongly influenced by the Muslim religious brotherhoods. But there are other important ethnic identities, such as Haal Pulaaren, Sereer, Mandinka and Joola, which are of particular interest in a discussion of female identities and gender relations in Senegalese society.

Up to the recent past religion, law and custom have demanded that the head of a Senegalese household is a man, women only taking over this role in the absence of the former. An increasing number of Senegalese households are now headed by women, somewhere between one in five or one in four households if the rising trend noted in the 1990s[4] has remained constant. This trend has been affected by migration particularly from villages to towns and cities. An unpublished ILO survey[5] on migration in Senegal noted that in the 1980s and early 1990s increasing numbers of Senegalese women were migrating, following a trend already established elsewhere in the continent.[6] Two decades of low rainfall (1971 to 1991) generally encouraged both men and women to migrate from failing farmlands to the urban centers.[7] By 1991 almost half of these rural migrants were women.[8] Irregularity of remittances from male migrants and the attraction of urban jobs have fuelled this trend throughout the 1990s and into the twenty-first century. Rising urban unemployment through the 1990s did nothing to abate this trend.

However, though urbanization is undoubtedly growing, the migrants are not necessarily permanent residents in urban areas. For example, there are many Joola and Sereer women from Casamance and the Sine[9] who migrate to the towns and cities up the coast at the end of the rainy season in October. They go north to take up work as domestic servants and cooks or they find other urban employment. In late May many will return home for the rice-growing season. This is a pattern particularly favored by unmarried women. Marriage for these women, as for women generally in Senegal, will have the most fundamental impact on how they will live the rest of their lives.

Polygyny is widespread in Senegal. A report published in 2000 noted that almost half of all Senegalese wives were married to polygynous men.[10] Meanwhile, increasing numbers of young women are opting not to marry or to put off getting married. While in 1978, it was calculated that 13 percent of women under the age of 60 were not married, one generation later this figure had gone up to 33 percent.[11] Given that the pressure on young Senegalese women to marry is considerable, this trend is all the more surprising and potentially significant. Low educational attainment was associated in the older generation with the very high incidence of polygyny among Senegalese people who had grown up before Independence. In the 1990s monogamy became the prevalent form of marriage in all age groups and at all educational levels.

THE DISCOURSE OF GENDER AND DEVELOPMENT (GAD) IN SENEGAL

The issue of gender relations and its impact on the quality of women's lives in society has been a salient political issue in Senegal since Independence but it is just recently, in the past twenty years, that regular studies and information gathering have been carried out. Most of the documentation generated by these studies is only available locally and has not been accessible in the international community. The findings have been integrated into the analysis that follows, as have many oral sources including interviews and discussions conducted in Senegal between 1998 and 2010.

These interviews were designed first and foremost to identify how gender and development policy is conceptualized and articulated in Senegal by the agents and subjects of gender and development policy. These interlocutors are included in the discussion that follows as participants or "voices" in a debate on how gender mediates development in Senegalese society. The "voices" included in this discussion operate primarily through the following four structures:

1. the state
2. the international agencies
3. the academy
4. civil society[12]

Socio-political discourse is neither linear nor are the positions articulated within the discourse the monopoly of a single discussant; consequently the arena within which the voices operate is conceived as a "debate." There are many points of intersection between participants in this debate, and the voices are sometimes plural and can appear contradictory.[13] The approach adopted here is designed to enrich the analysis in that it allows space for diversity and digression in the discourse on gender, and seeks to maximize inclusiveness where some more modeled approaches seek to distil contributions into consistent positions.

The analysis will seek to clarify the relationship between "universal" concepts of gender and social development and those operating in a more culturally-specific francophone African context. It will address the question of whether the relatively homogeneous view on how gender impacts upon quality of life articulated at the international level resonates with discourse/s at national level and, if so, whether these endorse the key objectives of international social development policy for women set out by the international community identified in chapter 5 and recapitulated in table 12.1.

GENDER POLICY IN THE POST-INDEPENDENCE STATE

At the level of the state, the discourse on gender and development began at Independence. In 1960, the political elite who took over from the French identified the existing situation of gender inequality in Senegal as being a colonial construct and chose immediately to distance itself from its colonial predecessor in its discourse on gender equality and women's advancement. This idea that gender disadvantage was imported by the European colonizers became part of a platform from which gender discourse was henceforth articulated by the state:

> [*Pour les femmes*] *et par rapport à la période précédente, la situation coloniale constitue un recul, car ses institutions politiques ont été hermétiquement fermées aux femmes.* [. . .] *Au lendemain des indépendances, dans le cadre d'un*

Table 12.1. International Gender-Specific Development Targets

Policy Targets	World Social Summit 1995	Beijing Women's Conference 1995	OECD Development Goals 1996	Millennium Development Goals 2000
Improve girls' access to schooling	Agreed	Agreed	Agreed	Agreed
Improve women's reproductive health	Agreed	Agreed	Agreed	Agreed
Improve women's economic status	No commitment	No commitment	No commitment	No commitment
Increase women's representation in politics	No commitment	Agreed	No commitment	No commitment

projet national de développement conçu pour l'ensemble de la société sénég-
alaise, les nouvelles autorités s'attèlent à l'élaboration d'actions de promotion
des femmes qui se voulaient une rupture par rapport aux politiques coloniales.[14]

The state saw its role as needing to give back to women the value they had lost under colonial rule (this policy was known as *revaloriser la femme*). The first post-Independence government launched what became known as the *IFD (intégration de la femme au développement)* plan in response to the legacy of women's economic marginalization during the colonial era. The plan was implemented at the local level through programs run by the local representatives of the ruling Socialist Party. The State's role was to provide the structures and support required to launch the Plan. It did this by promoting the development of women's groups, known as the *groupements de promotion feminine (GPF)*.[15]

The *IFD* plan was essentially a rural initiative, naturally enough as the overwhelming majority of Senegalese women in the 1960s and 1970s lived and worked in rural communities. The *IFD* Plan provided training in hygiene, health, nutrition, and kitchen gardening. In practice, it trained women to be better wives, mothers, carers and homemakers. In this respect it was typical of early attempts at women's advancement programs in the developing world which relieved the symptoms of gender inequality without addressing the causes. In fact, far from constituting a break with colonial policy, it can be seen as a step backwards from Popular Front social development policy of the 1930s when, for a brief moment in French colonial rule, such education and training objectives were actually criticized for prioritizing domestic skills over intellectual objectives.[16] However, what is unusual and progressive about this early Senegalese program is that the *GPF* groups were self-managed. In most other African states, such activities as the *GPF* engaged in were taken over by the ruling party apparatus. Cameroon and Gabon are both examples of how the international discourse on women's advancement in the 1970s was quickly absorbed into the centralized state apparatus, which then controlled its development. The extent to which the relative autonomy of these women's groups in Senegal subsequently led to the flourishing of an independent pluralistic and broad-based women's movement (in contrast to most other countries in the sub-region) is explored further in chapter 15, which examines how women's associations and NGOs have forged a powerful civil society presence in Senegal.

Despite the Senegalese State's rhetoric on integrating women into the development process, its economic planning continued to locate women as marginal to the economic development of the country. There is no mention of the role of women in the economy in the five-year economic plans from

Independence in 1960 to the 5th economic plan of 1977. This is all the more striking given that the state was at the same time criticizing its own institutions and policies for a lack of focus on the economic productivity of women, notably in its own re-evaluation of the *IFD* Plan. The perceptible lag between discourse and policy becomes a characteristic of the state's engagement with gender and development from this point onwards.

After 1977, the state's economic planning documents began to include references to the importance of women's labor in the Senegalese economy. The 5th Plan (1977–1982) acknowledged the role of women as economic agents whose productivity was being eclipsed by the traditional emphasis on their reproductive role. A national commission was set up and tasked with producing a report on *La femme dans le processus du développement*. The Commission's brief was two-fold: define the socio-economic and legal situation of women and propose strategies to overcome existing barriers to advancement.[17]

The discourse adopted by the Commission at this time derived from the "Women in Development" (WID) approach[18] to development. This approach, much reviled nowadays, constituted at the time a significant step forward in that it encouraged the state to recognize the material contribution of women's labor in the economy and their value, actual and potential, as human capital in the process of economic development. Where it failed was in omitting to engage with the social and political dynamics of gender inequality. This approach sought to find solutions to the worst excesses of gender inequality and to relieve the burden of work put upon women but without disrupting existing gender dynamics.

The recognition of women's contribution to economic development and acknowledgement of their relative disadvantage coincided with the first UN decade for women launched at the Mexico women's summit in 1975, which Senegal attended. Senegal sent delegations to both the following two conferences in Copenhagen and Nairobi. Africa also hosted a number of regional conferences, where Senegalese delegations were invariably in attendance. These international events brought the issue of "women in development" and, to a far lesser extent, the issue of gender inequalities, to the forefront of the African development agenda. It introduced the discussants and agents in the participant countries to the internationally-approved vocabulary with which to discuss, debate, lobby and legislate on the issues raised at the UN summits from 1975 to 1985.

It was during this decade that the structural foundations of "women's policy" were laid in Senegal. By the end of 1978 the Senegalese government had set up the first ministerial department for women's affairs. In 1983 this Secretariat was amalgamated into the Ministry of Social Development. As the structures surrounding social development and women's affairs multiplied and became integrated into the state apparatus during the 1980s, the process was accompanied by the emergence of conflicting interests and ideas on how the state should respond to the growing body of information on gender inequalities and gender discrimination in Senegal. For example, in 1980, the government introduced by decree the annual "Women's Fortnight."[19] It launched the first fortnight on the theme "Well-being of the family and its role in development."[20] Women as mothers, carers and homemakers provided the predominant configuration of "womanhood" during the first fortnight. Despite its explicitly conservative agenda, the idea of a women's fortnight met with suspicion and even open hostility in the national press.[21] Nevertheless, the Ministry of Social Development went ahead with this initiative and continued preparing a national program for women's advancement, *Plan national d'action de la femme sénégalaise (PAFS)*, launched two years later in 1982.

Meanwhile the state was responsive to initiatives being developed at the international level. Having participated in the first two world conferences for women in 1975 and 1980, the relevant ministries actively supported the various "Women in Development" (WID) policies and programs of the major bilateral and multilateral aid agencies during the 1980s. The national action plan, *PAFS,* focused on improving access to formal education; access to health services, particularly for maternal and infant care; access to paid work; and improving women's legal status.

Shortly after the launch of *PAFS* in 1982, the Senegalese government entered into a structural adjustment programme with the IMF. It required a reduction in public expenditure in the 7th Plan (1985–1989) and 8th Plan (1989–1993). In common with other less developed countries with few nationalized industries and a small state sector, Senegal had little to offer in terms of public expenditure cutbacks outside of cuts in social spending. The impact of this was felt most keenly in the female population. As the burden for unpaid social work and welfare falls overwhelmingly on women in Senegal where there is little state welfare provision, this rolling back of the state had an immediate impact on the work burden and responsibilities of society's principal carers. Women had to step in and fill gaps created by social expenditure cuts. In this sense SAPs served to reinforce the marginalization of the female population in the paid economy, by increasing their hours of unpaid work and reducing the time they could spend on education and training. Though the government for its part had moved forward in establishing structures for women's advancement, these structures remained to a large extent empty vessels in this period.

During the course of the 1980s the debate on women's role in Senegalese society and economy evolved quite significantly. While the first women's fortnight of 1980 had focused on women as providers of family welfare, the 1989 fortnight was entitled *Femme et Crédit*. The rationale behind this choice of theme was to raise awareness of women's lack of access to credit in Senegal and reveal how this was undermining their economic potential.

As the debate moved forward the gap between discourse and policy widened. In 1992, the ministry with responsibility for women's affairs initiated a micro-credit scheme for women.[22] In practice the scheme was so limited and under-funded that its impact was minimal. Women's lack of access to economic resources, including credit, continued to be a critical obstacle to economic advancement into the twenty-first century. In 2001 the West African UNIFEM office based in Dakar persuaded two of the major Senegalese banks to accept rural women farmers' applications for credit, offering UNIFEM as guarantor for the loans.[23] This was not the first time UNIFEM had intervened positively in national economic affairs. A decade earlier in 1990, the Ministry of Social Affairs had asked UNIFEM to evaluate the first *PAFS* plan launched in 1982. The report that came back from UNIFEM had been critical, revealing that:

- the *PAFS* plan was not integrated into the five-year national economic plan;
- *PAFS* was adopting a "band-aid" approach that relieved symptoms without addressing causes;
- *PAFS* was not contributing effectively to national development;
- co-ordination between *PAFS* and the activities of the NGO and other development assistance communities in Senegal was almost non-existent;
- planning and funding were inadequate, by 1990 only 10 percent of projects had been financed.[24]

UNIFEM's report had revealed the limitations of a program based on a conceptualization of women as an essentially different and separate economic group, and ultimately marginal to national economic life.

The government's response at this time was to develop more State structures with responsibility for women's affairs. In 1991 it set up the first ministry for women's affairs, *Ministère de la Femme de l'Enfant et de la Famille*. The title of this ministry displays unambiguously the role and responsibilities attributed to women by the state: a Senegalese woman is primarily a mother responsible for the care of her children and the family. The language marginalizes as clearly as it defines: women's role in the economic, political and social development process of the nation is defined by their gender. This corporate approach to identifying social forces offered women neither the autonomy to define their economic roles nor plurality in their identities and capacities. They are defined by and contained within specific family functions and roles, and as such are predominantly seen as "dependants" and in need of special assistance.

In practice, this surface language of marginalization did not reflect developments taking place within the structures of the state. The *Ministère de la Femme, de l'Enfant et de la Famille (MFEF)*, despite its conservative title, was forging for itself a dynamic identity separate from the rest of the state apparatus. It started by criticizing the state for not including women in national economic and environmental planning. It argued that though women's consciousness had been raised since the Nairobi women's conference in 1985, their socio-economic position was no better in the 1990s than it had been before the Nairobi Conference.[25] By doing this it distanced itself from the outset from the traditional centralized apparatus of the post-independence African state, preferring to align its discourse with that of the emerging civil society.

At this point we see the state dividing into a plurality of voices as this spending Ministry began staking its claim for recognition in planning and budgeting at the national level, as well as at the regional and local levels where the Ministry had been concentrating on building up a network of representatives.[26] The Ministry set out its platform for action in the preparatory document for the Beijing Summit, which it called *Rapport national sur les femmes—lutte pour l'égalité, le développement et la paix*.[27] In this document the Ministry called for the introduction of quotas to increase the number of women in politics. It pointed to the urgent need for access to credit for rural women, and the need for a media campaign to make women aware of their legal rights. It called for immediate action in the following policy areas, which it identified as most crucial to women's advancement, namely:

- basic health care;
- women's participation in the management of the environment and natural resources[28];
- education and training for women;
- sustained and integrated support of rural women;
- development of flexible credit and finance options for women.[29]

This list highlights how far the definition of women's issues had moved in Senegal since the early 1980s compared with developments in the international debate. The emphasis placed on improving the legal status of women in earlier documents has disappeared. In its place finance, rural poverty and environmental issues are prioritized.

When Abdoulaye Wade succeeded Abdou Diouf as President in March 2000, gender was not at the top of the political agenda. After years of political stagnation under the old regime, the big issues of the millennium elections were youth, unemployment and urban poverty.

In the three years following President Wade's victory, the government occupied itself with promoting political transparency and a host of new development projects bearing ambitious titles to revitalize a jaded populace and inspire the new coalition. In a bid to inject new blood into the Senegalese political elite, mistakes were made, and the frequent cabinet reshuffles led to inconsistency in policy-making and neglect of some key areas, including gender policy, increasingly referred to at this time as "gender justice."

The gap between discourse and action was addressed in the shape of appointments to key offices of State. In his first government of March 2000, President Wade nominated Mame Madiar Mboye to head the Justice Ministry. She was subsequently promoted to the post of Prime Minister, heading the government from March to November 2002. The Ministry of Decentralization was given to Soukeyna Bâ, a founding member and president of *Femmes Développement et Entreprise en Afrique* (*FDEA*), an organization that provided micro-credit to women working in the informal sector. Since its inception in 1987 the organization helped fund over 7,000 small businesses.

In the context of Senegalese political history (colonial and postcolonial) these were radical appointments but they disguised a deeper complexity and contradictions in the system. The government has been operating under the constant threat of censure by reactionary religious groups.[30] Leaders and representatives of the religious right who had shared Wade's platform in the run-up to the 2000 presidential election had also vociferously opposed proposals to advance women politically and economically in Senegal. The support of this powerful section of the Muslim brotherhoods was considered crucial to Wade's bid to oust the old regime of President Abdou Diouf and his Socialist party, not least given the superior resources allegedly afforded the incumbent by the French President Jacques Chirac and the Gaullist Party public relations machinery.

Despite the anti-feminist elements in Wade's electoral coalition, various women's groups in Senegal had equally vociferously supported the opposition's bid for power only to be disappointed with the governmental program of the new regime. Government-sponsored studies since 1991 had highlighted the problem of women being marginalized in economic development planning but the 10th national economic plan (2002–2007) still failed to integrate gender into its economic and political priorities. The priorities of this plan

were the priorities of the 2000 election campaign to reinforce democratic institutions and practices; develop local government; improve social infrastructure (health, education, water and public sanitation); increase competitive and
productive capacity; promote regional integration; harness research and ICT
to development goals; pursue environmentally-friendly policies; and enable
the vulnerable in society to improve their productive capacity. The final point
was a nod in the direction of World Bank and IMF social policy which puts
a heavy emphasis on developing "human capital," building up the economic
potential of individuals, not least women workers who are seen as particularly
"underdeveloped" in human capital terms in the LDCs.

Under the new presidency neither was this latter point emphasized nor
were the institutional structures with responsibility for women's policy visibly enhanced; indeed in some respects women's issues and gender issues
became less prominent than under Abdou Diouf's presidency in the 1990s.
The ministry created to take charge of women's affairs was given the reas-
suringly conservative title of *Ministère de la famille et de la petite enfance
(MFPE)*. Housed in a building away from the main ministerial zone that
borders the Boulevard de la République in central Dakar, the Ministry was
allocated premises neighboring the UN agency zone by Dakar's central
square.

The *Ministère de la famille et de la petite enfance* was given responsibility for "gender policy" within a unit called *genre et développement (GED)*.
Structurally gender issues were being conflated with a particular conception
of women's role in society that would not raise alarm in conservative cultural
and religious quarters. A Muslim country[31] governed by an ostensibly secular
pro-Western regime in the first decade of the twenty-first century presented
particular challenges to those promoting the cause of gender equality.

Behind the conservatively titled walls of the Ministry, the *GED* unit
framed a policy in the most progressive language of any program to date.
The theme of gender justice encouraged the integration of human rights
discourse and the plan emerged with the title *le Plan national d'équité de
genre (PANEG)*.[32] Designed to be implemented in the period 2002–2006 it
faced numerous practical setbacks common to several government departments during this period. Ministerial changes meant that little documentation was produced, and for the first 24 months of the new regime the *GED*
unit operated from a strategy document rather than a finalized program of
action.[33] Indeed the strategy document fell far short of a policy program.
Locating Senegal's gender policy within the history of the UN initiatives,
conferences, outcome documents and conventions on women and gender, it
explicitly positioned the gender strategy in operation from 1997 to 2001, the
Plan d'action national de la femme sénégalaise (PANAF), as an offshoot of

UN policy and as an example of policy formulated in response to the 1995 Beijing program for action.[34]

The *PANAF* program was maintained in 2000 by the Wade administration in the absence of any alternative. The new gender equity document, *le Plan national d'équité de genre* (*PANEG*), was then conceived in the course of 2001 as a five-year plan. The most obvious difference between the former *PANAF* plan and later *PANEG* is one of language. The 1997–2001 Plan sets out to promote women while the 2002–06 Plan sought to achieve gender equity. However, the *PANEG* strategy document contained no definition of what gender equity means either in general terms or in terms specific to Senegalese social-policy-making. At one point it states that one of the most important aspects of gender equity is to reduce and eliminate disparities between men and women,[35] but neither explained what these disparities are nor how they can be addressed. Just as there was no definition of problems or issues, there was no mention of minimum standards by which to judge the success or otherwise of the *PANEG* strategy. On the other hand, the *PANEG* strategy document listed action points for the *MFPE*'s gender unit to pursue[36]:

- [C]reate a framework to co-ordinate activities in the field of gender;
- Mobilize the national and international community to engage in the debate around gender;
- Create a critical mass of gender activists to promote gender issues in the public and private sectors;
- Develop an extensive statistical accounting system for gender.

The document stated that gender should be integrated into the eight strategic objectives of the 10th Economic Plan (2002–2007), but there was no indication of how or why this objective should be pursued. As it transpired, the 10th Plan did not address these points.

In its discussion on the legal climate of gender equity in Senegal, the document was even less explicit. It made no mention of the constitutional reforms which took place in 2001 defining forced marriage as an infringement of human rights and giving women the right to own land.[37] As the discussion in the following chapters will argue, these are key issues governing the status of women in Senegalese society. However the document did make reference, obliquely, to two very sensitive gender issues in Senegal. By stating that no person can arbitrarily be incarcerated against her will and no person should undergo any medical treatment or mutilation against her will, it evoked the issues of seclusion and the illegal practice of female genital excision.

The draft objectives of the *PANEG* strategy for the period 2002–2006 aimed at providing women with equal treatment before the law, not just in theory but in practice, and giving women the same chances as men to benefit from national economic growth.[38] What we find in this document are objectives rather than policies, but the document did include a detailed budgetary statement. The predicted budget for the gender equity program over the period 2002–2007 was estimated in 2001 at 4,800 million CFA francs,[39] 20 percent of which was to be provided by the Senegalese government and 50 percent by the "development partners" with the remainder coming from the NGO sector.

Of this budget, fCFA500 million addressed the "absolute necessity" and first priority of producing gender equity statistics. While one might doubt the validity of this priority the list of variables cited was extensive and impressive in that it went beyond the traditional demographic, health, education, literacy, employment and unemployment data. The authors called for disaggregated employment data from the civil service, private sector management, agriculture, the primary sector and the leisure industries. The majority of women work in the informal sector in Senegal, which is more difficult to survey and monitor, so information on the average income of women and men in the informal sector was also indicated as crucial. The list went on to identify a wide range of variables reflecting the heterogeneity of the population and giving due attention to women who live in rural communities and work outside the modern sectors of the economy. The variables included access to drinking water, health services, educational services, leisure facilities, commercial services but also to arable land, real estate, and mortgages. As such the variables listed are different from those presented in the UNDP's Human Development Index (HDI), Gender Development Index (GDI), and Gender Empowerment Measure (GEM), while including international empowerment measures, such as participation in elections, and extending these to include participation in party politics, workers' organizations, employers' organizations and in NGOs; numbers of women in positions of authority in public service including the armed forces and the police; and the number of women employed in the legal system.

Statistics have to be processed, interpreted and quantified, so a new "Centre for research, documentation and information" was envisaged as a second priority to process and disseminate data on these variables in paper and electronic form via a dedicated website.

The third key objective cited in the *PANEG* strategy was to raise awareness among economic, political, religious and media leaders of the need for gender equity. This is the first mention of the role of religious leaders in gender equity policy. It is also notable that at other points in the document it is acknowledged that there is in fact already widespread public awareness of gender issues thanks to the plethora of studies and surveys that have already been carried out on women's issues and gender issues. The report therefore identified a need to address a residual and resistant hard-core of opposition among men occupying influential positions in Senegalese society.

The *PANEG* policy for the period 2002–2006 produced a number of written outputs[40] aimed at educating and persuading a public still dubious about the nature and desirability of gender equity:

- *Guide Méthodologique pour la prise en compte des questions de Genre dans les politiques, plans, programmes et projets de développement;*
- *Argumentaires Religieux sur l'équité de Genre (chrétien; musulman)*
- *Boîtes à images et affiches sur l'équité de Genre*
- *Récit de la loi sur la Santé de Reproduction*

The focus of the state on addressing religious/cultural resistance to gender equality and equity came to the fore when the *MFPE* published its principal outcomes for the period 2002–2006:

Réalisations en 2006:

- *Restitution de la formation et sensibilisation en Genre dans les régions du Sénégal au profit des leaders religieux musulmans;*
- *Formation en Genre—Plaidoyer—Négociation des membres du Réseau des Femmes Africaines Ministres, Parlementaires et Conseillères de la République /Antenne Sénégal;*
- *Formation en analyse Genre de leaders d'organisations féminines;*
- *Reproduction du Guide méthodologique pour la prise en compte des questions de Genre dans les projets et programmes de développement;*
- *Formation en analyse Genre des responsables syndicaux du Sénégal.*

The fourth strategic priority at the beginning of *PANEG* had been to increase the operational budget of the gender unit. The fifth also envisaged more funding for gender training in key public and private institutions. Incorporating gender into higher education and training, an initiative spearheaded in the late 1990s by the UNFPA,[41] was mentioned in the sixth key objective of *PANEG*. The seventh key objective involved supporting NGO efforts to implement programs, and to increase the use of NGO expertise in identifying the specific needs of the target populations. An innovative development in the discourse, this priority responded to the government's stated aim of decentralizing decision-making and widening participation in politics. The *Charte nationale sur le dialogue social* of 2002 encapsulated this interest in opening up channels of communication between the state

and society, in this case with a view to improving industrial relations and
promoting development:

> *La mutation qualitative du système actuel de relations professionnelles hérité de
> la colonisation et la promotion de nouveaux types de comportement, d'attitudes
> et de relations de travail pouvant assurer une plus grande cohérence avec les
> nouveaux paradigmes du développement.*[42]

What the National Charter reveals here is a fragmentation in the political
discourse. The principle of gender mainstreaming adopted in the fifth gender
programme (2002-2006) was not integrated into the new paradigm for development as it is articulated in the Charter.[43]

The eighth objective raised the question of information, feedback and the
exchange of ideas in the form of a forum for debate. This objective produced
immediate results. The government convened a forum on gender equity eighteen months later.[44] In calling for a wider range of voices to be integrated
into the formulation and implementation of the gender equity plan, objectives
seven and eight were in many respects ahead of the dominant discourse of the
1990s. They raise the key issue of how women experience gender discrimination in society.

The *PANEG* Progress and Evaluation Committee, set up to monitor progress at the yearly reviews, included representatives from other ministries
and government agencies as well as non-government representatives. NGOs
were designated to act as local agents to implement the activities formulated
at the national level, thus increasing participation and gender expertise in the
program. Under such conditions, feedback from the locality is restricted to re-
actions to national policy and subject to the same problems that faced the participatory development initiatives of the 1990s. The absence of "bottom-up"
structures through which a broader band of knowledge can flow from local
and regional agents upwards, means that local views and knowledge do not
get fed into the first stages of national planning and policy-making. The un-
der-use of local expertise reflects the traditional over-reliance on centralized
mechanisms and sources of knowledge, a feature that is common to many European and francophone African political systems. The State's gender equity
strategy acknowledges the need for public support and identified one of the
functions of the *PANEG* plan as a "social marketing" exercise in which the
"the Plan would be an instrument of communication."[45]

During the implementation of the *PANEG* strategy efforts to reduce the gap
between discourse and action encountered a linguistic obstacle that gender
activists worldwide have had to confront. While the concept of "woman" is
not generally seen as posing a major conceptual conundrum, understanding
the concept of "gender" demands a different order of political, intellectual

and philosophical engagement. The sixth gender program for the period 2007–2011 addressed the problem directly, obviating the need to distinguish between equity and equality through its title, *Stratégie Nationale pour l'Equité et l'Egalité de Genre (SNEEG)* 2007–2011.[46] The published priorities of the *SNEEG* plan revealed a discursive shift occurring in the choice of policy issue. The first three objectives for 2009 attempted to synthesize the exogenous discourse of gender with indigenous priorities:

1. *Continuer les activités de sensibilisation sur les violences basées sur le Genre à travers l'organisation du festival de films sur les violences basées sur le Genre;*
2. *Organiser des sessions de renforcement des capacités en Genre au profit du REFAMP/Sénégal;*
3. *Vulgariser les Conventions et lois (Convention sur l'Élimination de toutes les formes de Discrimination à l'Égard des Femmes, Loi sur la Santé de la Reproduction, etc.) dans les régions de Tambacounda, Kolda et Matam;*
4. *Poursuivre la démultiplication de la formation par les Points Focaux Genre et vulgariser le Guide Méthodologique en vue de son appropriation par les Acteurs.*[47]

A key document in the implementation of the *SNEEG* plan, the 68-page *Guide méthodologique*, elaborating gender and development theory and practice, contained a glossary of terms for use by planning agents. The emphasis on language reflected one dimension of the difficulties Ministry officials encountered in disseminating the discourse of gender equality and gender equity in French-speaking areas.

As the international vocabulary of gender and development was originally articulated in the English language, francophone African development agencies have had to confront the issue of "gender and development" policy being a culturally-remote construct located in Western feminism. This issue along with the concomitant issue of language were addressed at the first global summit for francophone women held in Luxemburg in 2000, which resulted in the *Agence internationale de la francophonie*[48] being tasked with creating a French-based vocabulary for gender policy and discourse for use in the developing areas of the francophone world.

In Senegal the casting of gender and development as a Western feminist construct has been addressed by the state through documents and debates presenting female socio-economic development as a indigenous value. This has translated into a direct appeal to religious authorities. The Ministry of the Family, supported by funding from the United Nations Development Programme, produced a document in the first decade of the twenty-first century which it went on to disseminate widely, including publication on its website, focusing on gender equality as an Islamic principle.[49]

Meanwhile the Ministry's work on preparing new legislation in favor of gender equity and equality took a significant step forward in 2010 when opponents were confronted and ultimately confounded by a twist in this linguistic tale. After what were interpreted as years of delay and distraction, the bill for legal parity, now known as *la loi sur la parité*, was adopted by Parliament in May 2010.[50] The reception this bill encountered in political circles was mixed as skeptical observers held their fire awaiting evidence of the application of the legislation and expressing concerns over the viability of attempting to impose socio-cultural practice in such a socially-contested site.[51]

While the language and discourse evolved during the first decade of the twenty-first century, and the voices of civil society and religious stakeholders were heard with increasing clarity, the opportunities for participation at the policy-making end of the discourse continuum remained relatively closed. In the Western policy-making model inherited at Independence, the center still has the wisdom which it disposes to the periphery.

Notwithstanding the centralization of political power in Senegal, the policy-making disposed to the periphery is not the monopoly of the state. The Senegalese social policy-making center is bi-cephalous, with the State presiding over the formulation and implementation of social policy in collaboration with the agencies of the international community who, throughout the course of the postcolonial era, have played an increasingly central role in the financing of these operations. The next chapter explores the contribution the UN agencies, the World Bank and the principal bilateral donors have made to the construction of the discourse and practice of gender and development in Senegal.

NOTES

1. "Be patient—I intend passing power on to women." These words were attributed to Me Abdoulaye Wade and reported in the Senegalese daily press following a presidential visit to the Dakar motorway works in May 2009 where the President had allowed himself to be overheard addressing two senior women politicians accompanying him on a matter of national interest. The accuracy of the reporting is less important than what it reflected of the *zeitgeist* in Senegal in a year of intense speculation on the direction the political regime was taking.

2. UNDP, *Human Development Report 2004*, Table 18, "Flows of aid, private capital and debt," at *www.undp.org/hdr/statistics/senegal*. Accessed 08/12/10. GDP per capita has been declining steadily since the late 1970s.

3. UNICEF, *Analyse de la situation des femmes et des enfants au Sénégal* (Dakar: UNICEF, 1995), 18.

4. CIDA/ACDI (Canadian International Development Agency/*Agence Canadienne pour le Développement International*) *Stratégie d'egalité des sexes programme du Sénégal—boîte à outils* (CIDA/ ACDI, November, 1998), 4.

5. Mbaye Sarr, *Emploi et Travail des Femmes au Sénégal—document provisoire* (Dakar: BIT/ILO, September 1993).

6. Aderanti Adepoju and Christine Oppong, eds., *Gender, Work and Population in Sub-Saharan Africa* (London: James Currey; New Hampshire: Heinemann; on behalf of the International Labour Organisation, Geneva, 1994), 32.

7. UNICEF, *Analyse de la situation*, 22.

8. Sarr, *Emploi et Travail*, table VI, 55-56.

9. Casamance is the most southerly region located south of the Gambia River and Sine is located in the western region south of Dakar.

10. Fatou Sow, Ngagne Diakhaté, Mamadou Matar Gueye, and Adama Fall-Touré, *Les Sénégalaises en Chiffres* (Dakar: UNDP, 2000), 11. The actual estimate at the time was 45.5 percent.

11. UNICEF, *Analyse de la situation*, 20.

12. Associations and non-governmental organizations.

13. In discourse theory the idea of plural positions is not new nor the monopoly of postcolonial theorists. See, for example, Sara Mills, *Discourses of Differences* (London: Routledge, 1993).

14. Fatou Sow, Mamadou Diouf and Guy le Moine, *Femmes Sénégalaises à l'horizon 2015* (Dakar: *Ministère de la Femme*/The Population Council, 1993), 10-14. "In the colonial period political institutions were completely closed to women. This represented a step backwards compared with their position in pre-colonial society. [. . .] In the immediate aftermath of Independence, the State launched a national development plan for the whole of Senegalese society. This included a commitment to developing policies for the advancement of women that would mark a break with colonial practice." Author's translation

15. Some of these "women's advancement groups" are still operating in Senegal.

16. For those interested in early gender and development policy I discussed this in "Colonial Subjects: Gender, Race and Discrimination," in *International Journal of Sociology and Social Policy* 26, nos 11/12, 2006, 449–454.

17. Sow et al., *Femmes Sénégalaises à l'horizon*, 15.

18. Known as *Femme et Développement (FED)* in French.

19. *La Quinzaine de la femme.*

20. *Bien-être familial—facteur de développement.*

21. Sow et al., *Femmes Sénégalaises à l'horizon*, 17.

22. *Ministère de la Femme de l'Enfant et de la Famille, Rapport national sur les femmes—lutte pour l'egalité, le développement et la paix* (Dakar: *Ministère de la Femme de l'Enfant et de la Famille*, 1994), vi.

23. Interview with Seynabou Tall, Engendering Government Program Officer, UNIFEM, Dakar, Senegal, 18 June 2003.

24. Sow et al., *Femmes Sénégalaises à l'horizon*, 19.

25. *Ministère de la Femme de l'Enfant et de la Famille, Rapport National sur les Femmes*, v.

26. *Ministère de la Femme de l'Enfant et de la Famille, Rapport National sur les Femmes*, v.

27. *Ministère de la Femme de l'Enfant et de la Famille, Rapport national sur les femmes.*

28. The emphasis on environmental issues is probably the result of the drafting of this report coming almost immediately after the world conference on the environment in Rio de Janeiro in 1992.

29. *Ministère de la Femme de l'Enfant et de la Famille, Rapport national sur les femmes*, vi.

30. It is notable that women, even the more radical feminists, fear speaking openly or publishing on the influence these Muslim brotherhoods have over women's affairs. At least two leading feminists to my knowledge have received death threats from men styling themselves as devout Muslims.

31. In national surveys typically 90-96 percent Senegalese people describe themselves as practising Muslims.

32. *Ministère de la Famille et de la Petite Enfance, Projet de plan national d'equité de genre*, (Dakar: *Ministère de la Famille et de la Petite Enfance—Gouvernement du Sénégal*, December 2001).

33. Interviews at *Unité Genre et Développement, Ministère de la Femme et de la Petite Enfance*, Dakar, May 2002.

34. The *PANAF* plan was formulated in 1996 in the aftermath of this conference.

35. *Ministère de la Famille et de la Petite Enfance, Projet de plan national d'equité*, 10.

36. *Ministère de la Famille et de la Petite Enfance, Projet de plan national d'equité*, 21.

37. Discussed in relation to UN assistance to gender policy funding in United Nations *United Nations Population Fund Proposed Projects and Programmes—Assistance to the Government of Senegal Document: DP/FPA/SEN/5*, 3 August 2001, paragraph 11.

38. *Ministère de la Famille et de la Petite Enfance*, "*Projet de plan national d'equité*," 21.

39. Approximately U.S.$7 million.

40. See http://www.famille.gouv.sn, *projets et programmes.*

41. This agency is known as *FNUAP* in French-speaking countries.

42. *Charte nationale sur le dialogue social, République du Sénégal*, 2002, Section 4.4. 5 *Promotion du dialogue social, paragraphe* 284. "A qualitative change in workplace relations replacing colonial industrial relations with new modes of behavior, attitudes and relationships in the workplace more consonant with contemporary development models."

43. From a political science point of view, this is not inconsistent with the parameters of the Charter. Social dialogue is conceived primarily as a means of reducing negative responses to policies delivered from the center. As such it is operating out

of a center-periphery model of economic relations (typical of the colonial era) rather than a cluster model (a more philosophically postcolonial construction). The latter would be a more appropriate approach if the initiative was to bring new participants into the formulation of development/economic priorities and as opposed to bringing them in at the point of reception of these priorities.

44. Interview with Nafissatou Faye, Coordinator of *Siggil Jigeen* NGO, Dakar, Senegal, May 2002.

45. *Ministère de la Famille et de la Petite Enfance, Projet de plan national d'equité*, 36.

46. *Ministère de la Famille, de la Solidarité Nationale, de la Sécurité Alimentaire, de l'Entreprenariat Féminin de la Micro Finance et de la Petite Enfance.*

47. "1—Continue activities for raising awareness of gender-based violence through the festival of films on gender-based violence. 2—Organize gender training sessions for the network of African women in government and parliament. 3—Disseminate information on laws and conventions (CEDAW, the law on health and reproduction, etc.) in the regions of Tambacounda, Kolda and Matam. 4—Continue organizing more training sessions for Gender Focal Points and disseminate the Gender Methodology Guide with a view to encouraging its uptake among stakeholders." Author's translation.

48. The *Agence internationale de la francophonie* (*AIF*) being the administrative arm of the *Organisation internationale de la francophonie* (*OIF*), executes the policy decisions of the Member States of the Francophonie organization.

49. The document focuses on the common mistranslations and misunderstandings of the Koran which sustain myths such as Eve being made out of the rib of Adam, a conception of womanhood that has its origins in the Bible, not the Koran. The analysis draws on the original sources to explain that the interpretation that women are inferior to men is unsustainable.

50. In the weeks following the vote on the parity law, President Abdoulaye Wade took every occasion to inform the international community that this law had been passed. He even interrupted his speech opening the international art exhibition, Dak'Art 2010, for several minutes to talk about the parity law, presenting it to the international community as a historic step forward for Senegal.

51. The reception it received in civil society was likewise far from unanimously positive. One national daily reported the matter in the following terms: "*Les femmes de Bennoo Siggil Senegaal dans un communiqué rendu public le 13 mai [2010] condamnent "vigoureusement les décisions unilatérales du président de la République . . . sans aucune consultation des acteurs politiques concernés . . .," Le Quotidien*, 15-16 May 2010, 12.

13

International Agencies and the Agenda for Change in Senegal

Fifty years of international community activity has confirmed the international agencies as key players in the process of social transformation in francophone Africa. As Rosalind Petchesky notes in her analysis of the international debate on women's health and reproductive rights, one of the major achievements of the international community has been the impact it had on the participation of developing world countries. Women were given a platform in the international debates where previously they had had little or no access to the global decision-making arena. Their attendance at the summits helped them lay the foundations for change in their home countries:

> Perhaps the most useful outcome of women's participation in the UN conferences of the 1990s was that it provided focus and co-ordination for advocacy and social change efforts at national level.[1]

The international agencies have been operating at the national level of social policy-making in francophone Africa since the 1950s and have built up such a high profile in Senegal that its capital, Dakar, frequently serves as the center for operations in the sub-region, both Anglophone and francophone. The prestige and influence of these agencies derive in no small part from the budgets they command. Since the World Bank started operations in Senegal in 1966 it has disbursed the equivalent of U.S.$2.8 billion in loans and grants to development projects, an increasing number of which have a gender dimension.[2] The major bilateral donors in the francophone sub-region, including USAID, CIDA/*ACDI*, *GTZ*[3] and the French *Coopération* mission, have also exerted an increasing influence over gender and development policies in the region as the nature of official development assistance (ODA) became increasingly politicized and "conditionality" increased in the aftermath of the Cold War in Europe and Africa. In this climate the state, far from taking a leading role in social development policy, occupies the role of development partner alongside the wealthier stakeholders.

International community multilateral funding for women's policies in Senegal began as a relatively low-key operation in the 1960s and increased markedly in the wake of the first World Conference for Women of 1975. Interest in women's projects continued to increase throughout the International Decade for Women from 1975 to 1985. By the first decade of the twenty-first century international development partners were investing around U.S.$23 million a year into social development initiatives in Senegal, most of which had a gender dimension.[4]

Clearly multilateral agencies not only played a central role in setting the agenda for gender and development policy in francophone Africa, they were also key players in the funding, approval and implementation of projects aimed at women. In retrospect, however, their influence in effecting real change in women's position in society was minimal up to the 1990s.

During the 1970s and 1980s, the agencies prioritized population policies in response to a perception in the industrialized world that there was a population explosion taking place in the developing world. From the early 1980s, as structural adjustment programs were being introduced in developing countries, social spending was cut and Senegal, like other low-income countries, became more heavily dependent on bi-lateral and multilateral agencies to fund social sector activities.

Some of the programs implemented by international agencies during this period were so poorly conceived and ignorant of local realities that, despite the best of intentions, they achieved the opposite outcomes from those intended. A UNICEF program of 1987 exemplifies this problem.[5] With a relatively generous budget of U.S.$5.5 million, the "UNICEF regional development program for women" was designed with a view to reducing the time rural women were spending on their daily domestic chores. The plan included digging village wells and building grain mills. The time women saved drawing their water from wells and grinding their grain in communal mills would then be spent on market gardening. The idea was that women would cultivate a surplus in the market gardens which they would sell on for a profit. The money generated from the market gardening would be used to buy health care for themselves and their children. As it turned out, and for a variety of reasons that had not been identified in advance because of the lack of research conducted in the locality, the project did not achieve its aims. In the 386 villages where the project was implemented, the health and welfare of women and children deteriorated during the duration of the program.[6]

While the intended outcomes did not materialize, a valuable but unpredicted side-effect came to light. The village women who had been involved in the project noted that although the proposed "solution" had been inappropriate they were grateful to the project organizers for having recognized their burden of work, this was the first time a donor agency had attempted to help them.

International agencies have since taken measures to avoid repeating past mistakes, the most comprehensive and widespread recent effort in this direction being the UNDAF[7] framework for assessing a country's development needs. UNDAF was introduced both in response to a recognition that time and resources were being wasted by the lack of coordination between UN system agencies, and to provide a more comprehensive picture of a country's needs. The recording of these needs within a single framework should facilitate agency efforts to co-ordinate their activities both at national and regional level.

In December 2000, the first UNDAF needs analysis of Senegal, the outcome of which was known as the "common country assessment" or CCA, was presented to a group of stakeholders from the Senegalese government, the development partners and civil society. The CCA identified three development priorities for Senegal:

- the fight against poverty;
- education for all[8];
- special assistance for the regions of Tambacounda and Casamance.[9]

Thanks to UNDAF it was expected that the UN agencies would be able to develop and implement a coordinated response to the CCA priorities and work more efficiently together through the first decade of the new millennium.

By the summer of 2001, the UN population fund (UNFPA/*FNUAP*) was already casting doubts on the new system: "the fact that co-ordination mechanisms exist does not mean that they work as designed: effective co-ordination calls for the involvement of all stakeholders."[10] *FNUAP*'s report went on to specify that in the field of gender activities the new system had not succeeded in accelerating change:

> the lack of a critical mass of staff in all ministries and eligible NGOs trained in integrating the gender approach into programmes has slowed the mainstreaming of gender issues into sectoral plans and programmes.[11]

In the first three years of the decade, it became apparent that the UNDAF and CCA initiative was not providing the hoped-for improvement in coordination of UN development activities in Senegal. The Resident Coordinator[12] of the United Nations agencies in Senegal reported to the UN Economic and Social

Council in June 2003 that Senegal's UNDAF was so complicated as to be unmanageable.[13] Traditionally agencies in Senegal have worked together on projects in an *ad hoc* fashion and often in response to individual calls from NGOs or government departments. The UNDP, for example, financed what were described as the "women's social development" activities within the national Anti-Poverty Program from 1995 to 2000. The vast majority of the women's social development budget in this program took the form of investments in human capital, directed at increasing economic productivity. In practice the initiatives reached only a very small number of women. Some 750 women were given training in food processing, a further 250 were trained in leadership with a view to increasing the number of women running women's organizations, and 30 women received training in disseminating knowledge on women's rights as laid down in the CEDAW convention.[14] More of this kind of women's leadership and rights training took place between July 2000 and November 2002 with funding from the UNDP.

THE MDGS AND THE NEW DEVELOPMENT FRAMEWORK

From 2000 onwards, international gender and development policy in Senegal started to operate within the framework of the Millennium Development Goals (MDGs) for the period 2000 to 2015.

Unlike previous development initiatives the implementation of the MDGs is the responsibility of all the international development agencies working together, including the IMF, the World Bank and the more centrally implicated partners such as the UNPFA, UNDP, UNESCO and UNIFEM.

The UNDP, as the lead development agency in Senegal, coordinated a statement on the activities of the international agencies within the MDG framework for the first Common Country Assessment of Senegal in August 2001. It was published in a policy statement, which for the purposes of clarity will be referred to here as the joint agencies' statement of 2001, or JAS-2001.[15]

The JAS-2001 identified 10 areas of concern for Senegal:

1. the national context of development;
2. extreme poverty;
3. HIV/AIDS;
4. access to basic social services;
5. food security;
6. basic education for all;
7. gender equality and national strategies;
8. the campaign to lower infant mortality;

9. reproductive health;
10. the environment.

The JAS-2001 narrative on "the national context of development" refers to gender issues on three occasions. Its first reference mentions the national policy to target women for economic advancement, largely through development of micro and small enterprises and a program of support for women's groups. The second reference compares the number of girls and boys in primary schools, and the third compares the number of girls and boys in secondary schools.[16] In common with most UN international documents where education and gender are discussed, there was no mention of the enormous gaps in vocational training and higher education or the impact that the absence of training has on the lifelong opportunities of adult women.

The second priority area identified in the JAS-2001, defined "extreme poverty" in a manner reflecting the tendency in international agencies to use exogenous quantitative values in national development documents. In this case, the statement defines a poor person as someone who has less that U.S.$1 of disposable income a day and/or a daily food intake of less than 2,400 calories. It then proceeded to define vulnerability to poverty. Despite the emphasis on the feminization of poverty in recent UN publications, among which was UNIFEM's *Progress of the World's Women* of 2000, the JAS-2001 did not use this opportunity to highlight the gender dimensions of poverty, but rather attributed inequality in poverty to regional variations and place of residence, either urban or rural.

HIV/AIDS AND THE FEMINIZATION OF A PANDEMIC

The presentation of the third priority area, HIV/AIDS, reveals a historical reluctance on the part of some agencies to discuss the social causes of the dissemination of this disease. The JAS-2001 noted that Senegal still had a low level of HIV/AIDS infection in 2000, 1.43 percent of 15–49-year-old age group, but that the gender ratio has changed.[17]

Indeed, until recently Senegal presented a pattern of infection similar to that in the West with more males than females infected by the virus, whereas in Africa generally the pattern had evolved quite differently, women having been particularly badly affected in the east and the south of the continent. By the end of 2004, women accounted for 60 percent of all cases in sub-Saharan Africa.

In the early 2000s for the first time, Senegal recorded parity in the numbers of men and women infected with the virus. The JAS-2001 did not offer any commentary on the dramatic change in the disease pattern in Senegal between

1988 and 2000. Furthermore the document did not point up the connections being identified in more critical and analytical discourses[18] between economic vulnerability, marital regimes, prostitution and the spread of HIV infection. The commentary focused on the success of the national campaign at keeping overall levels down.

The HIV/AIDS pandemic was framed in this document as an essentially scientific-medical issue rather than a social one. In fact the JAS-2001 used five statistical tables and graphs to convey a largely optimistic outlook on the disease. One of the graphics shows the rate of infection falling from 1.43 percent in 2000 to 0 percent in 2015. On the other hand one of the statistical tables revealed that over a third of prostitutes working in Ziguinchor are HIV positive.

The lack of consistent "position" in international agency discourse and practice at country level is exemplified by the engagement some UN agencies have made to the HIV/AIDS campaign. A UNIFEM-funded academic study published in Dakar in May 2002,[19] took a far less optimistic view of the problem of HIV/AIDS in Senegal. It confirmed that the Senegalese government responded early to the crisis, setting up a national committee against AIDS in the months following the detection of the first cases in 1986, but it also noted the absence of measures to arrest the trend towards the feminization of the virus in Senegal since 1986. Table 13.1 illustrates how the virus had been spreading among Senegalese women since 1988 at a rate dramatically higher than among men. Indeed there was an almost four-fold increase in the number of women infected with the virus during the first fifteen years of the anti-AIDS campaign in Senegal.

A UNFPA report on Senegal[20] cited several studies suggesting almost half of all 15- to 18-year-old girls in Senegal surveyed in the late 1990s and 2000 were sexually active and that the incidence of unwanted pregnancy was rising. The UNFPA report notes that 75 percent of young girls pregnant with a first child were married, leaving nevertheless a relatively high number of one in four births to unmarried girls. The medical problems associated with childbirth in adolescence are well-known, but in Senegal there is the added problem of the severe cultural stigma associated with unmarried motherhood. In

Table 13.1. HIV/AIDS in Senegal by Gender, 1988–2002

Year	Number of Infected Men	Number of Infected Women	Ratio of Men to Women	Growth Ratio— Men Only	Growth Ratio— Women Only	Total No. of Cases
1988	24,048	9,108	2.64:1	1	1	33,156
1996	36,251	23,553	1.54:1	1.51	2.59	59,805
2002	41,326	35,947	1.15:1	1.72	3.95	77,273

Source: Raw data from *Surveillance sentinelle* statistics of April 2002 published in Wone "*VIH/SIDA*" (2002).

the context of the HIV/AIDS pandemic, there were further worrying findings suggesting that only 3 percent of sexually-active teenagers were using contraception at the time of the UNFPA report.[21] This research, dated August 2001, stated that the "total contraception needs for Senegal amount to $1,124,000 a year, almost all of which is provided by USAID [. . . which gave] $900,000 in 2002."[22] Meanwhile the government focused on increasing the availability of low-cost anti-retroviral drugs for people living with HIV/AIDS.[23]

Though the JAS-2001 avoided any social commentary on the spread of HIV/AIDS in the Senegalese population, a UNIFEM-funded study from the late 1990s had found that the most prevalent form of HIV infection in Senegal is between husbands and wives. The majority of women in 2000 were still living in polygamous households. Léopold Senghor had made an attempt to outlaw polygamy in 1972, at the time the Family Code was introduced, but fierce opposition from Muslim religious leaders forced him to abandon the attempt. The issue of polygamy came to the forefront again when Abdoulaye Wade took power from Senghor's successor in 2000. President Wade, married to a Frenchwoman and known not to favor polygamy, chose to back away from the issue in a climate where the religious right was wielding even more power in Senegal than it had during Senghor's reign.

The relationship between Muslim marital customs, polygyny and levirate, and women's vulnerability to the HIV/AIDS pandemic has not been the subject of sustained research. However the UNIFEM-funded study cites an academic research project completed in 1997 that found only 11 percent of a sample of women infected between 1986 and 1997 were from polygamous households.[24] The infected women recorded in this study were all patients at the university hospital in Dakar, situated in the prosperous, highly urbanized residential area of Dakar-Fann, where rates of monogamy are far higher than the national average. The rate of infection of wives of polygynous men in the country as a whole remains undocumented.

Not unexpectedly, the rate of infection in Senegal appears to be highest among female sex workers.[25] A survey of some 2000 female sex workers discovered that almost two-thirds of them were divorced women. The study noted with no apparent irony that in Wolof, spoken as a first language by over 60 percent of the population, the word for *prostitute* is the same as the word for *divorcée*. Though the rate of infection in the male population in Senegal was relatively low by the late 2000s, a survey among male sex workers in Dakar had reported an infection rate of over 20 percent. A separate survey of female sex workers in Dakar revealed that 45 percent of the sample were divorcées, 36 percent were single women and 19 percent were married.[26] The vast majority of all categories, more than 9 out of 10 women, attributed their engagement in sex work as a result of extreme poverty. Over 80 percent of the registered female sex workers were also responsible for bringing up the children in their care.

Though at the time of the JAS-2001 the feminization of HIV/AIDS in Senegal was not highlighted, the gender dimension of this pandemic became mainstreamed into the international agencies' presentation of the development priorities for Senegal between 2002 and 2007. But here again the gap between discourse and policy opened up as the UNGASS[27] report of January 2008 confirmed the gender differential had widened, the overall prevalence rate in the young female population being reported at over twice the rate in the young male population, at 0.9 percent and 0.4 percent respectively.[28]

Other priority areas listed in the JAS-2001 assessment did not explore the gender dimension of social deprivation explicitly. Both "access to basic social services" and "access to drinking water," issues where gender plays a crucial role, were not subject to any gender analysis. In rural communities, women are responsible for providing water and they can spend up to a third of their working day going back and forth to remote water sources—as the early ill-fated UNICEF project had recognized. Over two-thirds of people who live in the more remote areas of Senegal still do not have access to piped drinking water.

Achieving food security, the fifth priority area, likewise was not framed within the context of the gender dimension of food production preparation and consumption.

Priority area 6, education, was the only policy area where the gender dimension was highlighted and presented essentially as a problem of girls' lack of access to schooling. The gender analysis here was essentially quantitative: there are fewer girls than boys, with just one mention of the problem of retaining girls in school.

The seventh priority area entitled "Gender parity" also dealt almost uniquely with educational access reflecting this conflation in the Millennium Development discourse between education and equality.

While the text identified some of the obstacles to girls getting an education, such as the lack of girls' lavatories in schools, widespread sexual harassment, fear of early pregnancy and the social stigma it entails, no policy responses to these issues were discussed in the document, nor any engagement made with the social and economic reasons why these obstacles persist. The objective for priority area 7 being the same as the objective for priority area 6, namely eliminate gender disparities in primary and secondary education, was confirmed by the JAS-2001 as the reduction of the concept of gender equality to access to formal education.

Priority area 8, infant mortality, and 10, the environment, contained no references to gender. The ninth priority area, reproductive health, is a complex variable as far as gender policy is concerned given the sex-specific nature of childbirth. The agencies' statement reflected awareness of sexual/biological difference but did not broach the issue of differential access to health services by gender. In conclusion, the common country assessment of 2001 exemplified a dislocation in the discourse around gender and revealed a failure to mainstream gender into the UN system in Senegal, not least because of residual confusion about what gender mainstreaming is and how it can be achieved.[29]

Since the publication of the first common country assessment, initiatives have been taken by the "gender focal points" (gender officers) in the UN agencies in francophone West Africa to implement gender mainstreaming. In Senegal, the gender focal points have also articulated concerns over the gap between the international gender discourse and local agency realities. The reduction of gender equality issues to educational access is described in a joint report by the group of UN and World Bank focal points as "*trop limitatif*."[30] The report went on to note that the other Millennium Development Goals (MDGs) have likewise failed to give sufficient consideration to gender. The report called for a campaign within the agencies to produce an integrated gender perspective for all the MDGs at national level.

The gender focal points' report then turns its attention to the recurrent issue of statistical indicators and calls for an extensive number of gender-sensitive indicators to be added to those already used in the UNDAF common country assessment model. HIV/AIDS was targeted for twelve new indicators. Ten gender-sensitive indicators to monitor progress towards "sustainable environment" targets were required, not least because the gender dimension of environmental issues had been overlooked by the authors of the MDGs. Altogether the gender focal points in Senegal identified 86 gender-sensitive indicators needed to monitor progress towards the MDGs in their sub-region.

A closer look at these 86 variables reveals a move towards synthesizing local norms within international modalities. There are several variables specifically related to motherhood and maternal health that would not, in another society, constitute core variables in gender monitoring. In countries such as Italy, Spain, and the United States where around half the women aged 25 to 45 will not require maternal health services, having chosen not to become mothers, it would be inappropriate to identify maternal health as the principal variable determining women's health. In Senegal, maternal health variables are often the only variables used to define a woman's health status suggesting that motherhood is still considered more or less synonymous with being female.

While the gender focal points work towards developing a more refined, culturally-embedded definition of gender in the locality, these new definitions will need to negotiate the boundaries set by the dominant configuration of gender and development. The functioning definition of gender and development in the UN system agencies working in Senegal continues to be drawn from the universal discourse elaborated in the earlier chapters. The weight and influence of this configuration of gender on the policy field cannot be overestimated for not only does it influence activities in all the international agencies operating in the sub-region, it also has a direct and acknowledged impact on the activities of the state.

The *PANEG* strategy document of 2001 confirmed that the future of the gender equity program in Senegal was dependent upon the approval and support of international agencies,[31] not least because the development partners (multilateral and bilateral) were expected to provide 50 percent of the funding needed to implement the Government of Senegal's gender equity program over the period 2002–2006. It is clear that Senegalese state could run the risk of capsizing its own policy if it was not operating within the framework approved by the international agencies. It remains to be seen whether the UN policy-making framework is sufficiently flexible to allow local gender officers to refine international definitions and recast targets in the light of local realities.

It is not the primary objective of the agents of international organizations to analyze and critique the prevailing international model of gender and development for the developing world context. While the agencies are primarily responsible for overseeing the implementation of internationally-financed and locally approved gender and development policies in Africa, the responsibility for primary research on the impact of the dominant discourse and its model of gender and development lies with the academy. The role the universities and research institutes of the region play in interrogating this discourse is explored in the next chapter.

NOTES

1. Rosalind P. Petchesky, *Global Prescriptions—Gendering Health and Human Rights* (London: Zed Books, 2003), 189.
2. *World Bank country profiles—Senegal 2009.* http://www.worldbank.org.
3. The official development agencies of the United States, Canada, and Germany.
4. United Nations, *United Nations Population Fund Proposed Projects and Programmes—Assistance to the Government of Senegal Document: DP/FPA/SEN/5* (New York: United Nations, 3 August 2001), paragraph 20.
5. Sow et al., *Femmes Sénégalaises*, 22 *passim.*
6. *Ministère de la Femme, de l'Enfant et de la Famille. Senegalese Women by the Year 2015—abridged version* (Dakar: Ministère de la Femme/The Population Council, 1993), 12.

7. UN development assistance framework.

8. "Education for all" is a reference to the UN's objective of providing primary schooling for all African children by the year 2010, an objective reiterated at the UN "Education for All" summit "Jomtien +10," held in Dakar in April 2000.

9. The latter having experienced the effects of civil war since 1982.

10. United Nations. *DP/FPA/SEN/5* (2001), paragraph 19.

11. United Nations. *DP/FPA/SEN/5* (2001), paragraph 19.

12. Minutes of the meeting of the Economic and Social Committee of the UN, 4 July 2003, at www.un.org. The Resident Coordinator heads the UN development agencies in Senegal.

13. Minutes of the meeting of the Economic and Social Committee of the UN, 4 July 2003, at www.un.org.

14. *Ministère de la Famille et de la Petite Enfance—Projet de Plan National d'Equité de Genre* (Dakar: *Ministère de la Famille et de la Petite Enfance—Gouvernement du Sénégal*, Décembre 2001), 13. This priority returned to the top of the agenda of policies for implementation in 2009–2010.

15. UNDP, *Suivi des objectifs de développement du millénaire au Sénégal* (Dakar: PNUD, August 2001).

16. UNDP, *Suivi des objectifs*, 9–10.

17. UNDP, *Suivi des objectifs*, 14.

18. The contribution of the academic community to the development of these discourses is explored in the following chapter.

19. Katy Cisse Wone, *Les fondements juridiques, socio-culturels et économiques de la vulnérabilité des femmes à l'infection au VIH/SIDA—le cas du Sénégal* (Dakar: UNIFEM, 2002).

20. United Nations *DP/FPA/SEN/5* (2001).

21. United Nations *DP/FPA/SEN/5* (2001), 4.

22. United Nations *DP/FPA/SEN/5* (2001), paragraph 34.

23. http://data.unaids.org, 2006, country reports.

24. Khoudia Sow, [no title], Doctoral thesis, UCAD 1997, cited in Wone, *Les fondements juridiques*, 26.

25. Generally male sex workers are not acknowledged or included in statistics and studies on prostitution in Senegal.

26. Wone, *Les fondements juridiques*, 31.

27. United Nations General Assembly Special Session on AIDS.

28. UNGASS, Country report—Sénégal, January 2008, 24.

29. This view was expressed to the author by several professional women working in the UN agencies in Senegal during interviews 2002–2008.

30. Coumba Mar Gadio, *Le Genre et les objectifs du millénaire pour le développement* (Dakar: UNIFEM/UNDP/UNFPA/OIT, 2003), 3.

31. *Ministère de la Famille et de la Petite Enfance*, Projet de Plan National d'Equité, 14.

14

Theorizing Gender and
Development in the Academy

Academics have been more active in the field of women's studies and gender than would appear from a desk-bound literature review of the subject. Many of the studies produced in Senegal have either not been published or have been published in short local print runs. Much of the information used in this chapter has come from interviews and discussions in Senegal[1] and from the wealth of documentary research located in the region.

CONFRONTING THE ECONOMIC CLIMATE OF RESEARCH

As higher education and research in francophone West Africa continues to operate within severe financial constraints, the demand for academic publishing far exceeds the supply. Notwithstanding these challenges, a body of literature has been produced under the imprint of regional academic publishers in the social sciences such as CODESRIA,[2] which produces a small list and a quarterly academic journal, *Afrique et Développement*. The journal has addressed the issue of gender on a number of occasions; first in 1997 with a bilingual special issue entitled "Gender revisited/ *Le genre revisité,*" and in 1998 with a double issue published under the title of "Gender Relations."[3] In response to the absence of infrastructural support in the higher education sector, women researchers formed the *Association des femmes africaines dans la recherche et le développement/* African Women in Research and Development, in 1977, maintaining a physical presence in the region through a small francophone research centre and library in Dakar and an intellectual presence through a quarterly journal, ECHO. It also publishes occasional volumes under the imprint AAWORD Book Series with the help of donations from external organizations, typically from the UN agencies in Dakar, Canadian development assistance, and influential international NGOs. The last general assembly of AFARD/AAWORD of the twentieth century chose for its theme "Visions of Gender Theories and Social Development in Africa: Harnessing Knowledge for Social Justice and Equality," the proceedings of which were published in the AAWORD series, thanks to a grant from the Ford Foundation. There are no copies of this book in any point of sale and no mention of the publication in international document retrieval systems and, in common with other texts published locally in this field, it carries no ISSN or ISBN identification.[4]

IN SEARCH OF THE INDEPENDENT ACADEMIC PUBLISHER

Opportunities for accessing the international academic publishing system have been undermined by an absence of funding for international conference attendance. Such events offer both the possibility to present work in an international forum, and to engage the interest of academic publishers who attend these international events. The result is that academics working in the field of women's and gender studies have frequently had to rely on the local international agencies to subsidize their research and cover publication costs. This has implications for academic freedom and the nature of academic research being undertaken in this field. An international agency is unlikely to fund and publish research which it does not recognize as being a useful contribution to women's studies and gender issues, as it defines these fields.

The first two major academic studies examining women and social development issues in Senegal were published in response to the international discourse on women in development and gender and development culminating in the Beijing+5 review of 2000. The first, *Femmes Sénégalaises à l'horizon 2015*,[5] published in July 1993, was funded by UNIFEM, UNICEF, UNDP, UNFPA, and the ILO, along with contributions from USAID and the World Bank. The second major publication in the field, *Les Sénégalaises en chiffres*,[6] published in August 2000, was funded and published by the UNDP[7] office in Dakar. The publications exemplify the constraints and opportunities offered by the academic-international agency partnership for research and development.

ACCOMMODATING LOCAL REALITIES
WITHIN INTERNATIONAL DISCOURSES

Femmes Sénégalaises à l'horizon 2015 provides a history of the origins and development of women's policies in Senegal from 1960 to the early 1990s, followed by the findings of a survey of 1,000 Senegalese women. The survey both defines gender disadvantage in Senegalese society by the way it presents the phenomenon in the survey, and opens the debate to local voices by inviting women respondents to rank variables based on what they felt were the dominant and influential factors barring the emancipation and advancement of women. The women identified a list of potential policy initiatives that they felt would be most likely to reduce existing inequities:

1. remove obstacles to women organizing themselves into self-managing economic groups;
2. promote the idea that a woman can value her own personal achievement;
3. develop democratic structures and procedures for policy-making;
4. promote women in politics;
5. provide literacy training;
6. facilitate women's access to land;
7. improve regional integration;
8. give women access to ICT;
9. grant women the power to oversee at regional and local level initiatives and decisions taken at national level to make sure they are followed through and backed up in the locality.[8]

The conceptual framework of gender disadvantage operating in this study sees rural illiterate women as marginalized at multiple levels, in society, the polity and the economy. The findings of this analysis provide a vision of how to bring these marginalized women from the periphery to the center of the modernizing economy.

The influence of the international agencies is visible in the discourse of the study insofar as it discusses women as human capital. The first key finding presented in *Femmes Sénégalaises à l'horizon 2015* is that rural women are not as economically productive as they could be.[9] The neo-liberal discourse of development that dominated the wider politico-economic environment in which this study was undertaken and funded is thus accommodated in the study's analytical framework.

The second publication, *Les Sénégalaises en chiffres* (2000), provided the most comprehensive overview to date of the socio-economic disadvantages faced by women as compared to men in modern Senegal. It was written by a team of researchers headed by a leading Senegalese sociologist,[10] who had previously edited the *Africa Development* special issue, *Gender Relations*. The purpose of *Les Sénégalaises en chiffres* was to provide statistics on the contribution women make to all aspects of life in Senegal and the conditions in which they provide this contribution. Ostensibly the focus of the study is on quantifying disadvantage through socio-demographic, economic and political data, and providing statistics to fill existing gaps. However the study includes analytical commentaries on each of its three thematic sections—*Données socio-démographiques, Données économiques, Données politiques*—which together make a significant contribution towards situating gender discrimination in its cultural and historical context.

While quantifying disadvantage and exclusion and making strong recommendations for relieving the symptoms of disadvantage, the study makes reference to the causes of discrimination and by so doing moves the analysis on from the *FED*/WID[11] approach that permeated the contemporary policy environment. This publication, visually styled after the Human Development Report[12] and following the HDR format of using statistics to deepen the debate, provides a qualitative gloss on the data that goes straight to the core of the cultural debate on gender and development. The conclusion to the first section, *Données Socio-démographiques*, states:

> *C'est donc au cœur de la famille qu'est d'abord ancré le débat sur les femmes et leur pouvoir, famille comme espace de signification des rôles sociaux des sexes. Il y a des rôles attendus des femmes et des hommes, des jeunes et des vieux au sein de la famille qui conditionnent leur participation à la communauté, à l'économie, à l'état et, plus globalement, au développement. Les politiques visant à l'égalité entre les sexes, à une meilleure prise en compte des droits des enfants, devront donc s'interroger sur la manière de les ancrer déjà à ce niveau.*[13]

It elaborates on this theme by identifying a further obstacle: women who do not conform to the gender division of labor within the family and a pre-established hierarchy between men and women may face rejection for their insubordination. Like the Human Development Report on which it was modeled, this publication is used for advocacy and the authors go on to argue that if women do not reject these pre-established relations they are participating in their own subordination.[14]

Similarly other statistical data presented in the study are interpreted as the results of socially-constructed phenomena. For example, maternal mortality is listed under the health and medical statistics, but the very high rate of mortality (around 500 per 1000 births) is described as the result of:

> *l'appropriation, par la communauté, du corps des femmes, de leur capacité de maternité transformée en besoin d'enfants bien intériorisé, l'attribution des tâches domestiques, fondent leur obligation de répondre à cette attente sociale. A ce niveau le contrôle social reste très fort.*[15]

The argument that society imposes an identity on girls points to a number of key issues determining girls' and women's quality of life and life expectancy in Senegal. These include [early] marriage and motherhood and unattended childbirth.[16] Just as issues of socialization are not addressed in the UNDP's quantitative evaluations of the gender dimension of development as expressed in the Human Development Reports, this academic study differs from most international agency studies in that it places an emphasis on explaining why certain variables are selected for quantitative analysis, what the data collected imply, and how the data reflect cultural specificity.

In the case of Senegal, a multi-ethnic society, the study highlights the ethnic dimensions of both social development and gender issues. It notes that Joola women, from Casamance in southern Senegal, are far more likely to give birth in a health centre attended by medical personnel than women from the other major ethnic groups in Senegal (Haal Pulaaren, Sereer, Wolof and Mandinka). Indeed three-quarters of Joola women were reported to have given birth in modern health centers at the time of the 1997 household survey[17] compared with only half of women from other ethnic groups. Furthermore Joola women have the lowest fertility rate by ethnic group, producing at that time on average 4.8 children compared with the 6.8 among Mandinka women.[18] A lower fertility rate tends to correlate with a lower maternal mortality rate.

The overall rate at the time of the study was 5.7 children, a rate that had been falling by approximately 1 child per woman per decade until the turn of the century.[19] Support for reproductive health care stalled in the early years of the twenty-first century as donor funding plummeted.[20] By the end of the decade it was clear that provision had worsened significantly over the ten year period 1997–2007. The Millennium Development Report 2009 noted that less progress was being made towards Millennium Development Goal 5—Improve maternal health and achieve universal access to reproductive health—than in any other field:

> Funding gaps are conspicuous for programmes needed to meet MDG 5, the goal towards which least progress has been made thus far. To take just one example: the strengthening and expansion of family planning programmes can make a major contribution to improvements in maternal and child health, but require adequate funding and access to supplies. Yet, since the mid-1990s, most developing countries have experienced a major reduction of donor funding for family planning on a per woman basis.[21]

In contrast, Millennium Development Goal 2—Achieve universal primary education—had experienced an upturn in donor spending with the result that "major breakthroughs have been achieved in sub-Saharan Africa, where enrolment increased by 15 percentage points from 2000 to 2007."[22]

In Senegal the focus on providing universal access to primary education has attracted universal support both within and outside the agencies. In *Les Sénégalaises en chiffres* access to education is presented as the key to breaking the cycle of disadvantage. Whereas the family has been identified as a site of conservative socialization, formal education is characterized in positivist functionalist terms:

> *L'éducation est une condition essentielle au développement de l'individu et du citoyen. En tant que productrice de connaissance et de conscience, elle forge la personnalité et permet une plus grande maîtrise de soi et de son environnement. Elle a très largement représenté un facteur de promotion sociale.*[23]

The study states the tradition of gender inequality in Senegal means that men and women do not always have the same opportunities to access and progress through education, and this applies to religious education, artisan training, and professional and vocational education, as well as to formal schooling. It argues that girls are being denied a formal education because:

1. domestic service is seen as a female responsibility (in other words women and girls learn from a very early stage to behave like household servants in homes where there are no paid employees to perform these tasks);
2. domestic chores are time-consuming which means that girls have little spare time in which to study;
3. domestic chores create a sense of inferiority in girls;
4. women learn that they are valued not for what they personally achieve but principally through their marriage and their husbands' achievements;
5. girls will almost inevitably get married, which locks them into the cycle of service and domesticity.

One could add to this list that the servant mentality instilled in girls makes them less inclined to insist on their right to education despite the fact that over 95 percent of Senegalese girls are born into Muslim families. Furthermore many domestic chores are heavy and tiring.[24] Being on average physically less strong than boys, girls pay a particularly heavy price for being allocated the lion's share of this labor.

EDUCATION IN REGIONAL AND INTERNATIONAL RESEARCH

In the wider academic community, in Senegal and in other parts of the developing world, there has been some questioning of the value of access to formal education.[25] Some academics argue for less emphasis on access to schooling and more on access to the production of knowledge. The production of knowledge in Africa and the delivery of education throughout the postcolonial period have remained almost exclusively in the hands of men, with girls and women being cast in the role of passive consumers, a situation whose origins can be traced to its colonial past.[26] In the French employment culture introduced into the former French colonies of Africa, few women had access to education, and even fewer had access to the production of knowledge. As girls' education became established, more female teachers were engaged but women never gained the presence in formal education in the French colonies that their French counterparts had traditionally enjoyed in the metropole. By the end of the 1990s only 19 percent of public sector primary school teachers were women.[27]

The education debate at the national level in Senegal rarely touches on the issue of gender in the production of knowledge, or on the demands society continues to make on young girls to provide a high number of hours of free domestic and agricultural labor that effectively keep them out of school. In this respect the academic voice is distinct from those emanating from the international community structures and the state. Among government officials and policy-makers[28] improving girls' access to education is presented as the sole or at least overriding education priority for Senegal, the reasons why girls are systematically excluded being invariably explained in vague terms and blamed on rural parents with "*mentalités traditionnelles.*" In campaigning for widening access to education, the government and the international agencies highlight the positive impact educating girls has on the health and wealth of the whole society, their focus tends towards presenting education as a means of developing women for the good of society, as opposed to affording education as a human right, an approach more prevalent in the academic discourse.

While there is some debate on the positive impact of primary education on women's quality of life, the arguments against the lowest levels of education are not carried through to the higher levels. Data on women's incomes suggests that access to higher education can have a significant impact on a woman's monetary income.[29] The *Sénégalaises en chiffres* study noted that although there were only 1,500 households headed by women graduates in Senegal in 1992, the average income of these households was higher than any other type of household.[30] This does not mean, however, that graduate women are earning the highest salaries. The data on income transfers between households show that graduate women receive a higher proportion of transfers and donations than any other group.[31]

The population of women graduates in Senegal is still not significant in numeric terms, representing only a minute proportion of the female population.

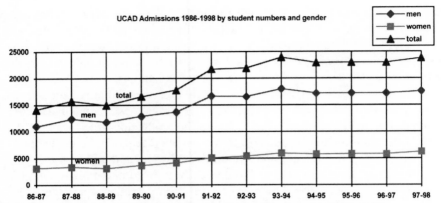

Figure 14.1.   Men and Women University Students in Senegal, 1986–1998
Note: By 2002-03 total numbers had risen to 32,000 university students in Senegal's main university, Cheik Anta Diop (ex-University of Dakar). 25% of whom were women.

However if the theory of critical mass holds true here as it has elsewhere,[32] a few women reformers can have an exponential impact on a political system once they reach a certain critical mass in key institutions of the State and society. A rising trend in girls enrolling at University in Senegal has been witnessed over the past twenty years, with a steep rise occurring in the period 1986–1994. While the upward trend has continued, the proportion of men to women in the student population has remained relatively constant as indicated in table 14.1.[33]

Despite this positive trend in access to higher education, women are still more exposed to unemployment than their male counterparts and education does not automatically offer protection against job losses. An important finding from the *Les Sénégalaises en Chiffres* (2000) study is that women with no educational qualifications had the lowest unemployment rates.[34] Indeed education is not in itself a guarantee of a job, nor is it any guarantee of improved social standing, nor does it automatically confer more power to women. Although the study revealed that qualifications improve your chances of getting a well-paid and desirable job, it also noted that because women still face so many obstacles to their participation in economic life, and because their earnings are on average so low, most women are not able to meet their basic needs through employment.

WOMEN AS HUMAN CAPITAL

Most Senegalese workers, men and women, are engaged in what is called the informal or "independent" sector. By 1992, almost 60 percent of all women earning a monetary income were working in the independent sector. Their income-generating work, then as now, mostly involves selling commodities either from home, on the street, at the market stall, or in a shop. They began making a presence in the business sector in the early 1990s, in dressmaking, hairdressing, property, and domestic appliances.[35] The degree to which the expanding female labor force indicates a rise in the quality of life of the female population is mediated by a number of socio-cultural factors.

As noted in *Les Sénégalaises en chiffres* the benefits which can devolve from being in paid work are numerous but depend on overcoming a range of obstacles not least a residual resistance to women working for income outside the home. The study stressed that for income to equate to more quality of life, several factors have to be accounted for, including the type of work women are doing, and how they are paid for this work. It is also crucial to evaluate the level of pay before paid work can be considered a *sine qua non* of women's advancement. A salaried job in the modern sector, such as primary school teaching, is recognized as providing the potential for improving the material quality of women's lives. In francophone countries, the state administration—which includes education—has traditionally been considered one of the better sources of regular income. However it was not possible for the research team to trace the impact of this employment sector on the female population as the state administration in Senegal declined to provide the *Sénégalaises en chiffres* study with employment statistics over time and disaggregated for gender.

For want of more local information, the study cited a survey conducted in Bamako, Mali, which concluded that women employed in the modern sector undoubtedly accrued social benefits. This was identified by their having fewer children and more power in the household. The power these women held derived from making a greater than average financial contribution to the family budget.

Other employment sectors have failed to foster women's advancement, and domestic chores and family commitments make it difficult for women to set up on their own in business.[36] However, here again the academic perspective provides a nuanced account. There are clear regional/ethnic variations in female employment patterns, with Joola and Sereer women from the rural areas of southern Senegal being more visibly active in the cash economy than women from other ethnic groups.

LAW, LAND AND CUSTOMS

Although the trend in urbanization is still rising, just under half of all women live in rural areas and are dependent on agriculture for their survival. Here women experience more difficulty than men do in gaining rights to cultivate land.

In most ethnic groups in Senegal men traditionally own land and give women the right to cultivate it.[37] Women can lose this right to land through divorce or widowhood, though here again Joola women from Lower Casamance are the exception. On marriage Joola girls receive their own rice fields and consequently their own means of support. On the other hand the pressure to marry is intense. In these rural communities marriage is still the prerequisite for accessing land, which itself is the prerequisite for acquiring credit and farming equipment. It is another example of how fact does not follow law where custom conflicts with legislation. The national land law of 17 June 1964 provided for equality of access to land to whomever farms it.[38] It is the role of the rural community council to manage the land and to help the most disadvantaged peasants get access to this land. Peasants have recourse to the land law mentioned above, but 97 percent of the women interviewed in the *Sénégalaises en chiffres* study had never tried to gain access by this route because of the social stigma it would bring upon the family if their conflicts were aired in public. Furthermore the women interviewed believed that the council would not act in favor of women or protect their right to the land.

In the decades since the land laws were passed, the problems confronting women had not been resolved. Women cannot make a private income from the land they presently hold because they only have enough land to serve the family's needs. They do not apply to rural councils for access to more land for the reasons mentioned above, and are unlikely to be granted any more land by either the family council or the village chief in his capacity as lawmaker and master of the land.[39]

Not all the members of the rural councils are men. But here we have an example of how political participation (local or national) does not lead directly to the emancipation or advancement of women. Women who do accede to the councils do little to promote other women. It is said that they have been elected on condition they do not upset the social order,[40] a not uncommon characteristic among both women and men who hold representative offices.

SOCIALIZATION FOR SUBORDINATION

The socialization of girls and women into subordinate and conservative roles through formal education entered the research agenda at *INEADE*, the national education institute in Senegal, in the 1990s, illustrating how the discourse has diverged across the various structures of the State. This process of divergence, fragmentation and collaboration across conflicting discursive positions within the political and academic arms of the state is exemplified in ongoing research on school textbooks which are being analyzed in relation to the role they play in constructing gender identities and perpetuating gender inequalities in Senegal. From a number of surveys and studies *INEADE* made recommendations for the revision of a first batch of textbooks during the period 2002–2005.[41] Meanwhile, the research unit of the Ministry of Education had for its part been collaborating with a UK development research institute to conduct a study on the factors influencing girls' enrolment at school.[42] This latter study pursued a more traditional line of education and development research focusing on access and attendance, rather than on the content and the outcomes of education.

The academic voice has also made itself heard in the political arena where it has met with hostility from religious fundamentalists. In the 1990s feminist academics[43] received threats of violence from religious extremists. At some points in the emergence of the gender and development debate in the 1990s, threats against academics became sufficiently serious to warrant the intervention of religious leaders who restored order by denouncing the instigators.

As the WID discourse became increasingly radicalized from the early 1990s, so the academic voice multiplied and then divided into opposing camps. Efforts to promote gender equality and equity in the academy face resistance and marginalization in Senegal[44] as they do throughout the international academic community.[45] But the structures within which arguments for equity and equality can be developed and delivered are being established in the research laboratories of *IFAN*[46] and *UCAD*, just as they are around the world, and these in turn lay the foundations of more intellectual space for independent research on the impact of gender on all aspects of social life.

THE FUTURE OF ACADEMIC RESEARCH ON GENDER

At the end of the first decade of the twenty-first century, the problem of a lack of academic publishing opportunities in the region remained unresolved. The international agencies continue to fulfill the role of publishing partner *par excellence* to the academy with the partnership operating within the traditional parameters of international community research with its focus on women as economic agents. The responsibility for publishing the whole spectrum of academic research from speculative and theoretical through to mainstream policy evaluation should not rest with the international agencies. Nevertheless studies have been undertaken in recent years that fall outside the traditional remit of the international agencies, as the title of a World Bank research project published in 2006 exemplified. While the project addressed the long-established theme of gender equity as a means of poverty reduction, the publication bore a title drawn from the traditional Wolof saying *Góor baax na, jigéen baax na*, testifying to a new articulation of gender and development issues in the locality.[47]

In the meantime as the academy deepens its engagement with gender theorizing and embeds its research in a new intellectual framework, the resulting deconstruction of gender supremacy is leading research into more controversial areas where traditional publishing opportunities are even rarer. The potential of the Internet to assist researchers in disseminating their work beyond the traditional limits of unitary academic disciplines will undoubtedly have an impact on the speed with which new theories can gain ground.[48] But the privilege of working at the boundaries of disciplines, of being the lone wolf outside the academic pack, has never been won without cost. The testimonies Awa Thiam collated and published in *La Parole aux négresses* in 1978 provide a lesson on the price of academic freedom. The issues she investigated over three decades ago have only recently acquired legitimacy in the wider gender and development community in francophone West Africa. At the time of publication, giving voice to "illiterate" African women speaking about polygyny, excision and infibulation was deemed too controversial. As Benoîte Groult revealed in her preface to *La parole aux négresses*, even the UN's global health agency would not engage with these topics at the time:

> *En 1975 [. . .] L'Association terre des hommes [. . .] a tenté de mettre l'Organisation mondiale de la santé face à ses responsabilités. Mais, là encore, il lui fut répondu que des opérations rituelles résultent de conceptions sociales et culturelles dont l'étude n'est pas du ressort de l'OMS.*[49]

By voicing social taboos, Thiam's work contributed to expanding the discourse of gender and development conceptually and, whether intentionally or not, prefigured a number of theoretical advances. Feminist standpoint theory has been developed as a means of valorizing the perspective of marginalized and otherwise "silenced" people and is used as a counterpoint to the more modeled positions of mainstream gender and development research.[50]

The academy continues to use its voice in the public and political arena in Senegal, where it has dared to be prescriptive and campaigning on issues of gender and development. In this respect it has operated largely in contrast to the state, which regularly over the decades tempered its language in deference to the religious right. During the era of the monopartism, the religious authorities and the state enjoyed a quasi-monopoly of power at the local level. In the 1990s, a new force emerged that attracted international backing and acquired an increasingly influential voice in the debate around gender and development.

The emergence of a civil society has altered the political landscape in Senegal and francophone Africa. This mass of social, political, economic, indigenous and exogenous forces has amalgamated over the past twenty years into the key player in the implementation of gender and development discourse in Senegal. The next chapter charts that rise to power.

NOTES

1. Discussions with academic colleagues were conducted primarily in Dakar from January 1998 through June 2010.

2. CODESRIA, the council for the development of social research in Africa, is funded by contributions from a number of African governments, Swedish, Danish and Canadian overseas aid, and the Rockefeller and Ford Foundations. It is located close to the Cheik Anta Diop University in Dakar and provides research facilities for students and social scientists.

3. AAWORD/*AFARD* is a pan-African organization with headquarters in Dakar and Naroibi.

4. I had to engage the help of an itinerant book finder/seller in Dakar to find a copy of this text, it was not available at any public point of sale.

5. Fatou Sow, Mamadou Diouf, and Guy le Moine, *Femmes Sénégalaises à l'horizon 2015* (Dakar: Ministère de la Femme/The Population Council, 1993).

6. Fatou Sow, Ngagne Diakhaté, Adama Fall-Touré, and Mamadou Matar Gueye, *Les Sénégalaises en Chiffres* (Dakar: PNUD, 2000).

7. United Nations Development Programme, the lead development organization in Senegal.

8. Sow et al., *Femmes Sénégalaises à l'horizon*, 173.

9. Sow et al., *Femmes Sénégalaises à l'horizon*, 11.

10. I am indebted to Dr. Fatou Sow for providing me with copies of this and *Femmes Sénégalaises à l'horizon 2015*.

11. *Femme et développement*/women in development.

12. It was published by the same UN agency that produces the annual Human Development Report.

13. Sow et al., *Les Sénégalaises en Chiffres*, 76. "The debate on women and power in society must start at the level of the family because this is where society defines gender distinctions. Men, women, children, old people, are all expected to play specific roles, and this affects the way they participate in their local community, in the wider economy, in their relations with the State, and more generally the role they play in development. So policies which aim at promoting gender equality and a better understanding of children's rights, need to address the question of how to get these aims working at the level of the family." Author's translation.

14. Sow et al., *Les Sénégalaises en Chiffres*, 79.

15. Sow et al., *Les Sénégalaises en Chiffres*, 33–34. "Women's bodies and their capacity to procreate have been appropriated by the community to the point that women believe they have a 'need' to produce children, and this identity is underpinned by the attribution of domestic roles. Society exercises a very strong hold over women in this regard." Author's translation

16. The term is something of a misnomer in the sense that births are almost invariably attended in Senegal either by a "traditional" birthing attendant or a midwife trained in the European manner.

17. *EDS (Enquête Démographique et de santé)*–lll.

18. Sow et al., *Les Sénégalaises en Chiffres*, 37.

19. The estimate being reported for the period 2000 to 2005 had dropped to 5.2 per woman aged 15–49. *Human Development Report 2007*, 245.

20. The Bush administration withdrew its support from reproductive health care programs early in the first term of office where it believed these programs were serving as a cover for practices for which it did not approve, such as termination of pregnancy.

21. United Nations, *The Millennium Development Goal Report 2009*, http://www.un.org, 31.

22. United Nations, *Millennium Development Goal Report*, 14–15.

23. Sow et al., *Les Sénégalaises en Chiffres*, 60. "Education is the starting point for personal and civic development. It not only produces knowledge and consciousness, it allows people to develop a sense of control over themselves and their environment." Author's translation

24. In France the role of the professional chef has traditionally been ranked on a par with the most physically demanding of jobs, such as coal mining.

25. Claire Robertson,"Women's Education and Class Formation in Africa," in *Women and Class in Africa*, Claire Robertson and Iris Berger, eds. (New York: African Publishing Company, 1986), 56–99.

26. Assie-Lumumba, Ndri Thérèse and CEPARRED, "Gender, Access to Learning and Production of Knowledge in Africa," in *Visions of Gender Theories and Social Development in Africa: Harnessing knowledge for social justice and equality* (Dakar: AAWORD Book Series, 2001), 95–113, [95].

27. Unpublished statistics provided by the Ministry of Education *Direction de la Planification et de la Reforme de l'Enseignement*, Dakar, Senegal.

28. Over thirty interviews were conducted with government education officials from various departments. Women officials were markedly more communicative regarding the reasons why girls were not in school, citing domestic chores and the lack of girls' toilets. It was explained that these facilities are particularly crucial to girls once they reach puberty. No men interviewed mentioned these practical issues.

29. Income statistics tend to report only on monetary income whereas the situation for women is often complex, involving different types and sources of income. Also women living in polygamous households may avoid disclosing the exact value of their income. See Sow et al., *Les Sénégalaises en Chiffres*, 122.

30. Sow et al., *Les Sénégalaises en Chiffres*, 123.

31. The study explains neither the nature of these transfers nor the reason for them.

32. A critical mass of women in politics has had an impact on political life in northern Scandinavia and recently there has been evidence supporting this theory from Rwanda.

33. My thanks to the Registry of the Université Cheikh Anta Diop de Dakar who provided statistics for UCAD and the Université Gaston Berger de Saint Louis.

34. Sow et al., *Les Sénégalaises en Chiffres*, 141.

35. Fatou Sarr, *Genre et Développement—atelier de formation,* (Dakar: UNIFEM/PNUD/SURF, 2002), 17.

36. Sow et al., *Les Sénégalaises en Chiffres*, 133.

37. Sow et al., *Les Sénégalaises en Chiffres*, 110.

38. Sow et al., *Les Sénégalaises en Chiffres*, 111.

39. Sow et al., *Les Sénégalaises en Chiffres*, 113.

40. Sow et al., *Les Sénégalaises en Chiffres*, 111.

41. Interviews at *INEADE*, Dakar, May 2002.

42. Marema Dioum Diokhane; Oumel Khairy Diallo; Alhousseynou Sy and Mafakha Touré, *Genre et Fréquentation scolaire dans l'enseignement élémentaire au Sénégal* (Dakar: Institute for Development Studies, University of Sussex/*Ministère de l'Education nationale*, October 1999).

43. The internally renowned African academic Fatima Mernissi was subjected to a hostile reception from a party of men on the occasion of a public lecture in Dakar, and local academic women likewise have reported threats of physical violence following public lectures.

44. Aminata Diaw, "Sewing machines or computers? Seeing gender in the institutional cultures at UCAD," *Feminist Africa*, no 9, 2007, 5–21.

45. Gender equality in the Academy is still a distant goal in most higher education institutions of the industrialized world.

46. *Institut fundamental de l'Afrique noire.*

47. "Girls are worth the same as boys."

48. In this regard CODESRIA launched a debate in 2008 on optimizing Internet publishing opportunities.

49. Benoîte Groult, *"Préface"* to *La Parole aux Négresses*, Awa Thiam (Paris: Denoel, 1978), iv.

50. An example of this is Patricia Hill Collins, "Learning from the Outsider Within: The Sociological Significance of Black Feminist Thought," in *The Feminist Standpoint Theory Reader: Intellectual and Political Controversies,* Sandra Harding, ed. (London: Routledge, 2004).

15

Voicing Dissent and Contesting Change in Civil Society

Since Independence in 1960, the women's movement in Senegal has engaged in negotiating a political space for itself beyond the postcolonial divide. Operating outside the formal political structures of the state, this space has grown immeasurably throughout the period. In the twenty-first century, civil society accommodates a spectrum of organizations, associations, lobbies, movements and groupings representing one of the major forces in francophone African development politics.

The flourishing of this force in the post–Cold War era owes much to a strategic alliance with the major paymaster of para-statal development policy, the international organizations. The following discussion looks at how the women's movement has succeeded in building on its international alliances to carve out a unique role for itself in civil society, thereby enabling a new set of independent voices to emerge and join the debate around women, gender and development in francophone Africa.

THE BIRTH OF THE NON-GOVERNMENTAL ORGANIZATION CULTURE

While the academic community has played its part in defining the modalities for change in postcolonial francophone Africa, and while the international development partners have played their role in funding policies for social change, a key impetus behind the implementation of that change has come from the women's movement operating through the many social, cultural and political organizations that emerged in post-independence Senegal. Between 1960 and 2000 over one hundred non-governmental organizations (NGOs) were formed in Senegal with the stated aim of advancing the socio-economic position of women in one form or another.[1] The sheer number of women's NGOs in Senegal sets it apart from other francophone countries in the region. The reason why Senegal has a particularly vibrant female civil society is the result of a combination of factors of which the following stand out as particularly relevant to this discussion.

THE ORIGINS OF THE WOMEN'S MOVEMENT

The political culture that excludes women from politics in Senegal is a relatively recent phenomenon and relates primarily to those institutions inherited from the colonial state. While the African elite that inherited power in 1960 has continued to exclude women from formal political structures, this same elite has demonstrated a relatively open and tolerant attitude toward civil society organizations. The confidence and stability of the *de facto* single-party state in Senegal under the presidencies of Léopold Sedar Senghor and Abdou Diouf derived in no small measure from the unwavering support it received from the Elysée Palace[2] for the first four decades of independent rule. It was in this relatively clement and secure political climate that structures to promote women's economic development were initially set up in the rural communities under the aegis of the ruling *Parti socialiste*. It is in these local structures that many of today's organizations have their roots.

The form female political participation has taken during the period since decolonization, and the degree of participation in civil society organizations, owes much to the way women are marginalized in formal political arena and to the cultural history of political participation in the region. In effect, women have defined a separate political arena from which they have shaped civil society politics while being unable to match this degree of involvement in party, parliamentary and governmental politics. In this sense there has been a clear separation between women's participation in civil society and their participation in the polity. This divide has its roots in gendered history of francophone Africa dating back to before the arrival of the colonizers.

WOMEN AND POLITICS: ACCESS DENIED?

While women have had very little access to the formal institutions of State power in recent history across the whole francophone region, prior to colonization the situation was far from uniform. Senegal has a history of female involvement in all levels and areas of decision-making including at the highest levels of statecraft. Indeed in some areas female involvement in politics, either in their own right or in collaboration with male counterparts, was a commonplace, an example being the Waalo State before its defeat by Faidherbe's forces in the mid nineteenth century.[3] Though scholarship in the field is still being developed, research shows that women living in the most westerly coastal area of West Africa in the pre-colonial era held a central role in the political system. In areas that are now part of modern Senegal women were key players both in the allocation and handing down of political power:

> *L'exercice du pouvoir n'était pas inconnu de la femme car pendant la période pré-coloniale dans l'espace soudanais (L'Afrique de l'Ouest), la transmission des droits politiques se faisait généralement par son canal (exemple des sociétés wolof et sereer).*[4]

Though women played key roles in the political systems of pre-colonial Africa, this does not suggest that political power was exercised by a mass of the female population. In common with European societies in the pre-modern era, women exercised political power largely through kinship and position in the social hierarchy:

> *A l'époque précoloniale, une élite féminine a émergé et a participé à la prise de décision au niveau le plus élevé. Mais force est de constater qu'elle n'a assuré ce leadership lié à sa position de classe que de manière exceptionnelle.*[5]

While there are still considerable gaps in our knowledge of how gender mediated access to political power in the pre-colonial era, there is little controversy over the impact colonization had on African women living under occupation. That impact would vary depending on where a woman lived and on her social status. The overall influence of colonization on the polity and economy of African nations was such that not even a remote rural village would be left unaffected by the arrival of the colonizer, and particularly the arrival of the French colonizer.

FROM ECONOMIC MARGINALIZATION TO POLITICAL MARGINALIZATION

The conditions within which a politicized women's movement took root in Senegal were determined by the nature of a colonization that centralized power within a male elite, and as a consequence, marginalized the majority both male and female. This marginalization had multiple consequences, experienced most intensely by the female population. As they became economically marginalized, their political status collapsed: "*Ignorées comme productrices car renvoyées aux cultures vivrières, les femmes furent également reléguées politiquement.*"[6]

The status of Senegalese women was further undermined by the formalization of gendered legal identities imposed on men and women across the French West Africa during the first half of the twentieth century. When Frenchwomen were allowed to participate in general elections for the first time in history following World War II, De Gaulle, as head of the consultative government and architect of the reform, had not thought to exclude African women from the extension of the franchise. However, the prospect of their enfranchisement provoked such consternation among some male African leaders that the Governor-General of French West Africa, Pierre Cournairie, sent a telegram to René Pleven, the Minister of the Colonies, on 12 October 1944 stating:

> *Sujets français musulmans sont émus par nouvelle que vote serait accordé aux femmes pour prochaines élections.* stop. *Ils déclarent la loi coranique ne le permet pas et que si réforme était étendue au Sénégal ils l'empêcherait par tous moyens.* stop.[7]

The telegram went on to say that the women, being by and large "illiterate," were incapable of voting. De Gaulle did not reform his bill to exclude women *de jure* from electing the deputies from the French African colonies to the French National Assembly, but he approved the introduction of conditions governing eligibility to vote which excluded them *de facto* from the process. As a result they were scarcely represented at all in the various categories of eligibility. After six years of campaigning by the Senegalese MP, Lamine Guèye, and a motion in the National Assembly tabled by Deputy Francine Lefebvre, a further category of eligibility was added and from 1951 an African woman who was married with at least two children would be allowed to vote regardless of educational status.[8] This exercise in social control was a way of incorporating only those women who appeared to be observing their traditional roles as mothers and homemakers, thus obviating the risk of including radical women in the electorate.

Not surprisingly, it was difficult for women to reach high office at this time. One of the few to rise to prominence, if not to a position of power, was Rose Basse. Without ever occupying a formal political role in her own right, this militant trade unionist worked her way up through the union ranks to become Lamine Gueye's secretary. Throughout the 1940s and 1950s, she had campaigned for the liberation of Senegal from French rule in the *Union démocratique sénégalaise (UDS),* the only party to establish a women's section. After Independence her political career, such as it was, came to an abrupt end. In 1963 Basse was imprisoned for supporting the presidential hopeful Mamadou Dia in his unsuccessful bid to replace Léopold Sedar Senghor as president.

Rose Basse was not typical of her time. There were very few women in the vanguard of Senegalese party politics in the final twenty years of French colonial rule. One of the co-founders of the *Union des femmes du Sénégal* (*UFS*), Jeanne M. Cissé, reported in an interview that her organization was affiliated to the French Communist Party but its founding statutes forbad women members from engaging in political debate! She recalled that when they had set up the union in 1954, it had been necessary to conceal its political motives.[9]

THE LIMITS OF POSTCOLONIAL POLITICAL PARTICIPATION

At the time Rose Basse was being imprisoned in 1963, the first woman was elected to the Senegalese National Assembly:

> Caroline Diop, a famous educator and great orator wielding substantial influence over the constituency, became involved in political activity as early as 1945. And yet, she was only elected and inducted as the first female member of the Senegalese parliament in 1963.[10]

Diop's election to parliamentary office was due to her impeccable credentials as a political campaigner but also to her support for Léopold Senghor. Her portrait now hangs in the *Musée de la Femme* on Gorée Island alongside other female firsts in their fields. The plaque commemorating "Women in Politics" sums up the ambiguities that surround Senegalese women as they operated in the inherited Western political systems that rule over postcolonial francophone Africa. The plaque states, in English:

> The political power of the women in Senegal has varied according to their community, their social position and their caste and class. Women have held the power of authority as well as the role of moderator.
>
>   They also have learned to be submissive. As the elite, they have played, at a high level, the role of transmitting and deciding political power. In the system of political duality common to African civilization which recognizes both women's power and men's power, women have left their mark. African and Senegalese history will retain the great achievements of women of all levels of society.

The apparent contradictions in this statement are echoed throughout this museum housed in the former residence of Victoria Albis, one of the most powerful business people of Gorée Island, who, along with subsequent generations of *Signares*, succeeded in confounding and scandalizing French colonial society for some two hundred years.[11] The wealth and position of these commercial operators declined abruptly in the nineteenth century, as they became increasingly integrated into French culture and society and their legendary power ebbed away.

The gradual marginalization and exclusion of women from the colonial economy was accelerated by the introduction of the politico-legal structures that defined Senegalese women as legal minors. The pre-colonial notion of political parity, alluded to in the *Musée de la femme* plaque, was implicitly revived by the *Parti socialiste*, in the 1970s with the introduction of a quota system of 25 percent of parliamentary seats to be held by women. However, in common with many of the exogenous "solutions" to gender and development issues explored in the earlier chapters, this measure failed to gain legitimacy among the local ruling elites and was never observed.

Indeed in the years following Independence the political elite were sending out confused messages about the role of women in postcolonial Senegal. The 1960s and 1970s saw the *Parti socialiste* adopting slogans such as "Every housewife must learn to run the country!" and proclaiming that:

> We will never achieve real freedom, we will never create a democracy and we will never build socialism without the participation of women in public service and political life and until we free women from the mind-numbing drudgery of housework and cooking![12]

At the same time the President of the Republic, Léopold Sédar Senghor, was railing against what he perceived as the falling standards of women in Senegalese society:

> We wonder at the number of broken families and divorces in our country. Why should this surprise us when husbands come home to find that their houses are not being kept as clean and tidy as their offices? Why should this surprise us if a wife is more interested in clothes and jewellery than in her own children, if a wife doesn't know how to sew on his buttons or polish his shoes, or if the little doll only opens her mouth to demand money? We know that a well-run house provides the best support for a household and essential assistance for national planning.
>
> Development is the primary goal of the Government of Senegal, and it is with this in mind that we are going to introduce a national programme of domestic skills training. It will form the basis of education for all young girls. The programme will be taught in women's training centres and in schools and colleges throughout the country.[13]

Three decades later, pressures to prioritize domestic duties and fulfill the roles of obedient housewife and homemaker had not disappeared from political rhetoric. In his New Year address of 2003, President Abdoulaye Wade proposed rural training centers where, providing their husbands permitted their attendance, women could learn childcare and hygiene.[14]

Though women have been effectively, if not legally, excluded from Western-style political structures such as the parliamentary debating chambers, their low participation in formal politics does not reflect a traditionally low-level of participation in other political structures. Joola women in the southern region of Ziguinchor have very low participation rates in national and local politics. However Joola women also have a long-established reputation for active involvement in local economic and labor politics.[15]

In regions where formal politics are inaccessible to women for cultural-religious reasons, women have opted to express political commitment through NGO activities. However as Sow et al. (2000) revealed, only twelve of the 109 women's NGOs registered with the Senegalese NGO council in 1999 were run by women.[16] The old colonial pattern of men running institutions, even those designed by and for women, was still the norm.

The area where women have been active in running their own affairs is in the *Groupements de promotion féminine (GPF)* set up by the state in the 1960s. By 1985 there were already 100,000 women involved in *GPF*s.[17] The *GPF*s gave women opportunities to develop management and networking skills. This initiative can be seen as an early contribution to the development of the relatively dynamic women's movement in Senegal reinforcing as it does the traditionally high levels of participation in community and village life. Though there are no formal records to confirm numbers, it is known that there are hundreds of thousands of women active in the *mbotaay*[18] and *dahira*[19] village associations throughout Senegal.[20]

PROSPECTS FOR CHANGE

Though women play an active part in rural and urban communities, the *Femmes Sénégalaises à l'horizon 2015* survey, conducted in 1992, revealed that the majority of the 1,000 interviewees expressed a need to be far more involved in the democratization process of their country valuing greater participation in formal politics as a key element in a long-term strategy for change in Senegal.

From the 1970s the WID, or *intégration de la femme au développement* approach, provided the dominant configuration for this change. In Senegal the government responded by attempting to integrate women into the economic development process, but in a way that would not destabilize existing social relations or change the (unequal) balance of power in society. This took the form of addressing practical needs:

> *des besoins pratiques . . . dans le cadre des structures existantes. [L'Etat] n'a jamais mis en cause ces structures. L'approche IFD n'a pas tenu compte des différences de classes, de race, de culture au sein de la société ou des stratifications et rapports d'exploitation entre les femmes elles-mêmes.*[21]

Recent schemes in Senegal to promote women in agriculture failed because they did not take into account of the fundamentals of neo-liberal capitalism by which economic agents need access to financial capital (women have little access to investment capital in Senegal) and access to the means of production, in this case access to land and labor to work that land. These practical issues have highlighted the WID dilemma for women in Senegal—the discourse is not culturally-located, nor is it adapted to take account of pre-existing structural biases. So long as a program is conceived as a specifically "women's issue" it remains divorced from the broader socio-economic context in which these policies are implemented.

The conservative tenor of the WID discourse articulated by the international community and by extension the state has modified since 1990 under the influence of the GAD/GED (*genre et développement*) discourse with its emphasis on the gendered nature of political and economic power in postcolonial society. While the gap between discourse and praxis is typically vast during the early formation of a policy discourse, changes in the political landscape have been announced in Senegal since 2000 that may influence the development of gender and development politics, notably through the decentralization of political decision-making structures. This is significant in that the normative barriers to local political power have been slightly more permeable than those that protect the national political arena. By opening up the decision-making structures to greater NGO participation, and by decentralizing some policy-making fields to the localities, the government has the opportunity to inject new impetus for change in gender policy-making in the twenty-first century.

MODELS OF CHANGE

This discussion of gender and development in Senegal began with a comment on the dynamism West African women have demonstrated in their protracted and not always successful bid for more political and participation equality.

Typically, they have expressed their desire for progress through civil society groups. However, NGOs and local community organizations can be conservative as much as they are radical, or can be a mixture of the two, and not all are campaigning for the same kind of change.

There has been a considerable rise in the number of religious NGOs in Senegal over the past 20 years funded by international development organizations based in the Gulf States where the gender and development agenda bears no relation to the dominant model that emerged from the world summits. This radicalization of civil society follows an earlier period of radicalization from a quite different cultural base, namely the women's movement that exploded onto the political scene in the United States and Europe in the late 1960s and 1970s. The discourse of power adopted by this movement had an impact worldwide and generated multiple opportunities for debate and exchange of ideas particularly during the international decade for women, 1975 to 1985. Senegal developed its own expression of this global movement through its indigenous campaigning organizations, the most prominent of which was *Yewwu-Yewwi PLF*[22] founded in 1984, and more recently the movement *Siggil Jigeen*.[23]

While the educated elite created *Yewwu-Yewwi* as the campaigning voice of the Senegalese women's movement, the grassroots were radicalized indirectly in response to global economic developments at this time. The economic crises that marked the late 1970s and the austerity measures that accompanied "structural adjustment" in the 1980s changed the relationship between the state and society insofar as the female population had to take up the responsibilities vacated by the state as a result of social expenditure cuts. Women's organizations multiplied and by the end of the decade found themselves working in a new political landscape.

As the relationship between the state and the donor community changed following the collapse of the Soviet Union, women's organizations found themselves in a more advantageous position vis-à-vis donor funding. In Senegal this led not only to a flourishing in the number of women's organizations after 1990—the year when the new state-donor relationship was confirmed for francophone Africa at the la Baule summit—but these organizations also became increasing powerful as magnets for external funding.

For the first time in the postcolonial era external funders were in competition with each other to influence gender policy in the former French-speaking colonies, and where French *coopération* failed to engage with the women in development discourse, the French Canadians were ready to fill the gap.

As well as attracting new sources of bilateral funding, women's organizations were also receiving a growing share of multilateral finance and funding from a relatively new operator in the field of African civil society, the international NGO.[24] Women's organizations coalesced only to a degree into a civil society movement in that many of them operated like Western pressure groups. They focused on single issues and competed for resources which undermined their ability to construct a common platform for change. The focus on practical outcomes drew attention away from the philosophical/ideological objectives of a politicized women's movement, reducing pressure for structural change, and the discourse remained resolutely within the WID framework.

While working within the WID framework progress was made on a range of issues. Furthermore the levels of activity and the legitimacy acquired by the civil society organization through association with powerful international partners allowed women's organizations to take the discourse into previously taboo areas. Gender-based violence and forms of discrimination previously ring-fenced by conservative forces as "authentically African" or Muslim, and beyond the limits of the discourse, were introduced into public debate. Domestic violence, child marriage, female genital mutilation, forced seclusions, bonded labor, sexual slavery, even the absence of female toilets in schools, have been brought out into the public arena by women's organizations.

Since 1990 these organizations have had a growing impact on the politico-legislative State.[25] Meanwhile the GAD (gender and development) approach to policy-making being proposed in the Academy and by some of the gender focal points in UN agencies has been slow in penetrating the policy-making arena not least because it requires from policy-makers a radical shift in thinking, a refocusing of attention from the signs of disadvantage to the causes of subordination:

> The GAD approach suffers from being more difficult to put into operation than the WID approach. In international development policy there is a growing tendency to use the vocabulary of GAD but the policies continue to be inspired by WID.[26]

Not surprisingly the 1,000 women interviewees in the *Femmes Sénégalaises à l'horizon 2015* survey in the early 1990s prioritized classic WID/*IFD* goals, with its focus on the actions of women as opposed to the transformation of structures. They spoke of access to literacy, greater participation in local politics, increased awareness of legal rights as priorities for policy-makers. For the most part these are variables that are going to improve women's contribution to development, and probably improve their quality of life too, but they do not have a direct impact on the balance of power or the reproduction of inequalities in society.

DEVELOPING MODELS FOR CHANGE

The academic community has engaged with these issues, often in collaboration with more intellectually-engaged members of the UN agency community and civil society organizations. When looked at as a sector, civil society has largely operated as a fragmented collection of single-issue groups. However the membership of women's organizations followed a different pattern from that seen in Western countries. In Senegal multiple affiliations among professional women are the norm and as such women who are members of the academy or political parties or work for international agencies are also prominent members of civil society women's associations. Women expect to fulfil several roles, and these include campaigning roles within political lobbies. As these women become increasingly numerous and vocal they are empowered to redefine the parameters of their political space and operating within a network of interests provides some shelter from the overwhelmingly male monopoly of the traditional vehicles of political expression, including the media, political parties and the state.

The political culture within which the debate takes place is commonly seen as hostile to women's issues. The press, headed by the official newspaper *Le Soleil*, has over the decades printed openly hostile and even misogynistic coverage of women's campaigns.[27] *Siggil Jigeen* and other women's groups excoriated the new regime for its conservative platform on gender issues during the 2000 presidential campaign and challenged the new government to convene a national forum. The government acceded to this demand. However, as evidenced by the other francophone African countries, national forums do not of themselves generate change. Gabon held in such a national forum on women's issues in 1994. Several dozen associations attended. In practice it provided a platform for one special interest group to neutralize another. The radical groups achieved little more than to let off steam while conservative organizations used the occasion to proselytize for a return to "traditional feminine values" (in this case Catholic). In fact state-sponsored initiatives of this type can serve to constrain, rather than promote, gender equality.

On the other hand, international forums operating outside the control of the State can offer a space for developing a discourse for change, provided they do not become so vast that they logistically outgrow their organizational competence. The World Social Forum, set up in Brazil in January 2001, was an attempt to provide this voice. The WSF has met on several occasions since to develop and articulate a global civil society position. Its official website illustrates some of the difficulties faced by international movements that do not benefit from the levels of financial and organizational support enjoyed by the bilateral and multilateral organizations that make up the international aid community.[28] Meanwhile, and notwithstanding these challenges, international civil society continues to provide a platform for NGOs to communicate with the international community.[29]

NURTURING THE SEEDS OF CHANGE

In Senegal, the seeds of change lie in structural developments taking place in the national and international political arena and in the gender equity debate itself. Political promises of widening participation continue to resonate with the public, but such structural reforms are slow to materialize. Where these are happening the NGO community is gaining more voice in the policy-making arena than in the past.

However the issue remains in Senegal, and in all regions of the world where patriarchal regimes still dominate the political landscape in the aftermath of European colonization, of how to enable women to use voice in ways that empower them. In the words of Marie-Angélique Savané,[30] speaking as guest of honor at the opening of a new women's hall of residence to women's studies in Dakar, "What you need is a big dose of self confidence to overcome an education which has taught you to be submissive and apathetic!"[31] Evidence suggests that not only does the new generation need to learn how to conceive of change in its own terms, but also to protect any *droits acquis* from the previous generation in a political landscape that defines itself in opposition to them.[32]

Civil society leaders in Senegal identified representation in politics and participation in policy-making as key issues in achieving gender equity, yet these aims are now rarely articulated in the twenty-first-century international development agenda. Improving access to education predominates in the discourse of the international community, the NGO community and the academic community, but the case of Senegal reveals how complex this situation is where access to education is not necessarily the guarantor of either a job or relative independence.

The national discourse and debate in Senegal around issues of gender equity demonstrates how the international community has provided a politically-sanctioned agenda within which these issues can be discussed. However, the discourse inherited from the international community has tended to be viewed as the sole paradigm for action and policy-making, rather than as a starting point for discussion. The political center (national or international) monopolizes the formative debate confining women's organizations to the margins and making it more difficult for women's voices to be heard in their own environment and in their own words.

The following chapter takes up this issue of accessing alternative visions of gender and development, turning to a largely unexploited source of information on social change. Taking as its starting point the work of francophone African social realist writers, it explores how women writers have identified and deconstructed the issue of gender inequality in their communities, using the literary form as the vehicle of political expression and the narrative text as the discourse for change.

NOTES

1. *CONGAD, Répertoire des organisations non gouvernementales membres du Conseil des organisations non gouvernementales d'appui au développement* (Dakar: CID/CONGAD, 2000).

2. The political cohabitation of President Jacques Chirac and Prime Minister Lionel Jospin in 1997 was the exception to this rule, Jospin favoring a more hands-off approach to "la Françafrique" while President Chirac was allegedly reinforcing the relationship. The allegations surfaced during the final run-up to the presidential election of March 2000, when it became clear that President Diouf might not be re-elected. The appearance of French marketing experts in the Diouf camp was attributed to an intervention from Gaullist party headquarters in Paris.

3. Fatou Sarr, *La Reconstruction du Mouvement social féminin africain et la production d'une pensée politique liée à la lutte des femmes* (unpublished, n.d.), 14.

4. Seynabou Ndiaye Sylla, *Femmes et Politique au Sénégal*, Mémoire de DEA (Université de Paris 1, 2001), 12. "The exercise of political power was not unknown to women in the Sudanese region before colonization. The inheritance of political rights passed down through the female side, as was the case, for example, among the Wolof and Serer." Author's translation.

5. Sow et al., *Les Sénégalaises en chiffres*, 144. "During the pre-colonial period a female elite emerged that participated in decision-making at the highest level. Nevertheless, we have to recognize the fact that women leaders were the exception rather than the rule and their power was class-based." Author's translation.

6. Sylla, *Femmes et Politique*, citing Odile Goerg in *Femmes d'Afrique* (Paris: Broché, 1998), 16. "The role women had played in production was overlooked and so they became relegated to providing subsistence agriculture. Likewise their political position was downgraded." Author's translation.

7. Saliou Mbaye and Jean Bernard Lacroix, "Le vote des femmes au Sénégal," *Revue Ethiopiques,* no. 6, 1970, 29. "French Moslem subjects concerned by news that women will vote in upcoming elections. stop. They say Koranic law doesn't allow it & if reform extended to Senegal will do all in their power to prevent it. Stop." Author's translation.

8. Aissatou Sow Dia, *L'Evolution des femmes dans la vie politique sénégalaise de 1945 à nos jours,* Mémoire de maîtrise, Département d'Histoire, Université Cheik Anta Diop, 1994–1995, 26.

9. Jeanne Cissé quoted in Dia, 60.

10. Babacar Fall, "Forced labor and labor laws in French West Africa 1900–1946," *Social History in French West Africa* (Amsterdam/India: SEPHIS/CSSSC, 2002).

11. Jean Delcourt, *Gorée—Six siècles d'histoire* (Dakar: Editions ClairAfrique, 1984), 54.

12. Katy Cissé Wone, "Idéologie socialiste et Féminisme d'Etat au Sénégal: de Senghor à Abdou Diouf,' 10ème Assemblée Générale du CODESRIA, 8 au 12 décembre 2002, Kampala/Ouganda, 2. Author's translation. "*Chaque cuisinière doit apprendre à gouverner l'Etat! . . . Il est impossible d'assurer la vraie liberté, il est impossible de bâtir même la démocratie et encore moins le socialisme, sans la participation des femmes aux fonctions publiques, à la vie politique, sans les arracher à l'ambiance abrutissante du ménage et de la cuisine!*"

13. Wone (2002), 3. Author's translation. " *. . . On s'étonne de l'instabilité de nos foyers, de la fréquence des divorces dans notre pays. Rien d'étonnant si le mari ne trouve pas, chez lui, l'ordre et la propreté de son bureau. Si la femme est plus préoccupée de ses boubous et de ses bijoux que de ses enfants, si elle ne sait pas coudre un bouton ou cirer des chaussures ? Si la poupée n'ouvre la bouche que pour réclamer de l'argent. Comme vous le voyez, l'art ménager est le meilleur soutien du foyer, l'auxiliaire indispensable de la planification. C'est pourquoi, le gouvernement du Sénégal dont la seule politique est le développement, entend introduire l'enseignement ménager partout, pour en faire la base de l'éducation de nos jeunes filles : dans les centres d'apprentissage féminins, dans les cours complémentaires, dans les lycées et collèges.*"

14. Published in *Le Soleil*, 3 January 2003. This example of a return to patriarchal values is noted in Fatou Sarr, *Op cit* (unpublished, n.d.), 28.

15. Sow et al., *Les Sénégalaises en chiffres*, 159.

16. Sow et al., *Les Sénégalaises en chiffres*, 172.

17. *Ministère de la Femme de l'Enfant et de la Famille* (1994), p.3.

18. A Wolof rural association

19. A Muslim institution

20. Sow et al., *Les Sénégalaises en chiffres*, 172.

21. Fatou Sarr and Fatou Sow, *Atelier de formation "Genre et développement"* (45pp, Dakar, UNIFEM-UNDP-SURF, Juin 2003), 22. "[The State has addressed] practical needs within the framework of existing structures. It has never questioned these structures. The WID approach confronts neither issues of class, race and culture in society nor the way in which lower-class women are exploited by women from higher classes." Author's translation.

22. *Yewwi Yewwu pour la liberation de la femme* is the longest running and most prominent of the national women's campaigning organizations in Senegal.

23. *Siggil Jiggeen* (Women rise up! in Wolof) presents itself as different from older organizations by representing economically and politically marginalized women in urban Senegal.

24. These international non-governmental organizations include major players in the African development arena, such as the Bill and Melinda Gates Foundation.

25. In the wake of intense advocacy, the law on female genital excision changed in December 1999 outlawing the practice throughout Senegal. Tostan, an international NGO based in Senegal played a key role in the anti-FGM movement.

26. Sarr and Sow, *Atelier de formation*, 22. Author's translation. *"Le GED . . . se confronte à un problème d'operationnalisation. Ainsi dans le champ particulier du développement international, même [que] l'expression GED se substitue progressivement à celle de l'IFD, paradoxalement les projets et programmes de développement continuent à s'inspirer de l'approche IFD."*

27. "Debates on feminism in Senegal: visions vs nostalgia," *ECHO (AAWORD newsletter)*, vol. 1, no. 2–3, 1986, 9–10.

28. In August 2010 the official website for the World Social Forum 2011 due to be held in Dakar, Senegal, 6–11 February 2011, was still under construction. The 2011 homepage presented the aims of the Forum as—To consolidate the capacities of analysis, proposal and mobilization of the organizations of the African social movement so that they can fully play their part in Africa and within the world social movement.—To build an African space of concerted development of alternatives to neo-liberal globalization, starting from a diagnosis of its social, economic and political effects.—To define strategies of social, economic and political rebuilding, including a redefinition of the role of the State, market and organizations citizens (sic).—To define the methods of control citizen (sic) so that political alternation supports the expression and the implementation of alternative answers, credible and viable.

Though clearly not written by a mother-tongue English speaker, most readers would have little difficulty accessing the intended meanings of these objectives. On the other hand, the introductory paragraph uses language and syntax that are quite foreign to mainstream international development discourse. Speaking of the WSF it states: ". . . 'Another world is possible' said this voice which real clamour, rose toward the sky. It was for the happiness of damned of the ground that we are we African. Overexploited, on involved in debt and marginalized, our voices also are choked, our standardized pain, our blocked fights. But on the few fourteen thousand participants in the World Social Forum, Africa, although run up against full whip by the neo-liberal reforms, was represented only by one about fifty people . . .". *www .fsm2011.org/en/wsf-2011*. Accessed 08/12/2010.

29. The francophone West African campaigning organization "No-Vox" (www .no-vox.org) is an example of the use national and regional NGOs can make of this platform.

30. Founding member of the *Yewwu-Yewwi pour la libération de la femme*, also referred to as Marie-Angélique Sanga.

31. Author's translation. *"[U]ne grande dose d'assurance et de confiance en soi car l'éducation vous oblige à la soumission et à l'apathie."* The hall of residence is named after a heroine of the anti-colonial movement, Aline Sitoé Diatta. The event was reported in the Senegalese daily press in March 2003.

32. "The postcolony is a world of anxious virility. . . . The unconditional subordination of women to the principle of male pleasure remains one of the pillars upholding the reproduction of the phallocratic system." Mbembe, "Provisional Notes," 9.

VI

WRITING GENDER AND DEVELOPMENT: CULTURE, CONTEXT AND CHANGE IN FRANCOPHONE AFRICA

16

The Literary Politics of Gender and Development

As Panagiotis Christias argues in his essay *"Du littéraire et du social—le double: recherche pour une métaodon,"*[1] academics have long been using sociology to analyse literature, but social scientists have been far less inclined to make this disciplinary leap and allow literature to illuminate their explorations of sociological phenomena. Indeed as Bertrand Ricard has pointed out, in the past those who dared to bridge the disciplinary gap ran the risk of encountering a reactionary backlash from their peers:

> *Les rares sociologues qui s'aventurent à utiliser des références littéraires pour étayer leurs thèses se font renvoyer dans les cordes en se faisant traiter d'essayistes.*[2]

However, as both argue persuasively, the voices calling for greater interdisciplinarity in sociological research and for the incorporation of literary analysis have become increasingly numerous and their reasoning is compelling, summarized here in the following three arguments:

1. It is neither rational nor possible to separate the literary and the sociological worlds as the one exists in the other.
2. The rise and fall in the popularity of literary genres reflect changes in society as much if not more than they reflect changes of a specifically literary nature;
3. Literary reconstructions of social phenomena enable the reader to view society at a multiplicity of levels, revealing the world portrayed in the story as a "mosaic of experiences."

That the social world is constructed from a plurality of "truths" and perceptions is accepted knowledge in literary production and analysis, while the implications of this knowledge have been slower to permeate academic sociology. As Richard explains:

> *La littérature peut servir le sociologue à relativiser, à montrer la pluralité des «petites vérités», à faire comprendre la quantité des émotions, au sens "phéno-ménologique" qui nous anime au quotidien.*[3]

Quoting Ernst Jünger's dictum that the writer's task is not to invent something new, but rather to impose order on what is, Ricard argues that what the reader receives from the text is not just the ordering of the world into a recognisable facsimile of reality, but rather an expressive understanding and interpretation of that world. The potential for politically-engaged literature to connect deeply with social trends and phenomena has allowed it to present and explore social changes that will subsequently be identified by sociology:

> *La littérature peut alors revêtir l'aspect de ce que Dantec qualifie de "labora-toire anthropologique experimental." [. . .] C'est à ce prix que certains pion-niers (Proust, Musil, Joyce) ont réussi à devancer les changements sociaux. [. . .] Pour comprendre le présent, l'écrivain d'aujourd'hui doit saisir les enjeux de cette "modification" anthropologique.*[4]

It is this potential in literature that allows writers from francophone Africa to explore the social position of women in a context that enables experimentation in the sense Dantec intended, and giving voice to women who have found themselves otherwise marginalized. The use of this experimental space has proved crucial to the development of literature in other parts of the continent, including francophone North Africa: "the Maghrebian Francophone novel is [. . .] a new site of comprehension and knowledge," where women writers are using the fictional form because "[t]hese new sites of comprehension are imperative for the development of a new feminism that operates on a politi-cally active platform."[5]

The novel provides the platform for expressing a multiplicity of positions that, in the case of feminist literature, can articulate the aspirations and goals women hold for their futures. The narrative must also contain the expression of the non-radical, the conventional everyday realities against which the radical voice can be heard and the experimental reality can be viewed. Paul Ricoeur in *le Temps raconté* (1985)[6] describes story (*récit*) as the guardian of "*le tiers temps*" or "*le temps humain*" where "*le vécu quotidien*" is contained outside the limits of either cosmic or historical time. He speaks of the inextricability of story and daily life as:

l'enracinement du récit dans le vécu quotidien, du logos fragmenté de la fiction d'un roman au Dire, instigateur et origine à la fois de l'histoire et de la fiction.[7]

It is primarily this reasoning that guides the discussion in this chapter. In no sense is the dimension of analysis adopted here an attempt to replace social science. Indeed arguments that fail to differentiate between what literature can contribute to our understanding of the way society organizes itself and operates, as distinct from what we may assume quantitative and qualitative methods of social science enquiry can hope and aim to reveal, are not comparing like with like.[8] A critique that does not allow for the potential of multi-methodology is ignoring fundamental developments in social science methodology that came in the wake of the poststructuralist examination of Western knowledge systems. These methodological advances have been integrated into a range of social science approaches and notably into feminist standpoint theory providing a gender perspective on the cultural location of knowledge from a gender perspective.[9] Literary analysis offers an avenue for developing standpoint theory by providing a cultural space in which to ground the *"petites réalités"* of socio-political analysis. Indeed integrating literary representations of gender disadvantage within a broader analysis of the impact of political responses on the individual in society reflects an appreciation of the "mosaic" of experience that makes up the reception of a policy on a target population and, crucially, it reflects how gender and disadvantage are experienced, as opposed to observed, in society.[10]

Social development policy for women in developing countries is largely formulated at the international level, as we have seen, on the basis of observational theories developed in international organizations and Western research centers. The international discourse on gender disadvantage and the policy responses that flow from this theorizing have constituted a social development "package" which has been disseminated and, in the absence of any alternative, widely assimilated at the African regional level. For equally pragmatic reasons, this discourse has been assimilated at the national level into countrywide responses to persistent poverty and deprivation in francophone Africa. As the case of Senegal shows, the position of women in society has a permanent position on the national political agenda. The issue has attracted millions of dollars in international development assistance and the birth of literally hundreds of organizations. Throughout these decades of activity, knowledge on the factors determining and influencing the exclusion of women from social development, has been based primarily on quantitative research with the result that there remain significant gaps in the qualitative knowledge base. The discussion here addresses the most significant gap in the qualitative knowledge base, that of the *petites réalités,* or the lived experience, of gender and development policy in the region as it has evolved over the past four decades. And for this we turn to African feminist literature.

Literature can be integrated into a social science project using methodologies that start either with a broad review of feminist creative writing or a selective approach to texts. Depending on the scope of the research a comprehensive overview of every work published in the field, in the country or during a particular era may be required. However, the objective here is determined by a social science rationale that defines the specific research object—factors affecting gender and development in francophone West Africa—as the point of departure, as opposed to developments in a literary system or practice. Consequently, a tight selection of texts that respond to the key questions has constituted the point of departure for this methodology. In the selection of texts studied here, the production of each text is culturally located in francophone Africa, as is its publication and reception. (The readership of any text written in an international language such as French will never be restricted solely to its point of origin, but the criterion here is that the text must be conceived of and distributed primarily in the francophone West African population.) Combined with the first criterion is the requirement that the text explicitly addresses the issue of gender, development and the impact of contemporary development discourse and praxis on francophone African women today.

The selection of works contribute to the debate on gender in francophone African society by incorporating new voices and new perspectives into the debate on gender disadvantage and policy responses in francophone Africa, and by offering an insight into whether the dominant discourse on gender in social development reflects lived experiences of gender relations in society at the level of the individual as opposed to the numerical aggregates used in the evaluation of policy up to this point.

On that basis, the discussion in this chapter revolves around feminist writers and literary texts that have been written with the explicit intention of communicating women's experience of gender disadvantage in their specific social and cultural contexts.

This discussion also serves a literary purpose which will be addressed here before moving into the social analysis. The discussion of women's experience of development is not starting from a *tabula rasa* but rather from an existing literary knowledge foundation based on texts that purported to represent the roles, functions and even experiences of African women in society. These texts are excluded from the selection of texts that inform the sociological analysis where it can be demonstrated that they are neither culturally located nor capable of accommodating a gender-sensitive perspective on sociological change and development.

AFRICAN WOMEN IN THE LITERARY TEXT— PAST AND PRESENT

In the colonial era, literary representations of West African women were uniformly constructed from a position outside their social experience. These literary presentations not only failed to engage with the lived cultural experience of African women but were also constructed in sites geographically remote from the realities of African women's lives. In most cases, publications on Africa and African people were the opinions, observations and interpretations of Western white male authors. Not surprisingly, portrayals of African women in colonial literature reflected little of the social realities of women's lives at the time. At the hands of the even the most gifted literary writers of their era, female African characters occupied the shadows, remaining passive until activated by the needs of the plot or the male characters. Joseph Conrad constructs Kurtz's lover in *Heart of Darkness* as a dark, hidden, silent figure, whose soul and spirit we are not required to know or enquire about.[11] Where women are given a more active role, it is to serve the purposes of the author and the men consuming these literary figments of the authorial imagination in extraordinary contexts. At the height of French colonial expansion in West Africa, this trend was exemplified by the lurid tales of French naval officer Julien Viaud, who was providing a largely European readership extraordinary tales from the French overseas territories under the *nom de plume* Pierre Loti. Loti's presentation of the "native" woman as an exotic and erotic creature emerged from a tradition established earlier in the century. Gone were the mature voluptuous women of earlier European "Orientalist" movements with their glimpses into imaginary private worlds of Asian and African women in their baths or harems, or in public spaces as servants, sex workers, and slaves. In Loti's hands it was as often female children rather than women who became the erotic interest of the novels and the focus of his readers' sexual fantasies:

> [T]he basic plot consists of the arrival of the European (usually Loti himself) in some foreign land, and a brief usually passionate relationship with a native girl, . . . He approaches native women in the same way as a landscape or a village street: he enjoys what he can on a sensual basis, conceptualises his experience as far as possible in terms of his imported ideology, and discards the rest as "incomprehensible."[12]

The aspirations, frustrations, achievements and disappointments of African women working twelve to sixteen hours a day cultivating crops, gathering food, fetching water, caring for children, cooking and cleaning appeared nowhere in this literary genre apart that is from those texts that reinforced a European configuration of the African woman as slave, as in Loti's characterization of Fatou Gaye in *Le Roman d'un Spahi*[13] set in French West Africa. Fatou Gaye displays an animal-like devotion to her lover, Jean, whom she treats more like her master and, emulating the faithful slave of antiquity, commits suicide over his body when he loses his life in a military manœuvre.

This is not to argue that these texts have no sociological or historical value. Loti's popular genre was responding to a growing sociological phenomenon in French society during the nineteenth century, where the constraints governing male and female sexuality within Catholic bourgeois society provoked an explosion in demand for texts offering vicarious transgressive sexual encounters. However, while colonial literature of this type may be highly illuminating within a study of European male sexuality, its usefulness in an exploration of African women's experience of gender relations is doubly thwarted. In her seminal essay "Under Western Eyes,"[14] Chandra Mohanty reminds us that portrayals of colonized populations in colonial texts are not only manifestations of an explicitly masculinist (and invariably anti-feminist) discourse, but further served the imperialist venture by reinforcing its justification for subjugating the local populations. Women who are characterized as being less than human do not need to be treated like human beings, and any such treatment becomes an expression of the colonizer's greater humanity and generosity rather than the right of the individual. This less than human quality is exemplified in *Le Roman d'un Spahi*. Loti describes his African mistress whose hands *"lui causait, malgré lui, une vilaine impression froide de pattes de singe . . . ces doigts teintés mi-partie, avait quelque chose de pas humain qui était effrayant."*[15]

As there was little factual reporting on Africa to temper the overwrought imaginings of the literary elite, the images of the Oriental and African woman came to Europe largely unchallenged. African literature written by Africans began to emerge in the early part of the twentieth century and with it came new literary representations of African women. One of the first African texts to present a woman as the principal character was Paul Hazoumé's *Doguimici* of 1938, the tale of a devoted African wife who, on the death of her husband, kills herself.[16] Though the eponymous heroine is supposed to be the main protagonist, it is a male character, Doguimici's husband, who controls the course of the narrative and ultimately the fate of this woman.

AFRICAN MYTHS OF WOMANHOOD

Doguimici was the forerunner of a generation of women characters whose idealization constituted a mythic vision of African "womanhood." The poetry of the first President of post-colonial Senegal, Léopold Sédar Senghor, carried this tradition forward into the postcolonial era. He remains among the most widely read exponents of ideal mythic womanhood, his *Femme noire* being the most famous hymn in this trope of woman as a repository for the values and ethics of an ideal traditional African society and culture in a form that can be read as an essentializing eroticization of feminity:

> *Femme nue, femme noire*
> *Vétue de ta couleur qui est vie, de ta forme qui est beauté*
> *J'ai grandi à ton ombre; la douceur de tes mains bandait mes yeux*
> *Et voilà qu'au coeur de l'Eté et de Midi,*
> *Je te découvre, Terre promise, du haut d'un haut col calciné*
> *Et ta beauté me foudroie en plein coeur, comme l'éclair d'un aigle*
> *Femme nue, femme obscure*
> *Fruit mûr à la chair ferme, sombres extases du vin noir, bouche qui fais lyrique ma bouche*
> *Savane aux horizons purs, savane qui frémis aux caresses ferventes du Vent d'Est*
> *Tamtam sculpté, tamtam tendu qui gronde sous les doigts du vainqueur*
> *Ta voix grave de contralto est le chant spirituel de l'Aimée*
> *Femme noire, femme obscure*
> *Huile que ne ride nul souffle, huile calme aux flancs de l'athlète, aux flancs des princes du Mali*
> *Gazelle aux attaches célestes, les perles sont étoiles sur la nuit de ta peau.*
> *Délices des jeux de l'Esprit, les reflets de l'or ronge ta peau qui se moire A l'ombre de ta chevelure, s'éclaire mon angoisse aux soleils prochains de tes yeux.*
> *Femme nue, femme noire*
> *Je chante ta beauté qui passe, forme que je fixe dans l'Eternel*
> *Avant que le destin jaloux ne te réduise en cendres pour nourrir les racines de la vie.*[17]

A large plaque bearing the poem dominates a display of women's cultural and literary achievements in post-colonial Senegalese society in the *Musée de la femme Henriette Bathily* on Gorée Island. The presence of this poem brings to mind Christopher Miller's comment in *Theories of Africans* where Senghor is described as placing himself "in a godlike position of promoting

woman to eternal status."[18] Senghor felt himself able to speak for generations of African women as he demonstrated when he famously claimed that
the African woman did not need to be liberated, she had been free for many
thousand of years. At the time he made this pronouncement the patriarchal
character of his words was largely obscured by a more pressing need to
address the low political, social and cultural status to which all but a small
elite of African women had fallen during colonization of the occupied territories of West Africa. While colonial ideology had classed African men
as less culturally and socially developed than European men, it had at least
allowed them to "improve" themselves through French education and gain
French citizenship. Women were categorized as a separate class of citizens,
occupying a position too far down the social and cultural scale for such aspirations. The recognition of their cultural and historic status by the *Négritude* poets—while bearing no relation to the reality of women's lives—was
nevertheless appreciated by this generation of women in the last decades of
colonial rule. The juxtaposition of Senghor's poem with feminist texts[19] in
the *Musée de la femme* offers a foretaste of the conceptual diversity gender
and development discourses will subsequently develop in the francophone
African context.

AFRICAN LITERARY WOMEN IN THE POSTCOLONIAL ERA

In an attempt to create an alternative African vision for women, African
intellectual history entered a new phase in the postcolonial era with regional
gender perspectives challenging standardized "Western" models. Within
these schools of thought, Western modes of promoting the status of women
in society were characterized as adversarial and against the nature of "African
culture."[20] While the *Négritude* movement's idealized version of women, typified by Senghor, has been characterized as sexist by subsequent generations
of male and female African writers (Mariama Bâ was among the first to reject
this image as erroneous[21]), stereotypes of African women and ideas resting
on essentialist notions of African "womanhood" have continued to feature
strongly in postcolonial African literature and social research. Florence Stratton has illustrated—with copious evidence from postcolonial African male
writing[22]—how women characters still function as representatives of qualities
and values. The homeland, law, tradition, fertility, the African state, the cor-
rupt nation, have all found an allegorical host in the female form. Commenting on one of the most venerated novels in the African literary canon, Chinua
Achebe's *Things Fall Apart*, she notes:

The critical silence on the work's sexism can be attributed to the same cause as that to which Achebe assigns responsibility for the silence on Conrad's racism (Heart of Darkness): sexism is such a normal way of thinking that its manifestations go completely undetected.[23]

Furthermore African writers, among them Wole Soyinka and Ousmane Sembène, noted that these tropes emanate from the essentially European intellectual device of Manichean or binary oppositions.[24] The concept of "womanhood" in the European literary tradition in Africa is articulated as "that which is not male." In this discourse, men are active, rational, articulate and practical. Female means passive, emotional, quiet, and allegorical.

Sembène recognized the European intellectual traditions that were uncritically adopted by earlier generations of African writers, and indeed by himself in his short story *La Noire de . . .* of 1962, a critique of Senghor's continued subservience to France after Senegal gained independence in 1960. In this novel Diouana, a Senegalese servant girl, fulfills the allegorical function of representing Senegal under Senghor's rule. Rather than branching out on her own when Independence comes to Senegal, Diouana remains the servant of her French family and returns with them to France. Overcome by a sense of alienation and misery, she eventually takes her own life.[25]

Though Stratton's analysis of African male writers has been condemned as "Western" and wrong-headed by several African male, and some female, critics,[26] Chinua Achebe subsequently acknowledged her critique of female characterization in *Things Fall Apart* and rectified this in his later work *Anthills of the Savannah*.[27]

Meanwhile in most postcolonial African literature by men, African women characters have consistently been reduced to a few representative types:

1. "The Mother" who silently and passively fulfills her destiny to bear many children and devote her life to nurturing husband and family;
2. "Mother Africa" who personifies an idealized notion of Africa as a supine female body, raped by the colonizer, and awaiting retribution or fulfillment at the hands of the new African (male) political elite; and
3. the Prostitute, an ubiquitous trope in African post-colonial writing signifying betrayal or depravity.

Though the female prostitute character has been a widely accepted trope in fiction and film, in Africa just as it is in mainstream Western culture, it has rarely been used in women's creative writing and where it is used, the woman often occupies the traditional role of the passive "deviant," or the victim who serves to highlight the righteousness of the woman who follows a more conventional path and becomes an obedient wife and mother. When the francophone Cameroonian writer Calixthe Beyala cast the heroine of *Tu t'appelleras Tanga* (1988) in the role of a teenager prostituted by her mother, the work caused a scandal among the francophone African reading public. In Senegal a committee of women formed to organize a public denunciation of Calixthe Beyala and her works even attempting to get her works banned from bookshops.[28]

Nigerian writer Wole Soyinka's has described "woman's function" in African development as one of "collaboration in man's vision." Soyinka went so far as to assume that African women were happy to comply.[29] This assumption is enlightening insofar as it reveals how male writing uses literature to communicate an ideology of gender supremacy in African society through the effective colonization and silencing of female characters. It is an approach to creative writing that denies agency on the grounds of gender. It brings to mind Gayatri Spivak's warning about the colonial tendencies of postcolonial indigenous elites:

> Between colonialism and indigenous patriarchy the figure of the woman disappears, not into pristine nothingness, but into a violent shuttling which is the displaced figuration of the third-world woman, caught between tradition and modernization.[30]

While Soyinka claims that African women are happy to co-operate in man's vision for Africa, not all African women support this view. Indeed some have articulated the view that where men speak for women, they condemn the latter to a position of inferiority:

> *Les forces traditionnelles se refusent à évoluer et s'obstinent à maintenir la femme dans une condition subalterne. . . . En prenant la plume les femmes africaines transgressent ainsi une loi tacite de leurs sociétés. Par l'écriture, elles signent leur premier acte de rébellion contre ces sociétés qui ont toujours fait d'elles de simples spectatrices.*[31]

While post-colonial literature by African male writers has characterized African women in ways that accommodate the realities of the cultural location, these realities have been defined without reference to the lived experience of the female characters.

As such this wider and culturally located use of female characters did not result in any sustained engagement with the gendered realities of francophone West African society. It has therefore been left to African women to take up this challenge.

THE EMERGENCE OF FRANCOPHONE
AFRICAN WOMEN'S WRITING

In her illuminating overview of women's literature in Francophone Africa, *"La percée des femmes dans le roman de mœurs africain,"*[32] Lilyan Kesteloot stressed the impact of the lack of access to formal education, the *"analphabétisme programmé"* of the French colonial era. At Independence in 1960 barely one in ten African women residing in the former French African empires could read and write in French. The legacy of this discrimination is seen in the significant gap in the number of boys and girls attending high schools and colleges in contemporary francophone Africa and the significant difference in literacy levels among men and women.

As the vast majority of girls were excluded from the education system in the colonial era, so women were also virtually excluded from the French-dominated literary system between 1920, when first literary text by a francophone African writer was published in French (Ahmadou Mapaté Diagne's *Les Trois Volontés de Malic*[33]) and the 1970s, when the first wave of novels by francophone African women writers were published. But even in the 1970s, African women writers found themselves subject to literary constraints created in the colonial era. The most famous novelist of her generation, Aminata Sow Fall, had to wait until 1976 to see her first novel in print. The publication of *Le Revenant* was held up for three years at the publisher[34] because the editor at *NEAS* did not think the subject matter would interest a European audience.[35]

Since this time the subject matter of the African novel has been more securely anchored in its own cultural location. But the legacy of colonization continues to exert an influence over the expression of cultural identity.

The reconstruction of identity in the post-colonial era has been fraught with tensions, as writers confronting the rapidly changing environment seek to disentangle the ideological roots of their reconstructive theories, separating the West from Africa, the colonial from the postcolonial, the modern from the traditional. Just as women everywhere in the world have struggled to apply feminist theories in ways that can work in their relationships and their environments, African women have their own struggle to articulate alternative roles and identities for women in modern African societies. In an interview with Barbara Harrell-Bond in 1980, Mariama Bâ explained how this struggle is usually conducted in a hostile environment: *"Dans toutes les cultures, la femme qui revendique ou proteste est dévalorisée"* she noted.[36] But she went on in the interview to lay down a feminist challenge to women in her society to articulate their experience of gender discrimination through writing:

*Plus qu'ailleurs, le contexte social africain étant caractérisé par l'inégalité
criante entre l'homme et la femme, par l'exploitation et l'oppression séculaires
et barbares du sexe dit faible, la femme-écrivain a une mission particulière.
Elle doit, plus que ses pairs masculins, dresser un tableau de la condition de la
femme africaine.*[37]

This expression of the political responsibility of fictional authorship is an
illustration of what Derrida would later argue linked fiction to the history
of democracy.[38] Meanwhile in this same interview Bâ would go on to state
that she was not a theorist or a "feminist," illustrating how in West Africa,
as elsewhere, the term "feminist" has become a label to mark women as socially unacceptable rather than as politically active in the pursuit of women's
advancement. Furthermore in francophone African context, "feminist" has
acquired a cultural stigma and as such can be used to point the finger at a
woman (and sometimes a man) who has abandoned African culture and adopted "Anglo-American" values.[39]

Language has constituted another aspect of the colonial legacy African
women writers have had to confront in their search for an authentic African
female literary voice. From the perspective of an Anglophone Cameroonian,[40]
Nfah-Abbenyi presents "Western" feminism as a culturally-specific ideology
intrinsically and irrevocably separate from the "African" understanding of
feminism.[41] Arguing that literary representations of women by women before
1980 were rare and largely ignored,[42] she looks at recent Anglophone and
francophone African women's writing as a body of work with a common
identity that transcends the colonial language legacy. To support this view
that the language of expression is irrelevant when set alongside the com-
munality of African women's experience she quotes Mariama Bâ: "there is a
fundamental unity in our sufferings and in our desire for liberation."[43] Others
argue that writing in a European language presents irreconcilable problems
for the African writer in terms of the ability of the one to express cultural and
philosophical concepts of the other. Indeed of the five key issues confronting
the study of contemporary African philosophy, Sam Oluoch Imbo posits the
language question as among the most intractable.[44] For the African feminist
writer the problems assume a further political significance in relation to form
and space: *"Ce contexte d'émergence renferme un topos, celui du silence,
délimite un espace, celui de la marginalité."*[45] The fact of having to find a
place in a male-dominated literary system has required an act of rebellion
at the outset on the part of the female writer: "For a [francophone] woman
writer . . . the act of writing in French is, of necessity, an attempt to make a
place for herself in that elite, male-dominated, European literary tradition."[46]

These issues were discussed with four francophone African women writers, Aminata Maïga Ka, Fatou Ndiaye Sow, Annette Mbaye D'Erneville, and Aminata Sow Fall, during a series of interviews on the politics of writing fiction in Senegal.[47] Aminata Sow Fall rejected the characterization of French as a primarily colonial language, claiming ownership of this language as her principal expressive medium, pointing out that as a child her first African language, Wolof, was not in any case a written language. She did concede that there are occasions where the action itself has a specific cultural location or an idea that cannot be accommodated by a language other than the one that has evolved in that culture.[48] As Barry Hallen has illustrated with reference to the expression of African aesthetics in Western language, the challenge these issues present, not confined to creative writing, have generated a number of pragmatic responses.[49] When asked to respond to this question of a European language constituting a barrier to the expression of authentic African experience, other francophone West African writers pointed to political and pragmatic issues that superseded the philosophical in the context in which they were writing. And indeed in some instances the need to communicate philosophical notions that were initially generated not within an African culture but more in a Western context pointed to the need to differentiate the requirements of authorship according to the type, function and readership of the text as it operates in an African context.

Fatou Ndiaye Sow, poet and writer of legal texts in vernacular form designed to inform Senegalese women of their human rights,[50] stressed the need to use "simple, everyday" French in legal texts to facilitate dissemination among young people in schools and colleges throughout the country and ensure equal accessibility across all the African language groups.[51]

When the question was put to the poet Annette Mbaye d'Erneville, the line of enquiry was deemed irrelevant. For her part, Aminata Maïga Ka believes that while one recognizes that the use of French can create problems, it also has advantages given that the publishing world operates in world languages (which she identified in this context as English, French and Arabic) as opposed to local languages. In any event the writer usually has no option in the matter of language choice.[52] She noted that even if a writer can find a publisher willing to publish the text in an African language, it would be a disadvantage to have the readership limited to the writer's regional community, particularly where the issues being addressed are national and even sub-regional in scope. Aminata Maïga Ka, like Aminata Sow Fall, commented that many African languages have only just recently become written languages. Maïga Ka learned how her first African language, Wolof, was being transcribed into written text by following a Wolof language teaching program on Senegalese national television in the 1990s. But she, like most of her compatriots, had no intention of abandoning what she considered her writing language, namely French. Not least as she pointed out because a high level of fluency in the French language is a hard-won skill. During the four centuries when French developed into a global language, it did so under the strict supervision of the French State and its linguistic arm, the *Académie française*. French Canadians are almost alone in the liberties they have taken with the language, developing their distinctive version of spoken French. But even here the written language retains its metropolitan form. Therefore the language used by francophone women writers to describe their experience of life in West African society is—with the exception of a few local peculiarities—the same language that is used and understood in any other part of the contemporary French-speaking world, and in this sense it is a truly international language. In this regard also the francophone African feminist text fits ideally the task of communicating the social experience of gender in the West African context to the wider international community.

The next chapter examines the earliest and arguably the most influential exponent to date of francophone African women's writing. In *Une si longue lettre,* her first and most famous work, Mariama Bâ signaled the birth of a new genre of social realist fiction in Africa.

NOTES

1. Panagiotis Christias, "*Du littéraire et du social—le double: recherche pour une métaodon,*" *Sociétés,* no. 64, 1999/2, 67–75.

2. Bertrand Ricard, "*Pour un rapprochement de la littérature et de la sociologie,*" *Sociétés,* no. 62, 1998/4, 5–7, [5]. "The rare sociologist who dares use literary texts in defense of a sociological thesis is dismissed out of hand as an essayist." Author's translation. Roland Barthes and Pierre Bourdieu among others have drawn on literary and aesthetic sources for evidence of sociological phenomena. Social scientists drawing on literature for policy analysis are far rarer, and in general social scientists engaged in policy analysis remain wedded to a quantitative approach.

3. Ricard, "*Pour un rapprochement,*" 6. "Literature can serve the sociologist by relativising and revealing the mass of little realities, all those emotions (in the phenomenological sense), that we experience in our daily lives." Author's translation.

4. Ricard, "*Pour un rapprochement,*" 7. "This allows literature to become what Dantec called the 'experimental anthropological laboratory.' . . . This was how some pioneers such as Proust, Musil and Joyce managed to prefigure social change. . . . To understand the present, a contemporary writer has to understand what is at stake in this anthropological 'modification.'" Author's translation.

5. Valérie Orlando, *Nomadic Voices of Exile—Feminine Identity in Francophone Literature of the Maghreb* (Athens: Ohio University Press, 1999), 9.

6. Cited in Christias, *"Du littéraire et du social,"* 70.

7. Christias, *"Du littéraire et du social,"* 70. "The grounding of story in lived experience, reconciling the fragmented logos of novelistic fiction with human expression, these are the origins of both history and fiction." Author's translation.

8. An example of this error of comparing apples with pears is Richard A. Epstein's "Does Literature Work as Social Science? The Case of George Orwell," published in *The University of Colorado Law Review* 73, 2002, 101–125. In this article Epstein presents his case against the use of literature in social science by comparing George Orwell with the economist Friedrich Hayek, and concluding that the latter was a better social scientist because he had a better grasp of the forces driving industrialization in the West. From this sample of one, and citing just one further piece of evidence to support his contention, a comparison of Balzac's description of the urban poor with that of an English economist, Andrew Ure, he rests his case.

9. Sandra Harding, "Introduction," in *The Feminist Standpoint Theory Reader: Intellectual and Political Controversies*, Sandra Harding, ed. (London: Routledge, 2004), 1.

10. I am wary of assuming that the literary encounter provides a point of entry into what Gayatri Spivak has termed "subaltern" experience. Women in the stories cited in this chapter are "subaltern" in the sense that they are all victims of what the author has identified as gender oppression and social marginalization. My interest is not to experience what these characters experience but to identify and appreciate what the author has selected as pertinent to the debate.

11. Joseph Conrad, *Heart of Darkness* (Harmondsworth: Penguin, 1998). Written in the last year of the nineteenth century, *Heart of Darkness* was first published by J Dent of London in 1902.

12. A. Hargreaves, *The Colonial Experience in French Fiction* (London: Macmillan, 1981), 34.

13. Pierre Loti, *Le Roman d'un Spahi* (1881).

14. Chandra Talpade Mohanty, "Under Western Eyes: Feminist Scholarship and Colonial Discourses," in *Third World Women and the Politics of Feminism*, C. T. Mohanty, A. Russo and L. Torres, eds. (Bloomington: Indiana University Press, 1991), 51–80.

15. Hargreaves, *The Colonial Experience*, 37.

16. Arlette Chemain-Degrange, *Emancipation féminine et roman africain* (Dakar: UNESCO/*Nouvelles Editions Africaines du Sénégal*, 1980). This study focuses on how women have been presented in African fiction between 1930 and 1970. It concludes that the female character in African fiction is most commonly associated with traditional values and not with progress or emancipation.

17. That this poems also graces the homepages of innumerable porn sites—as attested by the number of links to pornography generated by a Google search for the poem—gives further pause for thought.

18. Christopher L. Miller, *Theories of Africans: Francophone Literature and Anthropology in Africa* (Chicago: Chicago University Press, 1990), 259.

19. These includes Mame Younousse Dieng's *L'Ombre en Feu* (Dakar: *Nouvelles Editions Africaines du Sénégal*, 1997), which will be discussed in some detail later in this chapter.

20. In such discussions, Africa is often characterized as a single culture. See Anthonia A. Kalu, *Women, Literature and Development in Africa* (Trenton, N.J.: Africa World Press, 2001) for a defense of the *Négritude* characterization of women and an argument against "Western" feminism. Though this study clearly has some theoretical weaknesses, I did find it enlightening in what it reveals about how Western feminism can be interpreted as a single, monolithic, and confrontational ideology. There are also other points of interest in this work which I shall refer to later.

21. "*Les chants nostalgiques dédiés à la mère africaine confondue dans les angoisses d'homme à la Mère Afrique ne nous suffisent plus.*" Mariama Ba, "La fonction politique des littératures africaines écrites," *Ecriture française dans le monde* 3, no. 5, 1981, 6.

22. Florence Stratton, *Contemporary African Literature and the Politics of Gender* (London: Routledge, 1994).

23. Stratton, *Contemporary African Literature*, 31.

24. Stratton, *Contemporary African Literature*, 4. However, there are African authors who use opposition or "complementarity" and other binary or Manichean mechanisms and claim this device originates from traditional African knowledge bases. In Kalu, *Women, Literature, and Development*, the author uses just such a device to present her concept of "womanhood" and "manhood" as a duality, and puts much emphasis throughout the text that her theorising comes from African, not European, "ways of knowing."

25. Though Stratton has been severely criticized by African writers for reading African literature through Western eyes, it is difficult to deny her evidence as she cites case after case of the African male writer who uses a female character to represent his view of the depravity of the postcolonial African state.

26. The African male academics and writers who have rejected her work are too numerous to list here, but some African women have also done so, such as Kalu, *Women, Literature, and Development*, who excoriates, at numerous points throughout her text, Western feminists, and Stratton in particular, for the critical treatment she dealt out to her countryman, Chinua Achebe.

27. Stratton, *Contemporary African Literature*, 166.

28. Interview with Professor Lilyan Kesteloot, *Institut Fondamental de l'Afrique Noire (IFAN)*, Dakar, 10 January 1999. Lilyan told me this story in the course of a discussion we were having about what constituted "feminist" writing in West Africa. She said that she had successfully intervened to persuade the women to drop their action. In 1999 Beyala's work was still considered very controversial among the Senegalese reading public.

29. Stratton, *Contemporary African Literature*, 51.

30. Gayatri Spivak, "Can the Subaltern Speak?" in *Colonial Discourse and Postcolonial Theory*, Patrick Williams and Laura Chrisman, eds. (New York: Harvester Wheatsheaf, 1993), 66–111, [102].

31. Angèle Bassolé Ouédrago, "Et les Africaines prirent la plume! Histoire d'une conquête," *Mots Pluriels,* October 1998, 3.

32. Lilyan Kesteloot, "La Percée des femmes dans le roman de moeurs sénégalais,*" Environnement africain*, 10, nos. 39–40, 1997, 31–44.

33. Christopher L. Miller, "Nationalism as Resistance and Resistance as Nationalism in Literature in Francophone Africa," *Yale French Studies* vol. 1, no. 82, 1993, 62–100, [62].

34. *Nouvelles Editions Africaines du Sénégal.*

35. Interviewed by the author, 22 January 1999, Dakar, Senegal.

36. Quoted in Juliana Makuchi Nfah-Abbenyi, *Gender in African Women's Writing* (Bloomington: Indiana University Press, 1997), 13.

37. Quoted in Nfah-Abbenyi, *Gender in African Women's Writing*, 13.

38. Jacques Derrida, "Remarks on Deconstruction and Pragmatism," in *Deconstruction and Pragmatism*, C. Mouffe, ed. (London: Routledge, 1996), 80.

39. I have heard this view expressed many times in Africa by women whom I would happily describe as feminists. They, however, see the term as denoting a confrontational and aggressive type of woman.

40. The author discusses her linguistic background in the preface to her book in terms of English and French, with no reference to African languages.

41. Nfah-Abbenyi, *Gender in African Women's Writing*, 14.

42. N. Hitchcott, *Women Writers in Francophone Africa* (Oxford: Berg, 2000), 1. In this study Hitchcott states that though by 1984 there were over fifty titles by francophone African women, Anglophone African women's writing had been more prolific than women's writing in French. Heinemann published Flora Nwapa's *Efuru* in 1966. This was the first text by a woman to be published in its prestigious African Writers Series launched in 1958 with Chinua Achebe's *Things Fall Apart*. See Stratton, *Contemporary African Literature*, 80.

43. Nfah-Abbenyi, *Gender in African Women's Writing*, 9.

44. Samuel Oluoch Imbo, *An Introduction to African Philosophy* (Lanham, Md.: Rowman & Littlefield, 1998). In chapter 4 Imbo uses creative writing to explore this issue, opposing the position of Chinua Achebe with those of Ngugi wa Thiong'o.

45. Ouédrago, "Et les Africaines prirent la plume!" 7.

46. Mary Jean Green, Micheline Rice-Maximin, Karen Gould, Keith L.Yeager and Jack A. Walker, eds. *Postcolonial Subjects—Francophone Women Writers* (Minneapolis: University of Minnesota Press, 1996), xi.

47. Interviews were conducted in Senegal between January 1999 and May 2003.

48. At such times, as Aminata Sow Fall explained, a writer uses the African language term and explains it either in the text or in a note. These issues are familiar to the professional translator versed in finding solutions to the problems posed by cultural distance between languages. These problems become increasingly frequent as the cultural location of the two texts move further apart. For a discussion of male African writing in French see Kwaku A. Gyasi, "The African Writer as Translator: Writing African Languages through French," *Journal of African Cultural Studies* 16, no. 2, 2003, 143–59. Gyasi uses the terms "cushioning" and "contexualisation" to describe the solutions Sow Fall described in the conversation mentioned above.

49. Barry Hallen, "African Meanings, Western Words," *African Studies Review* 40, no. 1, 1997, 6.

50. See Fatou Ndiaye Sow, *Un Code pour toi et moi* (Dakar: *Ministère des Finances et du Plan*, 1998); Fatou Ndiaye Sow, *Des Droits pour les Enfants* (Dakar: *Ministère de la famille, de l'Action Sociale et de la Solidarité*, 1998).

51. Interviews with Fatou Ndiaye Sow, 23–26 January 1999, Grand Yoff, Senegal.

52. Another Senegalese writer, Mame Younnouse Dieng, has had her work published in Wolof in the 1990s. This followed the adoption earlier in the decade of a policy by the government to promote the use of African languages in Senegal.

17

Writing Gender and Development

The Birth of a Literary Voice

A travers l'arme du roman, les écrivains ont toutes les audaces et leurs analyses nous en suggèrent davantage que les études souvent empesées de chercheurs dits scientifiques qui n'arrivent pas à se dépêtrer de leurs contradictions sociales et culturelles. Quant aux "écrivaines," elles ont sur elles-mêmes un regard lucide, sans concession mais aussi tendre, qui nous enchante, un regard aussi résolument moderne qu'elles le sont elles-mêmes puisqu'elles ont atteint l'écriture dans la modernité, une modernité particulièrement récente pour elles qui ont été les mal aimées de l'école coloniale et qui le restent encore de l'université.[1]

Not only were women in francophone Africa excluded from education in the colonial era, obstacles to gaining a higher education have remained in place throughout the postcolonial era. In an interview on the subject, Aminata Sow Fall cited access to university as a crucial factor in her development as a writer.[2] Given the extremely low rates of female access to higher education in francophone Africa in the fifty years since Independence it is not surprising that novels written by African women writing in French only started to appear in the bookshops in the 1970s.[3]

Mariama Bâ is widely acknowledged as the writer who first used literature to launch the campaign for women's rights in francophone African society on the national and international scene. More than perhaps any other author from francophone West Africa, Mariama Bâ has been widely read and discussed in her local community within the reading and non-reading public alike.[4] In the case of Senegal, Bâ's own country of origin, the spread of literacy is particularly uneven, with the more Islamic regions such as Diourbel and Tambacounda recording very low levels of access to secondary and tertiary formal education through to the twenty-first century. The impact of published literature is limited in regions where the ideas and debates contained in published texts can only circulate secondhand and by word of mouth. The work of these novelists therefore has its biggest immediate impact in the literary and social elite, in those social classes which have a greater degree of participation in and influence over the political life of the nation.

There have been many different readings of Bâ's literary output, which amounted to just two novels, *Une si longue lettre*,[5] written in 1979, and *Un chant écarlate*,[6] published just before the author's untimely death in 1981. Some of these readings are conservative, some radical, and all are of interest to this discussion insofar as the voice of the author is heard through her readers as well as through her text. But it is above all Mariama Bâ's own stated intention to be a writer of politically-engaged texts that makes these novels interesting in the present study. She described *Une si longue lettre* in the following terms:

> [T]his is the first cry from the heart of Senegalese women, because it talks about the problems of Senegalese women, of Muslim women, of the women with the constraints of religion which weigh on her as well as other social constraints. [. . .] I am happy, however, that if this book is translated, there will be many countries who will be able to hear our cry, our own cry. The cry that they utter, the women from these other countries, their cry will not be exactly the same as ours—we have not all got the same problems.[7]

Bâ presents her work as an expostulation of the roles to which women are confined in society, and an exploration of the position of women in Senegalese society. That Bâ engages with issues of transnational significance is clear in her focus on the playing out of European marital arrangements among four central protagonists. As Barbara Klaw has pointed out, the roles Bâ attributes to husbands and wives in *Une si longue lettre* reflect a broader theme explored by Roland Barthes' in *Novels and Children*. The hierarchical typology Barthes employs in his essay suggests that the roles occupied by husbands and wives in Western societies are determined ideologically from social myths that supersede social class. While Bâ's novel can be read within such transnational discourses of gender domination, the focus on a marital regime specific to Senegalese/African society, namely, polygyny, problematizes a real-world location-specific issue confronting women in Senegal at the time of writing. Critics have put a forceful case for Bâ's voice being heard as that of a feminist reformer:

> The strategic value of these portrayals is twofold. They allow Bâ to raise issues that are of crucial importance to debates on the status of women in society. The themes she emphasizes are polygyny, the socialization of women, and women's

education. Through these portrayals Bâ also revises conventional male representations of women.[8]

Brahimi has argued that the political approach is not only resolutely feminist but, more importantly located in a pragmatic female critique of African practices defended and promoted in the name of "tradition." Practices such as polygyny became enmeshed in a discourse of cultural authenticity in the aftermath of Independence exacerbating the existing social and political disadvantages experienced by women.[9]

The importance of revisiting the issue of polygyny has become all the more pressing in the African cultural context, the distinction between polygamy and polygyny has been lost in the European languages of Africa.[10]

Using the institution of marriage as both a political and a social metaphor, Bâ's novels explore the differential impact of Independence on women and men in Senegalese society. The action in both cases is located in what Western literary criticism has traditionally designated as the "domestic" space.[11] In practice, the African novel (and indeed any novel regardless of cultural location) can and does operate across such imagined boundaries of public versus personal space. In the case of Bâ's novels, the personal and the political combine through the development of the marital relationship. In *Une si longue lettre* Bâ explores one African woman's experience of a polygynous marriage through the composition of a letter written by the central protagonist, Ramatoulaye, to her close friend, Aïssatou, who left Senegal some six years earlier to take up a post of interpreter at the Senegalese Embassy in New York. The pretext for compiling "so long a letter"[12] is the sudden and untimely death of the husband, Modou Fall.

While the work reflects an engagement with structural and ideological components of gender-based discrimination that defy geographical boundaries, the narrative is written around a series of culturally-located events. Describing her husband's death as "*l'atroce tragédie,*" the letter then turns into a reflection of incidents that take place during the days of mourning following Modou's death, which in turn generate flashbacks to the memorable events that punctuated thirty-five years of married life. Returning to the narrative's present, Ramatoulaye then recounts in graphic and painful detail the first ritual of widowhood to which she must submit: the symbolic handing over of herself and her goods to her dead husband's family. She experiences this as being disposed of like a chattel, and she feels all the more humiliated because she is treated in the same manner as the junior co-wife of five years, Binetou. There follows the reading of the *Mirasse*, a Koranic rite where the secrets of the dead are revealed, and the depth of Modou's betrayal is exposed.

Readings that have posited this novel as a hymn to African female solidarity are confronted here with evidence to the contrary in one of a long series
of examples of how the complex hierarchy of caste, class, race and gender
shape relations between women in Senegalese society.

Within the context of the wider political changes taking place at the dawn
of Independence, the central character recalls the early days of marriage when
she and her husband numbered among the first generation of young African
intellectuals to experience decolonization from France. They had witnessed
the departure of the colonial administrations in Morocco and Tunisia during
the half decade preceding their own independence as a prelude to their own
liberation. Both Ramatoulaye and her epistolary interlocutor, Aissatou's,
marriages were born in this era of confident expectation of a new, progressive world wrought in the image of the West. But it is not long before the
pressures originating from outside the marital couple lead to ideals within the
marital institution being abandoned. On the pretext of family honour, tradition and responsibility to one's social caste, Aissatou's husband is persuaded
by his mother to take a second wife from the family's village. The progres-
sively-minded Aïssatou refused to submit to this situation. The marriage is
broken and the couple divorce. *"Les livres te sauvèrent*—Rama notes—*De-
venus ton refuge, ils te soutinrent."*[13] (*SLL*: 52). The gender-based discrimination experienced by Aissatou originates in the imposition of "traditional"
female roles by female agents, and the source of her salvation is not found in
"traditional" female solidarity. Instead she relies on the transformative power
of knowledge, retrains as a linguist and becomes an interpreter. To achieve
self-fulfillment Aissatou is compelled to abandon her country (and by extension her friend Ramatoulaye) and relocate to the cultural diaspora. Here Bâ
sets out the irreconcilable tensions that pit the solution adopted by Aissatou
against the more conventional and socially acceptable course of action Ramatoulaye will follow twenty years later when she faces the same crisis in her
marriage—the imposition of a second wife. In the case of Ramatoulaye, her
middle-aged husband develops a humiliating and ultimately fatal passion for
one of their daughter's teenage friends. The young girl in question, Binetou,
is then subjected to enormous social pressure from her mother to accept the
advances of this married man. In one of several twists in the storyline, Bâ has
Ramatoulaye accepting this second marriage, despite the fact that she and
her husband had agreed upon a "modern" monogamous regime at the outset
of this union. Ramatoulaye is then subjected to yet further humiliation when
she discovers that regardless of her acquiescence, Modou has no intention of
fulfilling his duty as a husband. Outraged and wounded by this public flouting
of her husband's religious and cultural duties towards her, Rama moves out
of the family home and by so doing moves from a life of affluence into one

of poverty and marginalization and an unrelenting struggle to bring up twelve children as a single mother.

Bâ went on to win the first Noma prize for African literature at the Frankfurt literature festival in 1980. In the many interviews she gave in the months following the award she was asked repeatedly to discuss the (negative) characterization of men in the novel. On one occasion she replied that all men are like Rama's and Aissatou's husbands, in that they are all instinctively polygamous. Just as Chinua Achebe critiqued Joseph Conrad for presenting Africans as essentially different from whites, Bâ suffered a barrage of criticism for presenting women's sexuality as being essentially, as opposed to culturally, different from men's. At the time these interviews were taking place, the debate on gender was in its infancy, and distinctions between sex and gender were still being defined and understood (as indeed they still are) and it is possible that too much has been made of Bâ's remark. It is more useful to turn to the texts themselves for a deeper exposition of her understanding of the issues governing gender and development in postcolonial Senegal. As Bahimi notes: *"Comme dans La nouvelle romance d'Henri Lopès, on voit le livre servir de laboratoire pour la société en formation et en transformation."*[14]

The experimentation taking place in this novelistic laboratory focuses on the impact similar social factors have on different women. The key element used throughout her work is marriage and the socio-economic impact of this institution—in its various forms—on the position of Senegalese women. Indeed the status, happiness and mental health of women are seen as almost entirely dependent upon the existence and nature of the marital contract. There is nothing specifically Senegalese or West African about this theme until she introduces the cultural[15] element into the discussion of marriage in *Une si longue lettre* and *Un chant écarlate,* through the practice of polygyny.

The myth of female solidarity continues to be deconstructed in the representation of this institution. Bâ does not hold men up as the evil perpetrators of polygyny but rather as the more or less willing participants of a set of social relations maintained by women and men. She casts Binetou's Mother as the chief architect in the destruction of the monogamous regime as the mother browbeats her teenage daughter into marrying the middle-aged Modou: *"Elle a supplié sa fille de lui donner une fin heureuse, dans une vraie maison que l'homme leur a promis. Alors elle a cédé."*[16] Binetou was aware she had been sacrificed: *"Victime, elle se voulait oppresseur. Exilée [. . .] elle voulait sa prison dorée. Vendue, elle élevait chaque jour sa valeur."* Polygyny is presented as devasting not only the life of the first wife, who feels deceived and humiliated, and the second wife, who is but a puppet in the hands of her family, but also the lives of the offspring of the co-wives who must henceforth do battle for the attention of the father.

This novelistic experiment exposes the social and economic pressures on women who to enter polygynous arrangements, or force others to do so, as an escape from poverty and hardship. In *chant écarlate* the dangers of this course of action are even more graphically displayed than in *Une si longue letter*. The outcome of this action sees polygyny provoking fatal explosions of emotion. Myriam Warner-Vieyra's novel *Juletane* of 1982[17] developed the same thesis around the eponymous heroine who loses her sanity under the pressure of enforced polygyny. The dangers facing the polygynous man are likewise exponded as Juletane's husband meets an untimely end, as does Modou in *Une si longue lettre*, and the main male protagonist in Bâ's second novel, *Un chant écarlate*, is stabbed by his French wife for imposing a co-wife on her. But these polygynous men are not presented as monsters. Daouda Dieng, the self-proclaimed "feminist" of the National Assembly in Bâ's *Une si longue lettre*, is clearly already married when he invites the recently widowed Rama to be his wife. She responds—in yet another letter—explaining that though she holds him in high esteem she does not love him and so her conscience stops her accepting his offer. The fact of his being married is cited as a secondary reason:

> *Et puis l'existence de ta femme et de tes enfants complique encore la situation. Abandonnée hier, par le fait d'une femme, je ne peux allègrement m'introduire entre toi et ta famille. Tu crois simple le problème polygamique. Ceux qui s'y meuvent connaissent des contraintes, des mensonges, des injustices qui alourdissent leur conscience pour la joie éphémère d'un changement.* (*SLL*: 102)

Toril Moi noted decades ago in her essay "Sexual/Textual Politics,"[18] that critics who fail to make the distinction between the author of a feminist text and the politics of the central characters are wrongly conflating the voices of the text. It is an oversight that has persisted in the literary criticism of Bâ's work in readings that claim that *Une si longue lettre* shows Bâ's ambiguity over the issue of polygyny. This is an unconvincing interpretation given that Bâ wrote just two novels in her short writing career and that all the action of both these novels focuses on the devastating impact of this marital practice on women. Where there is ambiguity and confusion is in the apparently contradictory responses the practice generates in the central characters. On the one hand Ramatoulaye is seen admiring the course of action taken by her friend and on the other takes a contrary line when confronted with the crisis polygyny creates in her own marriage. The guiding principle governing the course of action adopted by Ramatoulaye is embedded in a logic of social stability as opposed to a logic of individual freedom. Neither is privileged in theory in these novels, but in practice the societal principle is revealed as fatally flawed in Senegalese society in the postcolonial era because, while it depends upon the observance of its laws by all parties to the system (husband and wife/wives), these norms no longer dominate in society. When Ramatoulaye decides to stay on as Modou's first wife she does so on the understanding that the other parties to the system will observe the norms and customs established around this practice over centuries. In fact her husband's actions have been motivated by the principle of individual freedom which he carries over into his new marital arrangement and excludes her from the new marriage. The inconsistency that exists between Ramatoulaye's position within her social system and her understanding of this position is again revealed when she is responding Daouda Dieng's proposal of marriage. She turns down Dieng's proposal on romantic grounds while citing social grounds—the issue of his existing marriage.

This gap between the theory of feminism and its practice is exposed in Bâ's writings on numerous occasions.[19] While Rama watches Aïssatou and admires her actions, she cannot react in the same way and this is in spite of having receiving the best French education. It is Ramatoulaye as opposed to Aissatou who represents the vast majority of women, those who invest in social systems that may go on to threaten or even undermine the very fabric of their existence. Aïssatou interprets polygynous behavior as an abuse, as a betrayal, and therefore the institution that legitimizes this is rejected. However, by so doing, this character puts herself beyond the pale of society and has to find an alternative means of survival. That she ends up leaving Senegal for the United States where she finds a place for herself in a wider multicultural community symbolizes the inability of this postcolonial African society at this moment in time to accommodate the feminist ideological and cultural perspective represented by Aissatou. As Bâ notes in the text, by moving to the States, Aïssatou is accused of betraying her culture, as opposed to society recognizing its failure to accommodate an alternative cultural perspective. The importance of gender in this narrative cannot be overstated, where the position of "woman" is foundational to the structure and survival of a patriarchal system. Under "normal" circumstances Aïssatou would not have been able to effect her own survival. However she has access to external resources because she has been educated. Bâ points to formal education as a key factor here, but not as a cure. She has Aissatou and Rama receiving exactly the same education. Reminiscing over their schooldays, Ramatoulaye notes with almost religious fervor: *"nous étions de véritables soeurs destinées à la même mission émancipatrice."* (*SLL*: 27).[20] The extent to which these girls were actually educated for emancipation is then played out in the trials they face in the course of the narrative, and in the ability they demonstrate to resolve a situation which is symbolically life-threatening in that it threatens their identities. Aïssatou is quick to realize that she does not have the resources within her present situation to survive the crisis polygyny presents to her identity. She draws on her experience of the formal education system to rebuild a life and an identity which can accommodate not just herself but also her children. Tertiary education in itself had not been sufficient, but it holds the potential for change and for the construction of alterative social systems.

Though the focus of the novel is on the individual agency of two women faced with what Bâ presents as an extreme situation of gender disadvantage, society is not presented as a purely formal and structural arrangement in this work. It operates both as the stage upon which characters perform and a character in the performance. As a background to the action, society is presented as the gender-segregated worlds of Ramatoulaye's home. Rarely do we see both genders acting together outside of the formal, ceremonial occasions, such as marriage and widowhood, where strict gender segregation is observed. Society also takes a more active part in the expression of social norms and customs. When Ramatoulaye observes her son-in-law performing roles she classifies as female-only—namely cooking and cleaning—she challenges him in the name of social propriety. He replies to the challenge countering Ramatoulaye's definition of male and female labor by exposing it as anti-feminist: "*Daba est ma femme. Elle n'est pas mon esclave, ni ma servante.*"

Other instances of anti-feminist behavior are set in both urban and village locations where the narrative exposes this issue of female anti-feminism and the exploitation of women by women in scenes where women are seen forcing polygyny on marriages which were initiated as monogamous partnerships. If there is an ideal of female solidarity in *Une si longue lettre* it is best represented by Aïssatou,[21] who shows solidarity in material terms, providing a car and other financial support in the difficult period of poverty following Ramatoulaye's separation. Bâ is in effect inverting what are mythic representations of African family life which still permeate social discourse in the region. Here Bâ uncovers the animosities and jealousies that separate women and highlight the role that women can play in preserving cultural institutions—even those most open to abuse and corruption such as polygyny—in a bid to protect and promote their own interests.

At the same time Bâ uses the novel to explore the potential that is already present in African society for change and development. Though Ramatoulaye initially expresses opposition to change, she evolves in the course of the short novel and develops a more flexible and some would say feminist practice. Faced with the unexpected pregnancy of her teenage daughter she overcomes the social disgrace threatened by this incident and creates a supportive and productive environment for her daughter to experience her motherhood.

Bâ returned to the predominantly destructive theme of polygyny in her second novel, *Un chant écarlate*, where the social staging of the narrative is further complicated by the addition of race. The story focuses on a young couple, a young Frenchwoman, Mireille, and her Senegalese husband, Ousmane in the immediate aftermath of Independence. Mireille's father, a high-ranking diplomat, returns to France with his family but Mireille opts to remain in Dakar with her Senegalese boyfriend, now husband. Ousmane represents for Mireille the epitome of a new world of racial and sexual equality, heralding a new era of cooperation between the former colonial power and the postcolony.

The narrative reveals a fundamentally different reality in which Ousmane's progressive veneer soon disappears as he succumbs to his mother's pestering to take an African wife. He marries his mother's choice of Ouleymatou, a young, beautiful and aristocratic village girl. Ousmane justifies his decision by arguing that he was losing his "authenticity" by living like a European with Mireille. He declares that Ouleymatou will reconnect him with his African roots and justifies himself further by arguing that this "reconnection" is crucial for the young (male) elite leading the reconstruction of postcolonial Senegal. In the face of this change in her marital situation Mireille loses her reason and tries to kill Ousmane and their son. Ousmane survives the attack and at the end of the novel we see him beginning to realize the implications of his dishonorable behavior and his depraved attempts at self-justification.

Unlike the African characters in the earlier novel, the tragedy of Mireille is that her French upper-middle-class upbringing has not educated her to deal with her marital breakdown in any constructive way. Faced with her crisis, Mireille's social world provides only two options: remain in the marital home or go home to her parents. The limitations—from a gender perspective—of this social system is reinforced through the characterization of Mireille's mother, an upper-middle-class Frenchwoman trained only to service the career and personal needs of her diplomat husband. The women in Mireille's world have no tradition of resistance to the hierarchical relationships of domination that Barthes, among others, identified as characterizing Western marital systems and as such Mireille can only resist by becoming "insane." Despite the calamitous impact polygyny has in both these novels, Bâ casts female characters as instrumental in precipitating these crises and in the facility with which they subconsciously and consciously maintain the *status quo*.[22]

Mariama Bâ was the first of a generation of women authors from the region to engage explicitly in advocating the use of literature in advancing the debate on the socio-economic advancement of women. Hers and the work that followed her untimely death in 1981 have served as a platform for engagement in the region and as a vehicle of communication with the world outside the region. What comes through so clearly in Bâ's work is the complexity of the cultural context of gender and development and crucially the lack of consensus on the form agency should take in promoting women's status and opportunities in this part of Africa. She reveals in her exposition of gender politics in Senegal the potential for ideological, cultural and structural change in her society but also exposes the multiplicity of ideological, cultural and structural obstacles standing in the way of development. The complexity of the task is explored in the works examined in the next chapter.

NOTES

1. Catherine Coquery-Vidrovitch, "Préface," in *Les Femmes dans la littérature africaine—portraits,* Denise Brahimi and Anne Trevarthen, eds. (Paris/Abidjan: Editions Karthala et CEDA, 1998), 5. "These writers have used the novel as a weapon and have bravely taken on difficult subjects in such a way that we learn more from reading their works than we do from so-called scientific research bound up in its social and cultural contradictions. As for women writers, they observe other women in a delightfully direct and sympathetic fashion. The perspective they adopt is also very modern, not least because they have only come to writing very recently, having been excluded from colonial schooling and still being largely absent from the universities." Author's translation.

2. Sow Fall noted in the same interview that she believed she would have become a writer had she not attended university, but being denied access may have had ramifications on the quality of writing and access to the international literary system.

3. If one excludes Marie-Claire Matip's autobiography, *Ngonda*, published shortly after Independence. See Ouédraogo, "Et les Africaines," 3.

4. In some parts of the former French African Empire over 90 percent of girls aged 15 to 19 can read and write nowadays, while over 90 percent of their grandmothers still do not do so.

5. Mariama Bâ, *Une si longue lettre* (Dakar: Nouvelles Editions Africaines du Sénégal, 1998).

6. Mariama Bâ, *Un chant écarlate* (Dakar: Nouvelles Editions Africaines du Sénégal, 1981).

7. I am quoting here from the published translation of Barbara Harrell-Bond's interview with Mariama Bâ quoted in Nfah-Abbenyi, *Gender in African Women's Writing,* 8.

8. Florence Stratton in *Contemporary African Literature and the Politics of Gender* (London: Routledge 1999), 155.

9. Denise Brahimi and Anne Trevarthen, *Les Femmes dans la littérature africaine—portraits* (Paris/Abidjan: Editions Karthala et CEDA, 1998), 75.

10. Cecile Accilien emphasizes the distinction between polygamy and polygyny in *Rethinking Marriage in Francophone African and Caribbean Literatures* (Lanham, Md.: Lexington, 2008), 67 passim.

11. Antonia Kalu draws our attention to the limitations of the non-African literary critic in *Women, Literature and Development in Africa* (Trenton, N.J.: Africa World Press, 2001).

12. In "Sinking One's Teeth into Mariama Bâ's *So Long a Letter*: Lessons of Cadmus," *Research in African Literatures* 40, no. 2, 2009, 63–81, [69], Charles O'Keefe reminds us of the cultural references to earlier epistolary novels in the title of Bâ's first novel. The clear allusion to a historic *"condition féminine"* reinforces the argument that this work references a critical tradition that is not determined by its geographical place of origin.

13. Here and henceforth *Une si longue lettre* is referred to in the text as *SLL*, with page number of the *NEAS* 1998 edition indicated after the colon.

14. Brahimi, *Les femmes*, 76–77.

15. This is a cultural rather than "religious" practice. The Koran does not call upon men to take second wives, indeed the Koran contains warnings about the difficulty men face in reconciling a devout Muslim life with polygyny.

16. "She begged her daughter to let her see out her days happily, in a real house, like the man had promised." Author's translation

17. Myriam Warner-Vieyra, *Juletane* (Paris: Présence Africaine, 1982). Warner-Vieyra, though born in Guadeloupe, has spent most of her writing career in Senegal.

18. Toril Moi, "Sexual/Textual Politics," in *The Politics of Theory*, F. Barker, ed. (Colchester: University of Essex, 1983), 1–14, [4].

19. This gap between the theory and practice of feminism in *So Long a Letter* has spawned a long discussion in literary criticism, an early contribution to which was Florence Stratton's "The Shallow Grave: Archetypes of Female Experience in African Fiction," *Research in African Literatures* 19, no. 1, 1988, 143–169.

20. "We were like sisters destined for the same mission of emancipation." Author's translation

21. Aissatou is the incarnation of the women's movement founded on notions of action and solidarity, typified in Senegal by the *Yewwu Yewwi* organization. She is also representative of the particular difficulties that face non-elite women in these movements.

22. The Cameroonian writer Calixthe Beyala has frequently returned to the theme of the oppressive function of women in African society in her novels. In *C'est le soleil qui m'a brûlée* (Paris: Editions Stock, 1987), 49, she characterizes the way in which women oppress or support each other through the responses of three women to the news of an unwanted pregnancy. The first woman states that it is essential for women to follow the rules society sets down and to have the child. The second states that a woman's body is her own affair, and the third says that far from being her own affair, a woman's body is a communal site in which society entrusts its honor and integrity. Beyala is arguing that women are just as likely, if not more likely, to internalize problematic social norms than they are to develop emancipatory modes of thinking and behavior. In this respect they represent women in all societies, not just in Cameroon.

18

Modernization and Marginalization in the Francophone African Feminist Novel

The destruction of an independent-minded young woman by the men and women of a rural community is the subject of Mame Younousse Dieng's novel *L'Ombre en feu*, written in the 1970s and published in French in 1997.[1] In this novel the impact of the international development agenda on the social development of rural women is scrutinized in the context of a remote village environment in Senegal. The central theme in *L'Ombre en feu* is girls' access to formal education in rural communities. In this story, as in the novels of Mariama Bâ, formal education—or *l'école française* as it called in this novel as it is still called in some of the more rural regions of francophone Africa—not only fails to empower the main protagonist, but more than this it unleashes countervailing forces in society that ultimately destroy her. All her intelligence and education cannot save the central protagonist, a young girl called Kura, from forced marriage, marital rape, unwanted pregnancy, and death in childbirth. In common with several of novels in this genre, the story is told by a narrator looking back over events following a death. In this case the narrator is a young educator, Saalif, who recounts the tragic events that take place in Jomb, a village located in the depths of the savannah, to his niece, Kura, the daughter of the village chief, Biram Njaay, and Biram's fourth and youngest wife, Mati. Saalif serves as a cipher for the international community exhorting the village to follow the mantra of formal education for all.

From an early age Kura shows a thirst for knowledge which encourages Mati's brother, Saalif, to ask Biram to let Kura attend school. Biram resists, arguing that Kura would be vulnerable in the company of men and boys and would return pregnant and dishonor him. When finally he agrees to Kura attending the local primary school, the reaction in the village is hostile to the point of insubordination. They accuse Biram of losing his religion, and the villagers withdraw marks of respect. It takes years for the village folk to reconcile themselves to Kura attending school, but gradually other girls are allowed to follow suit. Kura is a brilliant pupil, and at her primary school graduation ceremony Saalif arranges for the local prefect to attend and to praise her for her exceptional exam results. Biram is so impressed with all the fanfare and the offer of a government scholarship that he agrees to Kura attending the regional *lycée*.[2] He takes her to Dëkëba where the nearest *lycée* is located, and hands her over to the care of a distant cousin, Demba Gey. The cousin in question is less than delighted at the prospect of taking in this relative, but his wife, Sooda, persuades him to take her in. No sooner is Kura installed than she is put to work as Sooda's servant.[3] Whenever the girl is not at school she is doing housework. When Kura complains to her uncle Saalif about this, he reveals to her that his own experience of living with relatives during his schooldays was even worse, having been not only set to work for long hours every day but also having suffered physical abuse and beatings. He persuades Kura to stay on in Dëkëba. She grows into a beautiful young girl at which point Demba Gey starts taking a sexual interest in her.

On the day she is due to return home at the end of the school year Gey decides he will drive her home. Once out of sight of the town, he stops the car and attempts a sexual assault. At this point Gey tells her of his intention to make her his wife. When she recoils he interprets her rejection of his advances as a sign of modesty and inexperience, and even wonders whether she might also be overwhelmed by the honor of his interest in her. Demba Gey has already had three wives, two of whom he abandoned. They drive on to the village of Jomb where Demba Gey informs Biram of his intentions. Biram, delighted with all the presents and money Demba Gey has brought with him to support his suit, agrees to the marriage. Kura pleads with Biram not to force her to marry this man, but he rejects her appeals. She runs away to her uncle Saalif who tries to reason with Biram, to no avail. It is Kura's mother, Mati, who eventually wears down Kura's resistance and the marriage ceremony goes ahead. As the guests leave, the women of the family divide up the dowry and distribute the presents among themselves. On the night of the wedding Demba Gey arrives to sleep with his new wife, but Kura puts up such a fight that Demba Gey, massive though he is, does not manage to force her to have sex with him. Kura's screams are heard throughout the village. In response to her calls for help a neighbor remarks: *"cette fille est mal élevée"* (*OEF*: 171).[4]

The following morning when it is known that Kura has not consummated the marriage, she is showered with abuse by her mother. Though Kura is wounded and covered in bruises from her encounter with Demba Gey, the village is outraged by her behavior. There is nothing worse than a disobedient wife they say. Uncle Saalif visits and advises Kura to have sexual intercourse with Demba Gey, suggesting that there is no way out of this requirement. He even shows her a letter from her boyfriend, Duudu, who appears to support this view, saying that once that is done she can get a divorce and then they can marry. Demba returns the following weekend. Kura is in a semi-conscious state when he arrives and unconscious when he leaves. Demba reports to Biram that he has had intercourse and points out that she seems unwell. The sheet soaked in Kura's virginal blood is retrieved from the girl's hut and a village celebration ensues. Kura falls into a pitiful state of health and bitterly regrets not having been able to resist Demba Gey.

On his third visit she is too ill for him to molest her. On his fourth and final visit she lunges at his genitals with a razorblade, at which point he rushes out of the hut towards the hut of village chief and after shouting through his door that he will be divorcing Kura, leaves the village never to return. He is denounced in the village for this action and Kura's family and the villagers start treating the girl in a more conciliatory manner. The second rape by Demba Gey has left her pregnant. The pregnancy is not going well, but Biram will not give his permission for her to be taken to the clinic. Saalif goes in search of Demba Gey to seek his authorization and finds Demba canoodling with a new wife. Embarrassed at being found in this manner he takes his visitor off to the bedroom for a private chat and tells Saalif that the new wife is only a way of taking his mind off Kura. Saalif stays only long enough to obtain his signature on the document authorising Kura's hospitalization. By the time Kura receives medical attention at the rural medical station she is fatally ill and the hospitalization never takes place. She dies at the medical station having given birth to a baby girl. Dieng does not dwell on the implications of the failure of medical care to save Kura.

The story ends to the sound of Mati and other villagers wailing the loss of Kura. As one woman remarks: "*Kura qui a appris le français se prend pour une Blanche. Voilà tout son drame*," (*OEF*: 178).[5] It is the women as much as the men who react against formal education and sending girls to school: Kura's great-aunt, Maam Booy, warns Kura that "*l'école mène à la perdition*," (*OEF*: 101). One of the villagers reinforces this point: "*Si j'étais homme, je proposerai la suppression pure et simple de cette maudite école. C'est d'elle que vient le mal*," (*OEF*: 179). However Saalif believes it is the duty of everyone, including women, to be educated in the Western fashion in order to contribute to national development. But the gap between theory and practice looms large. Like Binetou in *Une si longue lettre*, education does not save Kura from becoming a sacrificial victim. Kura describes herself as no more than a slave whose fate is decided upon by her parents. As Biram puts it so succinctly, it is of no matter what she has learned at school, when it comes to marriage and domestic arrangements: "*sache que tu n'es qu'une femme, c'est-à-dire un être sans savoir ni pouvoir. . . la femme n'est rien d'autre qu'un corps; l'esprit c'est l'homme."* (*OEF*: 169).

Regardless of how much formal education Kura has received, her society continues to dictate what her role will be and this takes no account of her educational status. Clearly the fate of Kura is tragic in this story, but Dieng's underlying message is not uniformly pessimistic. As Kura's friend Bintu explains: *"Nulle part dans le monde, l'émancipation s'est opérée en un jour. C'est une lente évolution, non une révolution qui fait une civilisation."* (*OEF*: 219).

The need for francophone African society to evolve and accommodate feminist developments is the message that also comes through Aminata Maïga Ka's work. She is widely held to be the most overtly "feminist" writer of her generation in Senegal.[6] While accepting the label of "feminist," an unusual position in itself, Ka is quick to point out that her writing is not polemical: *"je présente ce que je considère comme un problème dans notre société, mais je ne le juge pas pour les gens, mes lecteurs peuvent en tirer leurs propres conclusions."*[7]

Her writing is nonetheless an indictment of those so-called traditions which keep women from fulfilling their potential in society. Her three novels, *La Voie du Salut* (1980), *Le Miroir de la Vie (*1983), and *Brisures de Vie* (1998), address the gritty reality of life for the urban poor in modern-day Senegal. Beset by poverty, ignorance and betrayal, the women who populate these novels are confronted by such immense problems that no facile solutions to their situations are proposed in the narratives. Ka locates the women and men of her stories within immensely powerful, seemingly indomitable social structures. Contemporary urban society serves as the stage upon which the struggles of the women are played out.

MODERNITY AND MARGINALIZATION IN THE URBAN CONTEXT

The first of her novels, *La Voie du Salut*, written between 1977 and 1980[8] introduces the main protagonist as a corpse at the point of decomposing some weeks after its burial. We know this is the body of a woman, the body being referred to as *elle* several times in the opening paragraph, and that she had died in hospital during an operation. We are given a description of the woman who inhabited the body as seen through the eyes of her daughter.

The daughter describes her as: *"une mère douce, discrète, modeste. Une femme qui avait su endurer, sans broncher, toutes les vilenies de l'existence"* (*VDS*: 8).[9] The first *"vilenie"* mentioned is *l'humiliation du mari*. The husband in question is a medical doctor called Baba, who married Rokhaya, the woman decomposing in the grave, when she was a young girl. Baba had spied her washing clothes in the stream near her village and fell in love with her from afar. Initially his petitions to her father for consent to their marriage fell on deaf ears; Baba was a "foreigner" with no family in the area and an object of suspicion, but this suspicion was eventually overcome and the father agreed to his request. The narrative turns to Baba's work and here he is presented as a force for progress. He attends the case of a three-month-old baby who has just died during an operation of female circumcision. He rants against the practice and calls the child's father and uncle to account for the death.

The action of the novel then moves forward to his own marriage. The event is recounted in two episodes: the display of the bloodstained marriage sheet testifying to Rokhaya's virginity and the speeches of the elders in which Rokhaya's new role as married woman is explained to her:

> *Dès l'instant que tu es mariée, tu appartiens corps et âme à ton mari [. . .] Il est ton unique seigneur et maître. Il est seul habilité à te mener au Paradis où, du reste, tu n'iras qu'en lui obéissant aveuglement. (VDS: 36)*

The idea that a woman cannot reach paradise without being assisted by a man is not an interpretation of the Koran supported by Islamic scholars. The original texts of the Koran state that the Prophet insisted upon the equality of men and women before God. However this speech, delivered by Rokhaya's most senior uncle on her father's side, claims its authority from the Koran. The senior uncle goes on to give general advice on how Rokhaya should live her life as a married woman. She should be:

> *[S]ourde, aveugle et muette, c'est le secret du bonheur. Sache mesurer tes paroles quand tu t'adresses à lui. Ta volonté entière doit être tendue à lui donner pleine satisfaction. C'est à cette seule condition que les enfants qui naîtront de votre union accéderont à l'échelon le plus élévé de la société. (VDS: 36–37)*

The senior uncle then concludes by describing marriage as a pit of bitterness and despair where love only lasts a short time!

The story moves on to Baba and Rokhaya's married life which, in contrast with the uncle's last words, is an extremely happy one. Rokhaya is looked after by servants and doted on by her husband who brings her little surprise gifts at the end of every month. But it is not long before a dark cloud, in the form of a jealous and resentful relative, appears on the horizon. Oumar, Baba's brother, turns what should have been a short visit into a very long and disruptive one. The rules of hospitality make it impossible for Baba to ask his brother to leave. Rokhaya is not yet pregnant, so Oumar uses her condition to

disrupt the harmonious relationship between the couple, accusing her of being sterile, a deeply injurious attack on a woman who lives in a world where:
*"La plus grande calamité pour la femme africaine n'est-elle pas de ne point
enfanter?"* (*VDS*: 45).

Under pressure from Oumar, Baba sends Rokhaya to consult a gynaeco-
logist. Meanwhile Rokhaya's neighbors suggest she also visit a traditional
healer. Within two months she is pregnant and goes on to give birth to a girl.
The daughter, Rabiatou, is cherished by both parents, goes to the best schools
and finishes her education at a university law school in France. Just as Rabiatou is finishing her legal training in France she receives news that her father
has died. She returns home to take charge of the household.

Rabiatou, known as Raby, then becomes a vehicle through which the author plays out the difficulties facing young women in Senegal caught between
"traditional" roles and the contemporary aspirations of the young professional. The conflict is not presented through the prism of the contemporary
gender and development goals included in international community WID and
GAD models. In this case it is the "traditional African woman," Rokhaya,
who provides the lens through which we view the problems confronting
young educated professional women in Senegal. We see Raby continuing to
behave in Senegal as she did in Europe, going out in the evening with male
and female friends, and sometimes, even more problematically, on her own. It
is in these conditions that Raby meets and falls in love with a young teacher,
Racine.

The relationship generates opposition and consternation in Rabiatou's family. Her aunts vehemently oppose her intention to marry Racine because they
had been planning on Raby getting a really "good catch," a Minister, or an
Ambassador, the kind of husband who would provide them with regular gifts
of clothes, foreign travel and prestigious homes. Only when they are faced by
the even greater social disaster of Raby becoming pregnant while still unmarried is their opposition to the marriage removed. The marriage goes ahead
but the disgraced Raby receives none of the "honors" of expensive gifts and
ceremonial recognition normally due to a young bride.

In common with the unions of Bâ's novels, married life starts well for the
young couple. While Rokhaya is lavishing attention on her grandson, also
called Baba, Raby and Racine entertain and enjoy a busy social life. But it is
not long before Racine succumbs to pressure from the men in their circle to
leave Raby behind when they go out. They complain to him that he is behav-
ing like a European: *"Vous êtes trop toubabs. Ici nous sommes en Afrique, les
hommes sortent sans leur femme."* (*VDS*: 86).

These characterizations of European versus African gender relations which
suggest that female subordination and segregation is "traditional" to African

society are not challenged by Racine. Though Racine represents the young intellectual of the story he comes to epitomize the colonized mind, neither aware of his own cultural history nor engaged in its enquiry. Far from arguing with his persecutors, Racine accepts their arguments that his treatment of his wife constitutes a betrayal of his African culture. He gives in to the social pressure and even starts a clandestine relationship outside of his marriage, which he will soon declare as a legitimate co-marriage. Meanwhile the advice Rabiatou receives from her female friends is to focus on keeping a nice home and cooking delicious meals to entice her husband back to the home. The tale ends with Raby's closest friend, Sokhna, bringing her the news that Racine has taken a second wife and has set her up in a luxurious apartment in town. Raby collapses to the floor and a passing doctor prematurely declares she has died of shock. Her friend Sokhna rushes from the room and in a paroxysm of grief, generally favored by the heroines of more romantic novels than this, throws herself down a well.

The story is not an optimistic one. The oppressions of "traditional" gender relations, articulated by the senior uncle within a cultural-religious frame, are replaced by the grief and disappointments of "modern" gender relations. Hierarchy, obedience and service have been exchanged for access to formal education and the ideals this engenders, followed by romantic love, betrayal and disaster. There is an obvious intention here to shoot down the myths which have identified modernity with progress and equality. Through the fate of Raby we see that the quality of life of the "modern" woman is as dependent on the decisions of men as was her mother's life.

In *Le Miroir de la Vie*,[10] written in 1983, the story revolves around a young Sereer woman who has been forced to leave her rural community in eastern Senegal because of the rural poverty brought about by the persistent droughts of the 1980s. She comes to Dakar to look for work and finds a job as a domestic servant. We first encounter her walking to work in the chill of the early morning, with her fellow *"esclaves des temps modernes"* (*MV*:104).[11] She is typical of the many thousands of "modern-day slaves" who can be found sleeping 10 or 15 to a room in squalid low-rise houses in the sprawling suburbs of Dakar, and working in luxurious houses in the upmarket residential districts of the city. Fatou, the young Sereer woman, works at the home of the Secretary of State for Fisheries Research. The description of his magnificent home focuses on the bedroom of the Minister's wife, Arame Cissé. Measuring five metres by four, the room is fitted with a white deep pile wall-to-wall carpet, and furnished with drawers full of boxes of designer perfumes costing fCFA 30,000[12] a bottle.

Arame Cissé is admired in society as a generous woman and immediately we see how this is expressed in her world as she attends the funeral ceremony

of her aunt in the nearby town of Thiès. She is accompanied by her closest friend, Aminta, and the family griotte[13] who will speak on her behalf at
the ceremony. Adji[14] Arame Cissé contributes fCFA 300,000 to the funeral
coffers and her friend makes a further donation of fCFA 100,000. All this
generosity inspires a round of applause as the three women take their leave.

The story then turns to Arame's children. Her eldest, Omar, is a student at
the University Cheikh Anta Diop of Dakar and an active member of the *Mouvement marxiste du travail*. His room at the *cité universitaire* on the campus
in Dakar-Fann is being used for party meetings. We witness one such meeting
in which the group criticizes neo-colonial interference by foreign powers and
plans a bomb attack on foreign embassies in Dakar. Omar is arrested during
the attack and is left in prison for two days until his father acquiesces to Arame's pleas to get him released.

Meanwhile Arame's eldest daughter, Ndèye, has fallen in love with the
griotte's son, Saliou, and is insisting on marrying him. Being the son of a
female praise singer makes Saliou a person of "caste." His family is defined
as lower-class, whereas Ndèye Cissé is from a noble family, facts which—in
the eyes of the mothers of Saliou and Ndeye—make the marriage impossible.
However neither Astou Mbaay, the griotte, nor Arame Cissé succeed in persuading the young couple to their point of view. Aminta and Arame go off
to consult a famous fortune-teller to see what the cowrie shells predict. They
predict a union, and the dismayed women return home blaming "*l'école des
Blancs*" for Saliou and Ndèye's disobedience.

Back at the Minister's house in the wealthy quarter of central Dakar, Fatou the maid finishes her day's work and returns exhausted to her shack in
the outskirts. She thinks about her poor mother. Though now aged sixty, Fatou's mother starts work soon after 5 o'clock prayers because two of Fatou's
brothers are still living at home. As a result of the drought that ravaged the
east of the country in the early years of that decade, Fatou's mother can no
longer make sufficient income from her own farming and she relies on Fatou
and her sister to supplement her income. We then learn of Fatou's impending
social catastrophe. She is pregnant from a boy, Mamadou, who has abandoned her. After spending months hiding her condition under voluminous
clothes she sinks into a state of despair and stays away from work. Ndèye
Cissé visits Fatou in her shack and promises to help her. But Fatou gives
birth alone at night in the toilet block of her compound. The baby appears
to be stillborn so she bundles it up into a plastic bag and throws it into the
shallow canal nearby.[15] At that moment, a man on his way to early morning
prayers spots her and hauls her off to the nearby police station. When she
is left alone in a cell she hangs herself believing that by so doing she will
be remembered not for the disgrace of her pregnancy, but for her courage in

eliminating disgrace through death. The story ends with Arame Cissé writing a letter to her closest friend in which we learn that Arame's troubles have driven her to drink.

The novel draws our attention to the gender dimension of rapid economic destabilization and change. It illustrates how the socio-cultural issues generated within an environment of change have an impact on the lives of the female members of that society in ways that are distinct from its impact on male society. It explores society's response to teenage pregnancy, urban poverty, and puts paid to the myth of traditional African solidarity and indigenous systems of welfare. Whereas these have endured and even thrived in some rural localities throughout the cycle of economic downturns of the past four decades, they have not translated readily into the urban environment. On the contrary, African society is shown here to be deeply divided along class lines, fatally lacking in social support mechanisms in the urban environment, and increasingly lacking in social cohesion. From the female characters who people this story, we get no sense, in this profoundly heterogeneous society, of a "*condition féminine*," a concept at the heart of governmental responses to social issues in many French-speaking countries. In fact, these women have very little shared experience. Many are victims, but in different ways and with different outcomes. When gender disadvantage is combined with class disadvantage in the urban context, the combination can become fatal.

Brisures de Vies, published in December 1998,[16] addresses the social condition of low-caste women caught in urban poverty. The novel focuses on issues that just a year after its publication would play a central role in galvanizing opposition to the political regime that had monopolized power in Senegal since Independence in 1960. Urban poverty and unemployment provided the cornerstones on which the political coalition led by Abdoulaye Wade launched his assault on Abdou Diouf and the ruling Socialist Party in the presidential election of February–March 2000.

Narrated against this background of growing political unrest, Ka's short novel tells the tale of Diégane, a young guard at the Ministry of Mines in Dakar, who earns so little that he is falling deeper and deeper into debt. He is married to Gnilane, who has turned down many rich suitors to marry him but is now, due to months of overwork, too ill to carry on taking in washing and ironing. The story is narrated through the eyes of Gnilane who reflects on her own wretched fate, and on the fate of other women in her family, notably her cousin Gnima and niece Coura.

Gnima lives on her own, having walked out on the wife-beating brute she married, in a small apartment in downtown Dakar. She has taken an unstable and mercurial married lover who leaves her after an argument. When he does not return Gnima sinks into a state of desperate loneliness.

The narrative voice then passes to Gnima who reflects on the fate of another member of this family—her little niece Coura. The child has been psychologically traumatised as a result of being raped. Coura was running an errand for her grandmother when she was attacked by a vagrant in the forest near her village. The grandmother has since died of grief and guilt.

In the end, the story takes a positive turn. Macadou, Gnilane and Diégane's eldest son, has become a successful economist and has chosen to return to Senegal and look after his family rather than stay away and make his fortune as an economist in an international organization.

The social function of female sexuality as the repository of social mores and family "honor," female fecundity, and the rigid class (caste) system in Senegal, the vulnerability of women in an environment of urban poverty, social taboos surrounding rape and unwanted pregnancy (which intensify in periods of profound or rapid social change), these are the issues identified by the author as the most significant factors determining the quality of women's lives in Senegal and the key issues of social development. Access to education, paid employment, health services and political power feature in these stories but they are peripheral to the context in which determinants of social development operate in Senegal.

In the face of multiple seemingly intractable problems, no universal solutions are offered. Access to education, to paid employment, to Western values and to "modernity" in general do not provide the remedies to these women's problems. Indeed the "modernity" of the urbanizing environment in West Africa is seen as a hostile site in which young girls are readily sacrificed by a society whose foundations are shattering under the weight of rapid and unpredictable change.

FICTIONAL REALITIES OR "SCIENTIFIC FICTIONS"?

Francophone African women writers have established a political voice in the debate on gender and development in modern Senegalese society and their presence in this debate is now acknowledged.[17] As Coquery-Vidrovitch has argued:

> La littérature de langue française sur les femmes africaines nous apprend beaucoup: plus, à vrai dire, et de façon autrement plaisante que ne le fait la littérature dite savante des anthropologues ou des historiens.[18]

I would go further and suggest that social realist fiction responds to a gap that has not been filled by the social science literature due principally to two factors: firstly, the continued emphasis the latter places on quantitative as opposed to qualitative research; and secondly, the understandable and, in some cases, entirely justifiable emphasis that is placed on avoiding engagement with culturally specific social issues in human rights-based social policy-making.

The contribution African women writers are making is less in exposing culturally-specific gender-based disadvantage and more in illuminating the of socio-cultural context in which female characters access the opportunities of social development policies as they are currently conceived and implemented in developing societies. The novels focus on revealing the way cultural forces mediate the interface between individual and social policy.

These novels also serve to undermine certain myths that are still circulating about the implementation of social development policy in "traditional" developing societies. It is frequently asserted that African familial solidarity combined with the complementary, as opposed to binary, nature of gender relations in Africa where male and female constitute a "duality" rather than an opposition, makes gender mainstreaming superfluous in African social policy. It is a view still propounded by long-serving political leaders in francophone Africa. The texts help bring to light the ways in which the policies of these predominantly male political elites have, in the course of the postcolonial era, served to deepen gender inequalities in African society.

A better understanding of context brings to light the absence of effective social networks, and how this problem is worsening in the urban context and will probably worsen still further during periods of recession in the twenty-first century. In this regard, the texts also illuminate problems linked to the social development goals to be achieved by the year 2015. The primary goal— universal education—is clearly problematized in this literature. The positive and negative aspects of formal education are revealed in both Bâ and Dieng's œuvres. Mariama Bâ in *Un chant écarlate* shows us how a full-term formal Western-style education socializes a young woman (Mireille) into a debilitating form of subservience and dependency which makes her quite incapable of independent action once her husband Ousmane has been shown to have feet of clay. Kura, in Mame Younousse Dieng's *L'Ombre en feu*, is a highly intelligent inquisitive girl whose life is transformed by attending a high school. Her personal security is violated when she is trapped in the family home of the grotesque cousin, Demba Gey, and furthermore her education cannot save her from having to marry him. Neither can it save her from the ensuing marital rape and from an early death in childbirth. In the context in which she learned her lessons, her education gave her no power. Indeed as one of the villagers notes, it became her curse thus underscoring the argument that educational provision must be evaluated in relation to cultural rather than purely functional criteria.

Far from being an argument against education for all, this is an argument for ensuring that the provision and content of formal education policies work for girls in positive ways in the communities in which they live. The writers who engage in this discussion do not argue against the efforts of the international development community but they do challenge its discourse and its limitations. They also provide through their writing an indication of where obstacles need to be confronted. For example, the key role played by the local communities, for both men and women, in the successful implementation of all social development policies is clear in the work of Mame Younouse Dieng. Aminata Maïga Ka created Fatou in *La Voie du Salut* with the express intention of exposing the problem of teenage pregnancy and society's response to this in Dakar. The social problem was the reason for writing the novel and not *vice versa*. Indeed teenage pregnancy as a metaphor for social and familial disintegration in a rapidly modernizing society is a theme that recurs in African feminist literature throughout the sub-region. It serves as a central story line in Gabonese writer Justine Mintsa's short novel *Histoire d'Awu* (2000) where the expulsion of the pregnant 12-year-old Ada from her family home exposes the fallibility of some of the mythic narratives underlying contemporary social policy-making in francophone Africa referred to earlier in these chapters. It engages to some extent with the myth of familial solidarity (although in this case Ada's aunts step in to provide the kind of support her parents deny her) and with the mythic status of Western medicine in francophone Africa. As in Dieng's earlier novel,[19] the superiority of Western medicine, particularly in the context of maternal and infant health care, is questioned. While the mere suggestion that a village birth is safer and more desired in Gabon than a hospital birth may seem shocking to Western ears, this is precisely an example of a conclusion that Mintsa hopes to challenge by infusing oral narratives into her novel.[20]

FROM FICTIONAL REALITIES TO POLICY SOLUTIONS?

The will to provide effective social support to individuals suffering gender-based discrimination and marginization is evident in the stated social policy aims of governments throughout the region. It is also clearly evidenced in the significant contributions international organizations make annually to gender and social development initiatives since the mid-1970s. The social policy budgets devoted by international organizations to social development initiatives in francophone Africa continue to represent a significant portion of the development assistance entering the countries of the region. With Senegal receiving up to $10 million from USAID; $4 million from the African Development Bank; $3 million from the World Bank; up to $5 million from the various UN agencies with the Japanese aid agency JICA funding education programs to the tune of over $30 million a year in the first decade of the twenty-first century, there is no lack of consciousness of the problems and even the gendered character of these problems. All these budgets are either partially or specifically targeting the social development of women. Efforts to provide the kind of social services so fatally lacking for individuals like Fatou have been undertaken but the outcomes have been disappointing. Clearly the problem is not one of alerting governments and development partners to the need for gender policies. The challenge is one of harnessing the cultural knowledge present in the local environment to maximize the return on these capital outlays.

NOTES

1. Mame Younousse Dieng, *L'Ombre en feu* (Dakar: Nouvelles Editions Africaines du Sénégal, 1997). This work has also been published by *Nouvelles Editions Africaines du Sénégal* in Wolof.

2. High schools were initially located only in the regional capitals of French Africa and so by definition were largely inaccessible, financially and geographically, to pupils from rural communities. Entry was usually dependent upon the award of grants and bursaries from central government.

3. This practice has become a very sensitive issue in contemporary francophone African social policy as legislators tackle the need to distinguish between legitimate child labor and family work and the growth of forced labor and child slavery in the regional economy, particularly in the cocoa export industry in Cote d'Ivoire and in domestic service in Gabon.

4. Dieng, *L'Ombre en feu*, 171. Here and henceforth *L'Ombre en feu* is referred to in the text as *OEF* with the page reference given after the colon.

5. Kura learned French and thought she was a white girl. That was her tragedy. Author's translation.

6. During fieldwork in Senegal between 1999 and 2004, I explored the question of who was the most feminist writer in Senegal at that time with academics, professionals in the publishing world, and women readers with an interest in the issue, including a reading group of high profile women activists. In all cases, Aminata Maïga Ka was cited most often as an author clearly associated with feminist causes.

7. Interview with Aminata Maïga Ka.

8. Aminata Maïga Ka, *La Voie du Salut & Le Miroir de la Vie* (Paris: Présence Africaine, 1985).

9. Ka, *La Voie du Salut*, 8. Here and henceforth *La Voie du Salut* is referred to in the text as *VDS* with the page reference indicated after the colon.

10. Aminata Maïga Ka. *La Voie du Salut & Le Miroir de la Vie* (Paris: Présence Africaine, 1985).

11. Ka, *Le Miroir de la Vie*, 104. Here and henceforth *Le Miroir de la Vie* is referred to in the text as *MV* with the page reference given after the colon.

12. fCFA 30,000 represents a significant sum of money equal to a modest average monthly salary in the city where Fatou works.

13. A griotte (feminine form) or griot (masculine form) is an oral historian and praise-singer.

14. The name is a mark of respect shown to those who have made the pilgrimage to Mecca.

15. For those readers familiar with the geography of Dakar, the events appear to be taking place in the vicinity of Canal 4 and the Great Mosque.

16. Aminata Maïga Ka, *Brisures de Vies* (St. Louis, Sénégal: Xamal, 1998).

17. They have become relatively widely read in their local communities, according to anecdotal evidence gathered from professionals in the publishing and literary world in Senegal, though it is difficult to assess to the extent of this dissemination because one book is read by multiple readers so sales figures have little sense in this context.

18. Catherine Coquery-Vidrovitch. "Préface," in *Les Femmes dans la littérature africaine—portraits,* Denise Brahami and Anne Trevarthen, eds. (Paris: Karthala, 1998), 5. "In fact this literature teaches us more about African women than traditonal historical or anthropological studies can and they are more pleasant to read." Author's translation.

19. In *L'Ombre en feu,* Dieng locates the place of Kura's death as the western medical station, and the inaccessibility of the regional hospital is culpable—by implication—in sealing the fate of this young girl who dies in childbirth.

20. Cheryl Toman, "Fang Culture in Gabonese Francophone Women's Writing: Reading *Histoire d'Awu* by Justine Mintsa," *Research in African Literatures* 41, no. 2, 2010, 121–132, [128].

19

Conclusion

Harnessing Culture for Gender and Development

This study has looked at the discourse of gender and development in francophone Africa from three levels. It began its journey in the institutions and instruments of the international community where a model of gender and development was configured for a developing world in which francophone Africa forms a largely undifferentiated part. The discussion then turned to the factor of context in gender and development discourse and traced the emergence of gender as a social signifier in the African context. Lastly, we addressed the issue of culture in the experience of gender and development in the localized context. This experience was communicated through the voices of local activists and development practitioners as well as those stakeholders in the development process who articulate social experience outside the formal development structures. These stakeholders include African feminist writers who contributed a culturally-located expression of the experience of development in francophone African context. This last chapter brings together the conclusions from these three levels of analysis and seeks to identify future directions for the research and practice of gender and development policy in francophone Africa.

THE SCIENCE OF GENDER AND DEVELOPMENT

Social development rose to the top of the international policy-making agenda in the late 1980s and early 1990s, propelled in large part by the international development lobby working for the advancement of women. This coalition produced a dynamic mix that resulted in the gender dimension of social development coming to the fore of policy-making for the first time in history through two global summits, the first in Copenhagen and the second in Beijing.

The interaction of these two international policy-making fields resulted in a gendered version of development based on the recently established "human development" paradigm. This pared down universal model for the advancement of women[1] required that women must have a higher level of participation in and representation in political structures,[2] a fairer share of economic resources and remuneration, and above all that their access to educational opportunities and health care must be improved. Within this logic, the combined effect of these changes will bring the social development of women in the developing world up to the level currently enjoyed by men (as measured by the human development index).

When this theoretical model for the advancement of women was applied to francophone West Africa in the mid-1990s, the point at which statistical auditing began to be monitored systematically in advance of the women and social development summits, the countries of this region produced lower female social development scores than any other region in the world. When this study undertook a longitudinal analysis in an attempt to reveal how the social development of women had been evolving over time (1990 to 2005), the statistics provided some indications of trends but, in terms of policy-making, were not proved fit for purpose. In both Gabon, the richest country in the region, and Senegal, the most data rich country in the region, contemporary calculative technologies failed to provide a clear picture of the gendered dimensions of development among the female populations of these countries.

Furthermore, a closer study of the demographic profile of these countries showed that the populations are so heterogeneous as to call into question the plausibility of this modeled approach to social development being applied at national level.

The study of the history of gender and development policy also revealed that policy-making has been a highly centralized process in the former French colonies of sub-Saharan Africa. The NGO movement and the women's movement are both strong in parts of the region, particularly in Senegal, but their actions are fragmented and their access to the policy-making center is subject to the invitation of the State. Where access is achieved it is increasingly dependent on the intervention of international agencies and NGOs. These "international" bodies operate within a development culture which I have termed the "New York Consensus," highlighting the distance that lies between the origins and organs of the dominant development discourse and the culturally various developing world countries that populate its periphery.

The impact of not accommodating alternative cultural paradigms in the discourse and praxis of development was brought to the fore in the thematic reading of social realist texts from francophone Africa. These texts served both to uncover the distance that separates universal and local discourses of development and to signal some of the obstacles that lie in the way of development policies that fail to engage effectively with the culture of recipient populations. This is not to posit a monolithic model of "local" culture in opposition to an exogenous "alien" culture, but rather to propose a model of culture as dissensual and organic, evolving from a set of constantly changing relationships and holding within these dissonant intersections, the seeds of development and change.

THE LIMITS OF MODELING DEVELOPMENT

As the literary text has illustrated, providing a cultural context in which to evaluate gender and development policy-making underscores how the key variables articulated in the dominant discourse of gender and development do not operate in the local context in the same standardized ways they operate in the cultural vacuum of rationalist policy-making. A dislocation occurs between policy-making and policy implementation and attempts at universalizing the particular and homogenizing highly disparate populations produce unpredictable and varied results. The limitations of this approach go some way towards explaining the spectacular lack of progress in reaching even the minimal Millennium Development Goals of 2015.

With failure has come neglect. The salience of sex and gender as determinants of social development has waned and has fallen behind competing issues on the international political agenda, not least the "war against terror" and climate change. The lack of attention paid to the gender dimensions of the eight Millennium Development Goals, most notably in the Goals dealing with the environment and conflict, even indicates a move backwards on the part of the international community. This raises issues of concern for policy-makers in the second decade of the third millennium as vulnerability to poverty, exclusion and deprivation among the populations of the world's least developed region continues unabated. This reversal of fortune in the face of growing poverty can be interpreted as the result of a combination of factors:

1. Widespread disappointment at the lack of progress towards meeting the objectives set at the four global women's conferences, and particularly the Nairobi "Forward-looking strategies" of 1985.
2. Insufficient time then spent considering why the Nairobi Strategies had not been implemented. The assumption that the targets had not been met because the time frame was too tight and the targets too numerous

remained the orthodoxy, to the extent that almost no changes were made to the target-setting process at Beijing. The Beijing platform delivered more of the same, namely a raft of social policy objectives to be achieved either by the end of the decade, in 2005, or soon afterwards;

3. Meanwhile the same undifferentiated package of rationalist needs-based social policy objectives was delivered to countries using a single time frame with the exception of the most critical objective of all—the elimination of poverty—where countries were exhorted simply to do their best and as quickly as possible.

There are strong arguments supporting the setting of clear common objectives, time frames and deadlines. How else can the international community put pressure on renegade governments and hold them accountable when they fail to honor commitments made at global summits? Creating a universal common platform helps strengthen a lobby, particularly a controversial one campaigning for the enhancement of women's social, political and economic advancement. It can also serve to support pressure groups in societies where opposition to women's advancement (or change that impacts on the position of men in society) is a legitimate or official position, as exemplified by the States refusing to sign up to the international platforms of action. However, the history of these platforms has shown that even where political regimes sign up to the agreed international targets, these targets are not necessarily actioned at the level of the nation-state, and the international community is not able to enforce the implementation of these commitments to action in countries where the objectives are not underwritten by the national political elite. On the basis of this evidence, a highly standardized package makes less political sense than a package that has to go through an adaptation and adoption process in the Member State before reaching the implementation stage. The challenge lies in configuring the development structures within which that adaptation process could be framed and accommodate the socio-specificity of cultural context.

FROM UNIVERSALISM TO CULTURE

The way the global policy package is being formulated within the international policy-making structures has created barriers to its own implementation. This does not bring into question the validity of universality in other policy fields. The case for universality in human rights has been convincingly made by some of the most influential voices in international development politics.[3] Furthermore the universality of human rights is now embedded in the organizational development of the structures underpinning the international community in the twenty-first century. In 2005 the outgoing Secretary General of the UN made the creation of a "Human Rights Council" the central pillar of his reform of the UN in the mid 2000s.[4]

However, the human rights debate has now spilled over into other policy fields to the point where criticizing universalistic discourse can invite accusations of undermining international efforts to promote the rights of women. But to argue thus is to confuse ethics with dynamics. A distinction must be made between human rights, operating in the context of international law, and gender equity in development, enshrined in a much looser framework of international "platforms of action" and "conventions." Both can operate to promote the status of women, but it must be recognized that they operate within different policy-making frameworks.

CENTER-PERIPHERY POLITICS: RECONSTRUCTING THE MARGINS OF THE POSTCOLONY

The discourse of gender and development precedes and defines its practice; in other words the language of gender and social development is created at the center of policy operations and exported to the "margins." The evidence produced in this study leads us to question whether this top-down, center-periphery model of social development policy is a sufficiently delicate instrument to support social change in manageable and predictable ways in francophone West African societies. The findings lead us to question the plausibility of a remote body of people, however well-intentioned, operating from the richest financial centers of the world, formulating policies likely to maximize the quality of life of millions of women living in the vastly varied regions of the developing world.

The issue of who should be formulating policy is a question that has been circulating in the international development arena throughout the era of global conferences. These international events highlighted the risk every development field runs of a group of "experts" taking over policy discourse and practice in the absence of an intimate understanding of local realities. Commenting on how population policies were being arrived at during the first international environment summit in Rio de Janeiro in 1992, one Senegalese observer noted:

> These discussions are of course very interesting but one can't help wondering whether we will just end up with some academic speculations from a group of experts which will be meaningless to outsiders. This could lead to decisions based on factors which have little relation to the real problem.[5]

The distance between the discourse of the experts and the experience of the locality is reflected in the methods used by the former to evaluate the "development" of the latter. The success of universal social policy objectives is evaluated in international agencies by means of a raft of established quantitative methods designed by those agencies. Like the objectives themselves, these methods are instruments crafted by well-intentioned specialists, and are not without value. Nevertheless,

> [Q]uestions can be raised about the imperfections and insufficiency of quantitative measurements to evaluate human development. Indices can not, for example, capture a dynamic sense of empowerment at the level of individuals, households, communities. However, this does not erase the importance of designing quantitative measures that can be used for comparative analysis—cross-country over time. The availability of indices, even if imperfect, can provide insights into gender equality and directions for further improvements.[6]

But as this study has revealed, these quantitative methods are particularly maladapted to the realities of data collection in West Africa. The data are so incomplete that it is not possible to locate a country's position accurately along an intricately constructed human development continuum, never mind measure its progress towards an ideal end point. On this theoretical continuum, the ideal is understood to be the point where women's access to quality of life improvement delivered by social development policy is equal to that of men's, in other words, a situation where gender no longer acts as a determinant of access to society's shared resources. To establish within this paradigm whether a developing country is moving towards a situation where men and women have equal access to the social benefits of development, it is necessary to have in place an intricate set of qualitative and quantitative accounting measures capable of mapping this. This is not the reality in francophone West Africa, even if it were a desirable goal. There is also little possibility of this situation becoming a reality in the foreseeable future in countries where a large part of the economy operates outside the Western industrialized model and thereby defies Western accounting systems, such as Senegal where a substantial proportion of the national economy operates in the "independent" or "informal" sector. In such a context a government may feel compelled to sign up to social development goals in the glare of publicity at an international conference and then find itself compelled to address other obligations "on the ground." Such a government defers reporting back on progress to the international monitoring bodies, such as the UNDP's Human Development Report team or the CEDAW committee, and the knowledge gap widens.

FRANCOPHONE WEST AFRICA:
REFLECTING THE FAILURE OF DATA

The problems of data collection and reporting are openly acknowledged by the national and international development communities in the francophone West African region. As Gabon and Senegal demonstrated, we cannot map the implementation of the many international "Platforms for Action" either in poverty-stricken Senegal or in relatively wealthy Gabon with the exception of women's participation in parliamentary politics. Thanks to the Inter-Parliamentary Union, this variable is carefully documented consistently and throughout the world. It falls outside the immediate scope of this book to discuss how the presence of women parliamentarians affects the advancement of non-elite women in their society, suffice it to say that we would be naive in thinking that privileged women automatically work for the advancement of other women in their community. But regardless of whether increased parliamentary participation should be a prime objective, it is noteworthy that the objective of striving towards parity in political representation has lost the prominence it enjoyed on the agenda of international gender politics in the 1990s as has the goal of empowering women economically.

Variables are contested at numerous levels, from the international forums through to implementation in the locality. Efforts are currently being made by those who question the effectiveness of the existing gender and development monitoring model in francophone West Africa to introduce a portfolio of new numerical indicators for data collection. We can see evidence here of how the international development discourse sets down the parameters within which change at the local level can be envisioned and articulated. Local practice is forced to respond to a data-driven agenda, and control over the discursive parameters of development remains in the hands of the bodies that fund social development and, particularly, gender initiatives in Africa. As international development agencies continue to develop and export their ready-made "tool kits" for gender mainstreaming in developing countries[7] there are as yet no tool kits designed specifically for re-evaluating and adapting policies to the realities of life in local communities.

BRINGING INTERNATIONAL DISCOURSE
TO THE MASSES OR THE MASSES TO
INTERNATIONAL DISCOURSE?

In the discussion of gendered social development in Senegal, social values research methods (primarily interviews conducted in the locality) and cultural studies research methods (thematic analysis of feminist social realist writing) revealed how the universal discourse of development has been effectively inculcated into the local context. From more than one hundred interviews and discussions conducted in the region over a period of ten years, it emerged that while the language of gender and social development has been forged primarily in the international community and draws little from the local or national context,[8] activists on the ground are quick to adopt the international discourse. This is a phenomenon common to other development issues including environmental politics, as the following example from Guinea testifies:

> Several authors have recently spotlighted the presence of particular off-the-shelf "narratives," current in development institutions, which come to define development problems and justify interventions, particularly in conditions where data are poor, time is short, national agendas are overruled and local consultation impossible.[9]

This phenomenon has occurred throughout the developing world. It has even been noted in the field of "participatory" development policy:

> During the late 1980s and into the 1990s, the discourse about community has been complemented by an increasingly ubiquitous discourse about "people's participation" and "empowerment." While community has by no means disappeared from public and private discourses on development, everyone, from village farmers to international donors, has begun to speak the language of "participation" and 'empowerment."[10]

In this study of Asian development, Woost goes on to argue that this does not signal a shift in the locus of policy making from centre to periphery. He sees it as a sign of a rather sinister and ultimately centralizing trend:

> [P]articipatory discourse, like the notions of community that preceded it, clearly has many different connotations only some of which hold the possibility for more "bottom-up" debate about the social, economic and cultural arrangement of the present and the future. [. . .] My contention [. . .] is that mainstream use of participatory rhetoric in Sri Lanka offers little in the way of alternative development. Rather the notion of participation has been laundered and reshaped in official discourse to fit the mould of an increasingly ruthless drive to implement market-led strategies intended quickly to turn Sri Lanka into an NIC (Newly Industrialized Country).[11]

The market-led discourse is not absent from the African context. In francophone West Africa, the neo-liberal ideology of the market is discernible in discourse promoting gender and development policy as a means of developing "human capital." Indeed, the economics of social development forms an increasingly visible part of the ubiquitous official discourse of gender and development in the region.

LITERARY DISCOURSE AS CULTURAL VOICE

By contrast, the literary contributions to this debate on gender and development have demonstrated how the language of development used by the international development community does not extend into a culturally-based engagement with development issues.[12] Local cultural and literary systems provide a platform for alternative discourses of development.

In *L'Ombre en feu*, Mame Younousse Dieng explored the impact of what is commonly referred to still in francophone West Africa as "French school," namely formal European-style education, and showed how the importation of this phenomenon into a rural community completely unprepared for this life-changing development generated completely unexpected results. Here formal education became not a catalyst for social development but a catalyst for social chaos. Mame Younousse Dieng was not arguing against formal education in this exploration of the impact of schooling for girls in rural Senegal, far from it. Her contribution to this debate is to point up the cultural context of policy implementation. She and other writers are exposing local cultural realities which currently have no place in the official discourse of development. The dysfunctional outcomes of maladapted social policies in these narratives serve to reveal the model of development as "unfit for purpose," not because it is intrinsically wrong, but because it has not passed through the prism of local cultural realities before reaching the implementation stage. What these writers implicitly argue, in creating the social chaos of their fictional, representational communities, is that unless local stakeholders, including the most conservative forces in the community, are involved in the process of social policy formulation and implementation, then outcomes will be unpredictable, even disastrous.

LOOKING TO THE FUTURE: BEYOND UNIVERSALISM

The phenomenon of gender discrimination is an issue affecting the entire postcolonial world and as such it is one that we can quite rightly approach cross-culturally, while still acknowledging the specificity of cultural context. Cross-cultural analysis offers a platform for incorporation of a range of perspectives, including critical and conservative perspectives from within communities, acknowledging the possibility of multiple perspectives, or sociological "realities." The current absence of multiple perspectives has led to a hierarchy of knowledge in the gender and development field that undermines its credibility and its potentiality for change in the locality as the following critique exemplifies:

> In Western/feminist discourses, African traditional practices are reified and cast as impositions on women. It is unthinkable in such imperialist discourses that African women actually choose to have co-wives and some choose to be circumcised. African women who are in polygamous marriages are not morons or powerless, exploited, downtrodden victims. Many of these women are intelligent, highly educated, successful, independent women who choose polygynous marriage as what is good for them.[13]

Conflating sign (polygyny, circumcision, etc.) with identity is a characteristic of colonial discourses of gender and development, but locating signs beyond the reach of broader structural critiques undermines the possibility of cross-cultural agency. The range of opportunities offered to women by a given social system is constrained by broader political structures (contained within patriarchy, religious cults, etc.). By uncovering the relationship between sign and structure we open up a space for cross-cultural critique and agency where context and sign can be subject to challenge and deconstruction from multiple perspectives.

Admitting social multiplicity and refusing to model identity around one "truth" offers an alternative to the dominating norms of an overly-standardized humanistic discourse and provides some shelter from the practical dangers and intellectual pitfalls of cultural relativism.

INTEGRATING CULTURE AND CONTEXT IN DEVELOPMENT THEORY

To development theorists and practitioners the challenge is not simply to recognize alternative ways of knowing, but to identify how to accommodate a multiplicity of realities in a formulation that by its nature is a standardizing procedure insofar as policy is applied to whole populations. The present study has explored this gap between the formulation of standardized policy and culturally-embedded knowledge of gender and development articulated from the perspectives of local development practitioners and feminist creative writers. The urge to bridge this gap chimes with developments in the intellectual history of the West. While traditional social scientists continue to argue against the use of literature in social science, diversifying the gender and social development knowledge base beyond the traditionally "scientific" source resonates with a trend that has been steering humanities research into increasingly interdisciplinary waters for the past quarter of a century. Since 1982, when "new historicism"[14] was introduced into literary theory, it has become orthodoxy to recognize the presence of social forces in the literary text. Now the intellectual traffic is beginning to flow in the other direction and, in the context of francophone Africa, is drawing on a particularly rich vein in feminist writing from the 1970s to the present day to illuminate knowledge of the social world. Indeed if we include male writers, postcolonial feminist African literature has for over half a century been providing a narrative interpretation of the socio-political environment offering an antidote to the homogenized and reductive construction of African womanhood that emerged from earlier literary traditions and the more recent official discourse of development.

UNIVERSAL DEVELOPMENT
DISCOURSE AND GLOBALIZATION

The standardization of culture and discourse that "globalization" claims to have produced bears little examination in the developing world context. In practice, there is no consensus over the acceptability of the Western value-system and the neo-liberal economic system on which it rests.[15] While it has been argued in this study that development policies that are insensitive to local cultural realities are less effective, the dysfuntionality of these policies has been seen to have had a much deeper and longer-term effect destabilizing the local economy:

> [A]s Chossudovsky rightly observes, the structural adjustment package of the IMF can increasingly be considered as the cause rather than the solution of the economic problems experienced in the Third World. The withdrawal of the State led to the increasing impoverishment of low-income groups.[16]

In some cases the result has been a rise in fundamentalism which, in its efforts to distinguish itself from Western paradigms, has adopted a strict, anti-modern religiosity with severe repercussions for the local population and particularly women.[17] Imposing foreign development models on societies already under strain from economic under-development or mismanagement creates a cultural backlash. This backlash is typically played out on the least powerful members of society who are used as a vehicle to articulate a mythical or extreme version of "traditional" indigenous society.

According to UNIFEM, which maintains a constructively critical view of the international community's policy responses to gender issues in social development, the international community is failing to recognize and accommodate in its policy responses the negative impact on women of recent global economic developments:

> The commitments [of the global summits] reflect an expectation that governments are responsible for implementing policies to improve the well-being of women, especially poor women, but they do not effectively address the ways in which market liberalisation and privatisation may undermine the capacity of governments to discharge their responsibilities, especially to poor women.[18]

In the face of failing policies, international agencies endeavor to change the local cultural context in which their policies are implemented rather than attempt to change the policy parameters themselves. The UN population fund[19] is an example of an agency that has aimed at drawing national governments and agencies into the international discourse. UNFPA implemented four population programs in Gabon since 1988 costing some $7 million in disbursements.[20] The agency reported the success of its programs in Gabon in the terms of the degree to which it succeeded in importing the agency's conception of female reproductive health into the locality. The UNFPA reported positively on its impact in Gabon but also pointed out that at the beginning of the twenty-first century there were still alternative perspectives on population issues persisting in the local environment and these remain a target for UNFPA advocacy:

> Important lessons drawn from the previous programme include the continued relevance and importance of persistent and well-targeted advocacy. Whatever the nature or magnitude of population problems, UNFPA's presence in the field and its continuous and judicious use of the findings of the research results for advocacy and sensitization activities directed towards decision makers, opinion leaders and civil society can and often does succeed in changing perceptions and attitudes.[21]

The success of UNFPA policy is measured in population parameters and legislative changes, such as the legalization of contraception in the year 2000. While the impact of such programs can be very positive in many respects, the opportunities for maximizing impact are severely constrained by the distance that separates policy and context. Gabon is a strongly Catholic country situated in a region of central Africa that has traditionally experienced a high percentage of sterility and neo-natal mortality. The framing of female reproductive health and the quantitative measurement of fertility and birth rates camouflage cultural and sociological factors that inform more complex local understandings of fertility trends.

For its part, the Gabonese State has been receptive as opposed to responsive to the international discourse of development. The official Gabonese definition of social development, elaborated by the Prime Minister's office in preparation for the UN Social Summit in Copenhagen, was clearly based on the international model. In the opening paragraphs of the Social Summit submission the Gabonese *rapporteur* envisioned social development as a project based on universal values, calling it "this new and universal project of civilization."[22] Notwithstanding the adoption of the universal discourse, the paragraph nevertheless ended with an acknowledgement of the generalizing humanist epistemology that underlies social development discourse:

> The Greeks then asked of Solon: What is the best constitution? Solon responded: First you must tell me for which people and then in which era.[23]

FROM EDUCATION TO EQUALITY?

Le défi majeur reste-t-il de renforcer le pouvoir des femmes dans la famille et la société, l'économie et la politique.[24]

According to this definition of female advancement, gender and development policy in Senegal in the postcolonial era has failed to empower women. If we take the definition of women's advancement enshrined in the current Millennium Development Goal 3, gender equality is reached through access to formal education and much progress has been made over the past two decades as exemplified by the data in table 19.1 Notwithstanding the problems with data collection in the region, the table suggests that if we adopt the Millennium Development Goal 3's definition then we can confirm that francophone West Africa is *en route* towards achieving gender equality.

The question remains whether African women would be satisfied with this definition, particularly as education has been held up as an example of where global visions and local realities part company:

> African women have been unable to [. . .] define their goals for liberation through education. [. . .] With economic control in the hands of men, women's education remains determined by men from the home base to the institutional base.[25]

This calls for the existing gender dimension of formal education to be problematized. There is no lack of understanding in the local development community on how to engage with this challenge. The question is whether the official discourse of the "New York Consensus" can bring the global and the local into a more creative partnership.

**Table 19.1.   Net Primary Enrolment of
Girls as Percentage of Primary School Age
Population**

Country	1991	2005
Benin	29%	72%
Burkina Faso	23%	35%
Cameroon	69%	n.d.
C.A.R.	41%	n.d.
Chad	21%	47%
Congo	77%	?
Côte d'Ivoire	37%	?
Gabon	85%	?
Guinea	19%	58%
Mali	16%	43%
Mauritania	30%	74%
Niger	17%	32%
Senegal	37%	64%
Togo	53%	72%

Source: UN Statistics Division Database 2006. Data
include UNESCO Institute of Statistics estimates.

THE "NEW YORK CONSENSUS" VERSUS
THE LOCALITY—IS THERE A WAY FORWARD?

In Senegal, Gabon, and other countries of francophone West Africa, WID, and, more latterly, GAD discourse has been incorporated into the local development discourse and into the apparatus of the State, primarily through the secretariats and ministries with responsibility for women's affairs. Notwithstanding the levels of activity and the sophistication of the gender and development infrastructure laid down in these countries, interlocutors interviewed for the present study in Senegal and Gabon expressed the view that gender and development discourses and practices have been largely colonized by the postcolonial African State with a result that the structures, and the policies implemented through them, have been emasculated and no radical change in the socio-economic status of women in francophone West Africa is achievable through the formal structural apparatus of the state.

On the other hand, many interlocutors, notably women working in the NGO sector, stated that though results have been poor, the climate of debate has changed. Where before opportunities for talking about women's advancement were severely limited, now public discussions on this topic are widely accepted if still contested by religious authorities in particular. The advocates of women's advancement in New York and throughout the international development community have contributed much to producing this climate for change.

At the policy-making periphery, in countries such as Senegal and Gabon, international agencies work in difficult conditions and in good faith to provide a better future for the people they serve. However, their relative lack of success in advancing the socio-economic condition of women, given the considerable investment to date—in recent years the annual budget for Senegal has been in excess of $20 million a year—suggests that global solutions to gender disadvantage can provide guidelines for social development around the globe, but they cannot, from the evidence we have seen, deliver social development, beyond the most minimal definition of this concept.

The case study of Senegal provides some indication of the degree to which the francophone West African region has the capacity to provide informed, culturally-embedded knowledge of the gender and development context. This suggests that the current policy of funding capacity-building actions for gender mainstreaming needs to re-evaluate the capacity base. The intellectual wealth that already exists has not been exploited in gender and development policy formulation in the region to date. Meanwhile in the course of the first decade of the twenty-first century an international francophone discourse of gender and development has evolved which, in the second decade of the twenty-first century, may serve to challenge the erstwhile dominant exogenous discourse of development from the Anglophone world.

Over the past half century, the international community of policy-makers who have constructed the dominant discourse of development have resisted handing down responsibility for policy formulation to the locality. The hierarchies of knowledge and power constructed during the centuries of colonial rule have left the "center" unwilling to devolve decision-making to the "periphery," and the narrative of gender and development policy continues to be written at a level far removed from the *petites réalités* of the target population.

Meanwhile local participation in this discursive process remains largely confined to local activists who are incorporated into the implementation of international development goals without ever having been present at the stages of conceptualization and formulation. If local women are involved at all they will almost invariably be elite women, many of whom have been educated in Western universities. These elite women have a vital role to play, but they are not generally the targets of gender and development policies aimed at improving education, reducing poverty and promoting rural development. In the words of one long-serving activist in the cause of women's advancement in Senegal:

> We need elites and intellectual women to devise policies for women's advancement and to bring injustices to light. But we should not limit women's participation to this level alone, we need to listen to women who represent the majority

of women, who are not the privileged few. We need to listen to what they have
to say. We need to listen to what these women want, what they need and what
changes they propose. African women can play a far greater role than they are
currently playing in this regard.[26]

The challenge facing social development policy-makers in the twenty-first
century is to harness this knowledge from the locality and make the global
visions of the international development community the visions of the women
they serve.

NOTES

1. The dimensions of this model were radically pared down from earlier attempts
at configuring the gendered nature of development, notably at the Nairobi conference
in 1985.

2. This is particularly pertinent to the former French African colonies. As A.
Mbembe has observed in his reply to the many critics who queried the absence of
gender theorizing in *On the Postcolony* (Berkeley: University of California Press,
2001): "In the Postcolony, [. . .] the *polis* is above all equivalent to a community of
men (*société des hommes*)."

3. See, for example, Martha Nussbaum, *Women and Human Development: The
Capabilities Approach* (Cambridge: Cambridge University Press, 2000).

4. In March 2005 Kofi Annan proposed a reform of the UN around three prin-
ciples: development, security and human rights.

5. Marie-Hélène Mottin-Sylla, "Le Libre choix en matière de sexualité et de fécondité," *Environnement Africain* 10, nos. 39–40, 1997, 139–154, [140]. Author's
translation. "*Ces discussions sont certes d'un grand intérêt. Il est cependant à crain-
dre qu'elles débouchent sur des spéculations d'école, aboutissant à un débat de spé-
cialistes, obscur au profane. Les décisions auxquelles elles peuvent conduire risquent
d'être prises, tout autant, au nom de considérations non explicitées, qui n'auraient
grand rapport avec le fond du problème.*"

6. Lourdes Benaría, *Gender, Development and Globalization—Economics as if
People Mattered* (New York & London: Routledge, 2003), 20–21.

7. *ACDI*/CIDA, the Canadian international development agency has been a leader
in the field of toolboxes, introducing the "*boîte à outils—stratégie d'égalité des
sexes*" in Senegal in 1998.

8. An example of alternative political discourse on women's social development in
francophone West Africa can be found in Thomas Sankara's speeches on women and
development: *Women's Liberation and the African Freedom Struggle* (New York:
Pathfinder Press, 1990).

9. James Fairhead and Melissa Leach, "Webs of Power and Construction of Environmental Policy Problems: Forest Loss in Guinea," in *Discourses of Development—
Anthropological Perspectives*, R. D. Grillo and R. L. Stirrat, eds. (Oxford: Berg, 1997),
35–57, [35].

10. Michael D. Woost, "Alternative Vocabularies of Development? 'Community' and 'Participation' in Development Discourse in Sri Lanka," in *Discourses of Development—Anthropological Perspectives,* R. D. Grillo and R. L. Stirrat, eds. (Oxford: Berg, 1997), 229–253, [229].

11. Woost, "Alternative Vocabularies of Development?" 230.

12. This is all the more visible when one compares the international discourse with what constitutes the salient political issues in the locality, such as female genital excision throughout the region, domestic violence in Senegal, or legal measures to protect women against enforced polygyny in Gabon.

13. Obioma Nnaemeka, "Urban Spaces, Women's Places—Polygamy as Sign in Mariama Bâ's Novels," in *The Politics of (M)Othering,* Obioma, Nnaemeka, ed. (London: Routledge 1997), 167.

14. Though the term is historically attributed to Stephen Greenblatt and his work *The Forms of Power and Power of Forms* of 1982, he claims not to have coined this phrase himself. See Lucasta Miller, "Profile—Stephen Greenblatt," *The Guardian Review,* 26 February 2005, 20–23, [21].

15. For a discussion of these claims see Ha Joon Chang, *Kicking Away the Ladder* (London: Anthem Press, 2002), particularly chapter 1.

16. Frans J. Schuurman, ed., *Beyond the Impasse—New Directions in Development Theory* (London: Zedbooks, 1993), 11.

17. Constantin von Barloewen, *L'Anthropologie de la modernisation* (Paris: Editions des Syrtes, 2001). The argument developed in this book is summarized by von Barloewen in *Le monde diplomatique,* November 2001, 23.

18. UNIFEM, *Progress of the World's Women 2000* (New York: United Nations 2000), 9.

19. Known as *FNUAP* in francophone countries.

20. United Nations, *United Nations Population Fund—Proposed Projects and Programmes Recommendation by the Executive Director Assistance to the Government of Gabon* DP/FPA/GAB/4 (24 December 2001), 6.

21. United Nations, *United Nations Population Fund,* 7.

22. Primature de la République Gabonaise, *Contribution du Gabon* (1995), 2. Author's translation. The original speaks of "*ce nouveau projet de civilisation universel.*"

23. Primature de la République Gabonaise, *Contribution du Gabon,* 7. Author's translation. *Des Grecs jadis demandaient au sage Solon "Quelle est la meilleure constitution?" Il répondait: "dites-moi d'abord pour quel peuple et à quelle époque."*

24. Fatou Sow, Ngagne Diakhaté, Adama Fall-Touré and Mamadou Matar Gueye, *Les Sénégalaises en Chiffres* (Dakar: PNUD, 2000), 175. "The main challenge still facing us is to reinforce the power women have in the family, in society, in the economy and politically." Author's translation.

25. Lioba Moshi, "Foreword," in *Women and Education in Sub-Saharan Africa—power, opportunities and constraints*, Marianne Bloch, Josephine A. Beoku-Betts, and B. Robert Tabachnick, eds. (Boulder, Colo.: Lynne Rienner, 1998), xi.

26. Awa Sarr, "Consolider la place des femmes dans l'économie sociale et solidaire: un défi d'actualité au Sénégal—Entrevue avec Awa Sarr," Lucie Fréchette,

Michèle Diotte, *Nouvelles Pratiques Sociales* 15, no. 1, 2002, 14. Author's translation. "*Nous avons besoin des élites et des femmes plus intellectuelles pour concevoir les politiques en faveur des femmes et dénoncer les injustices en lieux de pouvoir. Mais il ne faut pas limiter noter participation à ce niveau, il faut entendre les femmes de la base, la majorité des femmes, écouter ce qu'elles ont à dire, ce qu'elles veulent, ce dont elles ont besoin et les changements qu'elles proposent. Les femmes africaines peuvent prendre de plus en plus de pouvoir.*"

Appendix A

Commitment 5, UN World Summit for Social Development, 19 April 1995

TEXT of Commitment 5 on gender and social development from the Outcome Document of the United Nations World Summit for Social Development (A/CONF.166/9), 19 April 1995.

COMMITMENT 5

We commit ourselves to promoting full respect for human dignity and to achieving equality and equity between women and men, and to recognizing and enhancing the participation and leadership roles of women in political, civil, economic, social and cultural life and in development.

To this end, at the national level, we will:

(a) Promote changes in attitudes, structures, policies, laws and practices in order to eliminate all obstacles to human dignity, equality and equity in the family and in society, and promote full and equal participation of urban and rural women and women with disabilities in social, economic and political life, including in the formulation, implementation and follow-up of public policies and programmes;

(b) Establish structures, policies, objectives and measurable goals to ensure gender balance and equity in decision-making processes at all levels, broaden women's political, economic, social and cultural opportunities and independence, and support the empowerment of women, including through their various organisations, especially those of indigenous women, those at the grass-roots level, and those of poverty-stricken communities, including through affirmative action, where necessary, and also through measures to integrate a gender perspective in the design and implementation of economic and social policies;

(c) Promote full and equal access of women to literacy, education and training, and remove all obstacles to their access to credit and other productive resources and to their ability to buy, hold and sell property and land equally with men;

(d) Take appropriate measures to ensure, on the basis of equality of men and women, universal access to the widest range of health-care services, including those relating to reproductive health care, consistent with the Programme of Action of the International Conference on Population and Development;

(e) Remove the remaining restrictions on women's rights to own land, inherit property or borrow money, and ensure women's equal right to work;

(f) Establish policies, objectives and goals that enhance the equality of status, welfare and opportunity of the girl child, especially in regard to health, nutrition, literacy and education, recognizing that gender discrimination starts at the earliest stages of life;

(g) Promote equal partnership between women and men in family and community life and society, emphasize the shared responsibility of men and women in the care of children and support for older family members, and emphasize men's shared responsibility and promote their active involvement in responsible parenthood and responsible sexual and reproductive behaviour;

(h) Take effective measures, including through the enactment and enforcement of laws, and implement policies to combat and eliminate all forms of discrimination, exploitation, abuse and violence against women and girl children, in accordance with relevant international instruments and declarations;

(i) Promote and protect the full and equal enjoyment by women of all human rights and fundamental freedoms;

(j) Formulate or strengthen policies and practices to ensure that women are enabled to participate fully in paid work and in employment through such measures as positive action, education, training, appropriate protection under labour legislation, and facilitating the provision of quality child care and other support services.

At the international level, we will:

(k) Promote and protect women's human rights and encourage the ratification of, if possible by the year 2000, the avoidance, as far as possible, of the resort to reservations to, and the implementation of the provisions of the Convention on the Elimination of All Forms of Discrimination against Women and other relevant instruments, as well as the implementation of 11/ the Nairobi Forward-looking Strategies for the Advancement of Women, the Geneva Declaration for Rural Women, 12/ and the Programme of Action of the International Conference on Population and Development;

(l) Give specific attention to the preparations for the Fourth World Conference on Women, to be held at Beijing in September 1995, and to the implementation and follow-up of the conclusions of that Conference;

(m) Promote international cooperation to assist developing countries, at their request, in their efforts to achieve equality and equity and the empowerment of women;

(n) Devise suitable means to recognize and make visible the full extent of the work of women and all their contributions to the national economy, including contributions in the unremunerated and domestic sectors.

Appendix B

Commitment 5, 24th Special Session of the UN General Assembly, 26 June 2000

TEXT of Commitment 5 on gender and social development from the Outcome Document of the 24th Special Session of the UN General Assembly: World Summit for Social Development (WSSD) and beyond: Achieving social development for all in a globalizing world, 26 June 2000.

COMMITMENT 5

To promote full respect for human dignity and to achieve equality and equity between women and men, and to recognize and enhance the participation and leadership roles of women in political, civil, economic, social and cultural life and in development:

76. Promote the full enjoyment of all human rights and fundamental freedoms by all women and girls as one of the prerequisites of gender equality. Governments should ensure that the human rights of women and girls are respected, protected and promoted through the development, implementation and effective enforcement of gender-sensitive policies and legislation.

77. The elimination of discrimination against women and their empowerment and full participation in all areas of life and at all levels should be priority objectives at the national as well as at the international levels and an intrinsic part of social development. Equitable social development requires full respect for human dignity, equality and equity between women and men, and the mainstreaming of gender considerations in all levels of policy-making and in the planning of programmes and projects. Despite some progress, gender mainstreaming is not yet universal, and gender-based inequality continues in many areas of most societies.

78. Take fully into account and implement the outcome of the twenty-third special session of the General Assembly entitled "Women 2000: gender equality, development and peace for the twenty-first century."

79. Ensure gender mainstreaming in the implementation of each of the further initiatives related to each of the commitments made at the World Summit for Social Development, considering the specific roles and needs of women in all areas of social development, inter alia, by evaluating the gender implications of proposals and taking action to correct situations in which women are disadvantaged. The use of positive or affirmative action and empowerment programmes is commended to both Governments and international organizations.

80. Strengthen national efforts, including with assistance from the international community, to promote the empowerment of women, inter alia, by:

(a) Closing the gender gap in primary and secondary education by 2005 and ensuring free compulsory and universal primary education for both girls and boys by 2015;
(b) Increasing the access of women and girls to all levels and forms of education;
(c) Achieving a 50 per cent improvement in levels of adult literacy by 2015, especially for women;
(d) Increasing the participation of women and bringing about a balanced representation of women and men in all sectors and occupations in the labour market and closing the gender gap in earnings;
(e) Ensuring the reduction of maternal morbidity and mortality as a health sector priority;
(f) Eliminating all forms of violence against women, in the domestic as well as in the public sphere;
(g) Promoting programmes to enable women and men to reconcile their work and family responsibilities and to encourage men to share equally with women household and child care responsibilities.

81. Promote international cooperation to support regional and national efforts in the development and use of gender-related analysis and statistics, inter alia, by providing national statistical offices, upon their request, with institutional and financial support in order to enable them to respond to requests for data disaggregated by sex and age for use by national Governments in the formulation of gender-sensitive statistical indicators for monitoring and policy and programme impact assessment, as well as to undertake regular strategic surveys.

82. Support Governments in their efforts to institute action-oriented programmes and measures to accelerate the full implementation of the Copenhagen Programme of Action and the Beijing Platform for Action, with time-bound targets and/or measurable goals and evaluation methods, including gender-impact assessments, with the full participation of women for measuring and analysing progress.

83. Consider signing and ratifying the Optional Protocol to the Convention on the Elimination of All Forms of Discrimination against Women.

84. Increased efforts are needed to provide equal access to education, health, and social services and to ensure the rights of women and girls to education and the enjoyment of the highest attainable standard of physical and mental health and well-being throughout the life cycle, as well as adequate, affordable and universally accessible health care and services, including as regards sexual and reproductive health, particularly in the face of the HIV/AIDS pandemic; they are also needed with regard to the growing proportion of older women.

85. Ensure that the reduction of maternal morbidity and mortality is a health sector priority and that women have ready access to essential obstetric care, well-equipped and adequately staffed maternal health-care services, skilled attendants at delivery, emergency obstetric care, effective referral and transport to higher levels of care, when necessary, post-partum care and family planning, in order to, inter alia, promote safe motherhood, and give priority attention to measures to prevent, detect and treat breast, cervical and ovarian cancer and osteoporosis, and sexually transmitted infections, including HIV/AIDS.

Selected Bibliography

AAWORD/AFARD. *Visions of Gender Theories and Social Development in Africa: Harnessing Knowledge for Social Justice and Equality* (Dakar: AAWORD Book Series, 2001).

Adepoju, Aderanti, and Christine Oppong, eds. *Gender, Work and Population in Sub-Saharan Africa* (London: James Currey; New Hampshire: Heinemann on behalf of the International Labour Organisation, Geneva, 1994).

Agbasière, Julie. "Sembene Ousmane and the Feminist Question: A Study of 'Les Bouts de Bois de Dieu,'" in *Current Trends in Literature and Language Studies in West Africa,* Ernest N. Emenyonu and Charles E. Nnolim, eds. (Ibadan: Kraft Books Limited, 1994), 53–62.

Agence internationale de la francophonie. *Contribution de la Francophonie à l'examen décennal de la mise en œuvre du programme d'action de la Conférence mondiale sur les femmes de Pékin* (Paris: Agence internationale de la francophonie, 2005).

Amadiume, Ifi. *Male Daughters, Female Husbands: Gender and Sex in an African Society* (London: Zed Books, 1987).

Annan, Kofi. *We the Peoples—The Role of the United Nations in the 21st Century* (New York: United Nations Department of Public Information, March 2000).

Anon. "Summary of the 24th Special Session of the General Assembly." *Earth Negotiations Bulletin* 10, no. 63, 3 July 2000, 1–11.

Assie-Lumumba, Ndri Thérèse and CEPARRED. "Gender, Access to Learning and Production of Knowledge in Africa," in *Visions of Gender Theories and Social Development in Africa: Harnessing knowledge for social justice and equality* (Dakar: AAWORD Book Series, 2001), 95–113.

Bâ, Mariama. *Une si longue lettre* (Dakar: Nouvelles Editions Africaines du Sénégal, 2001)[1979].

———. *Un chant écarlate* (Dakar: Nouvelles Editions Africaines du Sénégal, 1981).

Barnes, J. F. *Gabon—Beyond the Colonial Legacy* (Boulder, Co.: Westview Press, 1992).

Barthel, Diane. "Women's Educational Experience under Colonialism: Towards a Diachronic Model." *Signs* 11, no. 1, 1985, 137–154.

Benaría, Lourdes. *Gender, Development and Globalization—Economics as if People Mattered* (New York & London: Routledge, 2003).

Beoku-Betts, Josephine. "Western Perceptions of African Women in 19th and early 20th centuries," in *Readings in Gender in Africa,* Andrea Cornwell, ed. (London: James Currey, 2005), 20–25.

Berger, Iris, and E. Frances White. *Women in Sub-Saharan Africa* (Bloomington: Indiana University Press, 1999).

Berrian, Brenda. "Through Her Prism of Social and Political Contexts: Sembene's Female Characters in Tribal Scars," in *Ngambika: Studies of Women in African Literature,* Carole Boyce Davies and Anne Adams Graves, eds. (Trenton, N.J.: Africa World Press, 1986), 195–204.

Betts, Raymond F. *France and Decolonisation 1900–1960* (London: Macmillan, 1991).

Beyala, Calixthe. *C'est le soleil qui m'a brûlée* (Paris: Editions Stock, 1987).

———. *Tu t'appelleras Tanga* (Paris: J'ai lu, 1988).

Booth, David, ed. *Rethinking Social Development* (Harlow: Longman, 1994).

Boserup, Ester. *Women's Role in Economic Development* (London: Allen & Unwin, 1970).

Bouche, Denise. *Flux et reflux, 1815–1962: histoire de la colonisation française* 2 (Paris: Fayard, 1991).

Boulaga, Fabien Eboussi, Achille Mbembe, and Celestin Monga. "Nourrir les Esprits: entretien avec Fabien Eboussi Boulaga." *Africultures*, article no 4539, 19 July 2006. http://www.africultures.com. Accessed 07/28/10.

Bouya, Alphonsine. "Education de filles: Quelles perspectives pour l' Afrique sub-saharienne au XXIème siècle." *Afrique et Développement* 19, no. 4, 1994, 11–34.

Boyce Davies, Carole, and Anne Adams Graves, eds. *Ngambika: Studies of Women in African Literature* (Trenton, N.J.: Africa World Press, 1986).

Brahami, Denise, and Anne Trevarthen. *Les femmes dans la littérature africaine—portraits* (Paris: Karthala, 1998).

Brown, A. D., and C. Rhodes. "Writing Responsibly: Narrative fiction and organization studies." *Organization* 12, no. 4, 2005, 505–529.

Bulbeck, Chilla. *Re-orienting Western Feminisms—Women's Diversity in a Postcolonial World* (Cambridge: Cambridge University Press, 1998).

Bunwaree, Sheila. "Education and the Marginalisation of Girls in post-GATT Mauritius." *Compare—an international journal of comparative education* 27, no. 3, 1997, 297–317.

Bureau International du Travail-ACOPAM. Genre et Développement—analyse de la place des femmes une expérience au Sahel (Dakar: BIT/ILO, 1996).

Callaway, Barbara, and Lucy Creevey. *The Heritage of Islam: Women, Religion, and Politics in West Africa* (Boulder, Co.: Lynne Rienner, 1994).

Carr-Hill, R. *Social Conditions in Sub-Saharan Africa* (London: Macmillan, 1990).

Case, F. "Worker's Movements: Revolution and Women's Consciousness in God's Bits of Wood." *Canadian Journal of African Studies/Revue Canadienne des Etudes Africaines* 15, no. 2, 1981, 277–292.

Chang, Ha-Joon. *Kicking Away the Ladder—Development Strategy in Historical Perspective* (London: Anthem Press, 2002).

Chemain-Degrange, Arlette. *Emancipation féminine et roman africain* (Dakar: UNESCO/*Nouvelles Editions Africaines du Sénégal*, 1980).

Christias, Panagiotis. "Du littéraire et du social—le double: recherche pour une métaodon." *Sociétés* 64, no. 2, 1999, 67–75.

Clifford, J., and G. E. Marcus, eds. *Writing Culture: The Poetics and Politics of Ethnography* (Berkeley: University of California Press, 1986).

Cohen, W. B. *The French Encounter with Africans* (Bloomington, Indiana: Indiana University Press, 1980).

CONGAD. Répertoire des organisations non-gouvernementales membres du Conseil des organisations non-gouvernementales d'appui au développement (Dakar: CID/CONGAD, 2000).

Conrad, Joseph. *Heart of Darkness* (Harmondsworth: Penguin, 1998) [1902].

Coquery-Vidrovitch, Catherine. "Préface," in *Les femmes dans la littérature africaine—portraits,* Denise Brahami and Anne Trevarthen, eds. (Paris: Karthala, 1998), 5–6.

———. *Les Africaines: Histoire des femmes d'Afrique noire du XIXe siècle au XXe siècle* (Paris: Editions Desjonquères, 1994).

———. *African Women—A Modern History* (Oxford: Westview Press, 1997).

———, ed. *Femmes d'Afrique* (Paris: Broché, 1998).

Coquery-Vidrovitch, Catherine, and Odile Goerg. *L'Afrique occidentale au temps des Français: colonisateurs et colonisés* (c. 1860–1960) (Paris: Editions la Découverte/ACCT, 1992).

Corcoran, Patrick. "W(h)ither Francophone Postcolonial Studies." *Francophone Postcolonial Studies,* 2004, 2, no. 1, 11–19.

Cornwell, Andrea, ed. *Readings in Gender in Africa* (London: James Currey, 2005).

Crowther, Michael. *Senegal—A Study of French Assimilation Policy* (London: Methuen, 1967).

D'Almeida, Irène Assiba. *Francophone African women writers: destroying the emptiness of silence* (Gainesville: University Press of Florida, 1994).

Delcourt, Jean. *Gorée—Six siècles d'histoire* (Dakar: Editions ClairAfrique, 1984).

Derrida, Jacques. "Remarks on Deconstruction and Pragmatism," in *Deconstruction and Pragmatism,* C. Mouffe, ed. (London: Routledge, 1996), 77–88.

Devlin, Claire, and Robert Elgie. "The Effect of Increased Women's Representation in Parliament: The Case of Rwanda." *Parliamentary Affairs* 61, no. 2, 2008, 237–254.

Diallo Maïga, Fanta. *L'Accès des filles à l'éducation de base au Gabon* (Dakar: Bureau Régional de l'UNESCO, 1993).

Diaw, Aminata. "Sewing machines or computers? Seeing gender in the institutional cultures at UCAD." *Feminist Africa* no. 9, 2007, 5–21.

Dieng, Mame Younousse. *L'Ombre en feu* (Dakar: Nouvelles Editions Africaines du Sénégal, 1997).

Djibo, Hadiza. *La Participation des femmes africaines à la vie politique: les exemples du Sénégal et du Niger* (Paris: Harmattan, 2001).

Dumont, Jean-Pierre. *Les systèmes étrangères de sécurité sociale* (Paris: Economica, 1988).

Emenyonu, E., ed. *New Women's Writing in African Literature* (Oxford: James Currey, 2004).

Equate Project (The). *Education from a Gender Equality Perspective, report prepared for the Office of the USAID* (Washington: USAID, May 2008).

Escobar, Arturo. *Encountering Development—the making and unmaking of the Third World* (Princeton, N.J.: Princeton University Press, 1995).

Etienne, Mona. "Gender Relations and Conjugality among the Baule," in *Female and Male in West Africa,* Christine Oppong, ed. (London: George Allen & Unwin, 1983), 303–319.

Etta, Florence Ebam. "Education and Development in sub-Saharan Africa—Gender Issues in Contemporary African Education," *Afrique et Développment* 19, no. 4, 1994, 57–84.

Evers Rosander, Eva, ed. *Transforming Female Identities—Women's Organizational Forms in West Africa* (Uppsala: Nordiska Afrikainstitutet, 1997).

Ezeigbo, Theodora Akachi. "Women's Empowerment and National Integration: Ba's *So Long a Letter* and Warner-Vieyra's *Juletane*," in *Current Trends in Literature and Language Studies in West Africa,* Ernest N. Emenyonu and Charles E. Nnolim, eds. (Ibadan: Kraft Books Limited, 1994), 7–19.

Fall, Aminata Sow. "Entretiens avec Aminata Sow Fall." Interview by Sonia Lee. *African Literature Association Bulletin* 14, no. 4, 1988, 23–26.

Fall, Aminata Sow, and François Pfaff. "Aminata Sow Fall: L'écriture au féminin." Interview avec Francois Pfaff. *Notre Librairie* no. 81, 1985, 135–138.

Fall, Babacar. *Social History in French West Africa* (Amsterdam/India: SEPHIS/CSSSC, 2002).

Fall, Rokhaya. *Femmes et pouvoir dans les sociétés Nord-Sénégambiennes* (Dakar: CODESRIA, 1994).

Fanon, Frantz. *Peau Noire Masques Blancs* (Paris: Seuil, 1998) [1952].

———. *Les Damnés de la Terre* (Paris: Maspero, 1961).

Fasiku, Gbenga. "African Philosophy and the Method of Ordinary Language Philosophy." *Journal of Pan African Studies*, 2, no. 3, 2008, 100–117.

Felice, William F. *The Global New Deal: Economic and Social Human Rights in World Politics* (Lanham, Md.: Rowman & Littlefield, 2003).

Goodridge, Richard. "Women and Plantations in West Cameroon since 1900," in *Engendering History—Caribbean Women in Historical Perspective*, Verene Shepherd, Bridget Brereton, and Barbara Bailey, eds. (London: James Currey, 1995), 384–402.

Gordon, April A. *Transforming Capitalism and Patriarchy—Gender and Development in Africa* (Boulder, Co.: Lynne Rienner Publishers, 1996).

Green, Mary Jean, Micheline Rice-Maximin, Karen Gould, Keith L. Walker, and Jack A. Yeager, eds. *Postcolonial Subjects—Francophone Women Writers* (Minneapolis: University of Minnesota Press, 1996).

Griffin, K., and T. McKinley. *Implementing a Human Development Strategy* (London: Macmillan, 1994).

Griffiths, Claire H. *Social Development in Francophone Africa: The case of women in Gabon and Morocco* (Boston: Boston University African Studies Paper No. 211, 1998).

———. "Education in Transition in Francophone West Africa," in *Education in Transition: International Perspectives on the Politics and Processes of Change,* R. Griffin, ed. (Oxford: Symposium Press, 2002), 239–258.

———. "Gender, Education and Literary Output in Francophone Africa," in *North-South Linkages and Connections in Continental and Diaspora African Literatures,* Edris Makward, Mark Lillilet, and Ahmed Saber, eds. (Trenton, N.J.: Africa World Press, 2005), 388–403.

Gruat, J. V. "La Garantie sociale en république gabonaise: Une innovation en Afrique en matière de protection sociale." *Revue Internationale de Sécurité Sociale* 38, no. 2, 1985, 173–189.

Gyasi, Kwaku A. "The African Writer as Translator: Writing African Languages through French," *Journal of African Cultural Studies* 16, no. 2, 2003, 143–159.

Hall, Catherine. "Gender Politics and Imperial Politics: Rethinking the Histories of Empire," in *Engendering History—Caribbean Women in Historical Perspective,* Verene Shepherd; Bridget Brereton, and Barbara Bailey, eds. (London: James Currey, 1995), 48–59.

Hallen, Barry. "African Meanings, Western Words." *African Studies Review* 40, no. 1, 1997, 1–11.

———. "Review Essay: African Philosophy in a New Key." *African Studies Review* 43, no. 3, 2000, 131–134.

Harding, Sandra, ed. *The Feminist Standpoint Theory Reader: Intellectual and Political Controversies* (London: Routledge, 2004).

Hardy, Georges. *Une Conquête morale, l'enseignement en AOF.* Présentation de J. P. Little (Paris: Editions l'Harmattan, 2005).

Heward, Christine, and Sheila Bunwaree, eds. *Gender, Education and Development—Beyond Access to Empowerment* (London: Zed Books, 1999).

Hitchcott, N. *Women Writers in Francophone Africa* (Oxford: Berg, 2000).

Hodgson, D. L., and S. A. McCurdy, eds. *"Wicked" Women and the Reconfiguration of Gender in Africa* (Oxford: James Currey, 2001).

Hugon, Anne, ed. *L'Histoire des femmes en situation coloniale* (Paris: Karthala, 2004).

Ibrahim, Huma. "Ontological victimhood: 'other' bodies in madness and exile—toward a Third World feminist epistemology," in *The Politics of (M)Othering,* Obioma Nnaemeka, ed. (London: Routledge, 1997), 147–161.

Ibnlfassi, Laila, and Nicki Hitchcott, eds. *African Francophone Writing: A Critical Introduction* (Oxford: Berg, 1996).

Ijere, Muriel. "Sembene Ousmane et l'institution polygamique." *Ethiopiques* 5, nos. 1–2, 1988, 173–184.

———. "La Condition féminine dans Xala de Sembène Ousmane." *Revue de Littérature et de Esthétique Négro-africaine*, no. 8, 1988, 36–45.

Imam, Ayesha, Fatou Sow, and Amina Mama, eds. *Engendering African Social Sciences* (Dakar: CODESRIA, 1997).

Imam, Ayesha, Amina Mama, and Fatou Sow, eds. *Genre, Sexe et Société* (Paris: Karthala, 2004).

Imbo, Samuel Oluoch. *An Introduction to African Philosophy* (Lanham, Md.: Rowman & Littlefield, 1998).

IMF/OECD/UN/World Bank. *A Better World For All* (Washington, D.C.: Communications Development, 2000).

Jones, Howard. *Social Welfare in Third World Development* (London: Macmillan, 1990).

Jones, Adele M. E. "Training for Empowerment? NFE in Small Island Countries." *Compare—an International Journal of Comparative Education* 27, no. 3, 1997, 277–286.

Ka, Aminata Maïga. *Brisures de Vies* (St. Louis, Senegal: Xamal, 1998).

———. *La Voie du Salut & Le Miroir de la Vie* (Paris: Présence Africaine, 1985).

Kalu, Anthonia C. *Women, Literature and Development in Africa* (Trenton, N.J.: Africa World Press, 2001).

Kesteloot, Lilyan. *Anthologie Négro-africaine—histoire et textes de 1918 à nos jours* (Paris: EDICEF, 1992).

———. "La Percée des femmes dans le roman de moeurs sénégalais." *Environnement africain* 10, Nos. 39–40, 1997, 31– 44.

Lebeuf, Annie M. D. "The Role of Women in the Political Organization of African Societies," in *Women of Tropical Africa*, Denise Paulme, ed. (Berkeley: University of California Press, 1974), 93–119.

Lee, Sonia. "The Awakening of the Self in the Heroines of Sembene Ousmane," in *Sturdy Black Bridges: Visions of Black Women in Literature,* Roseann P. Bell, Bettye J. Parker, and Beverly Guy-Sheftall, eds. (New York: Anchor Press/Doubleday, 1979), 52–60.

Le Vine, Victor T. *Politics in Francophone Africa* (Boulder, Co.: Lynne Rienner, 2004).

Linkhorn, Renée. "L'Afrique de demain: Femmes en marche dans l'oeuvre de Sembène Ousmane." *Modern Language Studies* 16, no. 3, 1986, 69–76.

Lionnet, Francoise, and Ronnie Scharfman, eds. "Post/Colonial Conditions: Exiles, Migrations, and Nomadisms." *Yale French Studies*, no. 82, vol. 1, 1993.

Longwe, Sara Hlupekile. "The Evaporation of Gender Policies in the Patriarchal Cooking Pot." *Development in Practice* 7, no. 2, 1997, 148–156.

Maiga, Djingarey Ibrahim. "La Situation des droits humains des femmes au Mali," in *La Situation des droits des femmes et de l'égalité des sexes en Afrique francophone* Compilation des Communications du Forum régional du ROFAF, Lomé, Togo, 23–26 March 2009, 9–23.

Mani, Lata. "Cultural Theory, Colonial Texts: Reading Eye-witness Accounts of Widow Burning," in *Cultural Studies*, L. Grossberg, C. Nelson, and P. Treichler, eds. (New York: Routledge, 1992), 392–408.

Manning, Patrick. *Francophone Sub-Saharan Africa 1880–1995* (Cambridge: Cambridge University Press, 1998).

Mbah, Jean-Ferdinand. *La Recherche en sciences sociales au Gabon* (Paris: Editions L'Harmattan, 1987).

Mbaye, Saliou, and Jean Bernard Lacroix. "Le vote des femmes au Sénégal." *Revue Ethiopiques*, no. 6, 1970, 29.

Mbembe, Achille. "Provisional Notes on the Postcolony." *Africa: Journal of the International Africa Institute* 62, no. 1, 1992, 3–37.

———. *On the Postcolony* (Berkeley: University of California Press, 2001).

———. "African Modes of Self-Writing." *Public Culture* 14, no. 1, 2002, 239–273.

———. "On the Postcolony: A Brief Response to Critics." *African Identities* 4, no. 2, 2006, 143–178.

McNee, Lisa. *Selfish Gifts—Senegalese Women's Autobiographical Discourses* (New York: State University of New York Press, 2000).

Mehta, S. C. "Social Infrastructure in Francophone Sahel." *Africa Quarterly* 34, no. 1, 1994, 115–118.

Midgley, J. *Social Development: The Developmental Perspective in Social Welfare* (London: Sage, 1995).

Miller, Christopher L. "Nationalism as Resistance and Resistance as Nationalism in Literature in Francophone Africa." *Yale French Studies*, vol. 1, no. 82, 1993, 62–100.

———. *Theories of Africans: Francophone Literature and Anthropology in Africa* (Chicago: Chicago University Press, 1990).

———. *The French Triangular Trade: Literature and Culture of the Slave Trade* (Durham & London: Duke University Press, 2008).

Mills, Sara. *Discourses of Difference: An Analysis of Women's Travel Writing and Colonialism* (London: Routledge, 1993).

Ministère de la Femme, de l'Enfant et de la Famille. *Senegalese Women by the Year 2015—abridged version* (Dakar: Ministère de la Femme de l'Enfant et de la Famille—Gouvernement du Sénégal, 1993).

Ministère de la Planification. *Recensement générale de la population et de l'habitat* (Libreville: Ministère de la Planification—Gouvernement du Gabon, 1995).

Mintsa, Justine. *Histoire d'Awu* (Paris: Gallimard, 2000).

Mkandawire, Thandika, ed. *African Intellectuals* (London: Zed Books in association with CODESRIA, 2005).

Mohanty, Chandra Talpade. "Under Western Eyes: Feminist Scholarship and Colonial Discourses," in *Third World Women and the Politics of Feminism,* C. T. Mohanty, A. Russo, and L. Torres, eds. (Bloomington: Indiana University Press, 1991), 51–80.

Moi, Toril. "Sexual/Textual Politics," in *The Politics of Theory,* F. Barker, ed. (Colchester: University of Essex, 1983), 1–14.

Mottin-Sylla, Marie-Hélène. "Le Libre choix en matière de sexualité et fécondité." *Environnement Africain* 10, nos. 39–40, 1997, 139–154.

Ndiaye, Raphaël A. *La Place de la femme dans les rites au Sénégal* (Dakar: Les Nouvelles Editions Africaines, 1986).

Nederveen Pieterse, Jan. *Development Theory—Deconstructions/Reconstructions* (London: Sage, 2001).

Nfah-Abbenyi, Juliana Makuchi. *Gender in African Women's Writing—Identity, Sexuality and Difference* (Bloomington & Indianapolis: Indiana University Press, 1997).

Nnaemeka, Obioma. "Urban Spaces, Women's Places—Polygamy as Sign in Mariama Bâ's Novels," in *The Politics of (M)Othering,* Obioma Nnaemeka, ed. (London: Routledge, 1997), 162–191.

Nussbaum, Martha. *Women and Human Development: The Capabilities Approach* (Cambridge: Cambridge University Press, 2000).

Nussbaum, Martha, and Jonathan Glover. *Women, Culture and Development: a Study of Human Capabilities* (Oxford: Clarendon, 1995).

Nussbaum, Martha, and Amartya Sen. *The Quality of Life* (Oxford: Clarendon Press, 1993).

Office of the President of the United States. *Budget of the United States Government: Fiscal Year 2003—Department of State and International Development Assistance* (Washington, D.C.: Executive of the President of the United States, 2003).

Ogden, John. "The Africanization of the Curriculum in Gabon." *The French Review* 55, no. 6, 1982, 855–861.

O'Keefe, Charles. "Sinking One's Teeth into Mariama Bâ's *So Long a Letter*: Lessons of Cadmus." *Research in African Literatures* 40, no. 2, 2009, 63–81.

Oppong, Christine, ed. *Female and Male in West Africa* (London: George, Allen & Unwin, 1983).

———, ed. *Sex Roles, Population and Development in West Africa* (London: James Currey, 1988).

Orlando, Valérie. *Nomadic Voices of Exile—Feminine Identity in Francophone Literature of the Maghreb* (Athens: Ohio University Press, 1999).

———. *Of Suffocated Hearts and Tortured Souls: Seeking Subjecthood through Madness in Francophone Women's Writing of Africa and the Caribbean.* (Lanham, Md.: Lexington Books, 2003).

Ouédrago, Angèle Bassolé. "Et les Africaines prirent la plume! Histoire d'une conquête." *Mots Pluriels*, Octobre 1998, http://www.uwa.edu.au/motspluriels.

Pande, R., A. Malhotra, and C. Grown. "Impact of Investments in Female Education on Gender Equality," in The Equate Project, *Education from a Gender Equality Perspective* (Washington, D.C.: Equate/USAID, May 2008).

Paulme, Denise, ed. *Women of Tropical Africa* (Berkeley: University of California Press, 1974).

Pervillé, Guy. *De l'Empire français à la décolonisation* (Paris: Hachette, 1993).

Petchesky, Rosalind P. *Global Prescriptions—Gendering Health and Human Rights* (London: Zed Books, 2003).

Pietilä, Hilka. "Women's Issues Five Years after Beijing—Progress and Drawbacks." *Cooperation South*, no. 2, 2000. 1–3.

PNUD. *Suivi des objectifs de développement du millénaire au Sénégal* (Dakar: PNUD/UNDP, August 2001).

Quist, Hubert Oswald. "Illiteracy, Education and National Development in Postcolonial West Africa: A Reappraisal." *Afrique et Développement/Africa Development* 19, no. 4, 1994, 127–145.

Ramonet, Ignacio. "Pour changer le monde." *Manières de Voir*, no. 52, July–August 2000, 1.

Rawiri, Angèle. *Fureurs et cris de femmes* (Paris: Harmattan/Collection Encres Noires, 1989).

Ricard, Alain. *Littératures d'Afrique Noire* (Paris: Karthala, 1995).

Ricard, Bertrand. "Pour un rapprochement de la littérature et de la sociologie." *Sociétés* 62, no. 4, 1998, 5–7.

Robertson, Claire. "Women's Education and Class Formation in Africa," in *Women and Class in Africa*, Claire Robertson and Iris Berger, eds. (New York: African Publishing Company, 1986).

Sammba, Saliou, and Malaado Kanji. *Des Droits de la Femme Africaine d'hier à demain*, Claire Robertson and Iris Berger, eds. (Saint Louis, Senegal: Xamal, 1997).

Sankara, Thomas. *Women's Liberation and the African Freedom Struggle* (New York: Pathfinder Press, 1990).

Sarr, Awa. "Consolider la place des femmes dans l'économie sociale et solidaire: un défi d'actualité au Sénégal—Entrevue avec Awa Sarr," Lucie Fréchette and Michèle Diotte. *Nouvelles Pratiques Sociales* 15, no. 1, 2002, 9–14.

Sarr, Fatou. "The Funding of Non-Governmental Organizations in Senegal: constraints and opportunities." *Development* 49, no. 2, 2006, 108–115.

Sen, Amartya. *Commodities and Capabilities* (Oxford: Oxford University Press, 1985).

———. "More than 100 Million Women Are Missing." *New York Review of Books* 37, no. 20, 1990. http:/ucatlas.ucsc.edu/gender/Sen100M.html.

———. *Development as Freedom* (Oxford: Oxford University Press, 2001).

———. *The Idea of Justice* (London: Allen Lane, 2009).

Shepherd, Verene, Bridget Brereton, and Barbara Bailey, eds. *Engendering History—Caribbean Women in Historical Perspective* (London: James Currey, 1995).

Sircar, Roopali. "Women and Resistance: Women in Sembene Ousmane's God's Bits of Wood." *Africa Quarterly* 34, no. 3, 1994, 146–68.

Snyder, Margaret C., and Mary Tadesse. *African Women and Development* (London: Zed Books, 1995).

Sow, Fatou, Ngagne Diakhaté, Adama Fall Touré, and Mamadou Matar Gueye. *Les Sénégalaises en Chiffres* (Dakar: UNDP, 2000).

Sow, Fatou, Mamadou Diouf, and Guy le Moine. *Femmes Sénégalaises à l'horizon 2015* (Dakar: *Ministère de la Femme*/The Population Council, 1993).

Sow, Fatou Ndiaye. *Un Code pour toi et moi* (Dakar: Ministère des Finances et du Plan—Gouvernement du Sénégal, 1998).

———. *Des Droits pour les Enfants* (Dakar: Ministère de la Famille, de l'Action Sociale et de la Solidarité, 1998).

Spivak, Gayatri. "Can the Subaltern Speak?" in *Colonial Discourse and Post-colonial Theory,* Patrick Williams and Laura Chrisman, eds. (New York: Harvester Wheatsheaf, 1993), 66–111.

Stovall, Tyler. "Love, Labor, and Race: Colonial Men and White Women in France during the Great War," in *French Civilisation and Its Discontents—Nationalism, Colonialism, Race,* Tyler Stovall and Georges van den Abeele, eds. (Lanham, Md.: Lexington Books, 2003).

Stratton, Florence. *Contemporary African Literature and the Politics of Gender* (London: Routledge, 1994).

———. "The Shallow Grave: Archetypes of Female Experience in African Fiction." *Research in African Literatures* 19, no. 1, 1988, 143–169.

Sudarkasa, Niara. "The 'Status' of Women in Indigenous African Societies," in *Women in Africa and the African Diaspora—A Reader,* Rosalyn Terborg-Penn and Andrea Benton Rushing, eds. (Washington, D.C.: Howard University Press, 1996), 73–87.

Terborg-Penn, Rosalyn, and Andrea Benton Rushing, eds. *Women in Africa and the African Diaspora—A Reader* (Washington, D.C.: Howard University Press, 1996).

Thiam, Awa. *La Parole aux Négresses* (Paris: Denoël-Gonthier, 1978).

Thomas, Dominic. *Nation-Building, Propaganda, and Literature in Francophone Africa* (Bloomington: Indiana University Press, 2002).

———. "Introduction: Global Francophone Africa." *Forum for Modern Languages Studies* 45, no. 2, 2009, 121–28.

Toman, Cheryl. "Fang Culture in Gabonese Francophone Women's Writing: Reading *Histoire d'Awu* by Justine Mintsa." *Research in African Literatures* 41, no. 2, 2010, 121–132.

UNDP. *Human Development Report 2000* (Oxford: Oxford University Press, 2000).

———. *Human Development Report 2003* (New York: United Nations, 2003).

———. *Human Development Report 2004* (New York: United Nations, 2004).

———. *Human Development Report 2007/2008* (New York: Palgrave Macmillan, 2007).

———. *Human Development Report 2009* (New York & Oxford: Oxford University Press, 2009).

UNIFEM. *Progress of the World's Women 2000* (New York: UNIFEM/UNDP, 2000).

———. *Répertoire des ONG africaines actives dans le domaine Genre/Femme et Développement* (Dakar: UNIFEM, 1995).

———. *Regards de femmes africaines sur la pauvreté* (Dakar: UNIFEM, 2003).

UNIFEM/IAD/CONSEF. *Femmes et Alternance au Sénégal—quelles stratégies pour les prochains scrutins?* (Dakar: Editions Démocraties Africaines, 2000).

United Nations/Nations Unies. *Rapport sur le développement humain 1994* (Paris: Economica, 1994).

United Nations. *Womanwatch—Summary Report on the Fourth World Conference on Women* (New York: United Nations, 1995).

———. *Comprehensive Report on the Implementation of the Outcome of the World Summit for Social Development—Report of the Secretary-General* (New York: United Nations, 1999).

———. *Report of the World Summit for Social Development* A/Conf.166/9 19 April 1995, http://www.un.org.

United Nations. *United Nations Population Fund Proposed Projects and Programmes—Assistance to the Government of Senegal* DP/FPA/SEN/5, 3 August 2001, http://www.un.org. Accessed 08/20/2009.

United Nations Population Division. *Charting the Progress of Populations* (New York: United Nations, 2000).

Wallerstein, Immanuel. "Elites in French-speaking Africa: The Social Basis of Ideas." *Journal of Modern African Studies* 3, no. 1, 1965, 1–33.

———. *Africa: The Politics of Independence and Unity* (Lincoln: University of Nebraska Press, 2005).

Warner-Vieyra, Myriam. *Juletane* (Paris: Présence Africaine, 1982).

———. "An Interview with Myriam Warner-Vieyra," Mildred Mortimer. *Callaloo: A Journal of African-American and African Arts and Letters* 16, no. 1, 1993, 108–115.

Weeden, Chris. *Feminist Practice and Poststructuralist Theory* (Oxford: Blackwell, 1997).

Werbner, R., and T. Ranger, eds. *Postcolonial Identities in Africa* (London: Zed Books, 1996).

Wone, Katy Cisse. *Les fondements juridiques, socioculturels et économiques de la vulnérabilité des femmes à l'infection au VIH/SIDA—le cas du Sénégal* (Dakar: UNIFEM, 2002).

Yiman, Arega. *Social Development in Africa 1950–1985: Methodological and Future Perspectives* (Brookfield, USA: Avebury Publishers, 1990).

UNPUBLISHED/RESTRICTED DOCUMENTS

Albarka, Maurice. *La Situation de la femme au Sahel*, Archives des Documents de la FAO, n.d.

Canadian International Development Agency/Agence Canadienne pour le Développement International. *Stratégie d'Egalité des Sexes Programme du Sénégal—boîte à outils* (Canadian International Development Agency/*Agence Canadienne pour le Développement International* CIDA/*ACDI*, November 1998).

Dia, Aissatou Sow. *L'Evolution des femmes dans la vie politique sénégalaise de 1945 à nos jours.* Mémoire de Maîtrise d'Histoire, Université Cheik Anta Diop, 1994–95.

Diokhane, Marema Dioum, Oumel Khairy Diallo, Alhousseynou Sy and Mafakha Touré. *Genre et fréquentation scolaire dans l'enseignement élémentaire au Sénégal* (Dakar: Institute for Development Studies, University of Sussex/*Ministère de l'Education Nationale*, 1999).

314   *Selected Bibliography*

Gadio, Coumba Mar. *Le Genre et les objectifs du millénaire pour le développement* (Dakar: UNIFEM/UNDP/UNFPA/OIT, 2003).

Koumba Pambolt, Ignace. *L'Intégration de la femme gabonaise dans le processus du développement* Mémoire de maîtrise de Sociologie, Université de Caen, 1978–79.

Mime, Fernande. *Les Filles à l'école sénégalaise—de l'égalité des chances à l'inégalité sociale: l'école en question* Mémoire de DEA, Ecole Normale Supérieure de Dakar, 1996–97.

Ministère de la Famille et de l'Action Sociale et de la Solidarité Nationale. *Evaluation à mi-parcours du plan d'action de la femme 1997–2001* (Dakar: Ministère de la Famille et de l'Action Sociale et de la Solidarité Nationale, 1999).

Ministère de la Famille et de la Petite Enfance. *Projet de plan national d'équité de genre* (Dakar: Ministère de la Famille et de la Petite Enfance, 2001).

Ministère de la Femme de l'Enfant et de la Famille. *Plan d'action de la femme 1997–2001* (Dakar: Ministère de la Femme de l'Enfant et de la Famille, 1996).

———. *Rapport national sur les femmes: Lutte pour l'égalité, le développement et la paix* (Dakar: *Ministère de la Femme de l'Enfant et de la Famille*, 1994).

Mohammed, Patricia. *Daughters of Khadija* (2001). http://www.cgds.uwi.tt. Accessed 08/09/2009.

Ntsame Engonga, Minette, and Jean-Pierre Zima Mefe. *Comment appréhender l'emploi au Gabon* (Ministère de la Planification, République du Gabon, n.d. [2007]).

Oyane Nzue, Pierrete. "Femmes et participation politique: L'exemple du Gabon." Paper presented at the Regional Forum of *ROFAF*, Lomé, Togo, 23 March 2009.

Pande, R., A. Malhotra, and C. Grown. "Impact of Investments in Female Education on Gender Equality." Paper presented at the XXV IUSSP International Population Conference, Tours, France, 2005.

Primature de la République Gabonaise. *Sommet mondial pour le développement social Copenhague 6–12 mars 1995—Contribution du Gabon* (Libreville: Primature de la République Gabonaise, 1995).

Sarr, Awa. *Yeewu-Yewwi pour la libération des femmes. Une saga de femmes sénégalaises visionnaires* (unpublished essay, 2002).

Sarr, Fatou. *La Reconstruction du mouvement social féminin africain et la production d'une pensée politique liée à la lutte des femmes* (unpublished article, n.d.)

Sarr, Fatou, and Fatou Sow. "*UNIFEM-UNDP-SURF Atelier de formation Genre et développement.*" UNIFEM, Dakar, 2003 (restricted).

Sarr, Mbaye. *Emploi et Travail des Femmes au Sénégal—document provisoire* (Dakar: *BIT*/ILO, Septembre 1993).

Savineau, Denise. *Rapport sur la Condition de la Femme et la Famille en Afrique Occidentale Française 1937–1938, Archives Nationales du Sénégal*, Série 17 G, Dakar, Sénégal.

Sylla, Seynabou Ndiaye. *Femmes et Politique au Sénégal*. Mémoire de DEA, Université de Paris 1, 2000–01.

UNDP/PNUD. *Coopération au Développement—Gabon* (Libreville: UNDP/PNUD, June 1992).

———. *Programme du Suivi-contrôle des politiques d'ajustement—Gabon* (Libreville: UNDP/PNUD, Février 1993).

UNICEF. *Analyse de la Situation des Femmes et des Enfants au Sénégal* (Dakar: UNICEF, August 1995).

———. *Analyse de la Situation des Enfants et des femmes au Gabon—document de travail* (Libreville: UNICEF, April 1995).

United Nations. *UN Fourth World Conference on Women* A/CONF.177/20, 17 October 1995.

Wone, Katy Cissé. "Idéologie socialiste et féminisme d'état au Sénégal: de Senghor à Abdou Diouf." Paper presented at the 10th General Assembly of CODESRIA, 8–10 December 2002, Kampala, Uganda.

INTERNET SITES

http://genre.francophonie.org
http://hdr.undp.org
http://www.ipu.org
http://www.oecd.org/dac
http://www.socialwatch.org

Index

Note: Page numbers in italics refer to figures and tables.

About the Author

Claire H. Griffiths is professor of French and francophone studies at the University of Chester in the UK. After graduating in French with politics from the University of Warwick, Dr. Griffiths earned a higher research degree in political science and a doctorate in francophone African studies. Following a period at the European Commission in Brussels, she spent four years teaching a masters programme for francophone and Anglophone African students, an experience that inspired a lifelong commitment to the African dimensions of French and francophone studies in higher education. Since 1996 Claire Griffiths has conducted several research projects in North and sub-Saharan Africa. She was made senior research fellow at the University of Hull in 2006 and took up her current position as chair of modern languages at Chester in 2009–2010. Her current research project analyzes the role of visual art in constructing political discourses of dissent in francophone Africa.

Lightning Source UK Ltd.
Milton Keynes UK
07 March 2011
168834UK00001B/48/P